The Making of Buddhist
Modernism

The Making of Buddhist Modernism

DAVID L. MCMAHAN

UNIVERSITY PRESS
2008

OXFORD
UNIVERSITY PRESS

Oxford University Press, Inc., publishes works that further
Oxford University's objective of excellence
in research, scholarship, and education.

Oxford   New York
Auckland   Cape Town   Dar es Salaam   Hong Kong   Karachi
Kuala Lumpur   Madrid   Melbourne   Mexico City   Nairobi
New Delhi   Shanghai   Taipei   Toronto

With offices in
Argentina   Austria   Brazil   Chile   Czech Republic   France   Greece
Guatemala   Hungary   Italy   Japan   Poland   Portugal   Singapore
South Korea   Switzerland   Thailand   Turkey   Ukraine   Vietnam

Published by Oxford University Press, Inc.
198 Madison Avenue, New York, New York 10016

www.oup.com

Oxford is a registered trademark of Oxford University Press

Library of Congress Cataloging-in-Publication Data
McMahan, David L.
The making of Buddhist modernism / David L. McMahan.
    p. cm.
Includes bibliographical references and index.
ISBN 978-0-19-518327-6
1. Buddhist modernism.   2. Buddhism—Social aspects.   I. Title.
BQ316.M36 2008
294.309'051—dc22   2008014450

9 8 7

Printed in the United States of America
on acid-free paper

Acknowledgments

This project got started with a Summer Stipend from the National Endowment for the Humanities. I am also grateful to the American Academy of Religion for a research grant and to the Andrew W. Mellon Foundation for a Central Pennsylvania Consortium grant.

An earlier version of chapter 4 was published as "Modernity and the Discourse of Scientific Buddhism" in *Journal of the American Academy of Religion*, vol. 72, no. 4 (2004), 897-933. Portions of this book also include material from "Demythologization and the Core-versus-Accretions Model of Buddhism" in *Indian International Journal of Buddhism*, vol. 10, no. 5 (2004), 63-99, and "Repackaging Zen for the West" in *Westward Dharma: Buddhism Beyond Asia*, edited by Charles S. Prebish and Martin Baumann, 218-229, Berkeley: University of California Press, 2002. Thanks to the publishers for permission to reprint this material.

Thanks also to Gerald Larson, Annette Aronowicz, Stephen Cooper, John Lardas Modern, Jason Carbine, Charles Prebish, Paul Numrich, Darryl Caterine, Dan Blair, Kabi Hartman, and Karen Sattler, all of whom read portions of the manuscript or supported the writing of this book in various ways.

Contents

Note on Buddhist Terminology

I have used Sanskrit unless referring to terms in texts in other languages. I have italicized and included diacritical marks for non-English terms unless they are generally familiar or are frequently used in this book. Proper names are rendered without diacritical marks. *Sutra* and *sutta* refer to Buddhist scriptures in Sanskrit and Pali, respectively. Tibetan terms are generally transliterated according to the system of Turrell Wylie; however, Tibetan terms that contain numerous silent characters or have entered into English parlance are rendered phonetically, with the Wylie transliteration in parentheses with the first use. Chinese terms are transliterated according to the pinyin system. Any unattributed translations from Sanskrit or Pali are my own.

The Making of Buddhist
Modernism

I

Introduction

Buddhism and Modernity

A New Buddhism

On a chilly Friday evening in my first year of teaching at Franklin and Marshall College, I was led at the behest of an earnest student down a dark street to the hippest nightclub in town. Inside, ghoulish sculptures protruded from flat black walls, flashing lights and ear-splitting music emanated from gyrating musicians on stage, and the darkened dance floor writhed with pink mohawks, lip and eyebrow rings, black leather, and torn jeans. And off to the side, sitting placidly in a dim corner by the bar, were five Tibetan Buddhist monks in their gold and saffron robes preparing to take the stage. When the band took a break, the monks emerged in the spotlight and, after a brief introduction by the student, performed some guttural chanting and a short *pūjā* ceremony. Some in the young audience appeared puzzled but maintained a respectful silence. Others looked satisfied, not understanding the Tibetan syllables or the mechanics of the ritual but knowing that something exotic, spiritual, profound, and very cool was happening. Afterward, a spokesperson for the local chapter of Students for a Free Tibet briefly discussed the Chinese occupation of Tibet and handed out some pamphlets, and the thrashing and gyrating resumed. The monks quickly moved on to their next stop, a show at Carnegie Hall the following evening.

It was one of the countless encounters between Buddhists and interested westerners—characterized by overlapping interests and agendas and mutual goodwill, as well as mutual incomprehension—that for more than a century have made up new contexts in which Buddhism can be found and which, indeed, have constituted a new Buddhism. For the monks and the clubgoers, life no doubt went on much as usual after this encounter. But the event undoubtedly generated dozens of conversations among the young partiers about the situation in Tibet, the demeanor of the monks, the otherworldly chanting, a Free Tibet concert someone had attended, and a book read or class taken on Buddhism. The monks surely had their conversations, too: attempts to ascertain the significance of the youths' clothing and hair-styles, expressions of hope that even this small event would help raise aware-ness and support for their cause of greater autonomy for Tibet under Chinese rule, assessments of American punk music, and perhaps comparisons of the nightclub scene to an anteroom of a Buddhist hell realm. The conversations en-tered the stream of discourse that makes up the growing and shifting patterns of overlap between Buddhism and western culture.

Another of these conversations took place in my classroom the next Mon-day, when I asked my students in an introductory class on Asian religions—our first day dealing with Buddhism—to relate some of their ideas and images of the tradition. After the various impressions from popular films and magazine articles, someone faithfully conveyed that semester's version of what has be-come a standard view: that Buddhism is a religion in which you don't really have to believe anything in particular or follow any strict rules; you simply ex-ercise compassion and maintain a peaceful state of mind through meditation. Buddhism values creativity and intuition and is basically compatible with a mod-ern, scientific worldview. It is democratic, encourages freedom of thought, and is more of a "spirituality" than a religion. While scholars steeped in the rich diversity of Buddhism in a wide variety of cultures over its twenty-five hundred years of history—not to mention serious practitioners immersed in the com-plexities of Buddhist practice and doctrine—may roll their eyes at such vagar-ies, these notions are not simply a result of ignorance. They have specific roots in representations of Buddhism in recent history—representations created, in fact, by scholars and practitioners themselves. Indeed, they are accurate repre-sentations not of Buddhism in its diverse Asian historical contexts but of a new Buddhism that has emerged more recently.

One of the prominent shifts in the religious landscape of North America in recent years is the explosion of Buddhism into various facets of American culture. Buddhist monks appear in television ads and sitcoms, chant onstage at rock concerts, and build stupas in California and upstate New York. Books on Buddhism fill the bookstores, while middle-class Americans gather for informal

Buddhist meditation on college campuses and in Unitarian churches. What many Americans and Europeans often understand by the term "Buddhism," however, is actually a modern hybrid tradition with roots in the European Enlightenment no less than the Buddha's enlightenment, in Romanticism and transcendentalism as much as the Pali canon, and in the clash of Asian cultures and colonial powers as much as in mindfulness and meditation. Most non-Asian Americans tend to see Buddhism as a religion whose most important elements are meditation, rigorous philosophical analysis, and an ethic of compassion combined with a highly empirical psychological science that encourages reliance on individual experience. It discourages blindly following authority and dogma, has little place for superstition, magic, image worship, and gods, and is largely compatible with the findings of modern science and liberal democratic values. While this picture draws on elements of traditional forms of Buddhism that have existed in Asia for centuries, it is in many respects quite distinct from what Buddhism has meant to Asian Buddhists throughout its long and varied history. The popular western picture of Buddhism is neither unambiguously "there" in ancient Buddhist texts and lived traditions nor merely a fantasy of an educated elite population in the West, an image with no corresponding object. It is, rather, an actual new form of Buddhism that is the result of a process of modernization, westernization, reinterpretation, image-making, revitalization, and reform that has been taking place not only in the West but also in Asian countries for over a century. This new form of Buddhism has been fashioned by modernizing Asian Buddhists and western enthusiasts deeply engaged in creating Buddhist responses to the dominant problems and questions of modernity, such as epistemic uncertainty, religious pluralism, the threat of nihilism, conflicts between science and religion, war, and environmental destruction.

The emergence of Buddhist thought on these problems is the product of a unique confluence of cultures, individuals, and institutions in a time of rapid and unprecedented transformation of societies. Many modernizing interpreters of Buddhism, both Asian and western, have proffered the theme of the rescue of the modern West—which they have claimed has lost its spiritual bearings through modernization—by the humanizing wisdom of the East. In order for the rescue to succeed, however, Buddhism itself had to be transformed, reformed, and modernized—purged of mythological elements and "superstitious" cultural accretions. Thus the Buddhism that has become visible in the West and among urban, educated populations in Asia involves fewer rituals, deemphasizes the miracles and supernatural events depicted in Buddhist literature, disposes of or reinterprets image worship, and stresses compatibility with scientific, humanistic, and democratic ideals. At the same time, these recent forms of Buddhism have not simply dispensed with all traditional elements in an effort to accommodate to a changing world but have re-invented them.

Buddhist Modernism and the West

It is tempting to think of the various modernizing forms of Buddhism as "Western Buddhism," given the influence of western science, philosophy, and psychology on modern variations of the dharma, as well as the visibility of American and European authors on the subject.[1] Indeed, westerners have contributed significantly to transforming Buddhism in highly selective and idiosyncratic ways in terms of the categories, ideologies, and narratives of their own cultures. The modernization of Buddhism, however, has in no way been an exclusively western project or simply a representation of the eastern Other; many figures essential to this process have been Asian reformers educated in both western and Buddhist thought. Nor can the motivations of major Asian figures in this process, such as Anagarika Dharmapala, Daisetz T. Suzuki, and of late, the Fourteenth Dalai Lama, be reduced to the simple accommodation of Buddhism to western forms of modernity. Some have infused Buddhist categories into modernist discourse only to turn around and critique modernity's perceived weaknesses, to resist the colonialism of the West, or to assert their own forms of religious or national particularity. This new form of Buddhism that I want to discuss—what some scholars have called Buddhist modernism—has been, therefore, a cocreation of Asians, Europeans, and Americans. Although I intend to look primarily at its manifestations in the West, such interconnections between them belie any attempt to categorize my subject as "western Buddhism," for it is a global phenomenon with a wide diversity of participants. What scholars have often meant by "western Buddhism," "American Buddhism," or "new Buddhism" is a facet of a more global network of movements that are not the exclusive product of one geographic or cultural setting.

By "Buddhist modernism" I do not mean all Buddhism that happens to exist in the modern era but, rather, forms of Buddhism that have emerged out of an engagement with the dominant cultural and intellectual forces of modernity. Buddhist modernism is a dynamic, complex, and plural set of historical processes with loose bonds and fuzzy boundaries. Yet there is something distinct enough to outline its broad contours, clarify some of its detailed features, and trace aspects of its emergence. Heinz Bechert established the term as a scholarly category in his *Buddhismus, Staat und Gesellschaft* (1966; see also 1984). He described it as a revival movement spanning a number of geographical areas and schools, a movement that reinterpreted Buddhism as a "rational way of thought" that stressed reason, meditation, and the rediscovery of canonical texts. It also deemphasized ritual, image worship, and "folk" beliefs and practices and was linked to social reform and nationalist movements, especially in Burma and Ceylon (now Sri Lanka). In some places it attempted to reassert Buddhism as a national religion in the face of European colonialism and to counter its negative colonial portrayals in western literature (1984: 276). In a later article, Bechert identified a number of key components of the early forms of Buddhist modernism. They include demythologization—the modernization of cosmology along with a "symbolic interpretation of traditional myths"—something that has allowed Buddhism to be interpreted as a "scientific religion" over against others that stressed belief and dogma. They also include the idea of Buddhism as a philosophy rather than a creed or religion, the insistence on the optimism of Buddhism (to counter early western representations of it as pessimistic) and an activist element that stresses social work, democracy, and a "philosophy of equality." Also crucial is the newly central emphasis on meditation, a development that not only has revived canonical meditation methods but also popularized and democratized them, making them available to all at uniquely modern "meditation centers" (1994: 255–56).

Richard Gombrich and Gananath Obeyesekere have mapped similar trends specifically in Sinhalese Buddhism in Sri Lanka. Emphasizing the Christian influence on modernizing forms of Sinhalese Buddhism in the late nineteenth and twentieth centuries, as well as those of Victorian English culture, they use the term "Protestant Buddhism" to suggest that modernizing Buddhism both protested against European colonization and Christian missionization and adopted elements of Protestantism. These included rejection of the clerical links between individuals and the religious goal, emphasis on the "individual's seeking his or her ultimate goal without intermediaries," "spiritual egalitarianism," individual responsibility, and self-scrutiny. The importance placed on the *sangha* (the community of monastics) was diminished as the laity became more important.[2] Under the influence of Protestantism, Gombrich and Obeyesekere assert, "religion is privatized and internalized: the truly significant is not what takes place at a public celebration or in ritual, but what happens inside one's own mind or soul" (1988: 216). The rise of Protestant Buddhism was also connected with urbanization and the rise of the bourgeoisie in Ceylon, as well as other Asian nations, and mingled traditional Buddhist ethics with Victorian social mores (Gombrich 1988: 172–97). It also replicated orientalist scholars' location of "true Buddhism" in canonical texts, while often dismissing local or village iterations as degenerate and superstitious.

More recently, Donald S. Lopez Jr. has mapped some of this territory in his analysis of what he calls "modern Buddhism," which, he contends, "stresses equality over hierarchy, the universal over the local, and often exalts the individual above the community" (2002: ix). It sees the Buddha's original message as deeply compatible with modern conceptions of "reason, empiricism, science, universalism, individualism, tolerance, freedom and the rejection of religious orthodoxy" (x). Modern Buddhism has much more active and visible roles for women than its more traditional predecessors, and its social location has often been among the educated middle classes. Lopez suggests that modern Buddhism has developed into a kind of transnational Buddhist sect, "an international Buddhism that transcends cultural and national boundaries, creating . . . a cosmopolitan network of intellectuals, writing most often in English" (xxxix). This "sect" is rooted neither in geography nor in traditional schools but is the modern aspect of a variety of Buddhist schools in different locations. Moreover, it has its own cosmopolitan lineage and canonical "scriptures," mainly the works of popular and semischolarly authors—figures from the formative years of modern Buddhism, including Sōen Shaku, Dwight Goddard, D. T. Suzuki, and Alexandra David-Neel, as well as more recent figures like Shunryu Suzuki, Sangharakshita, Alan Watts, Thich Nhat Hanh, Chögyam Trungpa, and the Fourteenth Dalai Lama.

These closely related conceptions of Buddhist modernism provide a fine composite map of the basic territory this book will explore; but they do not tell the whole story. It is often said as a matter of course that modernist forms of Buddhism have been westernized, demythologized, rationalized, Romanticized, Protestantized, or psychologized, yet little has been done to illuminate the specific modern ideological forces, textual sources, social and cultural practices, overt philosophies, and tacit assumptions that have been involved in these ongoing processes. In this book, I want to excavate some of the specific modern western literature, concepts, ideologies, and practices that have intermingled with Buddhism to fashion a uniquely modernist form of the dharma.

I shall try to illuminate not only how Buddhism's encounter with modernity has changed it but also how the conditions of modernity have created implicit parameters for what interpretations of Buddhism become possible and impossible. What are the nonnegotiable elements of modernity to which Buddhism has conformed? What on the other hand are those aspects of modernity that Buddhism challenges and attempts to transform? How has Buddhist modernism situated itself within modern discourses of knowledge, social relations, science, and philosophy? How, in turn, have Asian Buddhists situated the discourses of modernity within more traditional Buddhist discourses? How has Buddhism been enlisted in preexisting concerns and debates inherent in western modernity? How and why have certain elements of the Buddhist traditions been selected as serving the needs of the modern world, while others have been ignored or suppressed? How has Buddhism fit into the metanarratives of American and European culture, and into those of an increasingly globalizing modernity? How did modernizers and reformers construct Buddhist responses to some of the issues inherent in modernity, and in doing so develop the intellectual underpinnings of new forms of Buddhism both shaped by and critical of modernity? And how have Buddhist texts, ideas, and practices come to be understood as addressing some of the modern West's—as well as the modern East's—deepest existential, social, and philosophical concerns? These are some of the questions I will ask as I try to ascertain some of the ways Buddhism and western modernity have become interfused.

Modernity and Buddhism

To comprehend the encounter between Buddhism and modernity, we must clarify the multivalent term "modernity" (though, as noted, the term "Buddhism" is not without its ambiguities as well). "Modernity" is a contested term in the humanities and social sciences, and perhaps no one definition can suffice, nor even one timeline. The modern state, for example, has a different history from modern philosophy or modern economics; moreover, multiple and competing narratives of modernity exist. It is safe to say, however, that modernity generally refers to the gradually emerging social and intellectual world rooted in the Protestant Reformation, the scientific revolution, the European Enlightenment, Romanticism, and their successors reaching up to the present. Most analysts of modernity agree that it has produced a profound destabilization of traditional forms, creating a dizzying onslaught of novel cultural situations. Marshall Berman's heated prose captures this sense, as well as some of the particulars of modernity:

> The maelstrom of modern life has been fed from many sources: great discoveries in the physical sciences, changing our images of the universe and our place in it; the industrialization of production, which transforms scientific knowledge into technology, creates new human environments and destroys old ones, speeds up the whole tempo of life, generates new forms of corporate power and class struggle; immense demographic upheavals, severing millions of people from their ancestral habitats, hurtling them halfway across the world into new lives; rapid and often cataclysmic urban growth; systems of mass

communication, dynamic in their development, enveloping and binding together the most diverse people and societies; increasingly powerful national states, bureaucratically structured and operated, constantly
striving to expand their powers; mass social movements of people, and
peoples, challenging their political and economic rulers, striving to
gain some control over their lives, finally, bearing and driving all these
people and institutions along, an ever-expanding, drastically fluctuating
capitalist world market. In the twentieth century, the social processes
that bring this maelstrom into being and keep it in a state of perpetual
becoming, have come to be called "modernization." (1982: 16)

Other associated factors include new forms of literature and art, the increase
and ease of global travel, and the various ideologies and rationales that have
helped create, renew, and legitimate many of these processes. The "maelstrom
of modern life" includes all of this and threatens to become so nebulous as to
be unmanageable, both in life and as an analytic category. Let us, therefore,
rein it in under some more manageable headings.

The Charles Taylor's wide-ranging account of modernity in his vast *Sources
of the Self: The Making of Modern Identity* (1989) provides some vessels in which
the philosophical, religious, and social facets of the maelstrom can be contained. Although he barely mentions Buddhism or Asian religions, his thematization of the sources of modernity provides a valuable analysis, at once
expansive and incisive, of the relevant conditions under which Buddhism encountered western thought and cultural practice. Without attempting to do justice to his lengthy, complex argument, throughout this work I will utilize some
of his major themes as a frame. I begin here by adopting his distillations of the
key elements of modernity into three broad domains of modern self-identity
and morality: western monotheism; rationalism and scientific naturalism;
and Romantic expressivism, along with their successors. Although these three
frameworks, which I will refer to as the "discourses of modernity," are rooted
in western historical periods and forms of life, they are essential to understanding the development of Buddhism modernism not only in the West but
across the globe.[3]

The theistic domain includes traditional concepts of God, person, and ethical obligations based primarily in Christianity. Most significant to my subject
are the ongoing ramifications of the Protestant Reformation, missionary activity in Asia, and later, attempts at dialogue and cooperation between Buddhism
and Christianity. Asian Buddhist reformers and western interpreters and enthusiasts in the nineteenth and early twentieth centuries often took Christianity as that to which Buddhism had to respond, either by imitation or critique

or both. From the scathing indictments of missionaries in Asian lands to the emulation of Protestant anticlericism, to the contemporary Buddhist-Christian dialogue movement, Christianity has been an ever-present source of creative tension with modernizing Buddhism. More recently, Judaism has become important to Buddhist modernism, as Jews make up a disproportionate percentage of American Buddhist converts and sympathizers.

The second domain is that of scientific naturalism and the tradition of rationalism rooted in the European Enlightenment. Part of the appeal of Buddhism to the West, as well as its renewed prestige in Asia, has been the prospect that Buddhism could be understood as a "rational religion" uniquely compatible with modern science. This has been an important aspect of the construction of Buddhist modernism historically and remains an essential part of its claims to legitimacy today. Yet many Buddhists have been critical of scientific materialism, the technologies of warfare, the destruction of the environment, and the hope that technology can bring about well-being. Buddhist modernism has, therefore, maintained an ambivalent relationship with science, allying itself with its basic claims on the one hand while attempting to serve as its corrective on the other.

The third domain of modernity, which Taylor calls Romantic expressivism, encompasses the literary, artistic, and philosophical movement that arose in part as a critique of the increasing rationalization, mechanization, and desacralization of the western world brought about by industrialism and the scientific revolution. This movement sought to reaffirm sacrality and mystery and to find hidden depths in nature, art, and the human soul that it claimed were increasingly occluded by calculating rationality and instrumental reason. It saw nature and feeling as sources of morality and spiritual knowledge and elevated art, creativity, self-expression, and personal fulfillment to virtually religious levels. The successors of the Romantic movement were among the most important influences in Buddhist modernism: the American Transcendentalists, Theosophists, and adherents of other alternative spiritualities and, later, the Beat poets and the countercultural figures of the 1960s. Romanticism in this broad sense provides many themes that have become important to Buddhist modernism, especially in the West. Romantic philosophy, art, and literature often give expression to a feeling of alienation from key features of the modern world, especially the stultifying effects of industrialism, materialistic capitalism, and militarism. Romantics have also tended to exoticize "the East" and project the hope that the ills of western society can be assuaged by the supposedly more spiritual, primal wisdom of Asia. Friedrich Schiller called the Romantics "exiles pining for a homeland," and some in this tradition clearly saw this homeland as the ever-distant and mysterious Other of the Orient. Echoes of Romanticism ring in modern Buddhist appeals to a return to the natural, to the probing of the deep interior of consciousness, to the suspicion of external authority, to the reveling in creative spontaneity, and to the perception of the oneness and interconnectedness of all life.

These themes bear on the role in Buddhist modernism of what Max Weber called the "disenchantment of the world" (a phrase Weber borrowed from Schiller) and modern attempts at reenchantment. Weber introduced the influential concept of disenchantment into sociology to describe modernity's displacing of traditional social orders—their ties of kinship, community, and the natural rhythms of work and ritual—with depersonalization, oppressive routine, bureaucratic roles, and technical rules. The deities, spirits, and mysterious powers of the premodern worldview had, according to Weber, given way to scientific explanation, rational calculation, and technological application. No longer could people live in a world in which a divine order, an ethically governed cosmos, was taken for granted. The "mechanized petrification" of the workplace and the empty glorification of accumulation and wealth had displaced that world (1958).

Weber's account of modernity, along with its associated secularization thesis—the idea that modernity necessarily entails the receding of religion from public life and, for many, its disappearance altogether—has not been borne out on a large scale. In fact, we see today a resurgence of traditional religion in many parts of the world. Secularization and disenchantment have no doubt occurred, but among limited populations, especially Europeans, the intelligentsia of North America, and the burgeoning middle class in various Asian nations. What is important here, though, is that regardless of whether disenchantment has been universal, the development of Buddhist modernism has often operated on Weberian assumptions. The disenchantment of the world has been felt among the class of people among whom are found the architects and adherents of Buddhist modernism, and the dynamics of disenchantment and reenchantment have been important engines of its development. There is a keen sense in the literature of Buddhist modernism that something has been lost—an intimate connection with nature, a view of the world as vital and animate rather than mechanistic, a peaceful harmony between human beings that has given way to the global threat of catastrophic violence. Such literature draws on a primitivism that has always been the shadow of rationalism, emerging full-blown in the Romantic period, where we see a longing to slough off the complexities of modern society, a valorization of the "noble savage," a modern mythical being innocent of modernity's fall into differentiation, artificiality, and nihilism—someone in harmony with his environment, without the acquisitiveness, the drive to power, or the spiritual vacuity of modern humanity.

Modernity, then, carries with it a nostalgia for the premodern and a hope that ancient traditions can help in reenchanting the world, through, ironically, their own kind of "sciences" and "technologies"—those of the spirit.

Closely related to disenchantment is what we might call a "crisis of meaning" many have believed is endemic to modernity. A term more fashionable among academics in the mid–twentieth century, it is yet crucial to understanding my subject, for this crisis, to which some have looked to Asian religions for solutions, arises under the unique conditions of modernity. It is different from spiritual crises of previous cultures, which were defined by what Taylor calls "inescapable frameworks" that make "imperious demands which we feel we are unable to meet" (1989: 118). Facing permanent exile, eternal damnation, or many unfavorable rebirths is different from facing the possibility of nihilism that has burdened modern life, with its displacement of a taken-for-granted, normative order of things. Even though many still live within religious frameworks that are virtually unquestioned, modernity has always been haunted by the specter of nihilism. Part of the way that Buddhism has engaged with modernity is in attempting to combat the particularly modern sense of nihilism and disenchantment, refashioning the dharma as a way of reenchanting and ushering escaped meaning back into the world while at the same time remaining within a broadly naturalistic cosmological framework and aligning itself with rationalistic and scientific sensibilities. There is, therefore, a constitutive tension in Buddhist modernism—one I will return to repeatedly in this book—between scientific rationalism and romantic expressivism. Buddhist modernism, I will show, takes on much of its shape through negotiating this tension.

Throughout each of these three discourses of modernity run themes that constitute some of modernity's inescapable axioms, to which any bid for inclusion in the modern project must respond: individualism, egalitarianism, liberalism, democratic ideals, and the impulse to social reform. Two themes Taylor stresses that run through all three discourses will be important here: first, a distinctively modern world-affirming stance, a sense that the locus of a meaningful life is not in another realm but in the way this life, everyday life, is lived, and second, the shift toward interiority, reflexivity, and self-scrutiny. This shift is characteristic of Enlightenment rationalism, in that truth comes to be seen as located in the mind's faculties of reason. Descartes's dualism imports all meaning to the mind itself, a move that drains all but instrumental significance from the material world. Protestantism gave unprecedented value to internal scrutiny and to the experience of God within, while Romanticism located the source of morality, creativity, and spirituality in the deep interior of the soul. This inwardness of various facets of modernity became crystallized in another, later discourse that had an immense impact on later Buddhist modernism: that of psychology. Beginning with Jung's archetypal psychoanalytic theory and working its way up to current intertwinings of psychotherapy and mindfulness practices, psychology would become one of the most commonly used lenses for the interpretation of Buddhism.

Yet if we leave the question of modernity here, we risk setting up a falsely homogeneous picture that the diversity of modernities across the globe challenges. In the classical western theories of modernity—Marx's and Durkheim's, for instance—the cultural program of modern Europe, its institutional bases, and its dominant ideologies are destined eventually and inevitably to spread across the globe, transforming all modernizing societies in their image. Yet the emerging reality has been more complex and variegated. Different societies have developed diverse instantiations of modernity at different periods of development, giving rise to an array of modernities with a variety of ideological and institutional programs, albeit with the "original" western modernity serving as an often ambivalent reference point. The modernization of nonwestern societies has seldom been a mere capitulation or accommodation of western iterations of modernity but rather has combined creative, heterogeneous adaptation of certain aspects of modernity with selective resistance to others. Many nonwestern cultures, moreover, have deployed particular features of modernity, for example the language of human rights, in the service of resistance to the West. Various Asian civilizations that have been colonized by European powers, for instance, have taken up the modern, western emphases on social protest, individual and cultural autonomy, and utopian social visions, exposing the ironies of colonization by those who espouse human freedom and turning western discourses of emancipation back on the western colonizers.[4] Significantly, the earliest forms of Buddhist modernism were in fact created in the forges of such resistance movements. For example, nationalistic Buddhist revival movements began in the nineteenth century in Ceylon and Japan in opposition to colonialism, Christian missionization, and western hegemony. More recent incarnations of Buddhist modernism also negotiate this tension between adopting aspects of western modernity and critiquing them. Socially engaged Buddhism both espouses and condemns various features of modernity, for example opposing western economic imperialism and militarism while employing western notions of women's rights and individual freedom. Other forms of Buddhist modernism that combine unique cultural elements with more global trends might be considered "indigenous modernities" that creatively entwine local or regional components of Buddhism with decidedly modernist elements. Modernity—and Buddhist modernity—are therefore not homogeneous.

The Theoretical and the Tacit

These discourses of modernity are not exclusive but overlap each other, constituting various languages of self-identity, social practice, and political thought. While some individuals, texts, or movements may embody one of these domains to the relative exclusion of the others, mostly they are interwoven not only with each other but with the fabric of everyday existence in much of the modern world. It is in no wise unthinkable to encounter a physicist who reads Romantic poetry and attends church on Sundays (and perhaps even a Buddhist meditation session on Thursday evenings). Moreover, these discourses should not be considered only intellectual, artistic, or religious movements but rather broad, often prereflective tendencies that define some of the possibilities for modern consciousness.

I am interested in attempting to account for some of the ways in which Buddhism has been infused into the world constituted by both the tacit understandings and social practices, on the one hand, and explicit theories on the other, that constitute modernity. In making this distinction between the tacit and theoretical, I underline the fact that a tradition that is introduced into a new cultural context (or into which a compelling new cultural form is introduced and becomes dominant, as modernity arguably has in Asian nations) must re-create itself in terms of the prevalent intellectual discourses, as well as the tacit background understandings of a society. The former are important especially for a tradition that, like Buddhism, has appealed mostly to educated cultural elites in the West and has therefore had to make a distinctive intellectual case for itself. But perhaps more important for success is that the tradition be able to engage with a culture's lived world: the daily repertory of practices, implicit ideas, and dispositions that structure perception and action, allowing people to engage in social intercourse, know what is appropriate and inappropriate, understand what to expect of each other, and discern power relations. The tradition must be able to engage with what various thinkers have called being-in-the-world (Heidegger), forms of life (Wittgenstein), *Lebenswelt* (phenomenology), habitus, and *doxa* (Bourdieu). The way a tradition is reconfigured in a new cultural context has much to do with what seems attractive, repulsive, or anomalous about it from the perspective of the tacit understandings and social practices of the dominant tradition—that is, what *resonates*. I use this rather vague term quite deliberately to suggest that the way a new cultural form succeeds or fails depends not only on its explicit theoretical formulations but also on a rather inarticulate *feeling* of whether it can make intuitive sense in terms of a culture's pretheoretical understandings and social practices. These form the hermeneutical context for understanding another culture, the "pre-understandings" and "prejudgments" (to adapt Gadamer's terms) that inevitably impose on it our own historical, cultural, and linguistic frameworks but that also are the precondition for comprehension. Such preunderstandings inevitably shape how a tradition will be taken up in another cultural context, the way it will find a niche in the new situation and mold itself to its contours.

This distinction between the theoretical and the tacit also informs my understanding of what I am calling the discourses of modernity. They have explicitly theoretical aspects, yet they are themselves tacit dimensions of modernity: they make up the inarticulate, normative ways of being that seem uniquely rooted in "reality" but are actually highly culturally and historically idiosyncratic. They include the languages that not only philosophers, scientists, and clergy use but also the ordinary people use to articulate their own self-understanding. As psychologist Kenneth Gergen points out, people in the West have long structured their identities in the languages rooted in rationalism and Romanticism—in rationalist terms, we are able to reason, form beliefs, act on conscious intentions, and make judgments; in Romantic terms, we have inner depth, passion, creativity, moral fiber (2000).[5] Locke's ideas on democracy and the rights of the individual have become diffused through the popular imagination to the extent that, even if the average person may not be able to give a skilful account of them—or may not have even heard of Locke—they form a part of his or her implicit understanding of "how things are." Buddhism has had to resonate with such implicit understandings as well as their theoretical expressions in its re-creation of itself as Buddhist modernism.[6] The reason Buddhist literature often appears to meet so seamlessly with our everyday assumptions is that modernist authors have found ways, no doubt often unconsciously, of articulating Buddhism in the languages of modernity.

Translation and Transformation

Identifying some of these broad coordinates of modern western life as deeply cultural and particular helps us appreciate the extent to which modernity is transforming Buddhism and creating novel Buddhist cultures. The uniqueness of these cultures is something generally unappreciated by even some very serious practitioners in the West. Here is an example. What could be more commonplace than a Buddhist—or perhaps someone simply "into" Buddhism[7]—going to a good bookstore, browsing a bit, purchasing a translation of a classic primary text, then going home and reading it? Besides meditation, most western Buddhists would consider reading Buddhist books one of their primary activities as

Buddhists, and many have come to Buddhism through books (Coleman 2001: 199). Yet, as Jay Garfield points out, in no other period in Buddhist history before about the past century or two has this been a common practice, or in many cases even a possibility. In most Buddhist cultures, the book has served as support for oral recitation. Traditional Tibetan monks, for example, read sutras aloud, memorizing their words and reciting them to their teachers. They do not peruse the Buddhist canon and choose to read Cāndrakīrti one week and Vasubhandu another, according to whim, but follow an established curriculum. Outside of this curriculum, virtually no one ever reads these texts. Not only were there no bookstores and no widespread print culture in traditional Buddhist contexts but, until the recent global explosion of literacy, there were few people who could even read such texts. It would have occurred to virtually no one, furthermore, simply to pick up such a book and try to understand it for himself (even less *her*self). The vast canonical literature of Buddhism was written as an aid to oral and personal instruction by an authorized teacher. To attempt to read such texts without the help of a teacher and outside all established pedagogy would have been—and still is considered by some—folly. Thus the translation of canonical texts into Western languages is not just a linguistic translation; it is also a cultural transformation, or rather the establishment of a new, unprecedented textual practice in a new Buddhist culture shaping itself to the textual practices of modernity.

But the transformation does not stop there, as text itself is transformed in its being translated. As Garfield insists, all transmission and translation are also inevitably transformation:

> When we translate, we transform in all of the following ways: we replace terms and phrases with particular sets of resonances in their source language with terms and phrases with very different resonances in the target language; we disambiguate ambiguous terms, and introduce new ambiguities; we interpret, or fix particular interpretations of texts in virtue of the use of theoretically loaded expressions in our target language; we take a text that is to some extent esoteric and render it exoteric simply by freeing the target language reader to approach the text without a teacher; we shift the context in which a text is read and used (forthcoming)

Key terms activate certain frames of reference, certain nexuses of ideas, emotions, and behavior. We might, for example, translate the Sanskrit term *mokṣa* as "freedom." In Buddhism, this means liberation from rebirth in samsara as an embodied being, as well as liberation from destructive mental states (*kleśas*), craving, hatred, and delusion, and from the suffering (*duḥkha*) they produce.

When, however, *mokṣa* is translated as "freedom"—a perfectly justified translation, by the way—it cannot help but pick up the tremendous cultural resonances this word has in modern European languages and cultures. It inevitably
rings the notes of individual freedom, creative freedom, freedom of choice,
freedom from oppression, freedom of thought, freedom of speech, freedom
from neuroses, free to be me—let freedom ring, indeed. It is virtually impossible to hear this word without a dense network of meanings lighting up, meanings deeply implicated in the history, philosophies, ideologies, and everyday
assumptions of the modern West. The translation of one of Buddhism's central
terms, *bodhi*, provides another example. It literally means "awakening" and
describes the Buddha's highest attainment under the bodhi tree. The most
common English translation, "enlightenment," invokes, however, a complex
of meanings tied to the ideas, values, and sensibilities of the European Enlightenment: reason, empirical observation, suspicion of authority, freedom of
thought, and so on. Early translators, moreover, consciously forged this link.
Buddhist studies pioneer Thomas W. Rhys Davids (1843–1922) first translated
bodhi as "Enlightenment" and explicitly compared the Buddha with the philosophers of the European Enlightenment (1882: 30).

It is not that we must find other words to translate *mokṣa* and *bodhi*, thus
solving the "problem." While we might find more adequate and less ideologically
loaded terms, there can never be a translation that carries all possible meanings
and associations seamlessly from the original language and refuses all novel
meanings and associations in the new context. Translation and transmission is
inevitably—word-by-word, text-by-text, culture-by-culture—transformation.

The Hybridity of Buddhist Modernism

Most people in modern societies of the West have little idea that what they
refer to as Buddhism is actually a rich mixture of a number of different cultural
and intellectual currents from Asia, Europe, and North America. The history
of Buddhism is long and complex, spanning more than 2,500 years and, now,
virtually the entire globe. Moreover, it has an immense corpus of literature and
many distinct traditions, each a product of the different cultures in which it has
taken root. It is, therefore, inevitable that the adaptation of Buddhism to cultures outside Asia has entailed a highly selective appropriation of teachings,
practices, and texts. In all of the geographic areas where Buddhist traditions
have emerged, the dharma has been understood in terms of the categories,
practices, conventions, and historical circumstances of particular peoples at
specific times. They have, in fact, shown a remarkable adaptability, taking on

widely different forms in various geographical areas and transforming, absorbing, superseding, and accommodating local ideas and practices.

Through incorporating elements of a new culture and leaving behind irreconcilable ones, traditions inevitably become hybrids of what were already hybrid traditions. This hybridity, however, is not simply a process of weeding out what does not conform to the implicit norms of the new cultural context. It involves a reconfiguration of both tradition and context through contestation and negotiation as much as enthusiastic embrace. In many places where Buddhism has become a significant presence, it has been introduced and adapted in highly specific ways. In Tibet, for example, it was the government that was interested in Buddhism—initially its magic more than its philosophy and meditation. In the case of China, Buddhism was brought in by merchants and immigrants from South and Central Asia and gained cultural currency among the aristocracy. The tenor of crisis that ensued during collapse of the Han dynasty provoked an unprecedented openness to outside ideas and practices. Negotiations over the meanings of Buddhism to the Chinese—how much it could be assimilated to Daoist and Confucian thought, how a celibate monastic tradition could be understood in a place where family was paramount, how much of what the Chinese knew of Buddhism was "original"—continued for centuries.

In Europe and America, too, Buddhism has been adapted and infused into preexisting discourses and debates, interpreted in terms of modern western categories and assumptions, and called on to confirm or refute western philosophies, ideologies, and cultural practices. To conceive of the cultural locations of Buddhist modernism and of how Buddhist ideas and practices have been enlisted and transformed within the context of western discourses, we must understand how Buddhism's infusion into these discourses has created novel forms of Buddhism shaped as much by the taxonomies, concerns, and anxieties of nineteenth- and twentieth- (and now twenty-first) century America and Europe as by traditional aspects of Buddhism. The "native traditions" of the West that Buddhism has engaged with include Theosophy and other metaphysical traditions, analytic psychology, Christianity, and Judaism, as well as the pervasive discourses of Enlightenment rationalism, Romanticism, and now postmodernism. Such encounters have, as noted, already produced novel forms of Buddhism, but the transformation has not been one-way; Buddhist ideas and practices have had a significant impact on America and the West. From its dubious embrace by Schopenhauer and Wagner to the Victorian enthusiasm for it in England and America, to its explosion onto the American scene in the 1950s and 1960s with its vital influence on the Beat writers and other figures in literature, philosophy, psychology, and the arts, Buddhism has been an important if sometimes veiled element in the cultural life of Europe and North America.

Constructive engagement with modernity began with an effort by Asian Buddhists to defend Buddhism against not only negative western representations but also European imperialism in Asia. Buddhist revivalism in Ceylon in the late nineteenth and early twentieth centuries, for example, was primarily an attempt to reinvent Buddhism in response to western colonial oppression and missionization. Similar movements occurred in other Asian countries. Thus, Buddhist modernism began in a context not of mutual curiosity, cultural exchange, and open-minded ecumenical dialogue, but of competition, crisis, and the violence of colonialism. The hybridity of Buddhist modernism, therefore, sometimes corresponds to cultural theorist Homi Bhabha's influential use of this term. Bhabha conceives of hybridity in a special sense germane to relations between colonizers and the colonized, referring to ways a colonized people imitate cultural and discursive forms of the dominant power, often turning them in subtle ways against it (1994). Such a model may well apply in, for example, colonial Ceylon, which developed forms of Buddhism that were simultaneously imitative of and resistant to colonial powers. Other places, for example Japan and Tibet, were never colonized by the West, and the dynamics of European colonization cannot fully explain the intermediary forms of Buddhism that arose in these locations.[8] The hybridity of Buddhist modernism, therefore, is multifaceted and not reducible to one model.

Similarly, orientalism—in Edward Said's sense of scholarly representations of the Orient that are implicitly tied to ideologies and political programs of European subjugation of Asian and Middle Eastern peoples—is clearly relevant but not adequate to explain all aspects of my subject. Orientalism has undoubtedly played a significant role in the creation of Buddhist modernism, but it would be mistaken to reduce all of Buddhist modernism to enactments of orientalist fantasies or to responses to colonialism or postcolonialism. Some of the developments I will discuss are saturated with orientalism, while in others its presence is more like an echo in the background giving way to more contemporary realities. A number of analyses of Buddhist modernism have treated it as primarily a western discursive construction or a kind of western fantasy rooted in orientalism and corresponding to no real object. No doubt the literature of Buddhist modernism has no shortage of western representations that utterly fail to provide a coherent understanding of Buddhism or that subsume it so completely under western modes of interpretation that they would be unrecognizable to most Asian Buddhists. Analysis of such representations are an important part of this study, yet the understanding of Buddhist modernism primarily *as* a collection of western representations of Buddhism is inadequate, for two reasons. First, many of the important creators of Buddhist modernism were not westerners but Asian Buddhists who actively engaged with orientalist representations of Buddhism, adopting some features of them and countering others in accordance with various strategic interests. Seeing Buddhist modernism strictly in terms of western representations occludes the agency of Asian Buddhists as cocreators of modernist versions of their traditions (Snodgrass 2003: 10–15, King 1999: 149). Second, the many modernist scholarly and popular constructions of Buddhism, some of which have indeed been fantasies, nevertheless have not been *idle* fantasies. They have been productive, fashioning of new ways of being Buddhist practiced by living, breathing people around the globe. Fantasy, as the psychoanalysts have told us, is not something easily dismissed. It tells us important things about the fantasizer and can transform that which is fantasized about. Modern representations of Buddhism, even when they have been inadequate as historical description, have conditioned what Buddhism has become. Seeing Buddhist modernism solely in terms of representations and scholarly construction, therefore, neglects the most important thing to the historian of religions: that a novel, historically unique form of Buddhism has emerged in the last 150 years.

Sources and Strategies

This study is thematic, analytic, and illustrative rather than comprehensive. That is, I have endeavored to critically examine certain themes that illustrate enduring patterns and motifs of Buddhist modernism rather than attempting a survey of the subject that addresses every important figure or movement. I have chosen particular contemporary ideas and practices that have an interesting and illuminating history and represent important trends in the interpretation of Buddhism and the creation of Buddhist modernism. I often use as a starting point some themes that my mostly American students are likely to encounter at popular bookstores. This portrait of Buddhist modernism, therefore, is not one that attempts to cover every contour and capture every color of this widely diverse movement. Certain features are rendered in bright light; others are left in shadow with vague outlines coming through. The colors are refracted through the developments that have been prominent in the West, especially North America, where Buddhism has proven most successful. This does not always mean I am studying "Buddhism in America," however, but that I will often use North America as a starting point. I do this for a number of reasons. As Lopez suggests, English has become the lingua franca of Buddhist modernism. Books in English have been disproportionately influential around the globe, as have American teachers and Asian teachers who have become popular in the United States. Using literature mainly in English as starting point admittedly imposes certain limitations on this book. Buddhist modernism might look quite different if, for example, we started from popular Thai tracts or ethnographies of Sri Lankan meditation centers. And no doubt this research needs to be done! But North America provides an illuminating point of departure, for it has had an important relationship to Buddhist modernism. This is not because, as is often implied in popular literature, European Americans have always been the bold innovators at the forefront of adapting the dharma to the times and Asians always a force for maintaining moribund tradition. In fact, Asian Buddhists have usually been the pivotal figures in the reformation and revitalization of Buddhism in terms coherent with modernity. North America is important, rather, because more than any other place outside Asia it has been the locus of many important attempts to re-conceive Buddhism in modern terms. For over a century it has been the place where European, American, and Asian Buddhists alike have launched representations of Buddhism gauged to western sensibilities but reverberating back to Asia and around the world, becoming forces that have shaped Buddhism globally. In addition to the fact that Buddhism has become more popular in the United States than in any other non-Asian nation and that there now exist hundreds of Buddhist temples and dharma centers there, that country has played a key role as an incubator of new Buddhist representations and realities for Asians as well as Americans and Europeans. Nonetheless, the primary category through which I want to view my subject is modernity rather than any particular geographical area. In that Buddhist modernism is nothing if not transnational, I do not want to conceptualize it primarily according to national boundaries, even though I am looking at it from a particular shore.

The stratum of literature I have often found most useful for analyzing Buddhist modernism is neither scholarly literature nor the growing body of thirdhand and generally uninformed books—for instance, those on Zen and golf (seven are listed on Amazon.com as of this writing!)—but rather the works for the general but educated reader that are either influential formulations of Buddhist modernism or later works that take it for granted as representative of Buddhism as a whole. My general method is to work backward from themes common in contemporary Buddhist literature popular in the United States (though not necessarily written by westerners) and then look for earlier sources of these representations in the works of seminal Buddhist modernizers, thus tracing some of the most recent manifestations of Buddhist modernism to those in the formative period, the late nineteenth and early twentieth centuries. This means that much of the early material I address consists of interpretations of either Theravada or Japanese Zen traditions. Although Tibetan, Chinese, Korean, and other Japanese traditions, for example Soka Gakkai, have become important to modernist Buddhism more recently, the transformations of Theravada and Zen established many of the enduring motifs of Buddhist modernism from the early period. Crucial to reconstructing the history of the thematic elements of Buddhist modernism that I address is the attempt to untangle their western historical, cultural, ideological, and philosophical sources from their traditional Buddhist sources. In this way I hope to show some of the ways specific strains of Buddhism have crossfertilized with particular western traditions. I have not endeavored in this work to unearth new, idiosyncratic, or undiscovered Buddhist modernists but conversely to ascertain the historical significance of some of the most influential, for it is they who have created my subject.

Chapters 1–3 lay out some general interpretive ideas, some historical movements, and some particular examples that place Buddhist modernism in its broad intellectual and cultural contexts. Each of the five succeeding chapters probes more deeply the development of a single illustrative idea or practice.

In chapter 2, I discuss some of what distinguishes a Buddhist "modernist" from a more "traditional" Buddhist, first by drawing a few composite portraits of Buddhists across the modern/traditional spectrum, and second by addressing some of the factors in modernization: demythologization, detraditionalization, and psychologization.

In chapter 3, I discuss some of the ways Buddhism has engaged with and positioned itself in relation to the three discourses of modernity—scientific rationalism, Romanticism, and Christianity. I argue that Buddhist modernism has not only been significantly influenced by these discourses but also has carved out a place for itself in the tensions between them. In short, it has aligned itself with scientific rationalism to make a case that it is a "rational religion" over against Christianity. Yet it has also been wary of the materialistic implications of science and has drawn on the language of Romanticism, along with psychology, with their emphasis on interior depths and internal realities, to counter these implications.

Chapters 4–7 examine more closely particular ideas and practices that exemplify the hybridity of Buddhist modernism, especially as it negotiates the tensions between rationalist and Romantic discourses. In chapter 4, I examine the development of the idea that among the world's religions Buddhism is uniquely compatible with modern science or, in a more radical formulation, is and has always been itself scientific. I trace this idea's emergence to two intertwined crises in the late nineteenth and early twentieth centuries: the crisis of colonialism, which led colonized Buddhists like Anagarika Dharmapala to reconstruct Buddhism in terms compatible with science and rationalism in order to restore its prestige, and the Victorian crisis of faith, which led westerners like Paul Carus and Henry Steel Olcott to set out on a quest for a rational spirituality in harmony with science.

Chapter 5 probes the development of a modern relationship between Buddhism and creativity that, I argue, comes from a hybridization between certain specific elements of the Buddhist tradition—particularly Zen—and Romanticism and its successors. D. T. Suzuki's discussions of creativity have been essential to this development, as has his amalgamation of Zen with concepts of spontaneity and the unconscious from Romanticism, Transcendentalism, and psychoanalytic traditions. His creative blending of these has led to art, creativity, and spontaneity becoming key values in Buddhist modernism up to the present.

Chapter 6 brings the rationalist and Romantic modes together, exploring the history of the idea of interdependence. In order to contrast classical views of interdependence from modern ones, I begin with the implications of dependent origination (*pratītya-samutpāda*) in various South Asian formulations, then briefly consider some East Asian views of nature. Then I explore some of the ways conceptions of nature deriving from both Romanticism and science have informed a reconfiguration of the idea of Buddhist interdependence, shaping it into a world-affirming ecological worldview with political and ethical implications unique to the contemporary world.

Chapters 7 and 8 discuss the interweaving of various modern western ideas and social currents with Buddhist practices, specifically those that have become central to Buddhist modernism: mindfulness and meditation. Chapter 7 discusses the interface between Buddhist meditation techniques and the "subjective turn," the development of a modern form of radical reflexivity and privatized spirituality in the West. Modern discourse on meditation, I argue, has been influenced by scientific rationalism, Romanticism, psychology, and liberal social theory, while novel applications of meditation outside specifically Buddhist contexts have served to deinstitutionalize and detraditionalize Buddhist meditation, setting it loose from the traditional forms of Buddhism while, paradoxically, making it more central to the tradition than it was before.

Chapter 8 looks at the contemporary practice of mindfulness, placing it in a distinctively modern mode of world-affirmation that has transformed the practice from a way of transcending the world into a way of embracing and reenchanting it without resort to the supernatural. A significant part of this reenchantment, I argue, is derived from a hybridizing of Buddhist mindfulness with modes of consciousness derived in part from modern literary sensibilities that give new attention and valorization to the details of ordinary life.

Finally, the concluding chapter considers some recent developments and issues regarding Buddhism in the contemporary period. I considers radicalizations of the tendencies toward detraditionalization in North America along with countermoves toward *re*traditionalization and reappropriation of traditional themes. I also discuss a tension in contemporary Buddhism between social engagement and private spirituality and sketch some ideas on the capacity of Buddhism modernism (or postmodernism) to challenge, critique, and contribute novel insights to western modernity in light of the degree to which it has adapted to it.

2

The Spectrum of Tradition
and Modernism

Portraits of Traditional and Modern Buddhism

The line demarcating a modernist from a traditionalist is often
blurry and uneven. Modernists may openly refute certain elements
of tradition or claim to be going back to the true, original tradition.
Modernist movements often do not set out to establish something
new but on the contrary may claim to be casting off the new and
reviving the old. Such revival, however, is deeply and inevitably
conditioned by the language, social forms, practices, and worldviews
of the present. Whether self-consciously conservative or innovative,
traditions must reconfigure themselves in ways that allow them to
participate in the conversations of the day. This may involve radical
accommodation or radical challenge, but it always means novelty.

In order to clarify further the ways Buddhists have rethought
their traditions in response to the essential features of modernity,
I want to sketch a few portraits of traditional and modernist
Buddhists. These portraits, I hope, will help clarify various
practitioners' relationships to each other and thus more precisely
delineate the contours of Buddhist modernism. These are composite
portraits assembled rather unsystematically from interviewees, public
figures, Buddhist authors, and scholarly ethnographies. They should
in no way be taken as representative of all the possible ways of being
Buddhist in the late modern world but, rather, illustrative of points
on the continuum between modern and traditional. Specifically,

I want them, first, to show the profound differences between the extremes of traditional and modernist forms of Buddhism; second, to illustrate some of the ways tradition and modernism are sometimes intertwined; and third, to deal with themes that are prominent today but can be traced back to the formative period of Buddhist modernism.

A Western Buddhist Sympathizer

We begin with the type of Buddhist the American and European readers of this book are perhaps most likely to encounter: those who may or may not identify themselves as Buddhists per se but could be called "Buddhist sympathizers."[1] Sara, a middle-aged British woman, is a middle-class, educated professional with a family. She was raised in the Church of England and still attends occasionally, seeing little conflict between membership in the church and Buddhist practice. She began exploring Buddhism by reading a book by a popular American Buddhist author, and most of her contact with the tradition is still through books, mostly popular works by American or British teachers and a few prominent Asian ones. She has read a little of the Buddhist canon of scripture—only short selections. She knows no monastics, and while she has attended a few weekend retreats at a meditation center run by other Brits, she has never been to a traditional Buddhist temple and has no institutional affiliation. She considers meditation to be the essence of Buddhism and tries to meditate for about twenty minutes every day. She is part of an informal, "nondenominational" Buddhist meditation group that meets weekly in a rented hall. The group was started by another Brit who has had extensive experience with meditation but no formal ties to any Buddhist organization. The weekly meditation sessions contain little ritual—some bowing and a few verses chanted in English and borrowed from the more extensive liturgy the founder of the group encountered on retreat at a monastery. As a part of the brief liturgy, Sara bows in the direction of a small statue of the Buddha, an act she sees as a perfunctory gesture of respect, an expression of her assent to the basic principles taught by the Buddha, and as acknowledging her Buddha-nature—the spark of awakening within each being. She in no way sees herself as "worshiping" the Buddha, much less his sculpted form.

Sara sees meditation as a technique for achieving personal peace and psychological health and for appreciating and enhancing the richness of her everyday life. Her association with Buddhism, however, is not only limited to her personal meditation; it also affects her ethical choices and her relationships with others. She understands her practice to be conducive to moral behavior and to the cultivation of good relationships with others, as well as clear thinking and creativity. The teaching of compassion for all sentient beings has led her to eat less meat, and she has come to support certain environmental and social justice causes through reading about engaged Buddhism, a recent global movement that takes an active role in promoting peace, justice, human rights, and environmental care. She tries to maintain a practice of mindfulness periodically throughout the day and regularly reminds herself of the *brahmavihāras*— loving-kindness, compassion, sympathetic joy, and equanimity. This helps her manage her relationships with coworkers, friends, and family with a more calm and compassionate attitude. Her practice, therefore, impacts her ethical and social life but not in terms of particular actions that she considers permitted or forbidden. The Buddhist precept against taking intoxicants, for example, does not prevent her from having a glass of wine with dinner. Mistrustful of institutionalized "rules," she is guided by general ideals of compassion and nonviolence and by the notion that a calm, mindful state will naturally lead to ethical behavior. She believes that performing ethically positive or negative actions is likely to bring about similar consequences in her life, but she does not believe her practice will bring her good fortune or prosperity.

Her worldview is an amalgam of popularized Buddhist and Hindu teachings and generally accepted scientific ideas. The supernatural does not play a big part in her life but remains a tantalizing possibility for her. She believes in the possibility of supernormal events like telepathy but assumes that these could in principle be explained scientifically. She believes in what she would describe as something "greater" than herself: a higher power, energy, or all-encompassing consciousness within all beings and permeating the world. The ideas of God, Brahman, and buddha-nature all point to this one ultimate reality. Although she prefers Buddhist teachings, she reads popular books and attends occasional talks by Hindu and neo-pagan teachers. She has no allegiance to any particular Buddhist tradition, for the books she reads by popular Zen, Theravada, and Tibetan authors are all quite similar. She feels free to adopt, adapt, alter, or reject elements of Buddhism that she sees as products of Asian cultures rather than of a more universal "spiritual" truth beyond the trappings of culture. She is encouraged in this freedom of choice by Buddhist teachings emphasized in popular literature: the idea that the dharma is merely a raft useful for crossing a river but of no further use once it is crossed; that all truths are relative except the one universal Truth beyond all language and concepts; that Buddhism does not accept assertions that are contradicted by science; that all teachings, even Buddhist ones, must be verified by personal experience; that all doctrines are merely skilful means (*upāya*) adopted to each individual—fingers pointing to the moon that become redundant once the moon is seen. Thus her explicit beliefs about matters metaphysical are vague and shifting. She believes, for instance, that she will continue in some sense to live beyond physical death, but vacillates on the idea of reincarnation. She has read an account of the Buddhist wheel of rebirth in which beings are reborn as humans, animals, gods, jealous gods, hungry ghosts, or hell beings but doubts their literal existence, seeing them as symbolic. Nor does she find the idea of escaping earthly life appealing; rather, she seeks to live it more deeply, richly, and compassionately.

A Thai Laywoman

Yanisa lives in a small city in northern Thailand. She was born into a poor family and married a shop owner of slightly higher socioeconomic status. Her main religious activities consist of following ethical rules laid down by the *sangha* and performing rituals to produce karmic merit and control unseen beings. She believes that such meritorious actions will not only benefit her and her family in this lifetime but also increase their chances of being reborn in the higher heavenly realms rather than the realm of animals, the realm of hungry ghosts, or hells. She also considers ritual and ethical acts to be conducive to prosperity and good fortune. One of the key meritorious actions she performs is *dāna*, regularly giving money and gifts to support the local monastery. Once a week, she goes to the monastery and listens to the monks chant scriptures in Pali, a language she does not understand, hears a sermon by a monk, and receives again the five precepts, renewing her commitment not to kill, lie, steal, have prohibited sex, or take intoxicants. She walks piously around the stupas— monuments containing relics of deceased monks—and makes offerings of incense, flowers, and candles at the altar before the large Buddha statue, praying for her own and her family's well-being. At home, she makes similar offerings daily at the household altar as well as at the spirit house, just outside the home, for the household and yard spirits who protect the family residence. At every major event in life—marriage, childbirth, death, the building of a house, the plowing of a new field—she and her family perform carefully prescribed rituals to honor helpful spirits, protect them from malicious ones, and draw on the power of the Buddha, dharma, and *sangha*. She has never meditated and would consider it presumptuous to do so.

She believes implicitly that a sacred power imbues certain objects: consecrated Buddha statues, stupas containing relics of the Buddha or Buddhist saints, and the palm-leaf manuscripts of Buddhist scriptures. The copper amulet with an impression of a famous Buddhist saint worn around her neck not only reminds her of her moral obligations, it protects her from misfortune and confers prosperity. She is aware that some in her community, including some prominent Buddhist monks, look askance at spirit reverence, discourage the use of amulets, and approve offerings to the Buddha only as a token of respect, remembrance, and gratitude, but she considers this attitude an interesting anomaly. Most people she knows take the existence of spirits as a given, and she not only has seen the results of honoring and propitiating them but also has heard tales of tragedy befalling those who dare ignore them. She believes that certain powerful monks can foretell the future and perform miraculous healings through their ability to enter into advanced states of concentration (*jhānas*). She has no doubt that she will be reborn in the future and that her actions now will affect the conditions of her future lives, as well as the remainder of her present life.

Another source of merit Yanisa and her husband received recently was their teenage son's ordination as a monk. Although he will not remain a monk throughout his entire life, his ordination brought him and his parents merit, as well as social prestige. Through ordination he will receive an education they otherwise could not afford, and after his schooling he will likely disrobe and find a secular job. Her son's ordination brought a deep sense of pride since, among other more practical motivations, his ordination was an act of gratitude toward his parents, especially his mother, for bringing him into the world and tending to him throughout his childhood. Ordination is not an option for her, since there is no authorized order of fully ordained nuns in her country.

Although Yanisa is literate, she reads very little about Buddhism. An occasional pamphlet works its way into her household, and she read comic-book tales of the Buddha's life and previous lives to her son when he was young. She would be unable to articulate any complex Buddhist doctrines but knows the formative stories of the tradition—especially the legend of the Buddha and the tales of his former lives—through her family, her modest schooling, and her immersion in a Buddhist culture.

An American Dharma Teacher

Rachel is a Jewish American woman from an urban, upper-middle-class family. She was raised attending an Orthodox synagogue in which her parents were active. She studied anthropology as a college student and lived in India on a study abroad program, where she first became interested in Asian religions and was introduced to meditation at an ashram catering to westerners. She continued reading books on Buddhism and Hinduism when she returned home and began a regular meditation routine. After some more traveling in the United States and abroad, she settled in a major metropolitan area, got a master's degree in counseling psychology, and took a job as a counselor.

Meanwhile, she began meditating more frequently, twice daily for about thirty minutes. She began attending weekly *zazen* meditation at a local Zen center run by a Japanese priest. Throughout the years she became more deeply involved in the center, sitting on the administrative board and spending her vacation time in rigorous *sesshins* with up to ten hours per day of sitting and walking meditation. She eventually received lay ordination (*jukai*) in a ceremony that marked official entrance into the Buddhist community and obligated her to follow sixteen precepts. At the suggestion of her *rōshi* (Zen master), she spent a year at a Zen monastery in Japan that was accustomed to working with dedicated western students and would accept a woman for training. After years of dedicated lay practice, she received dharma transmission from her *rōshi* in the United States, giving her sanction for teaching. After years as a junior teacher at the center, she was invited to become the head *rōshi* at another Zen center. Although it attracts a handful of African and Latino Americans and a couple of second- and third-generation Asian Americans, her center is mostly middle- and upper-class European American professionals.

Rachel has learned the intricate ritual grammar of the Japanese monastery as a part of her training and incorporates it into her practice. She sees these rituals as tools for mindfulness and ways of bringing meditative awareness to everyday activities. Bowing to the Buddha-image is bowing to the Buddha-nature in oneself, not to an external being from which one expects help. Ritual setting aside of food for hungry ghosts is not done with the expectation that such beings—if they exist—will actually benefit from the nourishment, but as occasions to develop mindful compassion toward the hungry and the poor. She does not expect her practice of Buddhism to make her more prosperous or ward off undesirable events and considers such motives for practice primitive and superstitious. Rather, she sees practice as working with her ability to respond with wisdom and compassion to misfortune when it does happen. She also feels free to reject or reinterpret many traditional aspects of Buddhist doctrine, such as those involving a plethora of super- and subhuman beings and prescientific cosmology, which she interprets largely in psychological terms. She considers the fundamental teachings of Buddhism to be in agreement with, and in many ways to surpass, the insights of modern psychology, ecology, and philosophy. She interprets the doctrine of dependent origination (*pratītya-samutpāda*), for example, as cognate with a modern ecological understanding of the world. Unlike either Sara or Yanisa, she struggles with the difficult philosophical teachings of Buddhism, reading Dōgen, Nāgārjuna, and other classical authors in addition to modern ones.

A dynamic speaker with a warm personality, Rachel has become known for making abstruse Zen teachings accessible to Americans and softening the sometimes harsh elements of Zen that she sees as deeply rooted in Japanese culture and unhelpful in an American context. She understands that Buddhism in Asia is often far from egalitarian and supports reform of the hierarchical and patriarchal aspects of Buddhist institutions. The Zen center that she runs functions democratically, electing not only board members but also the head *rōshi*. She travels regularly to give lectures, retreats, and workshops at other Zen centers, churches, retreat centers, and colleges. She is also publicly supportive of progressive political movements, speaking out on the environment, peace, justice, human rights, and gay and lesbian issues in her dharma talks.

A Traditional Monk

Lobsang is a Tibetan in his forties living in India among a large refugee community. He arrived in India as a child, went to public school, and became a monk in his late teens. He was ordained in the Gelukpa school, which emphasizes scholarship and study. As a monk in one of the larger training monasteries in exile, Lobsang's primary activities are participating in rituals and pursuing the rich intellectual life that characterizes Gelukpa institutions. Each day at the monastery is divided into a cycle of rituals, including propitiatory rites for the guardians of the monastery, prayers to various deities, and recitations of sutras. The monks also perform seasonal rituals, which are often large, costly, and time consuming, celebrating particular deities with dancing, construction of mandalas, and tantric practices that symbolically identify the practitioners with the deities. In addition, Lobsang and many of his fellow monks perform rituals for the laity for various practical purposes such as repelling evil spirits, curing illness, and bringing about good luck. These rituals have a practical purpose for Lobsang as well: since monks must generally support themselves, performing rituals for compensation is the way they are able to obtain their basic necessities. He lives at a fairly rudimentary level in terms of material comforts, but some of his fellow monks who come from wealthier families, spend more of their time performing paid rituals, or have western supporters live much better than he.

The most important rituals Lobsang performs are tantric in character; that is, they involve evoking and identifying with a particular deity. To become qualified to perform such rituals, he was initiated in empowerment ceremonies that allow him to practice with particular deities, visualizing them and mastering the mantras and *mudrās* (hand gestures) associated with them. While these can be performed with soteriological goals, they have also been domesticated for more instrumental ends. Lobsang has been empowered to perform the tantric rituals of a number of deities, each with different characteristics and employed for different purposes—peaceful ones for peaceful purposes and wrathful ones for more aggressive purposes like driving away evil spirits. Like Yanisa, Lob-sang has no doubt that various kinds of invisible entities populate the world and must be propitiated and employed for help in worldly matters. Such be-ings include ghosts, local spirits, dharma protectors, and, on a more elevated level, tantric deities, as well as the Buddhas and bodhisattvas of the traditional Mahāyāna pantheon.

Lobsang's education as a monk began after he had completed secondary school in a public, secular institution—albeit with mainly monks as teachers. The first three years were dedicated to memorizing and reciting texts, a task that occupied many of his waking hours. For the next three years, he developed his rhetorical skills and honed his hermeneutical acumen through long hours of vigorous debate with other monks. He then spent another twelve years in inten-sive study of sutras and commentarial texts. After nearly twenty years of train-ing, he attained his *geshe (dge bshes)* degree—the highest degree possible in the Gelukpa school—and now spends a great deal of time teaching other monks. His duties also include time-consuming administrative tasks, an inevitable part of the complex bureaucracy of the monastery. He maintains close contact with his family and some friends outside the monastery and socializes with them when he can.

Like most of his fellow monks at the monastery, he does not engage in for-mal meditation, though the memorization, recitation, and tantric rituals he per-forms contain quasi-meditative elements that train the attention. He knows a small number of monks who have pursued serious meditation training, spend-ing years in hermitages and secluded caves, but the vast majority of his associ-ates have chosen study over meditation. He plans some day to pursue a course of meditation at a special monastery and possibly even spend time in a solitary hermitage later in life. Although he believes in the possibility of awakening and anticipates that some day he will attain it, he has no expectation of such an attain-ment in his current lifetime, despite references to this possibility in the tantric scriptures he has memorized. He recognizes that such a goal would involve the intensive practice of solitary meditation over a period of many years—perhaps even many lifetimes. He does, however, view his monastic vocation as a merito-rious life that will help him, as well as those he serves, attain a favorable rebirth and decrease the number of rebirths he will have to undergo before attaining full awakening.

An Asian Modernizer

Ananda is another Asian monk, but of a different sort from Lobsang. He was educated not only in his own Buddhist tradition but has also attended a

European university. He is well read in western literature, speaks English fluently, and is the author of books in English as well as his own language. His books have brought him recognition in the Buddhist populations of a number of countries in Asia and Europe, and he has traveled widely, having been invited to many places to give talks and conduct retreats. He has talked with Jews, Christians, scientists, and political figures, reads international newspapers, and is conversant with current events.

Because of his experience with western education, society, and cultural forms, his understanding of Buddhism is infused with other worldviews. Lobsang's education has taken place exclusively within one tradition; Ananda attempts to synthesize not only different schools of Buddhism but also Buddhist and western thought. He advocates modern conceptions of democracy, freedom, justice, egalitarianism, and human rights. He sees Buddhism as capable of making its own unique contributions to these ideas and believes that it affirms basic scientific principles, such as experimental verification and rigorous reasoning, and is compatible with evolution and scientific notions of causality in a way monotheistic traditions are not. In his writings and talks, he presents Buddhism as a system of sophisticated philosophical, psychological, and ethical ideas, along with practices for cultivating higher states of awareness and universal compassion. He also presents Buddhism as a force for peace, justice, and democracy and is involved with Buddhist-sponsored social programs in his country, as well as international Buddhist peace and justice movements.

While Ananda retains many traditional values, he is always attempting to adapt and modify them to the modern world. He values the complex systems of traditional Buddhist ritual, seeing them as ways of maintaining community and reaffirming commitments, but he advocates simplifying liturgy and making it more accessible to common people. He favors reforms that provide more opportunities for women's religious vocation, and he supports greater lay involvement with the *sangha*, promoting new types of lay ordination that mark a commitment to more advanced levels of Buddhist practice but do not require full monastic life. He advocates meditation for all, understanding meditation techniques as a Buddhist contribution to the welfare of all humankind, even if they are practiced only at a rudimentary level. He is uncomfortable with people seeking prosperity and profit through the dharma and disapproves of spirit mediumship, magic, and appealing to unseen beings for personal or family gain. While he does not deny the existence of unseen beings, he seldom speaks publicly about them and never tires of trying to disentangle popular spirit worship from the dharma. Monks, in his view, should be exclusively concerned with the people's spiritual well-being and not let themselves be turned into vehicles for fulfilling people's mundane needs and desires. An advocate for reform of what he believes are outmoded and moribund aspects of Buddhist tradition, he attempts to sort out the core practices and principles taught by the Buddha from later cultural accretions.

Although his impulse toward modernization, innovation, and reform are to a great extent inspired by modernist ideologies of the West, he does not embrace western modernity in toto. He openly admires the achievements of the West but is quite aware of its dark history of colonialism and imperialism in Asia and is critical of its military aggression as well as its materialism. He sees the great disparity between the rich and the poor as a fundamental evil and is critical of contemporary consumerism and the harsh realities of the free market economy. While these critiques are themselves quite similar to western critiques of the same phenomena, he interlaces them with Buddhist concepts, symbols, and stories, giving them a uniquely Buddhist flavor.

The Continuum of Tradition and Modernity

Again, these portraits are not meant to be inclusive of the great variety of contemporary Buddhists but to illustrate some essential distinctions and themes that are important to my subject. We could multiply the examples and develop a wider and more globally representative group, but these five give us material for some essential concepts, comparisons, and contrasts I want to address. First is the contrast between the two lay practitioners, Sara and Yanisa. They could both be considered practitioners of "popular" Buddhism, though of very different sorts. One of the most obvious differences is that for one, Buddhism is deeply embedded in the social life of the community, while for the other it is imported from outside and adopted by choice. Sara may well keep much of her association with Buddhism to herself if she chooses, and aside from her attendance at weekly meditation and occasional retreats, there is little in her "public" life that would identify her as a Buddhist. She herself sees it as a rather private affair, a personal choice among a smorgasbord of religious and spiritual options. She is even somewhat ambivalent about identifying herself as a Buddhist, being suspicious of "organized religion," as well as uncomfortable with such an identification among certain friends and acquaintances. Buddhism for her is a matter of meditation, personal transformation, psychological health, and the transcendence of social conditioning toward inner freedom. It is first and foremost personal, but in contrast to assertions by many sociologists about "privatized" religion, it is not without ethical and social implications. Many of the popular dharma books she reads have discussions of ethics, albeit under the rubric of cultivating compassionate and altruistic states of mind rather than explicit moral "rules." Nor is her practice irrelevant to community. The group of meditators she belongs to is a valuable source of friendship and support. Her practice of Buddhism, however, bears little relationship to her community beyond this small group.

Yanisa's religious orientation, in contrast, is deeply embedded in her family, community, and culture. She is aware of other religious orientations but has never seriously considered them to be "options" for her own life. She takes her religious perspective as a given, not as something she has consciously chosen. Far from her Buddhist practice being a matter of freedom from social conditioning, it is indistinguishable from the social and cultural life of her community—an embodiment of commonly shared practices, beliefs, and ethical values.

Yanisa's specific practices, as well, would be nearly unrecognizable to Sara. For Yanisa, ritual action is paramount and prior to explicit belief; it is practical and instrumental as well as reverential. It has to do with honoring, appeasing, and managing the spirit powers that pervade her existential world and with generating the karmic effects to provide good fortune in this life and lives to come. While Yanisa sees the consecrated Buddha-image at the monastery as embodying the power of the Buddha, Sara would recoil at any such notion, seeing the image to which she bows at her weekly meditation as merely symbolic. The notion of propitiating and honoring spirits through ritual plays no part in her practice. She sees such things as superstitious cultural accretions that have nothing to do with the essence of Buddhism.

Sara's and Yanisa's gender and socioeconomic classes also condition their practice of Buddhism. Sara's midrange income provides her with the resources for books, donations at lectures, and fees for meditation classes and residential retreats. Like the majority of western converts or sympathizers in meditative Buddhist traditions, she is white and middle-class.[2] Her formal education has nurtured her facility with abstract thought, which has increased her ability to access basic Buddhist philosophical concepts. Her gender has created virtually no barrier to her practice. Her home-grown *sangha* is about evenly divided between men and women, her meditation retreats have all been gender inclusive, and some of the Buddhist teachers and authors who have most influenced her have been women. She sees Buddhist doctrine as affirming the equality between men and women, mainly because most of the Buddhists she has encountered have implicitly affirmed it.

Yanisa, on the other hand, has never received more than a basic education and has little knowledge of Buddhist philosophy except for the most basic doctrines. Nor has she ever considered taking up a serious meditation practice, this being the province of special meditating monks and a few highly educated and devoted laypeople. Her role as the head female in the home necessitates her performing many of the household rituals for the benefit of the entire family. Although there is no order of nuns (*bhikṣuni*) in Thailand, she could if she desired become a female renunciate (*mae chī*). Few women actually do this, although there are increasing opportunities for Thai and other Southeast Asian Buddhist women to pursue intensive religious vocations. Most see their roles as supporting the monastic community through participation in rituals and helping to prepare provisions for them.

Both Sara and Yanisa combine their practice of Buddhism with non-Buddhist elements of their respective cultures, often without realizing they are doing so. Sara's practice occurs against a background of nonnegotiable assumptions derived from her culture: the equality of men and women, the superiority of democracy, the soundness of science in describing at least the physical world. Her ideas about and practice of Buddhism are informed, more than she even knows, by modern western psychology, philosophy, and the particular history of interactions between the West and Asian Buddhism, all of which provide a filtering and focusing lens through which she sees a small, select number of key Buddhist concepts. Yanisa's practice of Buddhism also occurs within a wider domain of religious concerns grounded in the social practices and presuppositions of her culture. She makes little distinction between the unseen beings that are specifically Buddhist—like the *yakṣas* and *gandharvas* mentioned in Buddhist sutras—and those that come from local spirit traditions. She knows that some revered Buddhist monks are especially powerful and can provide blessings and protection, but she does not hesitate to make use of non-Buddhist sources, like a local shaman, for similar purposes.

Although I mean to contrast Sara with Yanisa in order to distinguish a highly modernized and westernized approach from a more traditional one, this distinction should not be taken as absolute. For example, while few in Sara's homegrown *sangha* would believe that a consecrated Buddha-image has anything but symbolic power, some western sympathizers believe in supernatural beings that can influence human affairs. Some also believe that certain objects or places have an inherent spiritual power or accept more literal accounts of karma and rebirth. We should not, therefore, overestimate the degree to which western Buddhist sympathizers reject the supernatural or traditional cosmology. Similarly, we cannot see Yanisa's practices as purely "premodern." Although her practice of icon reverence is an ancient and traditional one, its current form in Thailand is inseparable from the modern commercial forces of globalized capitalism. The trade in sacred material objects—amulets, Buddha-images, votive tablets—have immense commercial significance, according to some reports, generating as much revenue as real estate (Swearer 2003: 16). Stanley Tambiah argues that the flourishing (though not the origin) of the cult of amulets is a response to the rapid destabilization of Thai society by modern economic and political forces, which has produced great uncertainty in many lives and fostered an increased tendency to rely on the supernatural (1987). The popularity of amulets, therefore, represents a kind of turn to traditional practice fueled by some of the distinctive forces of modernity. This illustrates the complex intertwining of tradition and modernity; the two are seldom exclusive of each other.

Rachel and Lobsang represent two very different ways of rigorous Buddhist practice. Practitioners like Rachel are so rare as to be numerically insignificant to the Buddhist world, yet their influence outweighs their numbers. In fact, a small minority of western Buddhists has had a great impact on how Buddhism is understood in the West and to a significant extent in Asian countries where Buddhism is prominent. This is because they have authored best-selling, internationally distributed books, gone on lecture tours, and set up their own institutions. They are culturally elite, well-educated, well-traveled, and usually from economically advantaged backgrounds. Rachel's situation would also be extremely rare in Asian Buddhist cultures, because she is a woman who teaches men and women alike and assumes the same authority as her male counterparts. Although esteemed female teachers exist in various Asian Buddhist communities, they seldom have authority over men. The Vinaya, the canonical body of literature containing rules of conduct for monastics, explicitly subordinates nuns to monks. While a number of canonical sources affirm that women have the same spiritual capabilities as men, women have historically had less access to advanced teachings and fewer opportunities for monastic practice or leadership roles.

Despite both being authorized teachers in Buddhist traditions, it is obvious that the differences between Rachel and Lobsang are vast. They occupy different cultural worlds and approach the dharma from a very different set of tacit assumptions. Both are credentialed in their traditions, Lobsang by a long, intensive process of monastic education and Rachel by a demonstration of commitment to the tradition and some formal monastic training (her year at the monastery in Japan). The differences in training reflect contrasts between the Gelukpa and Zen schools but also the modern practice of Zen *rōshis* in the West giving formal dharma transmission—an acknowledgement of a certain degree of accomplishment, as well as sanction to teach—to anyone the *rōshi* deems fit, regardless of whether that person has had the requisite training expected in a Japanese context.

Rachel and Lobsang also approach to their respective traditions differently. Although Tibetan Buddhism is modernizing in many ways, the curricula at its monastic training centers are still essentially traditional—that is, their purpose is to investigate, interpret, and reaffirm normative truths, in contrast to the liberal education model in the West, which is pluralistic and ideally encourages inquiry not directed to the predetermined conclusions of a specific tradition. Rachel is a product of the liberal education tradition and sees Buddhism as one path among many for the living of a contemplative and "spiritual" life. She has had access to a wide variety of ideas and has struggled to piece them all together into a coherent worldview. Lobsang, however, has a more profoundly internalized understanding of his tradition and knows it with more precision and nuance than Rachel knows hers. His years spent memorizing texts and debating various interpretations has given him a command of the tradition that is simply unavailable to someone with a different type of education. His is not a pluralistic education that presents a wide variety of views and then encourages students to reason their way to their own conclusions. Alternate views are presented mainly to be critiqued and dismissed. Thus all of the ideas and practices in his monastic training serve to construct a universe that appears uniquely realistic, plausible, and coherent.

Their respective approaches to practice are also quite divergent. Rachel considers meditation the essence of Buddhist practice, whether monastic or lay. In Lobsang's world, meditation is highly valued and considered necessary for the ultimate goal of the Buddhist path, but it is not an expectation and is undertaken by only a small minority of monks and even fewer laypeople.[3] Meditation is considered a rigorous endeavor to be taken on by highly trained individuals who are willing to commit years of their lives to it. Monks in Tibetan monasteries are impressed by the few westerners who have succeeded in pursuing this path, even for a short time, but are baffled and amused by those who come to monasteries hoping to pursue advanced meditation or tantric practices that are considered beyond even most of the monks' capacities. Given the idea common in Asian Buddhism that we are living in an age of decline, when advanced spiritual development is nearly impossible, most Buddhists—including monastics—in Asia are content to cultivate meritorious karma rather than ambitiously aiming for liberation in this lifetime. In Asia, awakening is considered a long-term project. In the West it is often assumed that meditation is the chief activity of the Buddhist monastic, but in fact it is mostly practiced by a minority of meditation specialists (as opposed to textual or ritual specialists). This is true even of practitioners in the Chan/Zen (i.e., "meditation") traditions, the majority of whom, in the words of Duncan Ryuken Williams, "never practiced Zen meditation, never engaged in iconoclastic acts of the Chan/Zen masters (as described in hagiographical literature), never solved koans, never raked Zen gardens, never sought mystical meditative states, and never read

Dōgen's writings" (2005: 3). Rather, their roles as priests have come to dominate their activities, which involve healing the sick and performing funerary
rites and exorcisms. While meditation has always been considered essential to
awakening and is respected and revered in most Buddhist communities, the
representation of it as the sine qua non of Buddhist practice for monastics and
laity alike is largely a modern development and a key constituent of Buddhist
modernism (a point I will discuss further in chapter 6).

The contrasts I have drawn between these first four portraits are largely
ones between western and Asian Buddhist practice, but this should not imply
that we can identify western with modern and Asian with traditional. The portrait of Ananda, the cosmopolitan modernist monk, represents those who have
been instrumental in the creation and maintenance of distinctively modern
forms of Buddhism. Although his name suggests South Asian origins, Ananda
could be from virtually any Buddhist-dominated country. This does *not* mean
that no substantive differences exist between the modernizing figures from
these very different places—certainly Ananda, if his name were changed and
his specific characteristics nuanced more, could become more clearly Thai,
Sri Lankan, Tibetan, Taiwanese, Japanese, and so on. But what I wish to emphasize here is his globalizing, ecumenical, transnational, and modernizing
tendencies, which explicitly incline him toward universalized rather than localized forms, even while he continues to be rooted in his own tradition. A crucial
part of modernization, whether we are talking about trade or religion, is its
tendency toward globalization, a tendency that in many cases compromises
local difference.

Like Rachel, Ananda represents a small minority of Buddhists but is highly
influential because of his visibility. He is obviously a composite of some of the
most prominent contemporary Asian Buddhist leaders, such as the Fourteenth
Dalai Lama, Thich Nhat Hanh, Sulak Sivaraksa, and others less widely known.
They, along with some of their predecessors in the nineteenth and twentieth
centuries, have negotiated the difficult and porous boundaries of tradition and
modernity as Buddhism has entered uncharted territory. Some have had modern, western education—attending Christian schools in Sri Lanka, obtaining
degrees form Oxford, or educating themselves in politics and science. They
are products of both Buddhist and modern secular cultures and inhabit the intermediary space between the two. They are often socially and politically active
and sometimes nationalistic. Many have experienced directly the dark side of
modernity through colonialism or modern warfare. Indeed, it is significant that
many countries with predominantly Buddhist populations have been ravaged
by war, occupation, or dictatorship in the twentieth century and that the two

most famous living Buddhists—the Fourteenth Dalai Lama and Thich Nhat Hanh—live in exile, while another prominent Buddhist and Nobel laureate, Aung San Su Kyi of Burma (Myanmar), has spent years under house arrest by an oppressive government. It is not coincidental, then, that many Buddhist modernizers have been motivated by peace and justice issues. Yet social engagement in Buddhism do not always resemble that of Ananda, who espouses views in many ways consonant with the political left in America and Europe. Figures who lean toward pacifism and support human rights, women's rights, ecological causes, and so on have become globally recognized and influential; nevertheless, other politically engaged Buddhists have supported militant forms of nationalism, for example those in prewar Japan and contemporary Sri Lanka. While modern forms of Buddhism have often advocated for peace and justice, they have also on occasion been co-opted by political forces with quite different agendas.

Most of the figures represented by Ananda have not embraced western modernity as a whole. They represent what we might call "indigenous modernities," which selectively embrace many elements of western modernity but are not fully assimilated to it. They may have a keen interest in science but still revere the relics of the Buddha. They may advocate liberal democracy but still insist on the certain traditional forms of hierarchical authority within the *sangha*. Their teachings combine Buddhist and western ideas and practices into complex hybrids that strategically adopt, reject, and transform elements of both modernity and tradition.

To illuminate the differences between the modern and traditional forms of Buddhism illustrated by these five portraits, I shall now describe some general tendencies through which modernized forms have emerged. Understanding detraditionalization, demythologization, and psychologization, three particular cultural processes that are largely a product of modernity and have cut across widely different cultures, can help us to understand some of the differences between our more traditional and more modern portraits.

Detraditionalization

A key aspect of modernization with regard to religion is the shift of orientation from external to internal authority and the associated reorientation from institutional to privatized religion that is known as detraditionalization. Linda Woodhead and Paul Heelas call this a shift "from an authoritative realm which exists over and above the individual or whatever the individual might aspire to,

to the authority of the first hand spiritually-informed experience of the self"
(2000: 342). In strongly traditional religion, authority is rooted in a "transcendent and authoritative past" that provides unerring guidance to the present. In
strongly detraditionalized religion, authority is conceived as deriving from the
individual's own investigation and experience; the "self" itself, or some aspect
of subjectivity, is considered sacred, and the internal realm becomes the locus
of authority.[4] While it may occur within the context of more traditional institutions, detraditionalized religion often lacks the institutional structures of traditional religion and may be found in ad hoc settings like workshops, retreats,
or Sara's grassroots *sangha*. It may also entail a shift from transcendence to
immanence, from negative to positive evaluations of human nature, and from
concern with the future (including future lives) to concern with experiencing
life fully here and now. Detraditionalization embodies the modernist tendency
to elevate reason, experience, and intuition over tradition and to assert the freedom to reject, adopt, or reinterpret traditional beliefs and practices on the basis
of individual evaluation. Religion becomes more individualized, privatized,
and a matter of choice—one has the right to choose and even construct one's
own religion. With this emphasis on individual choice can also emerge the
"consumerization and instrumentalization" of religion, as it may become
a commodity to satisfy the self (341–44).

The relevance of detraditionalization to Buddhism is complex, especially
when applied crossculturally. Clearly this process is guided by the ideologies
and social practices of the modern West. And it is important to note that the vast
majority of Buddhists throughout the world practice more traditional forms like
those of Yanisa and Lobsang. Like other large-scale religions, however, Buddhism has become detraditionalized among many adherents, including the rapidly emerging affluent and educated middle-class populations of various Asian
countries, as well as in the West among converts. Among western converts, detraditionalization occurs in part because most of them learn about Buddhism
from books that portray it as part of an amorphous "Eastern mysticism" or an
even more inclusive universal "mysticism" that is considered largely independent of institutional structures. Popular literature in the West often presents the
"essence" of Buddhism as primarily about inner experience rather than its institutional and social realities. This approach has created a new kind of quasi-lay
community of Buddhist sympathizers who read popular Buddhist books and
do some meditation and an occasional retreat but do not necessarily identify
themselves exclusively as Buddhist. These sympathizers, illustrated by Sara,
may not be committed to Buddhism in any institutional form, may reject or
simply be unaware of doctrines unpalatable to late modern sensibilities, and
may also be "Hindu sympathizers," "Daoist sympathizers," and "neo-pagan

sympathizers." It is not just their eclecticism, though, that makes them particularly modern—the religious lives of many, if not most, traditional East Asians throughout history has been constituted by an amalgam of beliefs and practices from a variety of traditions. What marks such contemporary spiritually eclectic Buddhist sympathizers as embodying detraditionalized Buddhism is the fact that they quite consciously feel free as individuals to adopt or reject whatever bits and pieces they choose from Buddhism, as well as mixing and matching them with fragments of other traditions, thus creating their own personal religious bricolage. Autonomous reason, freedom of choice, and intuitive insight are implicitly considered superior to external authority, even though part of that freedom may include placing oneself under the guidance of a spiritual teacher.

It may seem odd to those whose views of Buddhism are largely informed by modernist authors to say that the emphasis on subjective experience and the authority of the individual is a modern development. After all, Buddhism is often portrayed as the very embodiment of these tendencies. Indeed, there is a plethora of Buddhist literature, modern and ancient, on the workings of meditative experience. There is also a passage from a Buddhist sutra (which I will discuss further in the next chapter) advising skepticism and personal verification of teachings, even those of the Buddha himself. These would seem to suggest that individualism and the authority of personal experience is the hallmark of Buddhism. Yet the vast majority of Buddhists today and throughout history, like Yanisa and Lobsang, have not been encouraged to question orthodox doctrine or to construct their own personal approach to the path. They have also not been so bold as to consider their own personal experience authoritative over against the teachings of the learned and institutionally sanctioned, and they have relied on the authority of the *sangha* and their teachers rather than their own intuition to guide them in their beliefs and behavior.

I will return to the specific reasons for the emergence of detraditionalized Buddhism throughout the book, addressing them from a number of different directions. The outcome will, I hope, confirm that elements of Buddhism that many now consider central to the tradition—meditation, internal experience, individual authority—are so constructed because of the gravitational pull of modernity. Modernity has attracted particular elements from the vast corpus of the tradition and not only made them central—leaving out others that have actually been more typical of Buddhist experience throughout history—but also reconstituted them in terms of modern discourses. As well as through detraditionalization, this process has also occurred through demythologization.

Demythologization

Of Wheels and Ghosts

The famous Tibetan image of the wheel of rebirth, with its snarling, wide-eyed demon clutching a circle full of vivid images of joy and horror, bliss and violence, is an irresistible tool for teaching Buddhism. In addition to being so visually compelling, it contains many of the basic doctrinal themes of classical Buddhism: karma, rebirth, nirvana, the three poisons, the twelvefold chain of causation. One of its main features is the depiction of the part of the Buddhist cosmos that consists of six realms of rebirth containing different orders of beings: the gods, the jealous gods, humans, the animals, hungry ghosts, and the residents of various hells. The wheel hovers on screen during my classes every semester, always evoking scrutiny and questioning. However, I have found myself recently using it not only to introduce basic teachings or to discuss Buddhist art but also to elucidate the differences between traditional and modernist interpretations of Buddhism.

Consider, for example, a quotation about the wheel by the Burmese meditation teacher Mahāsi Sayādaw, a modernizer in many respects, but here giving a rather traditional account:

> The Wheel of Rebirth (samsara) is very dreadful. Every effort should therefore be made to acquaint oneself with the miserable conditions of Samsara and then to work for an escape from this incessant cycle, and for the attainment of Nirvana. If an escape from Samsara as a whole is not possible for the present, an attempt should be made for an escape at least from the round of rebirth in the realm of hell, or animals, or pretas. In this case it is necessary to work for the total removal of oneself of the erroneous view that there is a self, which is the root-cause of rebirth in the miserable states. (quoted in Fronsdal 1998: 171)

In contrast, Chögyam Trungpa, one of the most influential and westernized Tibetan Buddhist teachers in North America, describes the realms of rebirth in quite different terms:

> The realms are predominantly emotional attitudes towards ourselves and our surroundings—reinforced by conceptualizations and rationalizations. As human beings we may, during the course of a day, experience the emotions of all of the realms, from the pride

of the god realm to the hatred and paranoia of the hell realm. Nonetheless, a person's psychology is usually firmly rooted in one realm. This realm provides us with a style of confusion, a way of entertaining and occupying ourselves so as not to have to face our fundamental uncertainty, our ultimate fear that we may not exist. (1976: 24)

For Trungpa, the primary significance of the realms is that they symbolize various states of mind, helping practitioners to map them out and ultimately free themselves from their dominance. The god realm is a symbol of self-absorption; the realm of jealous gods corresponds to paranoia; the human realm corresponds to passion; the animal realm corresponds to stupidity; the hungry ghost realm corresponds to a feeling of poverty; and the hell realm corresponds to anger. While connecting the six realms with specific emotions or states of mind to be overcome has solid grounding in Buddhist textual traditions—beings are reborn in realms that provide karmic consequences of their actions of mind, body, and speech—the presentation of their significance as *primarily* or even exclusively psychological is uniquely modern. Such reinterpretation of cosmological-cum-ethical teachings is characteristic of the transformations of certain strains of Buddhism in the nineteenth and twentieth centuries. It is a part of a process of demythologization, one of the primary mechanisms in the modernization, revitalization, and reinvention of Buddhism. What I am calling demythologization is the process of attempting to extract—or more accurately, to reconstruct—meanings that will be viable within the context of modern worldviews from teachings embedded in ancient worldviews. In order to transpose such themes into a modern key, elements that are incompatible with modernity are relegated to "myth" and shorn of literal truth-value.

Demythologization, however, not only is a matter of doctrine but also can have implications for practice. Many schools of Buddhism perform ceremonies honoring the dead and symbolically offering food to hungry ghosts (*pretas*), who live in one of the undesirable realms of rebirth and now, reaping the consequences of greedy karma, have bodies with pencil-thin necks and bloated stomachs and live in a constant state of hunger. The Japanese Sōtō Zen version is the Kanromon, performed during the summer Obon festival, when the dead are believed to return to the realm of living and ghosts roam the land. Priests perform the ritual, which is primarily a matter of chanting scriptures, to create merit for deceased family members and ancestors, and the fees serve as a primary source of income for the temple. Rōshi Bernie Glassman, an American teacher, founder of the Zen Peacemaker Order, and one of the prominent

American figures in the broader engaged Buddhist movement, has re-created the ritual for feeding hungry ghosts to reflect the idea that whether or not such spirits inhabit other realms, they are first and foremost both ourselves and society's disadvantaged. One of his activist innovations is known as the "street retreat," in which Zen practitioners live on the streets with the homeless for a period of time without money, food, or provisions in order to erase the illusion of separation between the privileged and the underprivileged, the self and other. He has also been active in setting up prison meditation at correctional facilities and various other programs addressing issues of war, poverty, and homelessness.

And for Glassman, the hungry ghosts are not only the homeless, the disenfranchised, the destitute but also everyone: all beings have an unsatisfiable hunger that produces suffering. His adaptation of the Kanromon (Gate of Sweet Nectar) incorporates elements from Jewish liturgy as well as other traditions of Buddhism. In a short video on the ritual, participant Michael Daigu O'Keefe describes its significance as involving "opening to the hungry ghosts in my own being." The ghosts, he says, represent "the dissatisfied side of yourself." Yet hungry ghosts are also "anyone in the cracks of our culture, who's excluded from the mainstream . . . someone we may be ignoring, not providing for" (Gregory and Weaver 2004). Glassman's ritual combines the internalization common to demythologization with the recent impulse in Buddhism toward addressing systemic social ills. It also illustrates the eclectic combining of traditions common to detraditionalized religion, in that it amalgamates Jewish and Buddhist liturgy from different Buddhist schools.

Demythologization, therefore, internalizes what in traditional accounts are ontological realities, and in some cases, for example Glassman's modernized ritual, also externalizes them into concrete, visible realities. This is not to say that traditional Buddhists have never been concerned with "internal" realities or that they have traditionally ignored social problems. The literature on meditation, the Abhidharma's extensive analysis of mental phenomena, and the Yogācāra philosophers' rich expositions of different facets of consciousness all attest to elite classical authors' profound interest in the mind. And while the current forms of Buddhist social activism are novel, Buddhists have never been wholly aloof from society. Nevertheless, the reconception of the realms of rebirth and their residents as facets of one's own mind, symbols of psychological states, and representations of various groups of living human beings is a unique product of the modern age. I do not mean to deny here that subjectivity, consciousness, awareness, and meditation have been important to Buddhist life but rather to examine the ways things *not* traditionally taken as psychological have been translated into psychic realities.

Demythologization, Buddhist and Christian

The phenomenon of demythologization is by no means unique to Buddhism; in some measure it has occurred within virtually all religious traditions in the past century. In the 1960s, Peter Berger saw what he called the "subjectiviza-tion" of religion as a widespread phenomenon attendant on the loss of an un-contested model of objective reality.

> Religious realities are increasingly "translated" from a frame of refer-ence of facticities external to the individual consciousness to a frame of reference that locates them *within* consciousness. Thus, for exam-ple, the resurrection of Christ is no longer regarded as an event in the external world of physical nature, but is "translated" to refer to existen-tial or psychological phenomena in the consciousness of the believer. Put differently, the *realissimum* to which religion refers is transposed from the cosmos or from history to individual consciousness. Cos-mology becomes psychology. . . . The traditional religious affirmation can now be regarded as "symbols"—what they supposedly "symbol-ize" usually turns out to be some realities presumed to exist in the "depths" of human consciousness. (1969: 166)

Berger's mention of the shift in the meaning of the resurrection is a reference to the father of the hermeneutical program of demythologization, the Christian the-ologian Rudolph Bultmann. Bultmann's project was to attempt to extract what he called the "deeper meaning," or "existential meaning," of passages and themes in the New Testament from their original home in an ancient worldview and present it in terms comprehensible to modern people with a scientific world-view. The "mythological worldview," he asserted, contains miracles, demons, a three-storied world with heaven quite literally above in the clouds, earth in the middle, and a hell in the world below ground. Such conceptions, along with early Christian eschatology, are "over and done with" for "modern man" (1958: 17).[5] Yet, he claimed, "the mythological sayings as a whole contain a still deeper meaning which is concealed under the cover of mythology. If that is so, let us abandon the mythological conceptions precisely because we want to retain their deeper meaning" (18).

The classic case of such recovery of "deeper meanings" is his demythologi-zation of the notions of heaven and hell, an example that recalls the Buddhist wheel of life. "The meaning is quite clear," Bultmann says. "In a crude manner it expresses the idea that God is beyond the world, that He is transcendent. The thinking that is not yet capable of forming the abstract idea of transcend-ence expresses its intention in the category of space; the transcendent God is imagined as being at an immense spatial distance, far above the world" (1958: 20). Similarly, the representation of hell as the darkness below the earth expresses the tremendous power of evil symbolized by darkness. The concepts of Satan and evil spirits rest "on the experience . . . that our own actions are so puzzling; men are often carried away by their passions and are no longer masters of themselves, with the result that inconceivable wickedness breaks forth from them" (20–21). Although Bultmann's analysis was more existential than Trungpa's psychological interpretation of the wheel of life, both reenvision key elements of their respective cosmologies in ways that eradicate the supernatural from the main significance of the message and relocate that significance in the mind of the individual.

Critics have pointed out a number of problems, both theological and historical, with Bultmann's approach. Recent poststructuralist and postmodern thought suggests that the line between the mythological and nonmythological is not as unambiguous as Bultmann supposed. Nor is it clear that this search for the "deeper meanings" is fundamentally different from simply a radical reinterpretation—a "remythologization"—in terms of the dominant worldview— or "myth"—of a very different culture, in this case the modern West. I am, however, not concerned with the soundness of Bultmann's project per se but rather with its resonance with the way Buddhism has been interpreted, revitalized, and reconstructed in the modern era.

Buddhist demythologization has often differed from Bultmann's, in two respects. First, his program was a conscious hermeneutical strategy of adapting Christianity to the modern world, while much of this process in the interpretation of Buddhism has been largely *implicit* demythogization: demythologizers of Buddhism have seldom been so self-conscious as Bultmann, who baldly advocated a "radical abandonment and conscious critique of the mythological world-view of the Bible" (1958: 39). Second, while Bultmann attributed a mythological worldview to Jesus himself and attempted to reframe his essential message in modern terms, many interpreters of Buddhism have attributed an already "modern" or demythologized worldview to the Buddha and his early disciples. The early Buddhist sympathizer C. T. Strauss, for example, claimed that "genuine Buddhism is the reverse of mystical, rejects miracles, is founded on reality, and refuses to speculate about the absolute and other so-called first causes" (105). Moreover, it deems prayers, rituals, and ceremonies as "not only useless but a hindrance to spiritual advancement" (53–54). On this interpretation, the dharma of the Buddha was utterly distinct from the rituals, celebrations, image veneration, and attempts to control spirits common in the popular Buddhism that westerners often found in lands they colonized. Orientalist scholars located "true Buddhism" in the texts of the ancient past and delimited it to carefully selected teachings, excluding any consideration of living Buddhists, except reformers who themselves were modernizing their tradition in dialogue with western modernity (Almond 1988). The direction of the demythologization, therefore, was the reverse of Bultmann's treatment of Christianity: rather than a wise founder (Jesus) who presented existential truths that had to be excavated from their embeddedness in a prescientific worldview, sympathetic orientalists presented the Buddha as a protoscientific naturalist in his own time. Over the centuries, his ancient-modern doctrine was buried in the rituals and superstitions of the common people and thus had to be excavated not from its ancient context but from its more recent accretions.

Staples of Demythologized and Detraditionalized Buddhism

The demythologized versions of Buddhism, though based on a selective and re-constituted reading of the tradition, are not simply a western invention. There are passages in the vast Buddhist canon that can easily be brought into dialogue with modern sensibilities, and prominent Asian Buddhist authors have promoted demythologized Buddhism. It is visible, for example, in a text still widely used in college classrooms: Walpola Rahula's *What the Buddha Taught* (1959 [1974]). In many ways an excellent book, on the whole it presents certain key doctrines of the Pali *suttas* intelligibly and accessibly. However, the first chapter, "The Buddhist Attitude of Mind," is an unwitting primer on demythologized and detraditionalized Buddhism. Its brief description of the life of the Buddha contains echoes of American transcendentalism and European free thought, painting Gautama as a radical individualist who emphasized "freedom of thought," "self-reliance," and "tolerance" (4–5). Asoka's rock edicts endorsing peaceful coexistence among religions are cited as illustrative of the "tolerance and understanding that has been from the beginning one of the most cherished ideals of Buddhist civilization" (5) in contrast to Brahmanical orthodoxy, which "intolerantly and insistently believ[ed] and accept[ed] their [Brahmans'] tradition and authority as the only Truth without question" (9). The exhortation found in Pali *suttas* to "come and see" (*ehi-passika*) is cast as a scientific, empirical attitude contrary to "come and believe"—an implicit contrasting of Buddhism's alleged empirical attitude to the requirement of faith in Christianity (8–9). The "unanswered questions" in the Pali *suttas*—speculative questions the Buddha refused to answer because they were not conducive to awakening—and the parable of the poisoned arrow illustrate his pragmatic attitude toward life. Likewise, Rahula insists, the parable of the raft, which likens the teachings to a raft used to cross a river but then discarded once the crossing is achieved, illustrates the Buddha's freedom from dogmatism. The law of karma is styled in modern scientific terms as "theory of cause and effect," a "natural law," in implied contrast to Christianity's reliance on a supernatural being who can break his own laws (32).

My point is not that Rahula's is not "real" Buddhism, is somehow illegitimate or disingenuous but that it is not simply "what the Buddha taught," as the title promises. Rahula was attempting to construct Buddhist answers to questions that had not arisen in previous Buddhist contexts and to harmonize Buddhism with powerful modern discourses that have great cultural currency not only in the West but worldwide. His reconstruction of the dharma situates it within the discourses of modernity by offering a Buddhism that is demythologized, and detraditionalized in ways typical of modernization:

1. Rahula selects from the vast corpus of Buddhist literature certain features that can be interpreted in such a way as to resonate with a modern worldview, especially the Enlightenment, Protestantism, Transcendentalism, and science.
2. This selection excludes or obscures other features of Buddhist literature, for example the many stories of miracles, magical feats, supernatural beings, and literal heavens and hells.
3. When Rahula does address these, he tends to present them as ethically significant myth, symbol, or allegory.
4. By focusing on elite literature, Rahula's presentation occludes many features of the tradition on the ground, such as ritual, devotion, and exorcism, that are actually more central to many Buddhists' lives than abstract doctrines.

Many ordinary Buddhists would not recognize much of what Rahula presents as their practices, attitudes, and beliefs. What he suppresses would give a fuller picture of Buddhism in its various historical manifestations. His emphasis on tolerance of other views, for example, is certainly not reflected in the many Buddhist polemical texts savaging opponents' positions, or the religious conflicts in his own Sri Lanka that Buddhists themselves have participated in. What he refers to as "the Buddhist" is an idealized figure having little to do with living Buddhists. For example, in contrast to the pervasive practices among Buddhists for accruing merit in order to gain a higher rebirth, Rahula claims, on the basis of the doctrines of *anātman* and impermanence, that "the Buddhist" is "never worried about" the problem of life after death (1959 [1974]: 34). Rahula's Buddhism is the idealized, textualized Buddhism of the orientalist scholars.

Instead of this hybrid of modern and ancient cultural forms and eastern and western ideas and attitudes, one could imagine a quite different version of Buddhism emerging in a nonmodern culture—introduced by laity rather than elite monks, and with a primary concern with magic and the afterlife. The central features of such a Buddhism might consist of its rituals for karmic purification, its prayers to supernatural beings for rebirth in favorable circumstances, its thaumaturgy, and its rites for protection against evil forces. Buddhism did in fact sometimes taken a shape close to this in various places where it was imported before the modern era. Modernity, however, has forced some demythologization and detraditionalization to occur in order for Buddhism to carve out a place for itself in new cultures. And it has done so often not through explicit, programmatic reinterpretation like Bultmann's but simply through authors and practitioners absorbing the dominant ideas, practices, and assumptions of modernity that virtually any educated person imbibes.

Psychologization

The modern transmutation of the six realms of rebirth from ontological orders to psychological states exemplifies one way that demythologization and detraditionalization are often continuous with psychologization. In fact, the interface of Buddhism and western psychology has been one of the most prevalent frameworks of interpretation by westerners and a powerful constituent of later Buddhist modernism. Clearly, a great deal could be said about this interface; for now I will explain how the interpretation of Buddhism as psychology and the development of modern modes of Buddhist-influenced psychotherapy serve the demythologizing and detraditionalizing functions of modernization.

The earliest characterizations of Buddhism as a psychology came from the pioneering scholars Thomas W. Rhys Davids (1843–1922) and Caroline A. F. Rhys Davids (1857–1942). Thomas was the father of Pali studies and the founder and chair of the Pali Text Society. Caroline, whom he married in 1894, held the position after his death, and between the two of them, they published the majority of the Pali canon, along with a considerable number of scholarly and popular books. Their influence in establishing a standard interpretation of early Buddhism was immense, not only in the West but in Asia as well. Both presented Buddhism as an ethical psychology, deemphasizing ritual and religious elements. Impressed by the sophisticated analysis of mind in the Abhidharma, they were among the first to refer to Buddhism as a "science of mind," a term that became widespread among Buddhist modernists. With respect to psychology, Caroline Rhys Davids insisted that "the Buddhists are the true Eastern compeers of Aristotle and western psychology, and from a universal standpoint, equal in achievement with that of the Greeks, and indeed Europe generally, up to the time when psycho-physiology was introduced. This mental analysis is quite unmythological and scientific" (1912: 61).

In addition to the Rhys Davidses' work, the articulation of Buddhism in terms of analytic psychology became one of the most powerful and enduring psychological reconfigurations of the dharma and one of the chief engines of demythologization. The systematic psychoanalytic interpretation of Buddhism began with Carl Jung's (1927) prefaces to W. Y. Evans-Wentz's publication of the first English translation of the *Bar do thos grol* (The Tibetan book of the dead) and the *Tibetan Book of Great Liberation*. The *Bar do thos grol*, which has through an odd series of coincidences become somewhat exaggeratedly representative of Tibetan Buddhism in the West (Cuevas 2006; Lopez 1998: 46–85), is a guide to the passage of the deceased through the three states (*bar dos*) in between death and rebirth. Central to the experiences of the deceased in *bar dos* presented in the *Bar do thos grol* are visions of buddhas and bodhisattvas, some in peaceful and some in wrathful forms. Each represents the possibility of either liberation or rebirth in a particular realm. Jung interpreted the *bar dos* as levels of the un-conscious and the peaceful and wrathful deities of the realms as expressions of universal archetypes in the collective unconscious. "The world of the gods and spirits is truly 'nothing but' the collective unconscious inside me" (liii). This reading has been especially compelling in the West, having been taken up by a number of scholars and becoming nearly the normative interpretation among popular writers. The pioneering Italian Tibetologist Giuseppe Tucci said of the deities in Tibetan mandalas that they are "archetypes which are innate in the soul of Man and which, therefore, reappear in different lands and at differ-ent epochs but with a similar aspect" (1961 [1970]: 25). Huston Smith, in the popular film *Requiem for a Faith* (Hartley Film Foundation, 1969), declared that "these gods that seem so solid, so objectively real, actually represent our own psychic forces."

It is hard to overestimate the importance of this psychoanalytic transmu-tation of the deities to the modernization of Buddhism, especially Himalayan forms. This is not only because this view remains popular in western literature today (see, e.g., Moacanin 2003; Preece 2006) but also because it served the es-sential function of neutralizing the vast pantheon of Mahāyāna-Vajrayāna dei-ties by rendering them facets of the mind. Especially in the early stages of the encounter of Tibetan Buddhism with western modernity, this tradition could not have otherwise withstood the commandments, deep in the marrow of the West, of western monotheism and Enlightenment rationalism: we are not to have other gods before the one God, and we are not to ask gods for favors or protection, for to do so is irrational, superstitious, and primitive. Indeed, until the late nineteenth century, these commandments prevented Europeans from seeing Tibetan Buddhism as anything other than demonic and idolatrous or backward and superstitious. Buddhism's cultural capital as it moved into Tibet in the seventh century lay in its adherents' superior ability to control unseen beings. Its admittance into western modernity similarly depended on its demonstrating control over the these beings—this time exorcising them from the world of molecules and atoms and confining them to the psyche. Here they could continue to exist as "representations," "symbols," or "energies" resident in all human beings. The wrathful deities came to be construed as ingenious images of inner realities discovered by intrepid explorers of the psyche rather than diabolical demons or primitive superstitions. This internalization of the gods was the passkey that granted Tibetan Buddhism entry into the modern West, whose monotheism and modernity could not abide a gaggle of gods inhabiting the real world.

Attention to the rich psychological implications of the *Bar do thos grol* is not unfounded, and there are reasons deriving from Buddhist texts themselves for interpreting the deities as less than ontological entities. The doctrine of emptiness (*śūnyatā*), prominent in Tibetan thought, insists that no beings, whether gods, demons, humans, or animals, have inherent self-existence (*svabhāva*). Moreover, in the *Bar do thos grol*, deities are in fact presented as "appearances" (*snang ba*; Skt. *pratibhāsa*), not distinct from the deceased subject wandering in the *bar do*.[6] And deities are correlated in Sanskrit and Tibetan literature with various emotional states, positive and negative. However, western interpreters have been too quick to latch onto the nonduality of the images of deities and the deceased and the emptiness of all phenomena as adequate grounds to denude the gods of ontological status. In retrospect, this has been a hasty hermeneutic that has failed to take into account the more complex reality that there are multiple levels of interpretation: the deities (like everything else) lack inherent self-existence, but in no Tibetan tradition does this render them wholly psychological entities. It has become clear to western scholars and serious practitioners alike that the interpretation of the deities merely as archetypes cannot account for their existence in the lives of Tibetans themselves. To Tibetans buddhas, bodhisattvas, and protector deities are not merely symbols of psychological forces but real beings (as real, that is, as any other beings) who can have actual effects in the world, both benevolent and malevolent. Nor are the evocative representations of deities painted on paper and sculpted in metal and stone merely vivid insignia of mental realities. Once they are consecrated in a ceremony (Tib. *rab gnas*) that invites the deity into them, such images are considered to be material embodiments of the deities themselves. Prostration before them signifies more than just devotion to the symbolic ideals they represent; if one is in the presence of a consecrated mandala of a buddha, one is in the presence of the buddha himself (see Lopez 1998: 150–55).

For traditional Himalayan Buddhists, the world is alive not only with awakened beings but also countless ghosts, spirits, demons, and protector deities. These beings are prayed to and propitiated in daily rituals and cyclical festivals, and they figure into one's everyday life in very concrete ways. Nor can we resort to the distinction between "elite" and "popular" religion to explain away such beliefs and practices, for they are not confined to the uneducated masses while the erudite monks merely tolerate them as "skilful means" for the common people. Scholars have noted, for instance, the starkly real character that protector deities have for educated Tibetan monks in discussions of the debate known as the "Shukden affair," which has pitted the Fourteenth Dalai Lama against more conservative members of his own Gelukpa school, over whether the propitiation of Dorje Shukden, a protector deity, is beneficial or dangerous.[7] The controversy began in the 1970s when the Dalai Lama discouraged rituals associated with this protector deity long associated with the Gelukpa school, which provoked an angry reaction. While the popular western press tended to represent the controversy as a matter of the modern, rational Dalai Lama hounded by superstitious traditionalists, in fact the Dalai Lama never expressed doubt about Shukden's existence or attempted to reduce him to a mere symbol. To the contrary, part of his decision to discourage devotion to Shukden came on the advice of the Nechung Oracle, a benevolent spirit contacted through a shaman to advise on matters of state. The Dalai Lama also said that he believes Shukden to be a "spirit of the dark forces" and expressed concern that devotion to him could have deleterious effects on the cause of Tibetan unity and on his own health (Batchelor 1998: 64). Clearly, all parties involved saw Shukden as an external agent that could have real effects in the world, and the fact that he, like all beings, was empty of inherent existence made no more difference in this world of conventional reality than the fact that the Chinese occupying Tibet were likewise empty. Passions were so aroused by the controversy that, at its peak in 1997, Geshe Lobsang Gyatso, a supporter of the Dalai Lama's position, and two of his students were murdered over it.[8] People are seldom murdered over psychological archetypes.

Neither this controversy nor the increasing knowledge of Tibetan Buddhism among westerners has eliminated the psychoanalytic interpretation of Tibetan deities in popular western literature, a testament to the perceived necessity of demythologization. Psychoanalytic theory has been essential to the admittance of Tibetan Buddhism into the West. The benefit of transmuting the gods into psychological forces, however, came at the cost of failing to understand them in their own terms; making this form of the dharma acceptable to the modernist practitioner has obscured the self-understanding of Tibetans themselves. This is, as we shall see, a common and perhaps inevitable tension in the process of modernization. It remains to be seen whether these two ways of seeing Tibetan Buddhism can be reconciled in the lives of practitioners.

The translation of Buddhism into psychoanalytic language has also been a significant component in the introduction of Zen Buddhism to the West, beginning with Daisetz Teitarō Suzuki, who interpreted the collective unconscious as an aspect of the *dharma-kāya* (see chapter 4). Jung, an inveterate writer of prefaces, gave his psychoanalytic imprimatur to this approach in a preface for Suzuki's *Introduction to Zen Buddhism*. Later, the psychoanalyst Erich Fromm, collaborating with Suzuki, suggested that Zen was a kind of radical psychoanalysis that strove to unearth the entirety of the unconscious and bring it to consciousness, thereby overcoming alienation and bringing the practitioner to wholeness (see chapter 6). The psychoanalytic interpretation of Buddhism has by no means lost its popular hold today, but it has moved well beyond Freud and Jung (see, for instance, Safran 2003). Meanwhile, throughout the mid- to late twentieth century, other psychological theories and methods have interfaced with Buddhism as well, including Gestalt therapy founder Fritz Perls's "awareness training," an interpersonal therapeutic practice adapted from Buddhist mindfulness techniques. Abraham Maslow's conceptions of "peak experiences" and "self-actualization" have significantly influenced the western understanding of awakening and meditative insight, as have concepts in transpersonal psychology, a kind of psychological perennialism that arose in the 1960s.[9]

If there has been a sea change in the interweaving of Buddhism and psychology in recent decades, it is the emergence of more clinical applications of Buddhist meditation. While the early phase of the courtship between Buddhism and psychology was characterized by attempts to theorize the relationship between the two, recent work has moved toward acting on it in therapeutic settings. Buddhist mindfulness techniques have been integrated into and even formed the basis of new experimental psychotherapies. Perhaps the most successful has been University of Massachusetts psychologist Jon Kabat-Zinn's Mindfulness-Based Stress Reduction program, in which mindfulness practices, for example attention to breath, body, feelings, and cognition, are adapted from their Buddhist context, stripped of much of their traditional religious significance, and integrated into therapies to reduce stress, control anxiety, manage physical pain, and treat depression and posttraumatic stress disorder. These mindfulness techniques have, in turn, been incorporated into cognitive behavioral therapies and have given rise to hybrid therapies like mindfulness-based cognitive therapy (see Nauriyal et al. 2006; Kwee et al. 2006).

It is not necessary to go into the details of these innovative therapies to make my point about psychology here: the construal of Buddhism as a kind of psychology has been essential to Buddhist modernism. If psychoanalysis has aided in the demythologization of Buddhism, recent practical psychotherapies have helped to detraditionalize it, allowing meditation to operate in non-Buddhist therapeutic settings, often for non-Buddhist goals and without requiring commitment to explicitly Buddhist values. Rather than an integral part of monastic life bound up with its rituals, ethics, and cosmology, meditation has become something not only for lay Buddhists but for those of any religion or none. The goals of Buddhist-influenced psychotherapy are usually stated in terms of the western psychotherapeutic tradition: alleviation of symptoms, overcoming of depression, mitigation of obsessive thoughts, integration of the person, self-realization, and so on. Often Buddhism serves as a reservoir of techniques that might be useful to accomplish such extra-Buddhist goals. Psychotherapy is one of the most visible arenas where Buddhism is transforming around the edges, as it were—where Buddhism blends into non-Buddhism.

Clearly, the interaction of Buddhism with psychology exhibits aspects of both detraditionalization and demythologization as already described. In addition, the legitimacy that is granted Buddhism in its reconstrual as a kind of psychology reverberates back to the very conception of Buddhism among Buddhists themselves, a feedback loop that serves as an engine of transformation of the tradition. The validation of Buddhist practices in prestigious non-Buddhist contexts like the offices of professional psychologists at major research universities grants cultural capital and prestige to Buddhism, encouraging Buddhists to reconceptualize their own tradition in psychological terms.

The Variegated Continuum

How can understanding the tendencies of detraditionalization, demythologization, and psychologization help us understand Buddhist modernism and modernization more generally? Following some of the classical sociological conceptions of modernization, there is a temptation to create a mutually exclusive dyad of "tradition" and "modernity." "Tradition" is often seen as condition of characterized by hierarchical social differentiation, cultural homogeneity, tacit acceptance of a mythological worldview, unquestioning acquiescence to religious authority, thoroughgoing capitulation to social norms, and little individual freedom—in Durkheim's words, one where "the individual personality is lost in the depths of the social mass" (quoted in Heelas 1996: 4). In this condition, people are seen as embedded in a taken-for-granted world, with their identities thoroughly determined by the social group. "Modernity," in contrast, is seen as a condition of liberation from the bonds of tradition and the collective. In this condition, individuals can critically reflect on the "givens" of culture and religion and choose which to accept or reject. Sacred metanarratives are relativized, due to their confrontation with a plurality of other metanarratives. The multivocality of modern culture throws into question all voices, so that no one authority or tradition can enjoy taken-for-granted status. Individuals must now choose for themselves, construct for themselves their own religious meaning, weighing each claim and trusting their reason or intuition as a guide to their own paths. Religion is an individual, private affair. Individuals are now free, but at the cost of giving up the sacralized world full of magic and meaning; they are now compelled to confront a world without inherent significance, risking anomie and nihilism.

These classical representations of tradition and modernity, while containing some helpful ideas, are too simple. The picture of ancient traditions as monolithic, with no room for self-reflection or individual choice, is an exaggerated representation of both tradition in general and traditional forms of Buddhism. Buddhist history is peppered with individuals who have broken out of their traditional roles, reforming and revitalizing their traditions and developing novel doctrines and practices. Likewise, the free agent unfettered by tradition or external authority, rationally choosing his or her own beliefs and practices and relying on nothing but his or her own autonomous decisions, is a caricature. This notion of the modern individual as someone who has cast off the domination of the group, who is largely inwardly directed, and who, as Anthony Giddens puts it, "no longer lives by extrinsic moral precepts but by means of the reflexive organization of the self" underestimates the degree to which culture and subculture still determine behavior and self-identity, even in the most modern or postmodern of contexts (Woodhead and Heelas 2000: 370). As Paul Heelas suggests:

> people—whether "pre-modern"/"traditional," "modern" or even
> "post-modern"/"post-traditional"—*always* live in terms of those
> typically conflicting demands associated, on the one hand, with
> voices of authority emanating from realms transcending the self *qua*
> self, and, on the other, with those voices emanating from the desires,
> expectations, and competitive or idiosyncratic aspirations of the
> individual. . . . Is it really reasonable to suppose that "traditional"
> societies can swallow up the person to the extent of muting or

denying the exercise of autonomous voices, or to suppose that
dwellers in "modern" or "post-modern" societies are content, let
alone able, to live with little or no guidance from determinate orders?
(1996: 7–8)

Thus when we talk of modernization, detraditionalization, and demythologization, we are talking about broad tendencies that coexist in creative tension with
traditional elements, with neither side necessarily winning out wholesale.

The portraits of contemporary Buddhists presented earlier showed some
who are quite immersed in a traditional Buddhist world and others who approach the tradition in a nearly thoroughly detraditionalized and demythologized
way. In between the two extremes is a widely variegated continuum that could
include, for example, an uneducated Vietnamese villager who has stopped doing
rituals to appease spirits because his more modernist priest has persuaded him
they don't exist; a Taiwanese Buddhist scientist who performs daily practices he
is convinced will grant him entry into the pure land when he dies; an Anglo-
American Zen student who grants virtually absolute authority to his Japanese
rōshi, considering everything he says or does an expression of awakening. Many
Buddhists live in such complex amalgamations of tradition and detraditionalization, myth and demythologization. While detraditionalization has no doubt
taken place within Buddhism, it has not obliterated traditional institutions, authority, or hierarchy but has made them more open to contestation and rene-
gotiation and created novel forms of Buddhist modernism. Even among some
convert communities in North America, where detraditionalization is arguably
strongest, one can find highly traditional temples, teachers, and students.

Modernization, therefore, with its detraditionalizing, demythologizing, and
psychologizing tendencies, seldom consists simply in the emergence of a thoroughly autonomous self from the shackles of tradition, as modernity's dominant
narrative would have it. It proceeds, rather, through heterogeneous adaptation
of the discourses and practices of modernity, selective assent to its dominant
axioms and assumptions, and ideological struggle over the extent and manner
of adaptation. Modernizers have often struggled with how to combine tradition
with modernity and how to position Buddhism in relation to its various facets.
In the next chapter, I will consider how these efforts have engaged some of the
prominent discourses of modernity and how in this process different strands of
Buddhist modernism, especially in its formative years, have come into being.

3

Buddhism and the Discourses of Modernity

Decontextualization and Recontextualization

Scholars have come to appreciate more fully in recent decades the extent to which the texts, doctrines, institutions, and practices of any tradition are products of unique cultural and historical circumstances. They are deeply embedded in local and national cultures, and a sea of social practices and unstated assumptions, premises, and presuppositions surrounds their manifestations and artifacts. When stripped of these larger cultural contexts—either through radical internal change, contact with another culture, or export to another cultural-geographical region—a tradition is brought into other conversations that do not share these premises and presuppositions, as, for example, when Buddhists began to arrive in ancient China and, in the last century and a half, in North America. Such decontextualization and recontextualization often entails significant reconfiguring, as some of the cultural girders supporting a tradition are knocked down and replaced with those of a very different culture. A tradition must then survive in an environment other than the one it has evolved in; it must adapt. It must connect with the tacit assumptions, cultural norms, and social and institutional practices of an entirely different ideological ecosystem. It must take on new meanings, as translators and interpreters strike notes that resonate with the underlying harmonies of the new culture. Ideas and practices that made sense in one cultural context atrophy like vestigial organs, and new ideas and practices are grafted

on, sometimes uncomfortably, as the tradition is called on to answer new questions, meet novel needs, and uphold—or join with those who oppose—the new
culture's axiomatic assumptions. Particular features of the tradition are high-
lighted, occluded, or reinterpreted according to the particular resonance they
have within the new context's networks of meaning, value, and power.

In order to illuminate how this process has occurred and continues to
occur in the encounter of Buddhism with western modernity, I will isolate the
three broad discourses of modernity already presented—scientific naturalism,
Romanticism and its successors, and western monotheism—and sketch how
major facets of Buddhist modernism in the West have taken form as Buddhism
has engaged with each of these discourses. In other words, I will show how a
few dominant colors in the prism of western modernity have picked up different
hues of Buddhism while obscuring others. It is important to see, however, that
this is a process involving more than simply *picking up* certain themes whole,
for when brought into modernist discourses, they function in ways sometimes
quite new. They thus acquire novel significance and take on a new life. And
we must nuance this process still further: it is not just that each discourse has
illumined, and in thus illumining transformed, various aspects of Buddhism.
For between these three discourses of modernity there have been continuing
tensions, negotiations, overlaps, and contestations, and the emergence of Buddhist modernism has entailed staking certain claims within and between them.
Buddhism has had to be "placed" in particular relationships to them—affirming
one, challenging another, reconciling tensions between them, or perhaps offering something novel that addresses an unresolved issue. In staking their
claims, Buddhists and Buddhist sympathizers have attempted both to harmonize with and critique all three of these discourses, in order to show, first, that
Buddhism is a worthy participant in modern conversations—that is, does not
operate on such radically different assumptions that it must be relegated to the
eternal otherness of the "premodern"—and second, that it can in fact contribute something valuable to them.

I will keep a somewhat soft focus on these three discourses of modernity,
understanding them as inclusive not just of explicit movements (English Romanticism or the French Enlightenment, for example) but also of enduring and
often tacit cultural orientations deeply ingrained in modern, western (and increasingly eastern) cultures, popular as well as elite and intellectual. One must
also take care not to essentialize and reify these three domains. They overlap
and change over time, and their boundaries are blurry. Nonetheless, we can see
them as broad cultural tendencies that pervade modern life in such a way that any
new idea, artistic form, or institution must engage with them in order to be culturally viable. For these discourses contain many of the virtually nonnegotiable

axioms of modernity—for example, the superiority of democracy, the necessity of individual rights, the role of science in establishing claims about physical realities, the role of the artist as a purveyor of individual creativity. Any novel or foreign element must in large measure harmonize with these, even when it may challenge or reenvision some of their associated assumptions.

Buddhism and Scientific Rationalism

By scientific rationalism I mean the ideas and practices derived from the Enlightenment's epistemological claim that knowledge comes from systematic empirical observation and reason. This variety of rationalism was one of the inaugural constituents of modernity and instituted a new approach to knowledge. It entailed a more instrumentalist approach to reason than in previous periods, a more pronounced disengagement of objects from the observing subject—indeed a reconstitution of both. Scientific rationalism tends to see the world in largely mechanistic terms and promotes the scientific method as the exclusive tool for ascertaining empirical truths. It claims that in principle everything that is explainable is explainable in scientific terms. The limits of knowledge are whatever the limits of observation and reason are in a given case. This orientation is often closely associated with varieties of naturalism that deny that there is a "more" behind what can be analyzed scientifically, explaining the world solely in terms of material causes and effects. Of course, this is only a quick sketch, generalized almost to the point of caricature.

One could elucidate a dozen varieties of rationalism and naturalism, but my concern is not with these theories in themselves but with rationalism as a general, sometimes even tacit, orientation endemic to modernity. Two of its features are important here. First, it views the world as made up of predictable phenomena governed by natural laws that are discernible through systematic and detached observation, experimentation, and rational analysis. Second, it opens up the possibilities for the emergence of modern forms of nihilism, along with various attempts to stave it off. A comprehensive scientistic naturalism is a totalizing discourse that leaves no room for "spiritual" realities and, according to its critics, leaves life flat, meaningless, without intrinsic value, and devoid of compelling ethical norms. (Not all scientific naturalism is of this variety of course; most Enlightenment rationalists were theists.) Buddhist apologists, from the early decades of Buddhist modernism, began to articulate Buddhism in ways that would address both of these features.

Modernizers from Japan and Ceylon, as well as promoters in Europe and North America, presented Buddhism in the early decades of its encounter with the West as a religion uniquely harmonious with both the scientific method and the startling new scientific discoveries and theories of the time. A great deal of the demythologization discussed earlier assumes an appeal to scientific naturalism and rationalism, even if it does not accede fully to the more positivistic wing of this orientation. The first Asians to present Buddhism to the West boldly proclaimed its essential compatibility with science. Sōen Shaku (1859–1919), a representative of the Japanese delegation to the World's Parliament of Religions in Chicago (1893) and the first monk to teach Zen in the United States outside immigrant communities, is an example. He was one of the most important early founders of Buddhist modernism. Ordained in the Rinzai tradition at age twelve, he also became one of the first of many truly cosmopolitan Zen monks. He studied English and western philosophy and religion at Keio University in Tokyo and spent two years in Ceylon studying Pali and living at a Theravada monastery. In his lectures and letters to westerners, he insisted that "Buddha's teachings are in exact agreement with the doctrines of modern science" (122). He and other early modernist figures assimilated the doctrine of karma, and the Buddhist doctrine that all things come about through the complex operation of causes and conditions, to modern conceptions of causality; the traditional doctrine of karmic connections between species in the cycle of life, death, and rebirth was similarly assimilated to the theory of evolution.

Some modernizers made connections between the observation of the mind in Buddhist meditation practices and modern scientific methods of observation. Others presented the Buddha as a kind of freethinking empiricist. A Pali *sutta* that has become central in this regard is the *Kālāma Sutta*, in which the Buddha exhorts a particular audience (notably, not his own disciples) not to believe any teaching because of tradition, scripture, or devotion to a teacher but to test its ideas for themselves—an admonition widely interpreted today as exemplifying a empiricist spirit of free inquiry and self-determination. In this text, the Buddha responds to questioners who are confused by the variety of doctrines propounded by various Brahmins and monks and disturbed by their dogmatism and debasement of rival doctrines:

> It is fitting for you to be perplexed, O Kālālmas, it is fitting for you
> to be in doubt. . . . Do not go by oral tradition, by lineage of teach-
> ing, by hearsay, by a collection of scriptures, by logical reasoning, by
> inferential reasoning, by reflection on reasons, by the acceptance of
> a view after pondering it, by the seeming competence of a speaker,
> or because you think, "The ascetic is our teacher." But when you
> know for yourselves, "these things are unwholesome, these things

are blamable; these things are censured by the wise; these things, if undertaken and practiced, lead to harm and suffering," then you should abandon them. (Nyanaponika and Bodhi 1999: 65)

An exhortation to doubt must have been surprising to the first Christians who came across this passage. Although the *sutta* does seem primarily concerned with moral issues—discerning that moral action leads to benefit while immorality leads to harm—it is easy to see how it would come to be seen as carrying something of the spirit of free inquiry characteristic of science and modernity. Yet these claims tend to be exaggerated in modernist literature. For example, the early Buddhist advocate Paul Carus asserted that "Buddhism is a religion which recognizes no other revelation except the truth that can be proved by science" (1897: 114). This was a bit of an overreach, an anachronistic attempt to establish a kind of Buddhist "Nullius in verba" ("On the words of no one," the credo of the Royal Society of London for the Improvement of Natural Knowledge).[1] Nevertheless, establishing this resonance with the credos of modern science has bestowed on the *Kālāma Sutta* a centrality it never enjoyed prior to the modern age. It is cited in a vast number of popular works by westerners as evidence that the Buddha eschewed blind faith and demanded that his disciples personally verify everything, even his own teachings.[2]

This rationalist-empiricist interpretation of Buddhism, however, was complicated by the widespread existence of rituals, devotion to buddhas and bodhisattvas, icon worship, and other "superstitious" elements that colonizers and explorers reported in Buddhist lands. In the shaping of Buddhist modernism, the way these elements of Buddhism "on the ground" were reconciled with the rationalist elements in the texts was crucial. Interpreters both Asian and western have often portrayed these elements as the original "core" or "essence" of Buddhism, compromised by later accretions and distortions. What I have called elsewhere the core-versus-accretions model of Buddhism is the view that the Buddha himself taught a rationalistic, empirically based, psychological, and ethical doctrine that was free of "superstition," largely compatible with modern science, and was preserved in the Pali *suttas* (McMahan 2004a).[3] To this core were added over time cultural accretions, accommodations to the common people, superstition, rituals, devotional practices, and institutional ossification, until it arrived at the allegedly degraded state in which modern European colonists found it in various regions of Asia. Emerging in the late nineteenth century, this rendition of Buddhism saw the Buddha as a supremely rational figure who, as Stephen Prothero has pointed out, was largely modeled on the Victorian gentleman (1996: 97). He taught an eminently sensible doctrine surprisingly compatible with the basic tenets of the European Enlightenment and

Victorian social mores, a teaching that was empirical, rational, tenderly compassionate, and relied on personal experience and verification.

This view of the Buddhist tradition as beginning with a rationalist, protoscientific worldview and then gradually accommodating itself to popular belief, developing rituals, ceremonies, superstitions, mythical cosmologies, and a host of supernatural beings, has been a powerful element in Buddhist modernism, despite the fact that it is historically problematic. Granted there is a sparseness to the Pali *suttas* that later gives way in some Mahayana texts to visionary wonders, magical feats, prayers, and rites. And Buddhist cultures have developed techniques for bringing about worldly benefits, such as healing and praying for rain, and control of spirits, that go beyond anything advocated in the Pali canon. Buddhism became amalgamated with local spirit cults and other indigenous beliefs and practices in the various places it went. But the image of the early Buddhist movement as a rationalistic, protoscientific religion completely free from anything that would clash with modern rationalism and empiricism is a projection of modern attitudes. The world of the ancient Buddhists, for example, was filled with unseen beings who could have real effects. *Suttas* provide narratives of monks' encounters with malevolent nonhuman beings and recommend verses to ward them off, as well as other problems such as difficult childbirth and snakebite. *Suttas* also enjoin the laity to make offerings to gods (*devas*) and hungry ghosts.[4] Furthermore, claims for a Buddhist protoscientific cosmology must take into account that the world of the early Buddhists was envisioned as a great mountain, Sumeru, four and a half miles high, rising out of a vast sea, and surrounded by seven rings of geometrically arranged mountains extending outward. At the top of the mountain were the realms of the gods, and under it were the various hells. Today we call such cosmologies mythological; but the conception of mythology in this sense only arises when the modern naturalistic worldview supersedes it. In ancient times—and even today among some traditionalists—this has been a quite literal picture of the world.

My point is not to suggest that those who have experienced their lives within such worldviews are benighted. All ancients have had what today are called mythological worldviews, and many, indeed most, people today envision their world as extending beyond that mapped by modern science. Nor am I suggesting that classical Buddhist literature does not contain sophisticated rational analysis of the world and the mind or that there is not a certain pragmatic and empirical bent to certain teachings. My point is that we cannot equate Buddhist modernism, as do some of its proponents, with the revival of an ancient core of doctrine that, as Carus and others up to the present day have suggested, contains no disagreement with a modern, scientific worldview. Efforts had to be made to *construct* a relationship to modern scientific rationalism out of the philosophical elements of Buddhist doctrine.

Nevertheless, this scientific interpretation of Buddhism was a crucial part of a number of indigenous modernization movements that attempted to excise "superstitious" elements and adopt the language of scientific naturalism to describe their tradition to the West as well as their own nations. Interpreting Buddhism as aligned with modern science was quite successfully adaptive: today, as well as a century ago, Buddhism is widely considered to be largely compatible with the scientific worldview. There is a considerable literature, both popular and scholarly, that treats Buddhism as a rational, empirical, and even scientific approach to the world. The favorable image that Buddhism enjoys in the West as a religion largely free of superstition and irrational belief, and in basic harmony with science, comes in part from this early presentation of the rationalistic elements of Buddhism in ways that resonated with the scientific rationalism of the West.

Placing Buddhism between Rationalism and Christianity

This alliance of Buddhism with scientific rationalism cannot be understood apart from its relationship to the second discourse of modernity under consideration: Protestant Christianity. Indeed this alliance was bound up with advocates' attempts to simultaneously adopt and critique different themes in Christian doctrine and scripture. We can see a formative example of these dynamics, again, in Sōen Shaku. His early twentieth-century lectures to American audiences, still in print today (1993 [1913]), demonstrate an enduring formulation of the relationship between Buddhism and Christianity. Sōen takes an equivocal stance toward Christianity, sometimes trying to assimilate it to Buddhism, assuring his audience that Buddhism and Christianity are in basic doctrinal harmony, and sometimes asserting the superiority of some aspect of Buddhism over its Christian counterpart. In a lecture entitled "The God-Concept of Buddhism," for example, he is careful to assure his audience that Buddhism "is not atheistic"—embracing such a term would have been a death knell to Buddhism in turn-of-the-century North America—and "certainly has a God, the highest reality and truth, through which and in which this universe exists" (25). Adopting western metaphysical language, he identifies Buddhism as a kind of "panentheism," insisting that from the Buddhist perspective, God is not separate from the world.[5] He paraphrases biblical quotations that lend themselves to a nondualistic theism: we are made in God's likeness, he insists, and "God is in us and we in him" (29). Sōen also appears to draw on Hegelian terminology, identifying deity or ultimate reality as "universal reason" or "original reason" (see Hegel 1975). In reaching for a Buddhist equivalent of the concept of God, Sōen finds it variously in *dharmakāya*, the cosmic aspect of the Buddha; *śūnyatā*, the lack of inherent existence in phenomena; and nirvana, the state transcending suffering and rebirth in the phenomenal world. He sees these as corresponding to the concept of "Godhead," noting their similarity to the Johannine concept of God (47–48).[6]

Although he insists on the existence of God in Buddhism, Sōen dismisses anthropomorphic images of deity through a kind of satirical realism no doubt calibrated to resonate with the modernist Christian, Transcendentalist, and rationalist skeptic alike:

> Buddhists do not think that God has any special abode, that his administration of the universe comes from a certain fixed center or headquarters, where he sits in his august throne surrounded by angels and archangels and saints and pious spirits who have been admitted there through his grace. . . . If we want to see him face to face, we are able to find him in the lilies of the field, in the fowls of the air, in the murmuring mountain stream. (1993 [1913]: 48)

Similarly, in a lecture on immortality, he makes only veiled references to the central Buddhist doctrine of rebirth and essentially denies continuing personal existence after death, claiming rather that all beings survive as a "manifestation of the Great All" (58). He also insists that "immortality of work or deed or thought or sentiment" is more spiritually satisfying than naïve notions of personal immortality and, moreover, "more in accordance with the result of modern scientific investigation" (59). Buddhism is also in harmony with natural science, he insists, in its presentation of life as governed by inexorable laws of cause and effect, in contrast to Christianity's reliance on the miraculous (122).

Sōen's discussion represents a seminal move in the strategic positioning of Buddhism between Christianity and scientific rationalism, a move that reverberates to the present day. He demythologizes his own tradition—for instance, in his deemphasis on literal rebirth—and then presents it as more scientific than a decidedly nondemythologized Christianity with thrones, heavens, and angels. In this regard, Sōen's assertions illustrate the degree to which the representation of Buddhism as scientific was inextricably intertwined with its stance in relation to Christianity, particularly of its more orthodox forms. While it adopted certain aspects of liberal Christianity, the rationalistic presentation of Buddhism was also a point-by-point negation of elements of Christianity that nineteenth- and twentieth-century skeptics questioned: Buddhism has no personal god; it presents a universe run by natural law and cause and effect rather than the capricious dictates of a creator; its founder encouraged skeptical questioning and experimentation rather than blind faith; it anticipated recent psychological discoveries in the West rather than embracing simplistic theories of an immaterial soul; its ideas of karma, rebirth, and the continuity of species anticipate, rather than clash with, evolutionary theory; it has no divine incarnation, special revelation, or miracles; it does not stand or fall on the truth of a miraculous return from the dead of a special savior but offers an insight available to all here and now through rigorous observation and experimentation. In this view, Buddhism becomes, in effect, an inverse reflection of what skeptics and liberal Christians believed to be problematic about orthodox interpretations of Christianity in light of scientific developments and biblical criticism. The extraction of "science-friendly" elements of Buddhism from its broader cultural contexts thus allowed Buddhists and Buddhist sympathizers to stake out a particular ground in the field of tension between two discourses of modernity, scientific naturalism and Christianity.

Missionization, Perennialism, Dialogue, and Hybridity

Sōen's half embrace, half supersession of Christianity is one chapter in a relationship, more than century old, characterized by both alliance and rivalry. The story is well documented elsewhere (see, for example, Lai and von Brück: 2001); a few general trends are pertinent to our discussion. While there were prior encounters between the two faiths, those that became important in the formation of Buddhist modernism did not occur until the latter half of that century. Before then, Christians' characterizations of Buddhism were almost thoroughly negative. It was difficult for most Christians of the time to conceive of anything redeeming in a doctrine that included neither an almighty God nor an immortal soul. Mid-Victorian Europeans and Americans frequently painted Buddhism as atheistic, nihilistic, quietistic, pessimistic, and idolatrous—charges Buddhist modernizers would spend considerable time refuting (Tweed 2000 [1992]: 1–17; Almond 1988); indeed these refutations became the first constituent elements of Buddhist modernism, a Buddhism that was persistently pressed to announce itself as optimistic, activist, anti-ritualistic, anti-idolatry, and socially beneficial.[7]

The early relationship between Buddhism and Christianity was also inevitably bound up with colonialism and missionization, particularly in Ceylon. Christian missionaries came into numerous Asian lands under the auspices of European colonizers, and Buddhists generally—and largely correctly—saw the two projects as indistinguishable. Part of the colonizer's efforts to "uplift" indigenous peoples was converting them to Christianity. From the European side, Edward Said's now familiar point in relation to orientalism in the middle East was quite applicable: western powers studied the Orient in order better to control and subdue it; knowledge was a means of political and imperial control. Thus in classic orientalist fashion, Robert Spense Hardy, the author of one of the first and most widely read treatments of āTheravada Buddhism, *Manual of Buddhism* (1853), wrote: "By the messengers of the cross . . . this manual will be received, I doubt not, as a boon; as it will enable them more readily to understanding the system they are endeavouring to supersede, by the establishment of the Truth" (xiii). The earliest European translators of Buddhist texts and ideas presented Buddhism not to suggest it was an option to be embraced but as an aid to those who would replace it with Christianity.

Some Asian articulations of Buddhist modernism began as revitalization movements explicitly resisting the Christian missionaries. Even in their resistance, however, many emerging Buddhist modernists adopted Protestant themes to augment their conceptual resources for this struggle and to enhance Buddhism's prestige and viability in an emerging global context. Sinhalese Buddhism among the middle classes in Ceylon, as Gombrich and Obeyesekere have pointed out, developed a Protestantized form in resistance to Christian missionaries, adopting themes such as the blurring of the distinction between monk and laity, a more this-worldly orientation, greater social engagement, a deemphasis on ritual, and an emphasis on individual salvation (1988). These developments were hybrids in Homi Bhabha's sense of the term, that is, they were mimetic forms the colonized developed in order to subvert the agenda of colonizers. They formulated a discourse in the language of the oppressor, adopting concepts of the dominant Christian order but shaping them in ways that attempted to destabilize that order. Even in lands that were not subject to western colonial rule—notably, Japan—Buddhist modernism developed according to this mimetic pattern, insofar as those who formulated it were highly motivated to increase Buddhism's and Japan's prestige on the world stage, and therefore felt compelled to articulate Japanese Buddhism in the hegemonic discourse of either Christianity or secular forms of western modernity (Snodgrass 2003).

It was these already modernized interpretations that impressed the first wave of Europeans and Americans enough for them take Buddhism seriously. The Transcendentalists' favorable reception of Asian religions changed some of the negative perceptions of Buddhism and signaled a new and tremendously influential paradigm for understanding the relationship between religious traditions. Suspicious of the missionary impulse, Transcendentalists and their kin developed an eye for the similarities between religions, seeing them as complementary—different paths pointing toward the same ultimate reality. Entwined with this view was the emergence of a new crosscultural conception of "spirituality" as the individual's search for, or experience of, this reality. Spirituality was thus dislodged from its traditional Christian home, where it was used as a term to contrast with *material*, and came to be considered distinct from "religion," especially "institutional religion." Despite the fact that it retained Christian overtones, this newly cosmopolitan spirituality gave unprecedented legitimacy to non-Christian traditions as part of a universal search for a divine, ineffable reality, transcendent yet pervading everything and to which the individual mind is directly connected or even identical. Advocates of this approach believed the means to this divine reality was serene contemplation and mystical experience (another term that would acquire its modern meaning in this historical context), in which they saw Buddhism and Hinduism as specializing. This paradigm was a globalization of the earlier conception of the perennial philosophy (*philosophia perennis*)—the idea of a common set of truths held by all peoples in all times and places, first suggested in the sixteenth century by Augostino Steuco and developed by Leibniz. As it began to take shape in the nineteenth and twentieth centuries, it adopted a cosmology amalgamating Neoplatonism, German metaphysics, Buddhism, and the Vedanta school of Hinduism. According to its influential later formulation by Aldous Huxley, the perennial philosophy exists "in every region of the world, and in its fully developed forms it has a place in every one of the higher religions" (1970 [1949]: vii). The divine, therefore, was in every tradition, yet no tradition had a monopoly on it.

The view of Buddhism as one of a number of ways to a metaphysical absolute that transcended any and all tradition-specific religions was an initial and crucial move in the entrance of Buddhism into the discourses of modernity.[8] While casting Buddhism as a player in the drama of *philosophia perennis* was essential to its construction as a "world religion," granting it new respectability in the West, it also set up a field of tensions between universality and particularity that persists today. Many traditionalists, as well as modernists with interests in revitalizing rather than abandoning certain facets of Buddhist tradition, have had concerns about Buddhism being swallowed up in what Transcendentalists sometimes called the "Universal Religion," which ironically was itself a product of very particular historical and cultural circumstances. The perennialist model marginalizes and relativizes that which is specific to any tradition. If the specifics of a Buddhist text or practice did not conform to the tenets of the perennial philosophy, they were deemed incidental, parochial, institutionalized, ritualized, corrupted, or simply for the common people. Thus, while perennialism militated against missionizing by evangelical Christians, it more gently imposed another western hermeneutic schema on Buddhism.[9]

Yet, as Sōen's example shows, Buddhists were not passive agents in this exchange; in many cases Asian modernists adapted perennialist assumptions to their own needs. Often this involved reversing the often implicit assumption of Christian superiority that accompanied perennialism and making Buddhism the superior expression of the Universal Religion. D. T. Suzuki is perhaps most notable in this regard, both for his widespread influence and for his adaptation of a sort of perennialism that advocates for the superiority of Zen. Suzuki radically refigured the very idea of Zen, on the one hand attempting to extract it from Buddhism as a religion and on the other construing it as the essence of all religions. Zen, as Suzuki presented it, was the pure unmediated experience of reality and the spontaneous living in harmony with that reality. It was not, therefore, a property of the "religion" of Buddhism per se. The essence of Zen, for Suzuki, was mystical experience, which he believed was common to other religious traditions as well. At the heart of the widely variegated forms of historical religions, he claimed, echoing western writers on mysticism, was a common, universal mystical experience—an experience that transcends all cultural trappings (1957 [1979]). While espousing the universality of mysticism, however, he also claimed that Zen was its purest and most direct form, calling it "the ultimate fact of all philosophy and religion" (1949: 268). While in some senses equalizing all religions, Suzuki's formulation also served, as Bernard Faure has pointed out, to privilege Zen—particularly Japanese Zen—in relation to this essence of all religions (1993: 53–74).

Recent historical-critical study suggests that Suzuki's presentation was highly selective and limited as a portrayal of Zen in its cultural and historical contexts.[10] Suzuki's Zen was not proffered to the modern world as a historical tradition so much as an ahistorical essence of spirituality—an experience that offered existential certainty safeguarded from the clashing of opinion, dogma, and institutional authority. This image, coming as it did during a crisis of intellectual and religious life in Europe and America, was crucial to its enthusiastic reception among westerners disillusioned with what they saw as the failed promises of Christianity and, more broadly, of western culture. Suzuki's perennialism, recapitulating Sōen's embracing yet superseding of Christianity, was shaped to answer this disillusionment.

Establishing a viable relationship to Christianity has remained an important concern for Buddhist modernists. In the latter decades of the twentieth century, since the demise of colonialism, many prominent Buddhists have written books attempting to establish friendly relations between the two traditions. Buddhist-Christian dialogue has enjoyed the status of a theological subfield, and the dialogical impulse has extended to Judaism as well. Perhaps the culmination of the eye for affinities between Christianity and Buddhism is the emergence of contemporary hybrids, not just doctrinal amalgamations but communities of practice. Thomas Merton inaugurated the practice of *zazen* at his Trappist monastery in Kentucky, and a line of Catholic monastics have followed suit. The culmination of this trend has been the emergence of Buddhist-Christian communities led in some cases by Catholic monastics and priests who are also ordained Zen teachers.

A great deal of literature exists on Buddhist-Christian relations; what is important here is how these relations have shaped Buddhist modernism in particular ways in different places. For example, Buddhist modernism in Sri Lanka still tends to be resistant to Christianity, due to the bitter history of European colonialism and missionization. Buddhism has reasserted itself against its degradation at the hands of evangelical Christians and centuries of colonial oppression. In the United States, conversely, Buddhism has been brought into some Christian communities, blurring the lines between the two traditions. This is possible, in part, because of the way Buddhist modernists have portrayed Buddhism less as a religion in competition with Christianity than as a "way of being" or even a "contemplative technique" that can be compatible with—even augment—the practice of other religions. Perennialist assumptions widespread among religious liberals also weaken boundaries between religious traditions, encouraging less institutional allegiance and more hybridity. If all religions aim at the same end, the variety of religious practices becomes a smorgasbord of choices suited to individuals. The Mahayana conception of an assortment of "skillful means" (*upāya*) tailored to the capacities of the individual comes to be reformulated as an injunction to pick and choose among not only Buddhist practices but also those of other traditions.

This is no more than a quick sketch of a few moments in the long and complex history of the interactions between Buddhism and Christianity. The feature of it I want to highlight is the way Buddhism, from the early modernist period to contemporary times, has often been placed, either explicitly or implicitly, in relation to Christianity as a spiritual path unencumbered by many of the "nonmodern" elements of Christianity. Buddhism is interpreted as a rational, empirical tradition largely in accord with modern science, but one that also acknowledges a transcendent-immanent divine reality common to other religions. This formulation remains one of the crucial ways Buddhist modernism positions itself between the discourses of scientific naturalism and Christianity.

Buddhist Modernism and a Rehumanized Science

There is another important aspect of the Buddhist engagement with scientific rationalism: not only has Buddhist modernism attempted to supersede conservative Christianity as a rational religion in the modern world, it has also attempted to supersede scientific rationalism itself. Proponents of the scientific interpretation of Buddhism did not just present the tradition as the rational answer to a supposedly irrational Christianity; they presented it as a humanizing answer to an overly rationalistic and materialistic model of science in the West. While they asserted that Buddhism was in harmony with science, modernists often expressed dissatisfaction with the dehumanizing, mechanistic, and instrumentalist approach to science common in the Victorian era. Paul Carus called the Buddha the world's "first positivist"; but many westerners and modernizing Asian Buddhists have often been decidedly ill at ease with positivistic science, which asserted that everything could be explained exclusively in scientific terms. Scientific writing of the Victorian period often assumed a rather triumphalist tone: science was not only a sure means to knowledge of the natural world but also the means by which the human race would progress into happiness, harmony, and prosperity. Many intellectuals, including scientists themselves, became uncomfortable with these rather overblown claims, especially as the twentieth century manifested the darker applications of the explosion in scientific knowledge—the machinery of mass slaughter, environmental destruction, and an increasingly mechanistic vision of human beings and nature. Even the most vociferous advocates of the scientific outlook saw in it the threat of nihilism and anomie. Bertrand Russell, for example, saw science in the early twentieth century as forsaking its philosophical origins. Rather than science on the ancient Greek model as a "love story between man and nature," it was in danger of devolving into a mere technique that could drain life of wonder and meaning:

> As physics has developed, it has deprived us step by step of what we thought we knew concerning the intimate nature of the physical world. Color and sound, light and shade, form and texture, belong no longer to that external nature that the Ionians saw as the bride of their devotion. All these things have been transferred from the beloved to the lover, and the beloved has become a skeleton of rattling bones, cold and dreadful, but perhaps a mere phantasm. The poor physicists, appalled at the desert that their formulae have

revealed, call upon God to give them comfort, but God must share the ghostliness of His creation (quoted in Nicol 2007: 00)

Buddhist modernists have also been keen to the possibilities of nihilism lurking within modern science and its tendency to strip the world of sacrality, mystery, and inherent meaning. In the face of the potentially nihilistic and destructive ramifications of modern science, these advocates did not disavow their alliance with science but saw Buddhism as representing the possibility for its revaluation. They have argued that if, as some have claimed, Buddhism itself is a kind of science—an internal science—it may be one that with its emphasis on compassion, selflessness, and careful scrutiny of the mind might mitigate the destructive ends to which science has been put.

The influential Taiwanese reformer Taixu (T'ai Hsu, 1890–1947), represents an attempt within modernist Chinese Buddhism to establish the compatibility of Buddhism and science while also insisting on Buddhism's capacity to surpass science. His point of departure is the combined ill of nihilism and the technologies of destruction. "The old gods and religions seem to have been shaken in the wind of science, and religious doctrines have no longer any defense, and the world at large seems to be handed over to the tyranny of the machine and all those monstrous powers to which Science has given birth" (1928: 43). Unlike other traditions, however, "Buddhism is the only religion which does not contradict scientific truth, but rather confirms it" (27). The Buddha, he claimed, not only understood the reality depicted by modern science but also saw considerably beyond it. Although science is extremely valuable, he insisted, it can only provide partial understanding. The development of a "scientific Buddhism," therefore, can help to "overcome the incomplete character of Science" (27). While scientific knowledge is partial, the "reality of the Buddhist doctrine is only to be grasped by those who are in the sphere of supreme and universal perception, in which they can behold the true nature of the Universe, but for this they must have attained the wisdom of the Buddha himself, and it is not by the use of science or logic that we can expect to acquire such wisdom" (47–48). Combining an embrace and suspicion of science, he asserted: "*scientific methods can only corroborate the Buddhist doctrine, they can never advance beyond it*" (48; italics original). Taixu's embrace of science was, therefore, an attempt to control it, give it its proper place, establish the boundaries between it and the means to a more profound truth compatible with it yet beyond it.

Not all Buddhists' attempts to embrace yet surpass science have been so confident, even triumphalist, as Taixu's. Many modernists frankly say that Buddhist "mythological" ideas should give way to the undeniable explanatory powers of science. Yet the theme of the combined embrace and critique of science has ripened in contemporary Buddhist discourse, in which sentiments such as those expressed by the scholar and advocate Robert Thurman are common: "western science can learn a tremendous amount from Buddhism, which I must say, in my opinion, it deeply needs to learn. Buddhism is a good carrier of what in India was called, the inner science. . . . Allowing science to think that everything that it does in relation to material things is reflecting true reality, that only the material counts, has crippled science from looking at the human being as a being with a psychological interior" (2003). Elsewhere he calls tantric masters "the quintessential scientists of nonmaterialist civilization" (1994: 110).

Buddhist Modernism and the Romantic-Transcendentalist Discourse

For its critique of the less palatable elements of scientific rationalism, Buddhist modernism also drew from the tradition of western Romanticism. It was the Romantics who first cast the western gaze toward "the East," especially India, often hoping that it could offer resources to counter the growing materialism and rationalism of the Enlightenment. They longed for a spiritual worldview uncorrupted by these forces, often projecting their own idealistic philosophy on Indian thought and literature. Some predicted that the translation of Indian literature into western languages would provoke an "Oriental Renaissance" akin to the revival of European culture through the reappropriation of Greek sources in the fifteenth century (Schwab 1987). The image of India as the ancient motherland of civilization and culture, a place of timeless, pristine wisdom and of hope for spiritual regeneration of a decadent modern world, originated with the Romantics, especially Herder and Schlegel. Many looked to the Upanishads and Indian epics rather than Buddhism, with the exception of Schopenhauer and his famously inadequate reading of the words of Gautama. Yet the Romantics established certain western attitudes and philosophical ideas that would later, sometimes indirectly, have a formative impact on Buddhist modernism. Many staples of Buddhist modernist literature—the exaltation of nature, the idea of spiritual experience as identifying with the natural world or a universal spirit, the emphasis on spontaneity and creativity through the cultivation of an interior experience, the transcendence of conventional morality through an intuitive and interior source of ethics, the reverence of the simple and the rustic over the complex and technological—owe much to the intertwining of Buddhism and the Romantic-Transcendentalist stream of thought. This intertwining also ushered the dharma into the narratives of suspicion toward the mechanized worldview of scientific rationalism that I have just discussed. Romantic and Transcendentalist influences drew Buddhism into the orbit of hope for a reenchantment of the disenchanted, industrialized, and materialist West with help from the supposedly more spiritual East. It was from Romantics like Herder and Schlegel, in fact, that we got the binary image of "the West" as rational, materialistic, masculine, active, and technological and "the East" as intuitive, spiritual, feminine, passive, and natural—a vast overgeneralization that would provide a scaffolding for the construction of modernist incarnations of Asian traditions.

I will argue for a considerable influence of Romanticism—along with its successors transcendentalism, metaphysical religion, and later forms of spiritual eclecticism—on Buddhist modernism. Although the age of Romanticism, usually pegged from the late eighteenth through the mid–nineteenth century, is over, the themes it introduced have permeated European and North American life and remain an enduring part of its cultural fabric today. Lofty German idealist metaphysics and English poetry saturated with sentiment and flowery language are out of fashion, but Romanticism has enjoyed an often concealed "afterlife" in cinema, music, literature, and eclectic New Age spiritualities. How we think today of creativity, the imagination, the individual, and art, is still deeply informed by this movement.

Out of the vast and multifarious literature of Romanticism, it is often difficult to discern exactly what works were direct sources for the formative thinkers of Buddhist modernism, first because they are often vague about their sources, and second because they frequently seem to have been picked up secondhand.[11] Many Buddhists and Buddhist sympathizers during the formative period of Buddhist modernism were well acquainted with the Transcendentalists, Swedenborg, and the variety of esoteric philosophies, for example Theosophy and New Thought, circulating at the time. But some of the most important themes that inform all of these, and therefore came to inform Buddhist modernism, go back to the varieties of European Romanticism.[12]

One of the significant impacts Romanticism has had on Buddhist modernism derives from its cosmological metaphysics. The western metaphysic that most frequently became hybridized with Buddhism (as well as other Asian religions) is derived largely from some German Romantics who were productive in the late eighteenth and early nineteenth centuries. The work of the German idealists, including Schiller, Schleiermacher, Fichte, Herder, and Hegel, represents the broad outlines of this metaphysic. Its main themes are well expressed by Friedrich W. J. Schelling's idealist philosophy. Schelling sought to understand nature not as a collection of objects determined solely by necessary laws but as an active and productive power governing its own evolution from unconsciousness to consciousness. Against the prevailing Newtonian view of nature as a mechanism, he offered one that likened nature to an organism. The organismic whole of nature consists of two interdependent poles: the products—the objective side of nature, constantly flowing and changing like eddies in a stream—and the productivity itself, the creative, subjective side, which can never be an object. Subject and object, therefore, are not thoroughly separate entities, as Kant and Descartes had argued, but different poles of the vast interrelated whole of being. Objects are not independent of the subject, and the usual immersion of the ego in objects blinds the subject to its own primordial positing of objects. Moreover, because the subject and object are not ontologically divided, human beings can come to know nature in this unified sense, not through empirical judgments but through an "inner love and familiarity of your own mind with nature's liveliness . . . [and] a quiet, deep-reaching composure of the mind" (1856–61: 7:62). Through "intellectual intuition," the subject recognizes this activity, along with its own ultimate identity with objects. Restoring this lost identity between the self and the world is true happiness and overcomes the "fall"—the arising of opposition and differentiation out of the primordial unity of the spirit. All human beings are ultimately one, though on the empirical level they appear as many. The infinite absolute, however, is ineffable and beyond all distinctions (Schelling 1800 [1978]; Marx 1984).

Closely related to Schelling's "intellectual intuition" is Friedrich Schleiermacher's famous discussion of the essence of religion, also an important part of the background of the development of Buddhist modernism. Scholars of religion have correctly identified the work of this contemporary of Schelling, particularly his *On Religion: Speeches to Its Cultured Despisers*, as crucial to the modern conception of religion, and its influence will not escape the reader of modernist works of Buddhism. Most important is his assertion that the essence of religion is a kind of feeling or experience. This understanding of religion was taken up by Buddhist modernizers who, like Schleiermacher himself, wanted to distance this experiential "essence" of religion from its "external forms": ritual, superstition, hierarchy, dogma. Schleiermacher understood religion as an intuition or feeling of the infinite: "the immediate consciousness of the universal existence of all finite things, in and through the Infinite, and of all temporal things in and through the Eternal" (1988: 47). This experience of "the Whole" or "God" does not occur through the intellect or reason but through a prereflective awareness that precedes the division between subject and object. Already we can recognize certain fundamental resonances with staples of Buddhist modernism, for example experience, oneness with a living cosmos, intuition, nondualism, and interconnectedness.

English and French Romantics developed their own versions of this experiential orientation and the organismic philosophy of nature. They offered various visions of a living, organic universe pervaded by God or by an animating and sustaining life-force, in contrast to the mechanistic conception of the universe proffered by Newton and Descartes—the cosmos as a great machine operating according to fixed laws, a watch created and wound up by the great watchmaker. Samuel Taylor Coleridge, for example, suggested the metaphor of God as a poet rather than a watchmaker and the universe as a system of relationships in which each thing has its own particular life yet is also part of the all-encompassing life: "one omnipresent Mind / Omnific. His most holy name is Love" (Wu 1998: 455). William Wordsworth's celebrated poem "Lines Composed a Few Miles above Tintern Abbey" offers the quintessential articulation of the Romantic view of nature as a living force:

> And I have felt
> A presence that disturbs me with the joy
> Of elevated thoughts, a sense sublime
> Of something deeply interfused,
> Whose dwelling is the light of setting suns,
> And the round ocean, and the living air,
> And the blue sky, and in the mind of man—
> A motion and a spirit that impels
> All thinking things, all objects of all thought,
> And rolls through all things. (ll. 94–103)

Also important in "Tintern Abbey" is the idea of nature as a source of morality. We recognize, according to Wordsworth,

> In nature and the language of the sense,
> The anchor of my purest thought, the nurse
> The guide, the guardian of my heart, and soul
> Of all my moral being (ll. 109–12).

Nature, being continuous with human beings, supplies their moral and creative impulses.

Rousseau may have been the first to explicitly articulate the idea that nature itself and its manifestations in the human heart are sources of morality, creativity, and spiritual insight. According to him, nature manifests within the individual as the voice of conscience. This is not merely the internalized voice of social rules but a direct accessing of the reflected order of things in the human soul. True morality can neither be imposed from without nor discovered by reason alone. Calculating reason can stifle the voice of nature, and learning can actually corrupt one's ability to access one's own inner resources. In short, nature is good; society corrupts. Though not wanting to discard reason, Rousseau was suspicious of the Enlightenment's hegemony of reason and its mechanistic implications. Aligning reason with the "feeling for nature" or "feeling of existence" (*le sentiment de l'existence*) makes the complete and fulfilled human being. By examining one's inclinations, sentiments, and motivations, one can discern something about the design of the whole. Thus interior scrutiny acquires both an epistemic and ethical value, since it can reveal the vast system of creation and one's inseparability from it, as well as access the "voice of nature" within.

Rousseau's emphasis on nature and the natural is inseparable from his critique of his own society. Alignment with the impulses of nature entails a certain austerity in the face of the increasing desires, emerging consumerism, and trifling pleasures of the age; he warns against the corrupting effects of wealth and excessive leisure, as well as the stifling social conformity imposed by society in his day. These all erode genuine human relationships and alienate human beings from their true nature, which is discovered within. This perspective entails a theme taken up by other Romantics and important to the modernist interpretation of Asian religions (which I shall discuss later): the idealization of the peasant or the premodern "primitive" man. For Rousseau, the development out of the "state of nature" into modern society actually represents a fall from wisdom and happiness into vanity and misery (1967: 175). He heartily critiques the idle amusements of contemporary European civilization, for example contrasting the artificiality of the theater with the rustic entertainment of the self-reliant mountain dwellers he knew in his youth in Switzerland and whose entertainments were held outdoors and were open to the entire community (1911). Rousseau, therefore, explicitly erects a tension between the civilized, rational, modern life and the simple, agrarian, and untroubled life of peasants and "savages."

Wordsworth, too, sets nature as the source of art and morality against the modern world's contrivances and valorizes feeling and intuition in reaction to the valorization of the intellect and instrumental reason that characterized the Enlightenment. In his preface to *Lyrical Ballads*, he declares that poetry should deal with "those feelings which are the pure emanations of Nature," in contrast to the dry "artifices" of modern verse. Poetry is hewn close to nature; therefore, uneducated peasants and children, whose characteristics are "simple, belonging rather to nature than to manners," are instructive. It was Wordsworth who famously asserted one of the dicta of Romanticism, that "all good poetry is the spontaneous overflow of powerful feelings." This implied a mistrust not only of social norms but of what Wordsworth calls the "meddling intellect" through which "we murder to dissect" (2000: 595–615).

These themes are carried over in the work of the American Transcendentalists, the first westerners to engage in a serious way with Asian religions. In his seminal work, *Nature*, Ralph Waldo Emerson repeatedly extols the serene contemplation of landscape as not only spiritually uplifting but also noetic, offering the possibility of comprehending the "tranquil sense of unity" in the vast diversity of things. Visible nature is the outer edge of the manifestation of spirit, and the contemplation that perceives the affinities and ultimate unity in all of the greatly variegated phenomena "has access to the entire mind of the Creator" (Albanese: 70–71). Such a vision of underlying connection, affiliation, and unity is possible mainly through the solitary contemplation of things away from the bustle of human activity. He famously describes the disembodied joy he experiences in the woods: "Standing on the bare ground,—my head bathed by the blithe air and uplifted into infinite space,—all mean egotism vanishes. I become a transparent eyeball; I am nothing; I see all; the currents of the Universal Being circulate through me; I am part or parcel of God" (Albanese: 48). Emerson contrasts this mode of relatively passive, unitive envisioning of things to "Empirical science," which "is apt to cloud the sight, and by way of the very knowledge of functions and processes to bereave the student of the manly contemplation of the whole. The savant becomes unpoetic" (Albanese: 71). While nature indeed calls to the scientist, many "patient naturalists" miss the mark by "freez[ing] their subject under the wintry light of the understanding" (Albanese: 74). Further, aside from the ecstatic, ego-transcending pleasures of contemplating nature, one can also derive moral lessons from reading the materialized thoughts of God in the natural world.

Although the eras of Romanticism and transcendentalism have passed, many of their themes live on, having become infused into the broader culture of the West. The idea of each person having a deep interior, a true self within that is not identical to his or her social roles, for example, is a prominent romantic theme, not just in contemporary eclectic spiritualities but in some schools of psychology, in literature, and in various facets of popular culture. Notions of the source of creativity, morality, and personal authenticity as located in the inner depths of the individual are an important part of the vocabularies of selfhood that still have considerable currency today.

Romantic Themes in Buddhist Modernism

All of these themes derived from the Romantic-Transcendentalist line of thought have worked their way into Buddhist modernism or provided interpretive frameworks that have shaped its development. They include a conception of nature as being a living, organic system, as well as being discernible as a "voice within"—a source of morality, creativity, spontaneity, and art. Nature also militates against contrivance; the voice within is not the voice of society with its conventions and rules, and the artistic genius or spiritual virtuoso might justifiably circumvent these conventions. Art comes from a spontaneous upwelling of feeling, an epiphany of authenticity, that rises above the contrivances of society. Since the origin of the deepest moral, spiritual, and creative epiphanies is the deep interior of a human being, introspection attains an elevated value. The essence of religion itself is not its visible institutions, doctrines, and rituals but a profound intuitive experience. Such an experience, moreover, contrasts with both frivolous passions and dry rationalism. Finally, simple, uneducated people attuned to nature are more in touch with these spiritual impulses than sophisticated modern people. These ideas will sound familiar to those acquainted with modern expressions of Buddhism, particularly (but not exclusively) in the West. And this is no coincidence, for many Buddhist modernists borrowed terminology from if not the Romantics themselves then their successors. These ideas deeply informed the language into which Buddhist concepts were translated in the West and helped Buddhists and Buddhist sympathizers, drawing on the accumulated weight of a western tradition, to construct an interpretation of Buddhism that emphasized inwardness, criticized a mechanistic and scientistic view of life, and gave epistemic and moral value to internal probing and analysis of thought and feeling.

Here are a few examples of how modern Buddhist authors have taken up Romantic themes. The writings of Dwight Goddard (1861–1939), an American Buddhist most famous for his anthology *A Buddhist Bible* (1938), show the influence of Romantic metaphysics on Buddhist modernism. Born in Massachusetts, Goddard began a promising career in industry but shifted his career goals abruptly after his young wife died. He attended Hartford Theological Seminary and became a Congregational minister and missionary. His first post was in China, where he visited many Buddhist temples and slowly became disillusioned with the Christian missionary effort in Asia. After returning home, he eventually returned to industry and retired early on money he had obtained from an invention he had patented. Late in life, he began a serious engagement with Buddhism, returning to China and studying Zen in Japan, as well as associating with D. T. Suzuki and other Zen teachers in the United States. In true American religious-entrepreneurial fashion, he attempted to found his own homegrown monastic order, the "Followers of the Buddha." Despite the order's failure, the influence of his commandingly entitled *A Buddhist Bible*—a hodgepodge of translated

Buddhist texts, along with a quasi-sutra he composed in the voice of the Buddha—survived him. This was the text introduced Jack Kerouac to Buddhism, and it remains in print today.

Goddard's interpretation of Buddhism demonstrates a mode of demythologization that gives an obligatory nod to scientific rationalism but is dominated by Romantic-idealistic cosmology with some turn-of-the-century popular metaphysics. His precisely (if not concisely) subtitled book *The Buddha's Golden Path: A Manual of Practical Buddhism Based on the Teachings and Practices of the Zen Sect, but Interpreted and Adapted to Meet Modern Conditions* begins with a discussion of the Buddhist "cosmological conception of the universe." He mentions the wheel of rebirth, with its orders of being and realms of existence, but quickly dismisses them, asserting that "such a naïve cosmology as this, in our more scientific age, is seen to be unconvincing and improbable. . . . We must interpret it in a more scientific way that can be tested by our enlightened experience and logic" (2004 [1930]: 3). He then offers a cosmological sketch that is clearly derived not from Buddhism itself but from German idealist metaphysics (as discussed earlier), probably refracted through transcendentalism and late nineteenth-century metaphysical movements such as Theosophy. The sketch begins with a single, unified, all-inclusive cosmos, that he calls—fusing Asian and western idealist conceptions of the absolute—*dharmakāya*, the Dao, "Universal Spirit," or "Ultimate Principle." This ultimate reality is a synthesis of a principle of integration, which unifies and holds all things together, and a principle of individuation, the "active aspect of Dharmakaya." This active aspect is, in turn, a synthesis of two lower principles, "intellection" (*jñāna*), which represents the differentiating principle, and "love or compassion," which represents the unifying principle. From these emanate other principles, which are also either differentiating or unifying. They manifest from the "Spiritual Realm" down through the "Psychic Realm" and "the world of living ideas," which in turn divide into subject and object and then sensations and various phenomena of the "Physical World." The realms of existence in the wheel of life are thus discarded for various planes of existence, beginning with the unified ultimate reality, *dharmakāya*, and descending through humanity, animals, vegetation, the "microscopic world of bacteria," and the world of atomic particles and ether. Permeating all of these are the unifying and differentiating principles "moving in apparently opposite directions, but inextricably interweaving the ever-changing pattern of actuality, and both at last emerging from and disappearing into the self-nature of the Dharmakaya" (4–5).

Those familiar with original Buddhist sources would be hard-pressed to recognize this cosmology as Buddhist, while those familiar with German

Romanticism and nineteenth-century metaphysical movements will find it a familiar amalgam of them. Schelling, for example, offers a very similar dialectic of the descent of the absolute into differentiation and the unifying progress of mankind back to unity with the absolute. Goddard fully recognized the need, as his subtitle suggests, to adapt Buddhism to "meet modern conditions." Thus, one function of this reinterpretation was to legitimize Buddhism in terms of a metaphysic that already had cultural capital for his western readers. Placing this cosmology up front in the first chapter assured his readers that Buddhism was another articulation of an already familiar universalist system. Buddhism was first domesticated in terms of its cosmology, then allowed to present its unique contributions within that framework.

It is not just in cosmology, however, that we can discern the residue of Romanticism in Buddhist modernism. The Romantic picture of human beings as creatures with inner depths from which emerge religious, moral, and creative impulses is a staple of many modern and contemporary Buddhist works. A passage on ethics from contemporary American Zen teacher Lin Jensen, writing in a popular Buddhist magazine, is a good example. Jensen, the founder the Chico Zen Sangha in Chico, California, and a Buddhist chaplain at a nearby prison, has become known around the small city of Chico for his daily vigils sitting *zazen* on the sidewalks to protest the Iraq war. He is thus no stranger to serious ethical reflection. In his essay, he interprets Zen ethics not as a matter merely of judgments of right and wrong and prescribed over prohibited behavior. Rather, "ethical conduct is found in the way things are, circumstance itself: unfiltered, immediate reality reveals what is needed" (2006: 34). Zen ethics does, he claims, advocate good behavior over bad and coming to ethical conclusions through a "synthesis of painstaking induction," but it does not end there. What makes Zen ethics unique is that they are "not an invention but an expression of the heart's core." "The Zen Buddhist" he asserts, "trusts this ancient heart above all authority" (35–36). He offers a vivid simile for drawing ethics out of the depths of one's being: it is like a tree growing out of a bare rock with its roots extending through a crack to a barely audible subterranean stream that nourishes it. While the Zen Buddhist "may cherish and recite her preceptual vows each day of her life, she nonetheless learns to keep her ear to the ground, listening to her own living spring and trusting that above all else. . . . She lets the waters enter her body like sap rising from roots. She trusts that the limbs will grow in their own way and that the leaves will unfold in time" (36–37).

These themes are familiar to readers of contemporary western Buddhist literature: the idea of an inner source from which springs authentic ethical action; the precedence of this source, here called the "heart," over external authority and "rules"; the transcendence of conventional understandings of right and wrong by a spontaneous and ethically insightful act in perfect accord with circumstances. Rich metaphorical imagery drawn from the natural world is also a common trope. Jensen identifies these themes as unique to Zen ethics, but we would be hard-pressed to find language like this in canonical Zen texts. Such language, however, is quite familiar to anyone acquainted with the literature of Romanticism, which is filled with bold assertions that true morality is a matter of drawing from the depths of the soul rather than the moral codifications of the social world. It often expresses distrust of social conventions and "external authority" and privileges individual autonomy. It draws abundantly from the natural world for metaphor and inspiration. Although it offers no system of meditation, it stresses the necessity of self-scrutiny in order to find and come to trust one's authentic inner "voice."

These themes were carried over into American transcendentalism and turn-of-the-century metaphysical movements, where they became crucial in the first western interpretations of Buddhism. Later they worked their way into the mid- to late twentieth-century countercultural movements that took up Buddhism—the Beat writers and their countercultural successors, crucial to establishing Buddhism in North America—as well as into the contemporary eclectic spiritualities that are often loosely associated with Buddhism today. All of them draw the unconventional antics of masters in Chan/Zen literature into this Romantic and post-Romantic interpretation, which provides a framework for explaining such behavior that is not clearly given in the Zen texts themselves. The many recommendations in contemporary popular western Buddhist literature to trust your deepest experiences, your inner nature, your internal vision have more to do with this legacy of Romanticism than with traditional Buddhism. One seldom hears such counsel from traditional Buddhist texts and teachers; for them, until one is an advanced practitioner, one's inner experiences are likely to be considered just another form of delusion.

What does this Romantic interpretation provide to Buddhist modernism, in relation to rationalism? Goddard insists that we must interpret the Buddhist worldview "in a more scientific way that can be tested by our *enlightened experience* and logic" (italics mine). Jensen does not deny that ethics entails a "synthesis of painstaking induction" but insists that its essence dwells in "an expression of the heart's core" or the "living spring within." Thurman invokes a similar relationship between Buddhism as an "inner science" and typical materialistic science, which has "crippled science from looking at the human being as a being with a psychological interior." Each of these examples acknowledges the rationalistic element, whether of cosmology, ethics, or psychology, but suggests that the more vital aspect of each comes from an interior or intuitive experience that ultimately supersedes the rational. This is precisely the shape of the Romantic critique of Enlightenment rationalism. Buddhist modernists, therefore, while eager to ally Buddhism with science, have also critiqued scientific materialism by adopting some of Romanticism's assessments of Enlightenment rationalism.

This Romanticism-inflected stance of Buddhist modernism toward science recapitulates the Romantics' view of the scientific enterprise: it was far from a simple rejection. In the late eighteenth century, much of what was called science had goals similar to those of the Romantics: "to discover the vital powers that animated mind, matter, man, nature—everything" (Fulford 2005: 90). Romanticism was not antiscientific but was against the mechanistic and potentially nihilistic implications of "reductive" science. Romantic poets and artists often saw themselves in a common enterprise with natural philosophers, seeing both as unveiling the secrets of nature and the primal forces of life. Researchers of this period often worked on large-scale philosophical-cum-scientific questions pertinent not only to the truths of the empirical world but also to cosmological, moral, and spiritual questions. It was in disappointment, therefore, that the great Romantic Coleridge coined a new term, in 1833, for the plethora of new researchers who were abandoning the more profound scientific-philosophical questions and satisfying themselves with more narrowly pragmatic concerns like new inventions for industry—the term was "scientist" (90).

In finding an ecological niche in the modern West and modernized Asia, therefore, Buddhism infused itself into the tensions between scientific rationalism, Romanticism, and Christianity, drawing on the languages of each in order to articulate its own positions, reformulated for the modern world. We can summarize the formative and still enduring positions Buddhist modernism took in relation to these discourses as follows:

1. It drew from all three discourses, adopting rationalistic, Christian, and Romantic elements.
2. It aligned itself, however, with scientific rationalism over against conservative forms of Christianity, while borrowing from Christianity's more liberal and mystical elements.
3. Nevertheless, it was also critical of positivistic and scientistic modes of rationalism, and in articulating this critique it drew on the Romantic-Transcendentalist cosmology and stress on the value of interior experience.

It is important to note that not every affiliation between the discourses of modernity and Buddhism has amounted to merely the imposition of western concepts on Buddhism. The idea of the nonduality of subject and object, for example, is present in both Romantic idealism and Mahayana thought and thus provides a point of contact between the traditions. Hybridity came in when, because of this initial point of contact, the doctrines and practices associated with nondualism in Romanticism—for example, ideas of an initial "fall" from nonduality into individuation, followed, after spiritual struggle, by a higher redemptive reunification—were imported into Buddhist thought and became a part of a new, hybridized Buddhism.[13] Theosophists and monistic interpreters of Buddhism in the Victorian period often made such assimilations, and perennialism made this easier: since all religions were viewed as essentially saying the same thing, "filling in" perceived gaps in one with material from another was not uncommon.

4

Modernity and the Discourse of Scientific Buddhism

In this and the following chapters, I will provide some specific thematic illustrations of the ways some concepts, practices, ideas, and tacit assumptions characteristic of Buddhist modernism have been constructed by cross-fertilization of traditional Buddhism and the discourses of modernity. These discourses do not just involve doctrinal considerations but are laden with social, political, and cultural factors. Nor does this cross-fertilization always amount to a peaceful "syncretism" in which people of different faiths gather and gently combine their best insights to forge a new synthesis. Buddhist modernism, along with other modernist religious movements, has been forged in the context of conflict and strategic rhetoric as well as dialogue and cooperation. I have outlined in broad terms the ways Buddhist modernism has positioned itself in relation to modern scientific rationalism vis-a-vis Romanticism and Christianity. In this chapter I will show in further detail, and with greater attention to the social, political, and polemical contexts of the late nineteenth and early twentieth centuries, the ways Buddhists and Buddhist sympathizers attempted to align Buddhism with scientific rationalism.

In the *International Encyclopaedia of Buddhism*, published in India, an anonymous essay entitled "Religion without Speculation" contrasts Buddhism to "unscientific or speculative religion, the sort which is almost entirely the only kind known to the West" (Singh 1996: 18:45). Buddhism, it says, is intellectual enlightenment, supreme intuition. And it is this which differentiates it from all other religions or philosophical systems: it is nonspeculative, scientific. . . . What Gotama did was not to devise a law or formulate a system, but to discover a law, to perceive a system. His part may be compared to that of Copernicus or Galileo, Newton or Harvey, in physical science. . . . Buddhism extends the natural laws, the laws of causality to the mental or psychic domain, or, more exactly, perceives their operation in this sphere, and thereby disposes of the idea of supernatural or transcendental agencies working independent of or in contravention to the natural laws of the universe (47–48).

The quotation exemplifies one of the most important ways Buddhism gained cultural currency in the West when it was introduced in the nineteenth century: through its representation as a religion uniquely compatible with modern science. This representation was also important in Buddhist reform movements in Asia, for example those in Ceylon and Japan. Nor was this a transient phase in the early encounter of Buddhism and modernity; what I will call the *discourse of scientific Buddhism* became not only more voluminous but far more sophisticated throughout the late twentieth century, and is now arguably at its productive zenith. In the last few decades, a steady stream of both popular and academic books has addressed the subject of Buddhism and the sciences (see, for example, Austin 1998, 2006; Dalai Lama 2005; Davidson and Harrington 2001; Goleman 1997, 2003a; Hayward 1987, 1990; Hayward and Varela 1992; Houshmand, Livingston, and Wallace 1999; Varela 1991, 1997; Wallace 2007; Wallace and Lutzker 2003). The compatibility of Buddhism and modern science has become not only a staple of popular Buddhist literature but also a hypothesis in a number of quite sophisticated experimental studies. While all historical religious traditions in their encounters with modernity have had to reinterpret doctrines in light of science's dominance, symbolic capital, tremendous transformative effects on the world, and unsurpassed legitimacy in establishing "what is the case," perhaps no major tradition has attempted to ally itself with scientific discourse more boldly than Buddhism. Accordingly, an examination of the genealogy of the discourse of scientific Buddhism is in order.

The primary contributors to the formation of this discourse had different but overlapping agendas, spurred by two crises of legitimacy in disparate cultural contexts. The American contributors' crisis was what scholars have dubbed the "Victorian crisis of faith"—a widespread questioning of traditional forms of Christianity in the late nineteenth century. For the Asians, the crisis was that of colonialism, western hegemony, and demoralization over Buddhism's loss of prestige in the wake of Christianization. I will examine three figures who were crucial to the early development of this discourse. Two Americans, Henry Steel Olcott and Paul Carus, represent different approaches to relating Buddhism and science, one embedded in Theosophy and spiritualism and one reflecting the extravagant optimism about the promise of science in the Victorian era. And Anagarika Dharmapala (David Hewavitarne) was the most important figure in the turn-of-the-century Sinhalese Buddhist revitalization movement and a key figure in the development of Buddhist modernism in Southeast Asia. Each of these men made an essential contribution to the early formation of the discourse of scientific Buddhism, which has had profound effects not only on scholarly and popular interpretations of Buddhism but also on its historical development.

Dharmapala: Buddhism, Science, and Colonialism

At, the World's Parliament of Religions, held in Chicago in 1893—a pivotal episode in the history of Buddhist modernism—Asian Buddhists proffered to an American audience some of the themes connecting Buddhism to modern science that endure to the present day. Anagarika Dharmapala, already a well-known reformer in Ceylon, was a young, fiery, and articulate Buddhist who by all accounts had a highly favorable reception at the parliament. Yet in his address he likely made even the comparatively progressive Christians hosting the assembly uncomfortable by declaring, unlike Sōen Shaku, that the Buddha rejected the notion of a "supreme Creator"; but immediately following this statement, he claimed that the reason for this rejection was that the Buddha instead accepted "the doctrine of evolution as the only true one, with its corollary, the law of cause and effect." Then, in an attempt to seamlessly interweave Buddhist and scientific concepts, he quotes a passage from Grant Allen's *Life of Darwin*, claiming that Allen's passage "beautifully expresses the generalized idea of Buddhism."

> The teachings of the Buddha on evolution are clear and expansive. We are asked to look upon the cosmos [according to Allen] "as a continuous process unfolding itself in regular order in obedience to natural laws. We see in it all not a yawning chaos restrained by the constant interference from without of a wise and beneficent external power, but a vast aggregate of original elements perpetually working out their own fresh redistribution in accordance with their own inherent energies. He [sic] regards the cosmos as an almost infinite

collection of material, animated by an almost infinite sum of total energy," which is called Akasa. (Dharmapala 1965: 9)

The rhetorical moves in this short passage exemplify the most common ways early authors attempted to blend Buddhism with science. First, key concepts in scientific discourse are allied with those of Buddhism. It was certainly not lost on Dharmapala, who was educated in an English school in Ceylon, that he was using two terms charged with significance for his educated and largely western audience: the first, "cause and effect," was the sine qua non of the modern scientific worldview; and the second, "evolution," was perhaps the most radical, controversial, and cutting-edge notion in intellectual discussion at the time. In claiming these concepts for Buddhism, he fused them with the doctrine that everything emerges from causes and conditions (*hetupratyaya*), dependent origination (*pratītyasamutpāda*), and the doctrine of karma. By rejecting a supreme creator, he risked alienating his liberal Christian allies at the parliament, but with his description of Buddhist doctrine in explicitly scientific terms, he threw his hat in with the one discourse in the western world compelling enough to challenge the largely Christian assumptions of the organizers of the parliament: empirical science.

Second, western scientific description and explanation are subsumed within Buddhist discourse. This rhetorical move was especially prevalent among Asian Buddhists and western enthusiasts who presented Buddhism as embracing, but also preceding and surpassing, western science. In the passage quoted, Dharmapala treats the Allen quotation as if it were a direct formulation of Buddhist ideas, nestling it within his discussion of the Buddhist view of the cosmos and then adding the assertion that what Allen *really* means by the "infinite sum of total energy" is *akāśa*, a Sanskrit term used in Buddhism to denote unconditioned space. Clearly, the implication is that the Buddha himself understood these scientific ideas 2,400 years earlier, though they had been discovered only recently by the West.

To understand the historical context of Dharmapala's and others' attempts at the parliament to ally Buddhism and science, it is helpful to take a step back and notice some of the central themes of the 1893 World's Fair, of which the parliament was a part. The fair that year, called the Columbian Exposition, was a celebration of the achievements of Christopher Columbus. Robert Rydell and Richard Seager have both convincingly argued that the fair's exhibitions and activities represented a liberal utopian vision of late nineteenth-century America in which white America was vividly contrasted with "exotic" and "less civilized" peoples (Rydell 1984; Seager 1995). The physical layout of the fair and its exhibitions were divided between the White City, a temporary public space constructed for the fair, featuring neoclassical buildings and celebrating the triumphs of Columbus and America, and the Midway Plaisance, which consisted of exhibits representing the nonwestern world. They included large-scale replicas of scenes of faraway places: a re-creation of a North African village; Cairo Street, with a bazaar, dancing girls, and camel rides; a Chinese theater featuring a Confucian play and a fortune-teller. Victorian ladies and gentlemen could meander through the exhibitions and gaze at the spectacle of the world's "primitive cultures," complete with native peoples shipped in for the event, right in the heart of Chicago.

The implicit ideology behind such representations was the evolutionary model of religion, according to which all world religions were stages along the way to the most highly evolved form of religion and society. While the Christian organizers of the fair were liberal and enthusiastic about representing nonwestern cultures, this notion of progressive revelation tacitly relegated them to a lower status (Seager 1995: xxii–xxiii). It is particularly ironic that two of the most significant Buddhist contributors to the parliament presented Buddhism as not only in accord with what most educated Americans believed to be the most advanced scientific thinking of the day but as having anticipated such thinking by over two millennia. The use of the language of evolution and cause and effect signaled an attempt to subvert the triumphalism of the evolutionary model of the development of religions and the widespread derogatory representations of Buddhism and Asians in general. The Buddhists' use of scientific language at the parliament—not to mention their eloquence and sophistication— disrupted the taxonomy of civilized-versus-primitive that was implicit not only in the condescending language and attitudes displayed by some of the American hosts but also in the very physical design of the fair. Employing scientific language to express, translate, and transform Buddhist ideas, these Buddhists were both stretching scientific vocabulary to fit emerging Buddhist agendas and attempting to subvert the dominant western culture's hegemonic ideology with its own language.

The concerns that brought Asians to develop this discourse were not unique to the parliament, of course, but part of their broader attempt to negotiate representations of Buddhism that had surfaced with the European "discovery" of Buddhism as well as more general representations of Asians. Those Asians who were conversant in English or, like Dharmapala, educated in British-run schools, were quite familiar with the characterizations of Buddhism that were prevalent in the West in the eighteenth and nineteenth centuries. Virtually all western literature of this period that made reference to non-Anglo-Saxon peoples attempted to explain them through reference to supposedly inherent characteristics and predetermined inclinations, temperaments, and intelligence. The typical

Victorian characterization of the "Oriental mind" was that it lacked intellectual ability, was plagued by an excess of imagination, and was indolent and childlike. John Davy said of the Sinhalese: "in intellectual acquirements, and proficiency in arts and sciences, they are not advanced beyond the darkest period of the middle ages. Their character, I believe, on the whole, is low, tame, and undecided: with few strong lights or shades in it, with few prominent virtues or vices" (quoted in Almond 1988: 43). Such attitudes were used to justify colonial control over Asian lands—indeed such control was seen to be the only hope of the oriental. Dharmapala was inflamed by such characterizations, particularly of the Sinhalese, and labored in many writings to combat them.

Buddhism itself was often characterized in nineteenth-century western literature as pessimistic, nihilistic, devoid of any power for promoting goodness, and in a state of degradation and decline. Especially decried were Buddhism's supposed idolatry, benighted superstition, and mechanical ritualism. Not just the uninformed made such assertions but the early orientalist scholars who were largely responsible for introducing Buddhism to western audiences, including Jules Barthélemy Saint-Hilaire, who described Buddhism as the nihilistic nadir of Indian pessimism. The interpretation of Buddhism as pessimistic touched off considerable debate among scholars and early Buddhist sympathizers. Much was at stake in these arguments; as Tweed points out, the optimistic spirit of the late nineteenth century made little room for a popular adoption of an overtly pessimistic doctrine, and such interpretations may well have spelled the end of the first wave of interest in Buddhism in America (2000). Thus it is no accident that Dharmapala's presentations of Buddhism to Americans and Europeans insisted on its optimism and activism nearly as much as its scientificity.

Although such disparaging characterizations of Buddhism abounded in the European and American literature of the time, the assessment of Buddhism, as we have seen, was not universally negative. Indeed, Dharmapala arrived at the Chicago fair during a surge of interest in Buddhism. Westerners who were favorably disposed toward it at this time, however, seldom if ever embraced the living tradition; they looked to the figure of the Buddha, popularized by Edwin Arnold's romantic poem *Light of Asia*, and to the Buddha's original, "pure" teachings, which they believed had later become adulterated by the ignorant. The Buddha often was portrayed in the latter decades of the nineteenth century as a noble ethical reformer who rejected the caste system and set forth a touching doctrine of infinite compassion for all beings. Henry Steel Olcott saw the Buddha as a figure much like the ideal liberal freethinker—someone full of "benevolence," "gratitude," and "tolerance," who promoted "brotherhood among all men" as well as "lessons in manly self-reliance" (1883: 42, 36, 37, 45; quoted in Prothero 1996: 97).

Dharmapala, who was a close associate of Olcott for a time, was well aware of such representations. But there was more that he felt compelled to respond to. Underlying his efforts to revitalize Buddhism was his deep resentment against colonial rule of his native Ceylon and its suppression of Buddhism. He aimed to rehabilitate the dharma not only in the eyes of its western detractors but in those of the colonized and demoralized Sinhalese Buddhist population. With colonial rule and its attendant missionary activity, Buddhism faced a crisis of legitimacy, having lost prestige and considerable economic and political power. Dharmapala vigorously opposed Christian missionization and promoted a nationalistic cultural revival to bring Buddhism back from its demoralization.

Dharmapala's writings and talks show that he believed that the best approach for his revival of Buddhism was to embrace the favorable representations of Buddhism put forth by western enthusiasts and vigorously counter the disparaging ones. Thus he portrayed Buddhism as a religion perfectly suited to the challenges of the modern age, combating the impressions of Buddhism as nihilistic, pessimistic, passive, ritualistic, and superstitious and promoting it as activist, optimistic, and scientific. He largely adopted the textualist reconstruction of his tradition offered by western orientalist scholars, as well as the positive characterizations of Buddhism by westerners who tried to make it appealing to late Victorian culture. Dharmapala proffered a rational Buddhism that centered on the individual and his or her own salvation as well as altruistic social service. He adopted the perspective common among orientalists that the living Buddhism of his day was in a state of corruption and degeneration, having declined from the pristine, scientific, rational teachings of the Buddha himself. He emphasized the meditative and ethical elements of Buddhism and was critical of many practices that could be interpreted as superstitious or ritualistic. To replace these, he attempted to codify a version of Victorian morals and decorum in the style of Buddhist monastic codes of behavior, in order to reform the everyday behavior of the peasants (Gombrich and Obeyesekere 1988: 212–15). Portraying the Buddha as a rebel against the authority of the Brahmanical priesthood and its rites, he insisted that the Buddha was "democratic" and saw no intermediary between the individual and truth. Thus, Dharmapala's representation of Buddhism, though it could be fiercely critical of Christianity and the West, was deeply informed by Protestantism, Enlightenment rationalism, and Victorian cultural forms. This influence is largely masked in his writings—nowhere does he admit influence from the West, and perhaps he was himself unaware of its extent. Always these themes were presented as "pure Buddhism."

Because Dharmapala's Buddhism resonated so well with liberal Victorian sensibilities, he could use it as a powerful rhetorical tool for harmonizing with natural allies, as well as a weapon against his adversaries. His presentation of a rational, scientific Buddhism to western audiences was a reverse orientalism—what Seager, following James E. Ketelaar, calls "strategic occidentalism": "the selective and often highly politicized appropriation of western ideas, techniques, and critiques for use in undermining the claims of the West, asserting Asian independence, and negotiating roles in the emerging global society" (Ketelaar 1991; Seager 1995: 96). Especially when directed at western audiences, Dharmapala's presentation of Buddhism was often finely tuned to reflect the sentiments of his listeners and readers. For example, in a talk he gave in New York while in the United States for the parliament, he exploited liberal, upper middle-class, Protestant prejudices against Catholicism, ritual, superstition, and perhaps even Jews and Arabs while acutely appealing to their progressive Victorian sensibilities:

> In Christian countries scientists are at work to elevate the masses by
> scientific methods, while the missionaries that go to Asia are utterly
> deficient in scientific knowledge, and all they can offer are the myths
> of Canaan and Galilee which had their origin in the backwash of
> Arabia. . . . The message of the Buddha that I bring to you is free
> from theology, priestcraft, rituals, ceremonies, dogmas, heavens,
> hells and other theological shibboleths. The Buddha taught to the
> civilized Aryans of India twenty-five centuries ago a scientific religion
> containing the highest individualistic altruistic ethics, a philosophy
> of life built on psychological mysticism and a cosmology which
> is in harmony with geology, astronomy, radioactivity and reality
> (1965: 25, 27).

Even a cursory knowledge of Sinhalese Buddhism on the ground belies this portrayal of Buddhism as free from ritual, priests, ceremony, heavens, and hells; yet early apologists repeated this sentiment often, and its echo continues today. Remarkably, Dharmapala clearly perceived the fissures in American society and cast his lot with educated liberals who embodied progressivist ideals against his nemeses, the evangelical, mission-minded Christians, whom he saw as political tools of western governments. He vociferously opposed these missionaries and their activities in Ceylon. Their behavior, he claimed, revealed that their Christianity was "political camouflage" whose three motives were "politics, trade and imperial expansion" and whose weapons were "the Bible, barrels of whiskey and bullets" (1965: 439). He even suggested, in an amusingly prescient passage, that America should be sending scientists rather than missionaries to Asia:

> Instead of sending missionaries who preach the unscientific doctrine of fundamentalism to India and Buddhist lands, I would suggest that scientific missionaries who can give needed knowledge on radioactivity, and teach technical industries to the youths be sent. It is more meritorious to give pure knowledge born of science than to give the antiquated theological dogmas which originated in the brain of muddleheaded priests of the medieval period (29).

Elsewhere he claimed that Christianity had been detrimental to the progress of the nations of Europe, who "groveled in darkness until the light of physical science began to dawn" (440). The western narrative of the evolution of "civilization" is thus turned on its head, with the ancient Indians possessing a scientific religion while Europe wallowed in ignorance until the Enlightenment. Clearly he was appealing to and adopting the rhetoric of late nineteenth-century American modernist Christians and skeptics who themselves had quarrels with evangelical Christianity, missionization, and theologies they believed could not withstand scientific scrutiny.

Dharmapala's contribution to the discourse of scientific Buddhism reflects concerns specific to Buddhism's crisis of legitimacy in his own land and abroad. Although his project was highly influenced by western notions of science, democracy, individualism, and enlightenment, he remained loyal to a distinctively Buddhist vision of the world. For him, Buddhism encompassed these western ideas; they were already nestled comfortably within the dharma, which had anticipated them by centuries.

Olcott's Theosophical Buddhism and Occult Science

Asian reformers' development of the discourse of scientific Buddhism was in part a response to the demoralization brought about by colonialism, racist representations, and missionization; some of the important western interpreters using such rhetoric had somewhat different interests. Each side construed Buddhism in scientific-rationalist terms in response to a crisis in its respective cultural context. Yet these responses were not isolated from each other. Dharmapala's relationship with Henry Steel Olcott and the Theosophical movement deeply influenced his emphasis on science and reason, and Paul Carus invited Dharmapala to the United States several times. Although Olcott's and Carus's approaches to the relationship of Buddhism and science were quite similar, their general philosophies were distinct: Olcott's approach was esoteric and Carus's more rationalist-positivist.

Olcott, a founder of the Theosophical movement along with Helena P. Blavatsky, was by all accounts the first American to formally become a Buddhist. He and Dharmapala joined forces for a time in an effort to reform Buddhism in Ceylon and to create a global Buddhist network. Theosophy grew out of the spiritualist movement, which attempted to investigate supernatural phenomena, contact the dead by use of mediums, and bridge the chasm between the human and spirit worlds. Spiritualists considered this a fundamentally scientific endeavor—albeit an "occult science"—using empirical research and rational arguments to prove their hypotheses. Olcott and Blavatsky drew on the German Romantics' yearnings for magic and mystery, along with Schlegel and Herder's idea that all things spiritual originated in India. Claiming that she was in telepathic communication with the "mahatmas," a group of spiritual masters in Tibet who still possessed an ancient wisdom tradition, Blavatsky brought together the Romantic images of the mysterious East with the current vogue in spiritualism, tempered by scientific and quasi-scientific concepts. Like Dharmapala, the Theosophists made liberal use of Darwinian theory to promote the idea of spiritual evolution and were among the first to suggest that Asian traditions had developed internal empirical sciences for fostering this evolution.

The Theosophical Society took a decidedly perennialist attitude that sought to find the hidden truth behind all religions. One of the movement's fundamental premises was that beneath the diversity of the world's religions lies a primordial esoteric tradition that is the wellspring of the visible ones. Buddhism, Olcott and Blavatsky believed, was its best representative. Blavatsky said of Buddhism that it was "incomparably higher, more noble, more philosophical and more scientific than the teaching of any other church or religion" (quoted in Batchelor 1994: 269). This view was deeply informed by orientalist scholarship, especially that of Rhys Davids and his pioneering work in translating Pali texts. Like the orientalists, Olcott and Blavatsky paid little attention to the living traditions of Buddhism, except to declare their debasement and attempt to reform them. Olcott was careful in his writings to distinguish "true Buddhism" from the supposedly degenerate Buddhism of the masses.

Olcott went to great lengths to take control of the representation of Buddhism and promote his vision of the dharma, not only to the West but also to the Sinhalese, during his extensive time in Ceylon, and to Buddhists worldwide. The most influential and enduring legacy of this attempt is his *Buddhist*

Catechism (1881), which he intended as a compilation of fundamental Buddhist beliefs, set out in question-and-answer format. It had five sections: the first three were on the Buddha, the dharma, and the *sangha*; the last two were entitled "The Spread of Buddhism" and "Buddhism and Science." Following the model of Catholics and Protestant catechisms, Olcott attempted to extract what he considered the most important doctrines of the Buddhist tradition and lay them out clearly and simply. His aim was to disentangle the "true" teachings—by definition, those he saw as consonant with the modern, "scientific" worldview mediated through Theosophy—from the weight of what he saw as accumulated cultural baggage. The *Catechism* became hugely popular and helped to define Dharmapala's revitalized Buddhism of Ceylon. It is still used in schools there today.

The *Catechism*'s chapter on Buddhism and science was probably the earliest attempt to work out a definite correlation between the two. Its view of both is idiosyncratic. Far from the increasingly prominent positivism of the late nineteenth century, Olcott's was an "occult science." Early in this chapter, he declares: "we [Buddhists] do not believe in miracles"; he then spends quite a few pages discussing artistic depictions and textual descriptions of the Buddha with *buddharansi* (rays of light that emanate from the Buddha; 1881 [1947]: 115) and other supernatural phenomena that are standard elements of Buddhist literature. The *buddharansi*, Olcott claimed, were the human aura, which had been photographed and scientifically proven to exist "by carefully conducted experiments" (114). This aura, he insisted, is a natural phenomenon, not a miracle, and "it has been proved that not only all human beings but animals, trees, plants and even stones have it" (115). Olcott introduces the human aura as an example of *iddhi* (Skt. *ṛddhi*), a term found throughout Buddhist literature designating supernormal phenomena believed to be cultivated through, or a byproduct of, meditative practice. One of the common *iddhi* in Buddhist and other ancient South Asian writings is the ability to create illusory bodies (*manomāya*)—duplicates of oneself, someone else, or an object.[1] Olcott refers to an instance of this in the tale of Chullapanthaka and insists that it is an example of hypnotic suggestion, an element of a "branch of science" well known to those acquainted with mesmerism and hypnotism. The *bhikkhu* in the tale who makes his body appear as three hundred identical bodies was, he claims, using his mental powers to impress an image on the mind of the viewer and did not actually create other physical bodies for himself (115–18). In another passage, Olcott tells his questioner that human beings do in fact have "latent powers for the production of phenomena commonly called 'miracles'" but these are "natural, not supernatural" (1881 [1947]: 119–20). He then describes the various kinds of "occult powers" and ways they might be developed (120–21). He carefully maintains his scientific rhetoric throughout:

> Q.   *Our scriptures relate hundreds of instances of* [miraculous] *phenomena produced by Arhats: what did you say was the name of this faculty or power?*
>
> A.   *Iddhi vidha.* One possessing this can, by manipulating the forces of Nature, produce many wonderful phenomena, i.e., make any scientific experiment he chooses. (123–24)

A double rhetoric, therefore, is present in the *Catechism* regarding the miraculous.

Olcott's interpretation of Buddhism was highly influenced by his own Theosophical worldview and the long tradition of alternative American spirituality that affirmed the existence and value of clairvoyance, faith healings, and communication with the dead and with the mysterious mahatmas. In response to the growing popularity of Catholicism in Ceylon and especially of a Catholic shrine where numerous healings were said to have taken place, he even made his own Buddhist faith healing tour of the island. Drawing on his early training in mesmerism, he is reported to have performed many healings that he publicly attributed to the Buddha, no doubt to show that the Catholic healing shrine was not the only healing game in town and to dissuade Sinhalese from converting. In private, however, he rejected the "miraculous" nature of his cures. Insisting on strictly physiological explanations, he accounted for them in terms of "the passing of a 'nerve-aura' between himself and a patient whose 'mesmeric fluid' was in 'sympathy' with his" (Prothero 1996: 108).

Although the *Catechism* relies extensively on occult science, Olcott also marshals some of the essentials of mainstream science to the defense of Buddhism. Siding with scientific rationalism against Christianity, he denies "creation out of nothing," claiming this would be a miracle—presumably in the sense of the abrogation of natural law rather than the "manipulation of the forces of Nature" in the passage quoted earlier. Buddhism also affirms, along with science, the "indestructibility of force," as well as the consistent operations of causality (1881[1947]: 119). Like Dharmapala, Olcott presses the theory of evolution into his service, claiming that according to Buddhism, "everything is in flux, and undergoing change and reformation, keeping up the continuity according to the law of evolution" (110). He also asserts that the Buddha taught that "there were many progenitors of the human race" and that the theory of evolution verifies the Buddhist doctrine of karma. "Modern scientists teach that every generation of men is heir to the consequences of the virtues and the vices of the preceding generation, not in the mass, as such, but in every individual case. Every one of us ... gets a birth which represents the causes generated by him in an antecedent birth. This is the idea of Karma" (118). On the basis of these parallels between science and Buddhism, he claims that Buddhism is a "scientific religion" rather than a "revealed religion," obviously giving more credence to the former (109).

Olcott sums up the essence of Buddhism with the terms "self-culture," "universal love," and "justice" because, through karma, everyone will unerringly reap the rewards of his actions, bad or good (1881 [1947]: 53–54). He also takes pains to insist that Buddhism opposes "idol worship" and the observance of "ceremonies and other external practices" (55–58). "Charms, incantations, the observance of lucky hours and devil-dancing," moreover, are all "positively repugnant" to the fundamental principles of Buddhism (58), and such practices found among contemporary Buddhists are due to the decline and corruption of the dharma. Olcott insists, as well, that Buddhism perfectly embodies the social virtues highly valued among liberal modernists: women are on a "footing of perfect equality with men," and the Buddha was a social reformer who rejected caste inequality outright (71–72). Buddhism, moreover, displays an experimental, pragmatic attitude and is based on empirical evidence and autonomous reason—an implicit but obvious contrast with traditional Christianity, for which he often showed contempt. "We are earnestly enjoined to accept nothing on faith; whether it be written in books, handed down from our ancestors, or taught by the sages" (62). Presumably referring to the *Kālāma Sutta*, he insists that a Buddhist is required to believe only "when the writing, doctrine or saying is corroborated by our own reason and consciousness" (63).

Olcott's strain of Buddhist modernism illustrates the placement of Buddhism in relation to the three discourses of modernity that I discussed in chapter 3. He allied Buddhism with scientific rationalism in implicit criticism of orthodox Christianity, but went well beyond the tenets of conventional science in extrapolating from the Romantic and Transcendentalist-influenced "occult sciences" of the nineteenth century.

Carus: Buddhism and the Religion of Science

Perhaps the most important western figure who attempted to interpret Buddhism through science was Paul Carus. A German immigrant to the United States, Carus edited the periodicals the *Open Court* and the *Monist* and wrote more than seventy books and hundreds of articles on a wide variety of subjects, including Kant, Spencer, Goethe, Christianity, science, and mathematics. He was a participant at the World's Parliament of Religions. Not a scholar of

Buddhism per se, Carus, like Olcott, rode on the orientalist scholars' coattails for his understanding of things Buddhist. He is important here because his popular presentation of a definitively rationalist, scientific Buddhism, like Olcott's Buddhism, reflected the broad themes of liberal Protestantism and Enlightenment philosophy but was much more devoted to a mainstream, rather than occult, understanding of science.

Carus's own religious background is significant in understanding his attitudes toward Buddhism. He grew up a devoted conservative Christian but had a crisis of faith that shattered his early worldview. His own speech at the parliament poignantly hints at his trauma of believing he was damned for his increasing doubts about Christianity. He declared to the audience that he himself had "suffered from the misapplication of religious conservatism. . . . I have experienced in my heart, as a faithful believer, all the curses of infidelity and felt the burning flames of damnation" (1916: 34). Condemnations of evangelical Christianity later in the talk suggest the cause of his loss of faith:

> You who preach such a religion, can you fathom the tortures of a
> faithful and God-loving soul, when confronted with ample scientific
> evidence of the untruth of his religious convictions? . . . Whenever
> there is a soul distorted by a conflict between faith and scientific in-
> sight, the latter will, in the long run, always be victorious. And what
> a downfall of our noblest hopes must ensue! The highest ideals have
> become illusions; the purpose of life is gone, and desolation rules
> supreme. (34–35)

Out of this desolation, however, Carus came to believe that a new "purified" Christianity could be built. Indeed, from the fragments of his lost faith he constructed a new one whose cornerstone was the very science that had destroyed the old. He believed that his own experience mirrored the evolution of religion itself, the "dross" of which the light of reason and science must erase to leave only the gold. The despair entailed in this purging was necessary in order to "learn to appreciate the glory and grandeur of a higher stage of religious evolution" (1916: 36). This higher stage is heralded by the ascendancy of the scientific worldview, and Carus's new faith sacralized science as nothing less than a new revelation. "The religion of the future cannot be a creed on which the scientist must turn his back, because it is irreconcilable with the principles of science. Religion must be in perfect accord with science. . . . Science is divine, and the truth of science is a revelation of God. Through science God speaks to us; by science he shows us the glory of his works; and in science he teaches us his will" (20). Carus was so insistent that science was a religious revelation that he criticized antipathy to science by the religious as "a grievous fault," a "moral error" and, in fact, itself "irreligious" (34).

Not content to leave Christianity behind completely, he came to believe that he could retain its essential truths while jettisoning its dogmatic and mythical elements. His new faith was in a religion that was not yet fully formed, he thought, but was emerging through the rise of science and the increasing contact among the world's religions. What was developing from this historical situation, he asserted, was a "religion that can never come into conflict with science, which is based on simple and demonstrable truth" and is "the goal and aim of all religions" (1892: vi–vii). Carus called it the Religion of Science.

Carus's encounter with Buddhism came at the parliament, where he was especially impressed by the speeches of Dharmapala and Sōen, whose talks, as noted, reflected an already modernized Buddhism. Their presentation of a Buddhism whose essence was evolution, cause and effect, natural law, and experiential knowledge convinced Carus that he had found the best representative of the Religion of Science among all the traditional, historical religions. He spent the next few years vigorously studying Asian religions and quickly became America's most enthusiastic supporter of Buddhism. His position as editor of two journals and the Open Court Publishing Company allowed him to disseminate books and articles on Buddhism to a wide audience. Although explicit connections between science and Buddhism were scant in his works, he presented Buddhism in its broad outlines as a religion containing many essentials of Enlightenment rationalism and late nineteenth-century science. Karma was natural law translated into the ethical realm; rebirth anticipated the Darwinian understanding of species transforming themselves into other species; the detailed analyses of mind in Buddhist texts were in fundamental agreement with modern psychology; the exhortations of the Buddha to be "lamps unto yourselves," not blindly believing but verifying his statements experientially, contained the quintessence of the scientific spirit.

Carus's most influential work, *The Gospel of Buddhism*, assembled material from the Buddhist canon, edited to resemble the chapter-and-verse arrangement of the Christian gospels. Although disparaged by some scholars, it became quite popular and was translated into numerous languages. Like Olcott's *Catechism*, Carus's *Gospel* was used to reintroduce Asian Buddhists themselves to Buddhism. Sōen reported that it was used at Tokyo Imperial University, Dharmapala promoted it widely in Ceylon, and a sect of Japanese Pure Land Buddhists used it for training priests (Sharf 1995b: 12). Carus's *Gospel* used translations of Buddhist texts available at the time, but he admitted to occasional "modernization" of the contents, and he added six chapters of his own that he called "elucidations of [Buddhism's] main principles"—considered "main" insofar as they appeared to be in harmony with the Religion of Science (1915: vi).

Carus made little attempt to conceal that he was highlighting certain aspects of Buddhism and ignoring others. The essence of the Buddhism that was relevant to the modern world was, like that of Christianity, whatever could be interpreted as in accord with the current scientific worldview. Although he did not expunge all of the miraculous elements in the texts—keeping those he believed to be morally significant or to "bear witness to the holy awe of the first disciples and reflect their religious enthusiasm"—he nevertheless "pruned away the exuberance of wonder which delights in relating the most incredible things, apparently put on to impress while in fact they can only tire" (1915: viii). The texts, summaries, and excerpts he chose to include were many of the ethical and doctrinal teachings in the Pali canon, as well as parables and stories from the Buddha's life. Keen to show that the heart of Buddhism was basically the same as that of Christianity, he also included an appendix drawing parallels between passages in his Buddhist gospel and the Christian one. These parallels served, in turn, another purpose: to demonstrate that the essential truths of both Buddhism and Christianity pointed toward a universal religion not yet manifest in the world. His program is clear in the following passage in his introduction.

> All the essential moral truths of Christianity, especially the principle of universal love, of eradication of hatred, are in our opinion deeply rooted in the nature of things, and do not, as is often assumed, stand in contradiction to the cosmic order of the world. Further, some doctrines of the constitution of existence have been formulated by the church in certain symbols, and since these symbols contain contradictions and come in conflict with science, the educated classes are estranged from religion. Now, Buddhism is a religion which knows of no supernatural revelation, and proclaims doctrines that require no other argument than "come and see." The Buddha bases his religion solely upon man's knowledge of the nature of things, upon provable truth. Thus, we trust that a comparison of Christianity with Buddhism will be a great help to distinguish in both religions the essential from the accidental, the eternal form the transient, the truth from allegory in which it has found its symbolic expression. We are anxious to press the necessity of discriminating between the symbol and its meaning, between dogma and religion, between the metaphysical theories and statements of fact, between man-made formulas and eternal truth. And this is the spirit in which we offer this to the

public, cherishing the hope that it will help to develop in Christianity
not less than Buddhism the cosmic religion of truth. (1915: xiii)

This passage contains many of the basic elements of Carus's translation of
Buddhism into a religion of scientific modernism. It begins with a reference
to a scientific notion of the fundamental order of things, in Carus's words, "the
cosmic order of the world" or the "constitution of existence." It is taken for granted
that the science of the day has uncovered this basic order and that there is a
bedrock of scientifically discernible facts that are discoverable, provable, and undeniably true. "Scientific truths," Carus claims elsewhere, "are such statements
as are proved by undeniable evidence or by experiments and formulated in
exact and unequivocal terms" (1916: 28). For Carus, "science is stern and un-
alterable; it is a revelation which cannot be invented but must be discovered"
(46–47). He often insists that scientific truth and religious truth are one and
the same—this means that truth is the correspondence of ideas and reality, and
that no matter the path to it, scientific or religious, truth is one. If a religion has
any claim to truth, that truth must also be scientific—for Carus, there simply
could be no other definition of truth. Furthermore, as was common in the late
nineteenth century, his understanding of science assumed that it was inextricably linked to the progress of humankind as a species—that it would, as Carus
puts it, "raise our civilization to a higher plane" (79).

Carus also refers in the foregoing passage from his *Gospel* to the spiritual
crisis of the educated (and no doubt his own spiritual crisis) and the problem
of the disjunction between the order of things revealed by science and the out-
dated doctrines and stories of the world's religions. He mends this disjunction
by recourse to the ideas of symbolism, allegory, and mythology—loosely used
in his vocabulary to indicate nonliteral stories or ideas that nevertheless contain ethical meaning or point obliquely to literal truths. The recasting of ideas
incompatible with a scientific worldview as having nonliteral, symbolic meaning was and is a very common tool of modernizing religious reformers. All
discourse in a tradition that is obviously counter to the dominant—in this case,
scientific—discourse is interpreted as nonliteral, allegorical, symbolic. In the
case of Buddhism, miracle stories and prescientific cosmologies are erased from
the realm of cognitive statements describing actual events or ontological facts
about the world and translated into the realm of ethical, allegorical stories that
can exist within the scientific conception of the world—or dropped altogether
as the "exuberance of wonder ... put on to impress." Like Bultmann with his
demythologization of Christianity over a half century later, Carus attempted
to find a home for Buddhism in the modern era by interpreting material unacceptable to science as mythological and symbolic. Carus, in fact, claimed

that to understand such things literally was *irreligious,* a kind of "paganism." "A religious truth symbolically expressed is called mythology, and he who accepts the mythology of his religion not as a parable filled with meaning but as a truth itself, is a pagan. Now we make bold to say, that no conflict is possible between genuine science and true religion. What appears as such is a conflict between science and paganism" (1916: 38).

Once material deemed unacceptable to science could be transposed into the realm of the symbolic, and thereby effectively neutralized, the "essential" in a tradition could be extracted from the "accidental . . . the eternal from the transient, the truth from allegory." Confident in his capacity to discern between the fundamental truths of Buddhism and its superstitious cultural accretions, Carus could then declare that Buddhism "knows of no supernatural revelation, and proclaims doctrines that require no other argument then the 'come and see.'" Thus all of religion is divided up into the two separate realms of "symbol and meaning, dogma and religion, metaphysical theories and statements of fact, man-made formulas and eternal truth."

Finally, the passage discloses what Carus considered his ultimate purpose in presenting *The Gospel of Buddhism*: to further the development of a universal, cosmic religion. He proposed an evolutionary survival of the religious views most congruent with science until ultimately science and religion would merge. "Mankind is destined to have one religion, as it will have one moral ideal and one universal language, and the decision as to which religion will at last be universally accepted, cannot come about by accident. Science will spread, maybe, slowly but unfailingly, and the universal acceptance of a scientific world-conception bodes the dawn of the Religion of Truth—a religion based on the plain statements of fact unalloyed with myth or allegory" (1897: 10). Like many of his day, Carus applied the broad contours of Darwin's evolutionary theory to cultural phenomena rather promiscuously, assuming that religions evolved in ways similar to biological species and would either continue developing to culminate in the Religion of Science or become anachronistic and wither away. Religions, as well as plants and animals, were in a struggle of the survival of the fittest, and a religion that rejects science was "inevitably doomed. It cannot survive and is destined to disappear with the progress of civilization" (1916: 39). Eventually Carus came to believe that Buddhism was the religion most likely to develop into the Religion of Science, for Buddhism, he claimed, "is a religion which recognizes no other revelation except the truth that can be proved by science" (1897: 114).

Although Olcott's and Carus's circles overlapped—both were associates of Dharmapala and Sōen Shaku—they had different views of science, if not Buddhism. Carus, in fact, was somewhat hostile toward "esoteric Buddhism"

(Tweed 2000 [1992]: 60). Both, however, were responding in varying ways to a social crisis.

Science and Social Crisis

The discourse of scientific Buddhism as represented by these figures was part of their response to crises of legitimacy not just in their religious contexts but also in their respective personal, cultural, and political ones. For Europeans and Americans, the larger context was two widespread social phenomena of the time: the Victorian crisis of faith and the emergence of the immense symbolic capital of scientific discourse. Carus's embrace of Buddhism and sacralization of science was a reaction to the sense of radical anomie and nihilism he experienced attendant on his loss of his traditional Christian faith—a loss brought about largely by his belief in its incompatibility with science. Like many westerners attracted to Buddhism in his time, he came to see orthodox forms of Christianity as deficient, effete, and prescientific. Although he found scientific accounts of the world irresistibly compelling, he still longed for a spiritual view of humanity and the cosmos. His loss of faith and attempts at reconstruction were not unique; a great deal of literature reflects similar crises of faith and religious disorientation, insecurity, and doubt among Victorians, as well as new, skeptical modes of secular, religious, and quasi-religious life that arose in response. The reasons for this phenomenon are multiple (see Helmstadter and Lightman 1991). Most important here are the increasing dominance of scientific explanations for things formerly explained through religion and the growing distribution of scientific ideas and the ideas of non-Christian traditions in the popular press. This crisis was also a reaction against a wave of religious revivalism and evangelical fervor in England and America and an associated increase in missionary activity (Turner 1991: 9–38).

Carus's solution to his own crisis of faith was the valorization of the very science that had formerly robbed his world of meaning. His embrace of science as the road not only to absolute certainty but also to the progress of human civilization is clear throughout much of his writing:

> Bear in mind that the nature of science is the endeavor to establish an unquestionable orthodoxy on the solid foundation of evidence and proof? [sic] (1916: 80)

> Science has changed our life and is still changing it, raising our civilization to a higher plane, and making us conscious of the great

possibilities of invention, which by far outstrip the boldest promises
of the illusions of magic. (79)

To escape the moral degradation of religion, we can no longer shut
out the light of science, we must learn to understand that God is
a God of evolution, and the evolution means progress, and
progress is the essence of life. (89)

Such pronouncements, though extreme in contrast to today's understanding of the role and possibilities of science, reflect the widespread confidence in
science in the late Victorian era. The scientism of this time not only claimed for
science the capacity to establish certainties about all questions that could reasonably be asked but also the ability to advance the material, ethical, and for some,
spiritual progress of humankind. Nor was Carus alone in giving a religious cast
to science; religious interpretations of evolution linked with an optimistic view
of inevitable progress along with religious or quasi-religious social forms were
not uncommon. August Compte, the father of positivism, attempted to found
a positivist church devoid of metaphysics. Henry Ward Beecher claimed that
geological research had discerned "the long-hidden record of God's revelation
in the material world" (quoted in Barbour 1997: 67) Lyman Abbot said the scientific endeavor described the history of the outward signs of an "infinite and
eternal energy from which all things proceed" (quoted in Barbour 1997: 67).

A new scientific religiosity was emerging that conjoined the scientific confidence of the time with a spiritualized optimism derived from modernist Protestantism. Even accounts of skeptics who rejected religion completely suggest
that their unbelief mirrored in important ways the religious life they rejected,
often involving "anticonversion" narratives, a sense of renewed moral commitment, dedication to human welfare, and a kind of evangelical desire to promote
their new views (Turner 1991: 16–17). Thomas Huxley described the scientific
establishment as the "Church Scientific" and preached what he called "lay ser-
mons" popularizing science and condemning organized religion (Knight 1986:
3–4). Carus's sacralizing of science, then, was a radicalization of tendencies well
ensconced in late Victorian thinking. His attempt to merge Buddhism with science, while unusual, was one instance of a wider religious experimentation on
the part of many who were experiencing the Victorian crisis of faith.

Universalism

Among British and Americans who were becoming increasingly aware of cultural and religious diversity through the popular press, an important aspect of

the Victorian crisis of faith was the challenge of religious pluralism and con-flicting truth-claims among the world's religions. Although missionary expan-sion was at its height and traditional forms of Christianity were thriving at the time, many people were profoundly challenged by the relativization occasioned by the unprecedented awareness of the profusion of worldviews. For some, in-cluding Carus and Olcott, the solution to this problem lay in a universalist inter-pretation of religion in which the conflicting claims of the various philosophies and religions could be reconciled by their own self-transcendence. Theosophy's motto "There is no religion higher than Truth" expressed a common peren-nialist theme: the individual religious traditions were partial and incomplete reflections of a hidden, transcendent Truth that no one historical religion could lay claim to exclusively. As I have suggested, this idea was a crucial element in the increasing acceptance of Buddhism and other nonwestern traditions. While Olcott and Carus came to believe that Buddhism—albeit a revised version— was the best window on this universal truth, neither saw any tradition as hav-ing exclusive possession of it. For Olcott, Buddhism was the best expression of the primordial esoteric tradition that infused all religions. Although he consid-ered himself a Buddhist and had taken refuge in the three jewels,[2] this identity was subsumed under his allegiance to the more universal vision of Theosophy. Olcott's Buddhism was not just a tradition among traditions but the best rep-resentative of the primal, perennial tradition: "Our Buddhism was that of the Master-Adept Gautama Buddha, which was identically the Wisdom Religion of the Aryan Upanishads, and the soul of all the ancient faiths" (Olcott 1895–1935 [1974–75]: 2: 168–69).

For Carus, Buddhism was the most promising pointer toward the Reli-gion of Science, not Olcott's ancient, primal tradition but an emerging univer-sal religion-science that would retain what is true in historical religions and discard the rest as nature casts off species no longer viable. Carus's primary existential commitment was clearly to this grand narrative of scientific reli-gion rather than to Buddhism per se. His enthusiasm for Buddhism lay in his interpretation of the Buddha as the "first prophet of the Religion of Science" (1897: 309). Insofar as Buddhism—as well as a similarly demythologized Christianity—could be integrated into the totalizing discourse of religious sci-entism, it could help to re-create science, the cold, harsh destroyer that brought on his crisis of faith, as a religious revelation.

This commitment to a notion of religious truth that transcends any histori-cal religion was a crucial theme in the western interpretation of nonwestern traditions. In the Victorian era, few Europeans and Americans embraced Bud-dhism exclusively; most of those who were interested saw it as a compelling part of a larger picture. Then, as now, many western Buddhists' and Buddhist sympathizers' allegiance was not primarily to Buddhism as such but to a truth reachable by Buddhism as one path among many. Certain themes in Buddhist scriptures, for example the metaphor of the raft and skilful means (*upāya*), are easily interpreted in such a light. But in appropriating Buddhist ideas as a solution to the problem of pluralism, westerners were not so much adapting Buddhism as elaborating issues at the heart of the European Enlightenment and the very birth of modern scientific discourse. Stephen Toulmin convincingly demonstrates that the opening gambits of the Enlightenment—Descartes's attempts to establish a totalizing discourse of truth and a method that would ascertain certainties transcending sectarian differences—were themselves rooted in an earlier crisis of religious pluralism: the Thirty Years War. The project of modernity itself, Toulmin argues, was founded on a reaction against the tolerance of Renaissance writers, for example Montaigne, of ambiguity and uncertainty, and on a sense of pressing need to overcome the doctrinal differences and pluralism perceived to have caused these wars (1990). Truth, on this model, must transcend specific cultural contexts, religious positions, and political agendas; it must establish universal laws, ethical norms—in Carus's words, an "unquestionable orthodoxy on the solid foundation of evidence and proof" (1916: 80).

The desire for transcendent certitude and universal truth is, however, inevitably shaped by particular traditions and cultural conditions, and this apparently universalist position was from the beginning a part of the pluralistic mix. Moreover, despite its disaffection with western modes of thought and practice and its frequent appeals to the wisdom of an exotic tradition, it was a position grounded in western modernity. As Prothero shows, however much Olcott distanced himself from traditional Christianity, the deep structure of his Buddhism remained embedded in Protestantism (Prothero 1996: 7–9, 176–77). Olcott and Carus were anxious to fit Buddhism into the late nineteenth and early twentieth-century metanarrative of modernity, with its themes of reason, scientific and social progress, optimism, and activism, but just as Descartes's dream of establishing indubitable foundations of philosophic and scientific discourse failed to banish ambiguity and plurality, Carus's and Olcott's universalism could not escape becoming one position among others. Nor could it avoid clashing with modernizers who had somewhat different interests—most notably Dharmapala.

Indigenous Modernity and Critique of Christianity

If Carus's and Olcott's contributions to the discourse of scientific Buddhism were inextricably intertwined with the scientific triumphalism of their time and place, Dharmapala—as well as some other modernizing Asians, for example Sōen—used scientific rhetoric to legitimate his own triumphalist Buddhist-nationalist discourse. Despite the considerable influence of Olcott and Protestantism on Dharmapala, his partnership with Olcott and the Theosophical movement ultimately was not able to withstand their fundamental differences. One of the important factors in his rejection of Theosophy centered on this issue of universalism; the price of Buddhism being assimilated into a non-Buddhist model of truth was ultimately too high for him. Theosophy's main tenet, "There is no religion higher than Truth," necessarily subsumed living religious traditions beneath an abstract, universal religion transcending all its imperfect and fragmentary reflections. Olcott had already acutely experienced the practical problems of approaching adherents of living traditions with this idea; Dayananda Saraswati, whose organization, the Arya Samaj, had once been merged with the Theosophical Society, eventually renounced his ties to it because he saw Olcott as being too Buddhist and not accepting the higher revelation of the Vedas. Dharmapala, in turn, broke with Olcott, asserting that Theosophy was "only consolidating Krishna worship" and that since "theosophy enunciates the existence of the Great Lifegiver, the fundamental identity of all souls with the Universal Soul, emanation of souls from the Central Logos, etc.," it was not Buddhist (quoted in Prothero 1996: 167). "To say that all religions have a common foundation only shows the ignorance of the speaker. . . . Dharma alone is supreme to the Buddhist" (172). Further, Dharmapala was incensed by Olcott's suggestion that the famous tooth relic of the Buddha at Kandy was really an animal bone. Olcott, in turn, was disturbed by Dharmapala's encouraging of Sinhalese Buddhists to go on pilgrimages and attend festivals (Obeyesekere 1976: 239).

Especially after his break with Theosophy, Dharmapala was often vitriolic in his discussions of other religions, vilifying Christianity, Judaism, and Islam. His critiques frequently used terms of opposition common to European and American literature of the time—civilized versus primitive, Aryan versus Semitic. Such oppositions were used to advance the idea that "Semitic religion," be it Christianity, Judaism, or Islam, was archaic, prescientific, and "unsuited for a civilized Aryan community" (Dharmapala 1965: 400). "The Semitic religions," he claimed, in contrast to Buddhism, "have neither psychology nor a scientific back ground" (439). Thus the scientific rhetoric he first deployed to establish harmony with other religions later became a tool for espousing the superiority of Buddhism and the backwardness of other traditions. No longer concerned with allying himself with liberal Christians as he had at the Parliament, he portrayed Jesus as a "personality of an irritable temper" whose "turbulent behavior at the temple . . . aroused the passions of the mob" and who preached of a God who sent people to eternal fire, demonstrated his lack of compassion by "sending 2000 hogs to be drowned in the sea," had "unclean habits," associated with the "socially and morally low," and finally, was rude to his own mother (439–40). Along with his references to the violent nature of both the Jews of the Hebrew Bible and the Christians of Europe, who had plundered the world in a crass grab for wealth and power, Dharmapala constantly set up an opposition between Christianity and Buddhism with regard to science.

> With the spread of scientific knowledge, Christianity with its unscientific doctrines of creator, hell, soul, atonement, will be quite forgotten. With the expansion of knowledge Europeans may come to know more of evolution, of the laws of causation, of the changing nature of all phenomena, of the divisibility of matter, of the progressive nature of the animal and human consciousness, then will Buddhism meet with a sympathetic reception. (465)

Through the rhetoric of scientific Buddhism, Dharmapala was able to embrace yet deflect the racialist themes widely accepted in European culture at the time. Appealing to the Romantics' image of an ancient, cultured, and advanced but now lost Indo-European civilization, he could not only present the "Aryan" element—overshadowed by the Semitic element—as the noblest in European civilization but also Buddhism as the true antecedent to the most impressive of modern western accomplishments, the rise of science. In contrast to those who characterized "the East" as primitive and mystical, Dharmapala presented Buddhism as having been quintessentially modern and rational even in ancient times. Europe, in contrast, was a kind of lost tribe of the Aryans who had been seduced into primitivism and barbarism by the Semitic religions and only now were becoming modern and scientific.

Dharmapala's vitriol against other religions and his continued reverence for many traditional aspects of Sinhalese Buddhist culture turned the universalism of Olcott and Carus on its head, claiming scientificity for Buddhism alone. His rejection of the assimilating tendencies of religious universalism and his rootedness in the social and religious world of Ceylon, while incorporating modernist themes into this tradition, expressed an aspiration to a type of modernity different from that of the West. He strategically appealed to western science in order to reinforce what he perceived to be the inviolable truths of the dharma. In this sense, his Buddhist modernism, though it used the same discourse of scientific Buddhism as did Carus and Olcott, became an *indigenous modernity*—one that selectively incorporated distinctively modern western discourses into indigenous discourse to form a unique hybrid that refused full assimilation to western philosophical, social, and praxiological formations. Multiple modernities were present, therefore, even a century ago.

The early development of the discourse of scientific Buddhism emerged out of two intertwining crises in different cultural contexts: the Victorian crisis of faith in England and America, and the crisis of colonialism and western hegemony in Asia. Although the discourse promoted by Dharmapala, Olcott, and Carus was relatively homogenous with respect to Buddhism's "scientific" aspects, their divergent motivations and allegiances reveal a fissure in this discourse between the universalist approach and the indigenous modernist one—a fissure that continues to today.

A Note on the Discourse of Scientific Buddhism Today

The discourse of scientific Buddhism, despite these somewhat inauspicious beginnings, is no less powerful now than a century ago. While the nineteenth-century optimism regarding the unmitigated goodness of science is now but a distant dream, the explanatory power of science and its dominance in the arena of empirical claims of truth remain virtually unchallenged. At the same time, this discourse has changed and matured significantly in recent decades, in part because those involved in the discourse often have far greater knowledge of Buddhism, and because of the empirical component that has emerged. As José Cabezón notes, "a dialogue that began in broad generalities—'Buddhism,' 'science,' 'universal laws' and so forth—has shifted to a more concrete conversation that is increasingly cognizant of, and more informed about, the complex internal texture of these two spheres" (2003: 57). Two broad themes emerge in this conversation. First, there is an effort to more precisely establish complementarities between the sciences and Buddhism, either in terms of method or content. Second, there is an attempt to more precisely map out their respective spheres, often configured as the mind (Buddhism) and the material world (science). Buddhism is construed as a "science of mind" that provides special techniques for intensive analysis of cognition, emotion, and personal experience in general. It operates empirically and analytically but also intuitively and introspectively. Conventional science, in contrast, studies the world of matter quantitatively, rationally, and analytically. Science provides Buddhism with more up-to-date views of the material world, and Buddhism can provide science with not only sophisticated techniques for accessing and analyzing the mind but also humanizing ethical correctives that can infuse the potentially nihilistic and ethically problematic aspects of science with new meaning and values. While some theorists of this relationship present more sophisticated accounts than this brief generalization suggests, some version of this logic of complementarity is at work in most.

The most recent chapter in the interactions between Buddhism and science, the new forefront of the discourse of scientific Buddhism, is now the lab, where researchers hook up meditating monks to functional magnetic resonance imaging (fMRI) machines, mapping their brain states and physiological functioning, and perform long-term studies of the health benefits of Buddhist mindfulness practices for heart patients. Although authors of these studies often voice the same vague assertions of scientific Buddhism as their predecessors, they tend to explore more specific questions related to health and psychology and, at their best, can rightly claim a far more extensive and mature understanding of both science and Buddhism.[3]

What is the possible historical significance of this new phase of the discourse to the development of Buddhism itself? For the historian of religion, to ask whether Buddhism and science are compatible would be to pose an unwieldy question, one that posits a monolithic "Buddhism" as well as a monolithic "science," reduces Buddhism to its highly philosophical elements abstracted from any living context, and further reduces these to "general principles" that themselves have already been reinterpreted and rendered compatible with scientific principles. Both Buddhism and science are too complex and internally variegated for such reductions to be useful. They would create an abstract Buddhism already influenced by modernist presuppositions. The wealth of scholarship on Buddhism in the last few decades has clearly demonstrated that it is too complex and diverse to be so reduced. This does not mean, however, that fruitful work cannot be done in the sciences with questions derived from Buddhist perspectives and practices—after all, much of western science has developed within the rubric of a Christian worldview. But it means that the discourse of scientific Buddhism is not the best one to inform the *historian* about Buddhism as a historical and cultural phenomenon, since the Buddhism in question is already reconfigured in terms of modern scientific thinking. At the same time, historians and cultural critics who rush to dismiss the discourse of scientific Buddhism as merely an orientalist or "occidentalist" representation may miss the fact that it is more than just a representation—it is a concrete and highly significant transformation of Buddhist traditions themselves. "Scientific Buddhism" is not just a western orientalist representation of the eastern Other, nor is it just a native strategy of legitimation for Asian Buddhists, though it does involve both. It is instead a part of the ongoing hybridization of certain forms of Buddhism with distinctively modern cultural formations and intellectual practices. The historical question regarding contemporary Buddhism, then, is not "Is Buddhism scientific?" but "How is Buddhism transforming itself through its engagement with science?" Rather than telling us what Buddhism "is," the discourse of scientific Buddhism itself is constitutive of novel forms of Buddhism, with shifting epistemic structures and criteria for authority and legitimacy.

An offhand comment by Daniel Goleman, a leading popularizer of research involving Buddhist meditation practices, illustrates these shifts. Discussing empirical studies of experienced meditators performing compassion (*metta*) meditation, in an interview with the popular Buddhist magazine *Tricycle*, Goleman reports that MRI machines showed that areas of their brains associated with joy were highly active—more than any others that had ever been measured (Davidson and Harrington 2001; Goleman 2003b). When asked about the significance of this, he says of traditional Buddhist approaches to overcoming *kleśas*, negative psychological states: "it's beginning to look like the Buddha just might have had it right" (Goleman 2003b: 78). The research itself is interesting, but from the perspective of the history of Buddhism, it is this statement that is compelling. It suggests that the epistemic authority of the sutras, the purported words of the Buddha (*buddhavacana*), which have been authoritative for virtually all Buddhists, is now to some extent being subsumed beneath the epistemic authority of the scientist.[4] For we can assume that honest scientific investigation may find that in some respects the Buddha, as it were, got it wrong. This suggests that some of the tensions present in the early development of the discourse of scientific Buddhism are still at work today. While some Buddhists may simply be looking for legitimation of the dharma through science, and may lose interest in such research if science fails to deliver it, others no doubt see scientific experimentation as the ultimate arbiter of what is the case and, like Carus and Olcott, are willing to subject Buddhist claims to a non-Buddhist standard of truth. For instance, C. deCharms is frankly enthused about the possibility of using of science to mitigate internal issues in Buddhism: "by using the methods of science, methods based on commonly verifiably observations, it might be possible to start to find a similar kind of consensus regarding debated points within Buddhism, or even debated points within traditions" (1998: 48).

That western scientists, qua scientists, are willing to subject Buddhist truth-claims to external criteria is not surprising. What is extraordinary, however, is that the fissure between indigenous modernists like Dharmapala and those maintaining a universalist discourse (in this case contemporary science) has recently been bridged by prominent Buddhists, notably the most prominent one in the world, the Fourteenth Dalai Lama, who has actively encouraged much of the aforementioned research. The Dalai Lama has repeatedly said that if there are Buddhist doctrines that are found definitively to contradict established scientific conclusions, then these doctrines must be abandoned. Indeed, he has declared some aspects of traditional Buddhist cosmology to be mistaken, though he still maintains many traditional beliefs, such as karma and rebirth. Taken at face value, if the dharma itself is subject to scientific epistemic authority, this would seem to signal a profound change in the structure of Buddhist claims to authority. There has, however, been no large-scale jettisoning of Buddhist doctrine; Buddhists have not suggested that the prescientific cosmologies and miracle stories be expurgated from the canon. Buddhism, like all religions, has certain doctrines that are beyond the possibility of discarding. No one would argue that since the third noble truth simply does not have enough scientific support, the four noble truths should be reduced to three. Rather, modernists tend either to ignore doctrines that are difficult to maintain in light of science or to reinvest them with meanings that are viable within a modern worldview. As noted, for example, many modernist Buddhist teachers present the wheel of rebirth, the traditional doctrine of the various realms into which beings are reborn, neither as obsolete nor as literal cosmology but as a psychological reality, with each realm representing a state of mind.

The discourse of scientific Buddhism, therefore, has become an important part of how Buddhists address a question that permeates religious thought in the modern world: how to decide what is to be understood as literal and what is to be reinterpreted as myth, symbol, or allegory. In some respects, this is a modern transformation of a traditional Buddhist hermeneutical issue regarding literal or allegorical meaning—indeed, the distinction was not invented by modern westerners (see Lamotte 1988). The contemporary hermeneutic situation is unique, however, in that for the first time, a non-Buddhist discourse is increasingly being used to decide this question.

To return to the overly simple question of whether Buddhism, in fact, is compatible with science or not—as I have suggested, a historian of religion must ask the question differently. Let us try it this way: Are there elements of Buddhism that, when taken up in the context of modern science and developed and adapted along the lines of scientific thinking, *become* compatible with science? Clearly, yes. This "taking up" of selected elements of a tradition in the context of another tradition is how religions develop, adapt, change, and come to occupy different ideological niches from the ones they evolved in. The taking up and development of Buddhism in the context of the aforementioned three discourses of modernity—scientific rationalism, Romanticism, and Christianity—has created a new Buddhism, a hybrid that is adapted to all three discourses and is able to both complement and criticize them.

5

Buddhist Romanticism

Art, Spontaneity, and the Wellsprings
of Nature

A stark juxtaposition of scenes. In the first, a row of black-robed, tonsured monks in a perfectly straight line sit dead still in identical postures, their backs erect, hands joined in a precise oval on their laps, eyes cast down, mouths closed. Another monk walks slowly past them holding upright a long stick, flattened on the end. His eyes drift to one of the seated monks, and he stops in front of him. He turns toward the monk, and they bow to each other. Then he raises the stick into the air and smacks it down on the seated monk's right shoulder four times in rapid succession, shattering the stillness of the meditation hall with sharp, staccato cracks. He repeats the beating on the left shoulder. The two again bow politely to each other, the seated monk slightly lower than his assailant. The wielder of the stick then continues his slow, deliberate pace past the row of seated figures, still as stone statues.

The second scene is of a large Victorian room with built-in bookcases and a baby grand piano. Four or five occupants are standing around talking, drinking, and smoking. Another, a long-haired, bearded man in a suit and tie, is dancing in the center of the room. He leaps in the air and twirls around, his tie swinging up into his face. His arm glides quickly from his hips, making a serpentine arc in the air until reaching its peak above his head and then gliding in a fluid path back down to his torso. His other arm then makes an identical pattern, and they alternate in rapid succession. His face beams happily, and his hands gesture as if he is a master of ceremonies

offering the contents of the room to an imaginary audience. For a second he fal-
ters; then he regains his balance and his unpremeditated and unself-conscious
manner. His movements tread the fine line between pliable elegance and
clownish goofiness, with a tendency toward the latter.

It is difficult to imagine the two scenes having any connection to each
other or bodies doing such different things. It is hard, too, to conceive that
these scenes could be have much to do with the same religious tradition. The
first depicts a few of the activities that occur in Zen monasteries, most of
which involve rigorously ritualized control of the body: *zazen* meditation, the
deliberate walk of the hall monitor, and his use of the "encouragement stick"
on a meditator who might be sleepy or struggling with the rigid posture. It is a
scene repeated daily in monasteries all over Japan.[1] The second is a scene from
Martin Scorsese's documentary on Bob Dylan, *No Direction Home* (2005). The
dancing man is Allen Ginsberg, of Beat fame, and a devout, if unorthodox,
Buddhist.

Explaining the discrepancy between these two scenes might seem easy. We
could resort to familiar arguments about differences between American and
Japanese Buddhism, about how Buddhism is distorted and cheapened in
America, about how the Beats and hippies who embraced Buddhism were really fairly ignorant about it and woefully misinterpreted it to correspond to their
countercultural lifestyle. We might even note that Ginsberg was not a Zen Buddhist but a follower of the controversial Tibetan teacher Chögyam Trungpa.
And Ginsberg's dance was recorded a few years before he became a serious
Buddhist. None of these accounts, however, is adequate. After he became a serious Buddhist practitioner, Ginsberg did not stop dancing or doing the many
other things Beat writers did that Buddhist monks do not, and since Trungpa
was deeply influenced by Americanized Zen, the Buddhism Ginsberg learned
was a combination of Americanized Tibetan and Zen traditions. Furthermore,
although some of the Beats and other countercultural Buddhists did not have
a nuanced grasp of the tradition, Ginsberg, as well as a number of other Beat
Buddhists, spent a great deal of time studying and practicing it and had at least
no more impoverished an understanding than many serious American practitioners. And he conceived of Buddhism as intimately related to poetry, art, and
loopy dancing until the end of his life. Granted, Ginsberg's and others' countercultural appropriations of Buddhism in the 1950s and 1960s were often highly
selective and based on misunderstandings, and this can account for many
of the excesses of the more libertine embodiments of American Buddhism.
These misunderstandings, however, do not tell the entire story. Countercultural Buddhists and Buddhist enthusiasts latched onto a particular idea that
had been presented in some of the most influential Buddhist books from the

period: those written by D. T. Suzuki and his intellectual successors. Although no performer of sinuous dances himself, Suzuki proffered an idea about Buddhism—and Zen in particular—that took on a life of its own in North America: that Zen has to do with spontaneity, and that this spontaneity is the font of creativity, art, and the emancipatory transcendence of stifling cultural norms. Thus one may often read in contemporary literature that "Buddhism is fundamentally about being in touch with your deepest nature and letting it flow out of you unimpeded" (Kabat-Zinn 1994: 6).

Such ideas come primarily through the modern interpretation of Zen and then are applied to all of Buddhism. That Zen involves an element of spontaneity and unpremeditated creativity is by no means a wholly modern invention, though as the description of the monastery scene above suggests, it does not reflect the way Zen is typically practiced on the ground. Classical Zen literature, however, is full of Zen masters saying and doing bizarre, unconventional, and inscrutable things. They shout out paradoxes, put shoes on their heads, smack their disciples, and cut cats in half in order to shake their students out of habitual thinking and into a more profound understanding of things. In East Asia, this behavior is interpreted against a background of traditional Buddhist thought and practice. In North America and Europe, it came to be interpreted largely in language derived from Romanticism. In this chapter, I will elucidate the articulation of a special connection between art and Buddhism and suggest how this idea was framed—especially by D. T. Suzuki—in terms of Romantic conceptions of nature, art, creativity, and spontaneity. This created a hybridized concept of a unique relationship of Zen to spontaneous creativity that not only became an important and influential element of Buddhist modernism but also has influenced artists and cultural forms beyond the Buddhist community.

Nature and Art in Romanticism and Transcendentalism

Of all the elements of Romanticism and Transcendentalism that I argued in chapter 3 formed important facets of the hybrid discourse of Buddhist modernism, what is crucial to us here is the Romantic revolution in the understanding of art and creativity. Historian of Romanticism Meyer Abrams, in *The Mirror and the Lamp*, argues that prior to the Romantics, the job of the artist was to act as a mirror reflecting and imitating the world. This conception runs from Plato up through the Renaissance and into the Enlightenment. The Romantics rejected the metaphor of artist as mirror for the metaphor of the artist as a lamp that illuminates something new through the artist's unique vision and imaginative powers. On this view, the work of art is "essentially the internal made external, resulting from a creative process operating under the impulse of feeling" (Abrams 1953: 22). In this "expressive theory" of art, a relationship is set up between the interior depths of the individual—wherein lies nature or spirit, the source of creative inspiration and imagination—and the outward expression of one's unique vision. Psychoanalytic theories later augmented this idea, making the source of art the unconscious, which expressed repressed horrors or universal archetypes.

Before this shift from mimesis to expression, ancient and medieval art often took religious themes as their subjects, but the expressivist conception of art imbued the act of creation itself with a spiritual dimension. The artist or poet came to be seen as someone with unique powers of insight that could bring forth hidden dimensions of being. The German Romantics were explicit about this elevated role of creativity and its religious significance. For Schelling, art was "an emanation of the absolute," as well as the way to understand what cannot be an object of representation by the sciences or philosophy (1989: 31). It showed what could not be said, revealing the unity of the conscious and unconscious and manifesting the absolute beyond the knowable conditions of the artwork itself, such as the materials it is made of or its status. Art, therefore, is elevated above even philosophy; it is the vehicle for grasping the unconditioned absolute reality (Schelling 1978 [1800]). Schlegel, too, saw art as bringing the infinite to the surface through symbols. Schleiermacher conceived of the artist as someone who brings God nearer to the masses, while Herder went so far as to liken the artist to a creator god himself (Taylor 1989: 377–78). For Friedrich von Schiller (1759–1805) aesthetic education in the experience of beauty was paramount for both the individual and the transformation of society. Artistic activity was a kind of free "play" consisting of acts of creation that overcame the separation of the individual from others and from the world and integrated the various components of the self, including thought and feeling, contemplation and sensation, reason and intuition, activity and passivity, form and matter. It was the aesthetic impulse, the "play drive" (*Spieltrieb*), that allowed for this unification and for the possibility of true freedom (Schiller 1967). Modern European and North American culture's reverence for the artist, its allowing of the artist to stand to some extent outside society's conventions, its picture of the artist as feeling things more deeply than others, its *romanticization* of the artist (of course!) emerged in this period and remains a powerful cultural element of modernity today. The artist came to be endowed with an almost priestly or shamanic ability to conjure hidden aesthetic and spiritual realities, to transform the mundane into the sublime through the freedom of the creative imagination, and to plumb the hidden depths of reality and give them unique expression.

A related theme in Romantic literature embraces a constellation of concepts often found in English Romantic writings: genius, originality, and spontaneity. The great artist or poet is a genius whose productions are altogether original and spring from the interior depths of his soul. Thus Blake claimed that he wrote *Milton* "from Immediate Dictation without Premeditation" (Blake 1965: 697). Shelley similarly claimed that poetry had "no necessary connection with consciousness or will" (Wu 1998: 1042). Coleridge claimed that genius was the product of "unconscious activity" that transcended merely personal willing. Poets are often ignorant of the source of their own work, a number of Romantics claimed, and may themselves be surprised by their own spontaneous creations. The work of genius is derived from inspiration, and inspiration comes not from an accumulation of knowledge but from the spontaneous eruption of creativity. While this seems highly individualistic, Keats claimed that genius must transcend the self, that the poet in fact "has no self." Alexander Gerard asserted that "the fire of genius, like a divine impulse, raises the mind above itself, and by the natural influence of imagination actuates it as if it were supernaturally inspired" (quoted in Bennett 2005: 660).

This idea is inseparable from the modern concept of the *epiphany*. Beginning in the Romantic period, a special place is given to sudden insight, inspiration, or revelation as the source of art and literature. Taylor defines the concept as it develops from Romanticism through modernism in terms of the "notion of a work of art as the locus of a manifestation which brings us into the presence of something which is otherwise inaccessible, and which is of the highest moral or spiritual significance; a manifestation, moreover, which also defines or completes something, even as it reveals" (1989: 419). This idea of the epiphanic, he argues, came from the Romantics, worked its way up through modernist art and literature, and remains quite alive today. Surely this doesn't mean that people previous to the Romantic period didn't have epiphanies, but rather that such experiences began to take on a central role in the very conceptions of art and the artist. The epiphany is believed to reveal something beyond the conventional and to carry a certain moral force, though it may take one beyond conventional morality. The Romantics and Transcendentalists, often thought of it as a unitive apprehension of spirit, nature, or the life-force that flows through all things; or as the sense of oneness with nature or God, themes that would later be attributed primarily to Asian religions after Romanticism faded. The epiphany, however, is not limited to explicitly religious formulations, nor is it removed from specific social and political circumstances. Embedded in the very notion of an epiphany in the modern sense is a critique of the instrumental, industrial, and mechanical forces that emerge and grow stronger with each passing decade of the modern period; it requires an Other of industrial-capitalistic values and is conceived as a force that pierces the veil of social illusions they foster.

All of these themes suggest that the ground was well prepared for the introduction of Buddhism into the modern conversation. Buddhism would bring to this conversation its own epiphanies, practices of interior exploration, suspicions of the intellect, and cosmological visions, even while itself being shaped by these western ideas and practices. One of the more important figures in this intertwining of ideas and practices was D. T. Suzuki.

Zen and the Art of Art: D. T. Suzuki and Zen Romanticism

We would be hard-pressed to find a more influential figure in the development of Buddhist modernism than D. T. Suzuki (1870–1966). This is borne out not so much by some of the rather extravagant estimates of his importance to civilization but to the number of significant thinkers who adopted his interpretation of Zen and Buddhism.[2] His work formed the conception of Zen for many scholars of religion, psychology, and philosophy, as well as popularizers of Zen, Buddhism, and mysticism. Through figures like Aldous Huxley, Robert Blyth, Dwight Goddard, Erich Fromm, Carl Jung, and Thomas Merton, Suzuki's vision of Zen was disseminated widely throughout North America and Europe. In Japan, he influenced the ongoing revitalization of Zen and the Kyoto School of Japanese philosophy, which drew on both Buddhism and continental philosophy. Although not a monk, he studied with Sōen Shaku and served as Sōen's translator at the World Parliament of Religions and on subsequent lecture tours in the United States. He was, therefore, even before he wrote his own work, an important figure in the earliest attempts to spread Zen beyond East Asia and harmonize it with western thought and practice.

Much in Suzuki's writings on Zen derives from Romanticism, Transcendentalism, and their successors, although he seldom gives them much credit for influencing his thought. It is difficult to discern how much he actually read of the Romantics themselves, though he clearly read the Transcendentalists, through whom he became familiar with some of the themes I have just discussed.[3] He amalgamated Buddhist and German idealist and American Transcendentalist cosmological concepts with Buddhist ones and presented the Japanese poets as deeply and religiously attentive to nature like the English Romantics and Transcendentalists—yet, he insisted, superior. He is critical of the aspects of modernity that often distressed the Romantics and Transcendentalists: commercialism, greed for luxuries, rampant industrialism, and the dominance of instrumental reason. He also conceived of spiritual freedom as a spontaneous, emancipatory consciousness that transcends rational intellect and social convention.

My main focus here will be on Suzuki's development of a hybridized Buddhist-Romantic concept of creativity and spontaneity. The pluralistic lineage of the concept goes back not only to the Zen masters and poets Suzuki amply quotes but also to the German Romantics and American Transcendentalists, and then the Beat writers in America carry it forward.[4] This hybrid conception also finds expression in the work of a number of notable modern artists, Buddhist teachers, and educational programs, not to mention the plethora of "Zen and the art of . . ." books on the market. Suzuki's work brought the implications of Romantic-Transcendentalist thinking to bear on art and creativity in a way that came to not only define Zen in the West but also interpret it as a unique "way" of creativity that could be applied to virtually all aspects of life.

Humanity and Nature

How did Suzuki articulate this idea? As noted, a chief concern of Romanticism and Transcendentalism was nature and its relationship to humanity. In the wake of the Enlightenment's explication of the cosmos as a mechanism and of humanity's essential separation from nature, this movement was an attempt to resacralize nature and restore an intimate bond between human beings and the natural world. There are no terms in Buddhist languages that precisely correspond to the word *nature* with all of the connotations it has in the modern period; yet Suzuki takes up the European terms "Man" and "Nature" with alacrity, entering the conversation on western terms and offering Zen as the solution to the fundamental problem of modernity: humanity's confrontation with and alienation from nature. He outlines the problem as it was conceived in the West—as man's separateness from nature, feeling external to it, and desire to fight and dominate it. In the western mind, Suzuki argues, nature is hostile to man and antithetical to man's spiritual aspirations. In biblical traditions, it is the source of temptation, a prison-house for the soul, and a realm over which humanity has dominion, while in modern secular traditions it is mute material— an often-threatening "brute fact"—to be exploited and dominated. Man and nature are separate and hostile toward each other, for try as he might, man can never truly subdue nature. All of man's creations will eventually crumble and succumb to time's destructive power; thus "modern man," who aspires to subdue this power, is particularly susceptible to anxiety, frustration, fear, and insecurity (1956: 229–33).

Suzuki offers another way of understanding this relationship, one that brings together Zen with Romanticism's holism: man is not really separate from nature at all but is part of it. "Man came out of Nature in order to see Nature in himself; that is, Nature came to itself to see itself in Man" (1956: 236). Moreover, Zen offers the possibility of coming to awareness of this primordial identity of man and nature, an identity that transcends the dichotomy between them yet does not negate the individual. Zen points one toward the abode where "timelessness has not negated itself so that we have a dichotomy of subject-object, Man-Nature, God-world" (240). Here "pure subjectivity is pure objectivity; the *en-soi* is the *pour-soi*; there is perfect identity of Man and Nature, of God and Nature, and of the one and the many. But the identity does not imply the annihilation of one at the cost of the other" (241).

To this language of western metaphysics Suzuki adds a kind of language unique to Zen, the koan. Suzuki often writes that union with the absolute involves transcendence of the "rational" and "logical"—something we find as well in Fichte and Schelling, for example. But Suzuki, to suggest that Zen masters have realized this transrational union in the most perfect way, highlights a unique form of Zen literature: *mondō* and koans, stories of encounters between Zen masters and disciples that are recognizable to anyone with a bit of familiarity with Zen.[5] Their general form consists of a question and an answer that have no obvious relation to each other. Famous ones, like the koan about the sound of one hand clapping, have become familiar in the West. To illustrate the union of humanity and nature, Suzuki offers one koan in which a master hits a post with a stick and a monk feels sudden pain. He suggests that this demonstrates the degree to which awakened beings are "totally identified with Nature" and that the seeming incomprehensibility and irrationality of the koan is due to the fact that logic exists only on the surface of things, in the "realm of relativity." Penetration into the absolute, where humanity and nature are one, gives rise to speech that at once deals with "concrete facts"—posts, dogs, noses—yet utterly defies rational explanation, for it emerges from the prerational unity of things. The masters, therefore, are "instruments of communication in order that Nature may become conscious of itself. Pure being descends from its seat of absolute identity and, becoming dichotomous, speaks to itself" (1956: 250). Zen masters, therefore, speak from the depths of nature or "pure being" in which all things are unified, yet still utter discrete truths in the realm of relativity, thereby reconciling the absolute with the dualistic, differentiated world. These utterances may not make rational sense, but in their very disruption of rationality they may propel the listener's mind to transcend itself.

Suzuki acknowledges that western thinkers, mystics, and saints have all in some measure seen into this unification of man and nature, which he insists is common to all religious and mystical traditions. One of the unique contributions he sees Zen making is this transrational utterance that expresses and points toward the nondualistic unity of humanity and nature. This, Suzuki insists, is beyond philosophizing and argument. It is a unique form of discourse that speaks directly from the intersection of the relative and the absolute, reconciling them. For Suzuki, the "irrationality" of the Zen koan signals the fact that Zen has accomplished what the West has failed to accomplish: the total reconciliation of man and nature. "[Nature's] 'irrationality' transcends our human doubts or ambiguities, and in our submitting to it, or rather accepting it, we transcend ourselves" (1956: 234).

In his discussion of humanity and nature, Suzuki takes Zen literature out of its social, ritual, and ethical context and reframes it in terms of a language of metaphysics derived from German Romantic idealism, English Romanticism, and American Transcendentalism. His vocabulary of pure subjectivity, pure objectivity, and nature, as well as his elaboration of philosophical concepts—the ultimate harmony between humanity and nature, the emerging of the subject out of nature, nature coming to self-consciousness in the individual, and the individual in turn realizing his oneness with nature—clearly draw from these sources. Like them, he offers a picture of living nature of which humanity is a part, in contrast to both the Christian theological view and the rationalist mechanistic view. Like Schelling and Coleridge, who saw the fall as separation from nature and redemption as "Reconciliation from this Enmity with Nature," Suzuki presents unity with nature as the highest spiritual goal (quoted in Abrams 1984: 124). He also uses the koan to further elaborate the Romantic critique of rationalism and to articulate a variation of the expressivist view: the Zen master expresses his unique transcendent utterances from the depths of nondual being.

Does this conceptual borrowing mean that Suzuki simply appropriated western sources and tried to pass them off as Zen? This would be too simplistic a reading. He was placing elements of Zen literature on a scaffolding constructed of a variety of western philosophical ideas in order to translate selected Zen ideas into that discourse. Sensing affinities between Zen and the Romantic-Transcendentalist vein of western metaphysics, Suzuki deployed its terminology to frame the issue of humanity and nature, allowing Zen to claim the broad outlines of the metaphysic and then presenting Zen themes to bring it to what he considered its fullest expression. This allowed him to bring Zen into the conversations of modernity—in both Japan and the West—though it did implicitly exaggerate the degree to which Zen can unproblematically claim the Romantic-Transcendentalist metaphysic as its own. Most historically significant, though, is that in claiming this conceptual vocabulary for Zen, Suzuki placed Zen firmly within modernity's constitutive tensions between rationalism and Romanticism, aligning it with Romanticism but also implicitly claiming to supersede it. This is the recurrent pattern of Suzuki's engagement with western thought.

Concepts and Reality/West and East

What might be called this "Zen Romanticist" metaphysic of nature is important to Suzuki's discussion of creativity and art and what he claims is their unique relationship to Zen, a conception he sets forth in *Zen and Japanese Culture* (1959). Essential to Suzuki's interpretation of Zen is the deprecation of "concepts" and "verbalism," which, he claims, obscure the true nature of things as they are. He presents Zen as against abstract philosophizing and speculation in favor of a simple way of life that can lead to an immediate grasp of things and, through this immediacy, a grasping of the whole. Citing instances in Zen literature in which monks receive a blow or a tweak on the nose from the master in an attempt to free them from conceptualization and speculation and direct them toward the immediate experience of the present, he asserts that breaking "the deadlock of intellectualization" is essential to attaining satori, which "finds a meaning hitherto hidden in our daily concrete particular experiences" and uncovers the "'isness' of a thing" "purged of all intellectual sediments." Suzuki defines "satori" as "emancipation, moral, spiritual, as well as intellectual" (15–17), and as a radical "acquiring of a new point of view in which life assumes a fresher, deeper, and more satisfying aspect" (1949: 229).

Suzuki then uses this opposition between concepts and the direct apprehension of reality to critique the overreliance on the rational intellect he believes is an essential characteristic of the West. He does this by invoking the dualities of East and West developed in the context of western orientalism and reframing them in order to give the typically subordinate term ("the East") the higher status. An example is his discussion of the Japanese aesthetic term *wabi*, which designates simple, rustic elegance (and which has now worked its way into the language of interior decorating in North America). For Suzuki, *wabi* implies a kind of "poverty" that is "not to be dependent on things worldly—wealth, power, and reputation—and yet [feels] the presence of something of the highest value, above time and social position" (1959: 23). Citing Henry David Thoreau's log cabin as an American example of such simplicity, he praises this poverty against the materialistic excesses of the West: "despite the modern western luxuries and comforts of life which have invaded us, there is still an ineradicable longing in us for the cult of *wabi*. . . . However 'civilized,' however much brought up in an artificially contrived environment, we all seem to have an innate longing for primitive simplicity, close to the natural state of living" (23). His nod to Thoreau signals his affinity with the Romantic-Transcendentalist love of simplicity and solitude, its valuation of nature, its distinction between natural and contrived, and its suspicion of the benefits of modern luxury and technological progress. "With all the apparatus of science we have not yet fathomed the mysteries of life"—implying, of course, that Zen *has*. And in contrast to the limited graspings of western science, "the most characteristic thing in the temperament of the Eastern people is the ability to grasp life from within and not from without" (23–24). He thus affirms the orientalist idea, again derived from the Romantics, that the West is "logical" and the East "intuitive," asserting that the latter is therefore far better suited to address "the most fundamental things in life," particularly religion, art, and metaphysics (219).

Through these characterizations, Suzuki clears a place for Zen decisively within the tensions of modernity I have been discussing—between reason and intuition, civilized and primitive, science and art, outer and inner. He assimilates the overreliance on intellect, luxury, and technology to the West and the simple, intuitive, artistic, and nonconceptual apprehension of reality to the East (despite the fact that Japan had been for a hundred years aggressively pursuing the things he associates exclusively with the West). Such overgeneralized homologizations, however, are not unique to Suzuki; as noted, they recapitulated western conceptions that orientalists, missionaries, and colonizers of Asia had long before deployed. The first great translator of Indian literature into English, Sir William Jones, declared in the late eighteenth century that "reason and Taste are the grand prerogatives of the European mind, while Asiatics have soared to loftier heights in the sphere of Imagination" (1799: 1:11). In his valorization of Asian "simplicity," Suzuki adopts the Romantics' representation of "the East," which was more an internal critique of western culture than an adequate understanding of Asian culture. Certain German Romantics especially—Schelling, Herder, and Schlegel—seeking the antidote to the ascendancy of reason, analysis, and industry, had speculated that intuition, nature, and feeling were ascendant in "the East" (Clarke 1997: 54–70; King 1999).[6]

Suzuki's descriptions of the Zen recluse in his wooded setting, at one with nature, evoke not only Thoreau but also the entire Romantic tradition of valorizing the peasant, the child, and the "savage," as well as the nostalgia for the primitive in an increasingly complex world run by instrumental reason. Suzuki draws on Romantic primitivism in order to positively reframe the often pejorative western images of Asians as childlike, innocent, intuitive, mystical, and nonrational. It was the Romantics who first made it possible in the West to see these characteristics as virtues over against the competing traits of acquisitiveness, rationality, and industriousness. Suzuki adopts this western image of the East and rehabilitates it, translating the rustic peasant of Romantic lore into the Buddho-Daoist "Zen-man" who has managed to circumvent the complexities of modern civilization, as well as the contrivances of the mind itself, and claim a more immediate access to things as they are in their simple profundity. The ground for Suzuki's claims, therefore, were prepared for by countless cultural products—most visibly, Romantic-Transcendentalist poems, essays, and art and the Progressive movement's anxiety about urban life. He also drew on the broader discontent with modernity, anxiety about industrialism, and inclination toward the primitivism of modernist, surrealist, and other forms of twentieth-century art and literature. Especially as the twentieth century progressed and the dark side of technological progress came into view, this dichotomy between the industrial West and the "mystical East" became established in modern consciousness and was nourished by a sense of lack, nostalgia, and anxiety. Suzuki's writings recapitulate anxieties formulated by Schiller, who in distress over the Reign of Terror after the French Revolution claimed that civilization itself, "far from setting us free," had "inflicted this wound" consisting of our "fall away from Nature" and aesthetic beauty. In a century of war, alienation, and increasingly frenetic activity, Suzuki offered Zen as a way to be "quietly content with the mystical contemplation of Nature and to feel at home with the world" (1959: 23).

Suzuki thus helped to transform the oriental Other, in his supposed simplicity, irrationality, and primitivity, into an antidote to the ills of modernity. This is not to say that the there has been no love of nature and rustic simplicity in certain strains of East Asian life and literature; clearly these are important elements in Zen and Daoist thought and are not simply modern inventions. My point is that Suzuki thematized and reconfigured these elements to make them address some of the dominant concerns of modernity.

Spontaneity and the Sword

Having constructed an East Asian version of the Romantic peasant who is one with nature, unhindered by overintellectualization, and free from enslavement to desires for modern luxuries, Suzuki posits an intimate relationship between art and this figure's nonconceptual grasp of the real. A key concept in this formulation is *spontaneity*, a notion, as noted, familiar to the Romantics. When the clutter of conceptual thought is emptied from the mind—not through dullness or torpor but through attentive and careful training—one is freed to act spontaneously out of the unmediated encounter between the world and oneself. The source of creativity in all forms of art, as well as the everyday activities of life, is this encounter and its associated spontaneity. This is where, according to Suzuki, "all arts merge into Zen" (1959: 94). Ironically, in view of the popular image of Buddhism as perhaps the least militant of the world's religions, one of Suzuki's central illustrations of this spontaneous creativity is the art of swordsmanship, exemplified by the Samurai warrior. As other scholars have suggested, the numerous martial illustrations in Suzuki's description of Zen are not coincidental. They grow not only out of his attempts to harmonize Zen teaching with the West but also something closer to home: his valorization of the Japanese warrior ethic and his support for Japanese militarism and nationalism, an aspect of Suzuki's work and life on which virtually no critical work was done until recently (Faure 1993; Sharf 1995c; Victoria 2006). As much as contemporary Zen stresses that one can practice Zen in the midst of any mundane activity—washing dishes, driving a car, and so on—for Suzuki, the sword was nearer to hand. And his exemplar of "Zen swordsmanship" was the sixteenth-century sword master Takuan Sōhō, a samurai warrior and Rinzai Zen master.

Suzuki uses Takuan's letter to a student to illustrate Zen contemplation in the midst of activity. Essential to this confluence of swordsmanship and Zen is the aforementioned abandoning of cognitive activity, such that the mind does not stop or get fixed on any object or thought. Sword fighting allows for no moment of deliberation or calculation, says Takuan; just instantaneous response to the always developing and rapidly changing situation that could lead to death at any moment. If the mind gets fixed on anything, "it is then placed under another's control" (1959: 102). Further, "it feels inhibited in every move it makes, and nothing will be accomplished with any sense of spontaneity" (114). The well-trained mind works like a flash of lightning or a spark from steel striking flint, operating not by intellectual deliberation but by the spontaneous charge of its inner nature. It is, according to Suzuki's translation of Takuan,

> moving and yet not moving, in tension and yet relaxed, seeing everything that is going on and yet not at all anxious about the way it may turn, with nothing purposely designed, nothing consciously calculated, no anticipation, no expectation—in short, standing like an innocent baby and yet with all the cunning and subterfuge of the keenest intelligence of a fully matured mind. (109)

Takuan asserts that "this 'empty-minded-ness' applies to all activities we may perform, such as dancing, as it does to swordplay. . . . If he has any idea at all of displaying his art well, he ceases to be a good dancer, for his mind 'stops' with every moment he goes through. In all things, it is important to forget your 'mind' and become one with the work at hand" (quoted in Suzuki 1959: 114). In this state of no-mind, there exist "no traces of artificial contrivance, everything being left to Nature itself" (116).

Suzuki's interpretation of Takuan gets at the crux of the modern Buddhist conception of creativity and spontaneity in art and everyday life. The essential distinctions of this conception—between the contrived and the spontaneous, the intellectual and the intuitive—resonate with the Romantic discussions of art I have presented. Intellectual reflection, calculation, anticipation, and a whole host of cognitive activities are set up in opposition to the intuitive, spontaneous, and creative act arising from a trained, nimble mind. This essential distinction between the natural and the contrived invites homologization with the other binary oppositions discussed earlier, which for Suzuki get mapped onto the basic distinction between East and West. Again, the East is natural, simple, creative, while the West is rational, mechanical, and contrived. Suzuki is recapitulating the tension between rationalism and Romanticism in the West and again allying Zen decisively with the Romantics. While there is no straight line from Takuan's mention of dance to Allen Ginsberg's serpentine gyrations, we begin to see how Ginsberg could have incorporated his valorization of spontaneity and disregard of social norms with his understanding of Buddhism. We can also see glimmerings of how Buddhism and Zen came to be intimately associated with avant-garde art and experimental, improvisatory music and theater.

Another highly influential way Suzuki presents this tension between the spontaneous and the contrived is by developing his anticonceptualism and Rousseauian-Zen primitivism in relation to the "unconscious."[7] Thinking, he asserts, is "useful in many ways," but often "interferes with the work, and you have to leave it behind and let the unconscious come forward. In such cases, you cease to be your own conscious master but become an instrument in the hands of the unknown" (1959: 133). He urges that it is a "great mistake to adjust everything to the Procrustean bed of logic" and claims that "all works of original creativity are the products of the unconscious that go beyond rationalistic schematization" (140). And further: "A 'view' or 'thought' is the outcome of intellection, and wherever this is found this creativity of the Unborn or the Unconscious meets all sorts of obstacles. . . . The intellect is meant for utilitarianism, and whatever creativity it may have operates within this limit and never beyond it" (141). For the swordsman free of all thoughts, fears, and desires, "both sword and man turn into instruments in the hands, as it were, of the unconscious, and it is the unconscious that achieves the wonder of creativity. It is here that swordplay becomes an art" (146). This applies, moreover, to all other arts, including poetry, painting, and the tea ceremony. Echoing the Romantic and post-Romantic suggestions of the artist as priest/shaman, Suzuki rhapsodizes about the artist as one who plumbs the deepest mysteries of the universe and expresses them in his own inimitable and original fashion. The great artist has a nearly godlike ability to tap into the mysterious depths of unconscious creative energy and bring it forth into the world.

It is notable how Suzuki liberally amalgamates the Buddhist "Unborn" or emptiness with both the psychoanalytic *unconscious* and the Romanticist *nature*. Nature is likened to a "master mind," and the highest function of human consciousness is "to delve deeper and deeper into its source, the unconscious" (1959: 143). Suzuki is clearly drawing from psychoanalytic theory, and perhaps from the Romantics, when he declares, like Schelling as well as Jung, that the unconscious is the seat of creativity. But he claims that there are more profound levels of the unconscious than those discovered by the psychoanalyst. The "secret to the artistic life" dwells deeper even than Jung's collective unconscious: in the "cosmic unconscious," which is the "principle of creativity" itself. "All creative works of art, the lives and aspirations of religious people, the spirit of inquiry moving the philosophers—all these come from the fountainhead of the Cosmic Unconscious, which is really the store-house (*ālaya*) of possibilities" (243). Here he draws together this unconscious with the all-encompassing life of "Nature," in the sense of the Romantics and Transcendentalists, and assimilates these in turn to yet another Buddhist concept, the storehouse consciousness (*ālaya-vijñāna*) of Yogācāra Buddhism, and more generally to Buddha-nature, emptiness (*śūnyatā*), or *dharmakāya*, all Mahayana Buddhist terms for ultimate reality. The homologization of these western concepts with emptiness and the storehouse consciousness signals a modern shift in the concept of emptiness from the lack of inherent existence in things, which goes back to Indian Buddhist sources, to emptiness or *ālaya* as a *container*, or as Suzuki puts it, a "reservoir (*ālaya*) of infinite possibilities" (298). Quite different from the traditional Buddhist concepts of emptiness, this reinterpretation could blend more harmoniously with the Romantic and psychoanalytic notions of the deep interior as a *container* of infinite depths and creative possibilities.

To summarize, this idea of creativity asserts, along with the Romantics, that nature is a unified, living force that is the source and sustainer of existence. This Suzuki variously calls the absolute, nature, Buddha-nature, the unborn, the unconscious, and emptiness. Human consciousness is a manifestation of this larger, all-encompassing life, but the various forms of intellection, desire, and emotion that characterize it, while useful in a limited sense, cut it off from this larger life. The way of access to the absolute is inward, through what to ordinary awareness is the unconscious. This is the source of creativity. To act from the unconscious is to act on the inspiration of the absolute itself—even to efface the self (though without obliterating it) and let it act through one. Creativity overflows naturally from the depths of being when the ratiocinating mind gets out of the way. Finally, Suzuki insists that Zen provides a way of directly accessing these creative depths in ways yet unrealized in the West.

The Mirror of Zen and the Lamp of Romanticism

Recent scholarship has been critical of Suzuki's representation of Zen, especially the way he reduced it to personal experience, bent his interpretation toward chauvinistic aspects of Japanese culture, and neglected Zen's lived contexts in monastic institutions, ritual systems, and networks of social and ethical responsibility. Recent ethnographic and historical work has significantly changed the way scholars view Zen, although this reenvisioning of the tradition has generally not reached beyond the scholarly community. (See Faure 1991, 1993; Sharf 1995c; Snodgrass 2003; Williams 2005). Suzuki decontextualized Zen literature in order to incorporate it into a framework of modern, largely western, ideas. Motivated by ideological and nationalistic purposes as well as intellectual passion and spiritual ideals, he aimed—and largely succeeded—at bringing Zen into the increasingly globalized discourse of modernity. His presentation of a modernized Zen was essential not only for the western understanding—and re-creation—of Zen but also for the reform, reconsideration, and reconstituting of Zen in Japan.

Whether Suzuki obtained his framework from the Romantics themselves or secondhand through Emerson, Jung, or others is unclear. It is clear, however, that he adopted not only their language but their metaphysics as his vehicle, and would have found himself comfortable with Schelling's references to the living power and unity of nature as "the holy abyss from which everything proceeds and into which everything returns" and to art as what connects the conditioned world with the infinite, the conscious with the unconscious. For Schelling, art had an infinite dimension that could not be accounted for in terms of empirical causality and returned us to a primordial harmony of the subjective and objective (1978 [1800]). Following Schelling, Schiller complains, in a letter to Goethe, that his fellow German idealists "take too little notice of experience; in experience, the poet begins entirely with the unconscious . . . and poetry, it seems to me, consists precisely in being able to express and communicate that unconscious." Goethe responded that "everything which the man of genius does as genius, eventuates unconsciously. The man of genius can also operate rationally, after careful consideration, from conviction, but all that only happens secondarily" (quoted in Abrams 1953: 210–11). These Romantics are, of course, the predecessors of modern psychoanalytic theory, which develops further the understanding of the relationship between creativity and the unconscious, conceiving of the unconscious as a deep reservoir of creative energy and symbolism. My point is not that one cannot discern spontaneity, creativity, and a love of nature in some of the antics of Zen masters in the classical literature, and that all of this is therefore an imposition of western thought on Zen. It is rather that Suzuki thematizes spontaneity, creativity, and a love of nature in ways that are decisively modern; in his hands, they take their place within the tensions between rationalism and Romanticism. However spontaneous Zen masters may be appear in Zen koan literature, they did not thematize spontaneity or make it an object of explicit discourse. This is where Suzuki's Zen becomes a hybrid entity.

Suzuki also attempted to harmonize the worldview of the English Romantics and American Transcendentalists with the rustic ethos of Zen literature and monastic life, as well as its reverence for the natural world. Suzuki's insistence that the enlightened person transcends social conventions and prescribed morality, realizing intuitive action as the vehicle of nature, reconfigures and radicalizes Rousseau's primitivism. Many of the themes in Suzuki's conception of Zen creativity are present in Romanticism and its successors, but the hybridity of his conception is elided by his appeal, often polemical, to the uniqueness and supremacy of Zen. What *was* unique was the way he used these themes as a framework for interpreting often inscrutable Zen literature. His typical method of incorporating western sources was to appropriate certain basic western categories—like the *absolute* of German Romanticism, the *unconscious* of psychoanalysis, and *creativity*—while arguing that Zen embraces but supersedes them. Thus, according to Suzuki, Wordsworth, while he expresses appreciation of a violet in a poem, is not interested in the "in the violet as such" (1959: 266). Likewise, Tennyson presents his flower in the crannied wall in a "merely philosophical and conceptual way" (354). He "does not leave the flower alone" but "must tear it away from the crannied wall, 'root and all,' which means the plant must die. . . . His curiosity must be satisfied," and "as some medical scientists do, he would vivisect the flower" (1960: 3). In contrast, Suzuki claims, the great haiku poet Basho approaches the beauties of nature in a way that simply reflects their "suchness"—their unique specificity, which is at the same time one with the all-encompassing absolute—and approaches each object nondualistically, effacing his own egoistic perspective to let the object present itself, and becoming a "passive instrument for giving an expression to an inspiration" (225). Western thought, Suzuki insists, acknowledges the same ultimate reality as Zen but is defective in its ability to penetrate this reality in the unmediated way particular to Zen.

The modern West fails in this immediacy, Suzuki insists, precisely because in Western art—specifically under the guidance of Romanticism and its successors—all apprehension and expression of reality must be, as Taylor puts it "indexed to a personal vision"; that is, all presentation of things is mediated through the personal perspective of the artist (1989: 428). Thus Wordsworth suggests in "Tintern Abbey" that the senses and mind contribute to the apprehension of the world rather than just passively receiving it: "All the mighty world / Of eye, and ear,—both what they half create, / And what perceive" (ll. 105–107).

Suzuki was quite right to note this decidedly personal characteristic of modern western art—it is representative of the Romantic revolution, according to Abrams. Art is seen as a creation of the poetic mind, which is like a lamp that projects its own vision onto reality, thus "half making" it, rather than acting as a mirror reflecting things through mimesis. Suzuki claims that Zen supersedes this personal perspective and its lamp-like projections by directly accessing reality per se. This is perhaps the most philosophically problematic aspect of Suzuki's thinking on the matter—his characterization of Zen art, indeed Zen life, as wholly unmediated by intellectual activity and by this personal perspective. One has a hard time imagining, for example, a haiku, with its exacting formal requirements, simply emerging wholly formed without cognitive activity. Suzuki takes a line of thought already in place in western thinking about art and creativity and, in effect, ups the ante: people—particularly Zen people—are not just creatively inspired by the mysterious interior depths; they can spontaneously manifest this divine impulse in a wholly unmediated fashion.[8]

However philosophically problematic it may be in light of post-Kantian, analytic, phenomenological, and postmodern epistemological critiques, this influential picture gives Buddhism, and particularly Zen, a special place in the western imagination as a tradition with a particular ability to evoke spontaneous creativity. If Romanticism did away with notion of art as a mirror, Suzuki introduces another mirror to the discussion: the Zen mirror, a ubiquitous symbol of the clear mind reflecting reality as it is. Recall that the uniqueness of the Japanese/Zen contribution to art, according to Suzuki, is this pure presentation of the "isness" or "suchness" of things in their utter individual uniqueness yet oneness with the all-encompassing absolute. "Just as two stainless mirrors reflect each other, the fact and our own spirits must stand facing each other with no intervening agents" (1956: 13). In a sense, Suzuki wants it both ways: he asserts the value of originality and creative particularity but insists that this should be neither *personal*, as the Romanticist claimed, nor social, as many contemporary thinkers argue, but should be based on an immediate access to and representation of reality that transcends the personal and social.[9] The true artist is a kind of spiritual genius who offers an original presentation of reality, but a presentation unfiltered by the fickle imagination or the stormy passions of which the Romantics were so fond. Nor is Suzuki's mirror the simple imitator of reality, as art was conceived in the premodern West. The Zen mirror, he claims, reflects the moon untouched by personal concepts or passions, yet Zen art is still the artist's unique expression, poured straight from the vast container of all things.

Other Buddhist-Romantic Views of Art

Suzuki was not the only Buddhist modernist to draw on Romantic themes in addressing Buddhism and art, though his ideas were disseminated most widely—
by a host of western successors, including Robert Blyth, who elaborated on the
Romantic-Transcendentalist strains of Suzuki's articulation of Zen, offering a
promiscuous array of "Zen" quotations from Wordsworth, Johann Wolfgang
von Goethe, Coleridge, and Emerson, among a plethora of other western literary figures who he believed were in some way contiguous with Zen thought
(Blyth 1942). Other influential figures developed similar themes, some inde-
pendently and some influenced by Suzuki. In his 1936 essay "Art and Meditation," Anagarika Govinda develops his own Romanticism-inflected Buddhism
in relation to art.[10] Govinda, born Ernst Lothar Hoffman in Waldheim, Ger-
many, in 1898, studied Buddhism in Ceylon, took vows in the Theravada tradition, and eventually became affiliated with the Kagyu sect of Tibetan Buddhism.
He wrote a number of popular books expounding Buddhism to the West and
founded the Order of the Arya Maitreya Mandala, whose German branch still
exists today. Drawing on many non-Tibetan authors in formulating his representations of Buddhism, including Heinrich Zimmer, Martin Buber, Alan
Watts, D. T. Suzuki, and various Romantics and Theosophists, his hybridized
religiophilosophical bricolage was one of the most prominent early presentations of Tibetan Buddhism in the West.

In "Art and Meditation," Govinda argues that art is purely an expression of
interior states. Like meditation, art does not try to imitate nature but rather to
"reveal a higher reality by omitting all accidentals," Art is, he insists, an artist's expression of an "intuitive experience," which "crystallizes his inner vision into visible forms" (1999 [1936]: 4–5). Meditation is the vehicle by which one purifies the
mind to attain this intuitive experience and taps into "our innermost being," the
"deep and hidden well of our being," within which "the rivers of life unite" (2).
Plunging down into this inner being, artists access deep spiritual experiences,
which they then materializes in the forms of visual art, poetry, and music.

Govinda's explanation of art and its source was inspired by Neoplatonism
and Theosophy as well as Romanticism. He calls the plunging into the interior
depths "contemplation of the Beautiful," in Platonic fashion, and art itself the "manifestation of the Beautiful" (1999 [1936]: 8). He quotes the German Romantic
Novalis's saying that "the external world is nothing but the internal world in a
state of mystery" and cites Goethe's insistence on the independence of art from
objective reality to support his own contention that Chinese landscape painting
is a product of "pure self-realization, pure subjectivity condensed into form"

(10–15). Such painting, along with the figure of the Buddha, achieves what western art has never accomplished: "the visible representation of the Divine as such" (15). Like Suzuki, Govinda insists that East Asian art is superior because it is "not of rational origin," while Leonardo da Vinci or Albrecht Dürer, representing the West, produced art that "is the outcome of the concentration of reason which necessarily leads to the discovery of objective rules" (15).

If the East-as-intuitive, West-as-rational dualism is by now all too familiar, Govinda adds a new dimension that connected him with Modernist art: the implication that *abstract* art reveals the inner depths, making more real and intense "the life that was hidden under the surface" (1999 [1936]: 19).[11] Careful to distinguish abstract art from abstract concepts, which are "attained by logical operations, following analytical and deductive methods," Govinda argues that abstract art, like music, does not imitate natural forms but "reproduce[s] a certain state of mind" (19). In this he clearly is drawing from Wassily Kandinsky and other early twentieth-century abstractionists, as well as some figures in the Theosophical movement who saw nonrepresentational art as expressing spiritual essences underlying visible forms, and perhaps from Schopenhauer, who saw music's nonreferential quality as what made it the highest form of art and the one most conducive to peaceful contemplation and quieting of the will (Kandinsky 1977 [1914]; Schopenhauer 1969; Tuchman 1986). While no Kandinsky himself, Govinda produced and exhibited his own abstract paintings, which he claimed were expressions of various meditative states.

Sangharakshita, another prominent western Buddhist with a Sanskrit name and an avid interest in the arts, followed Govinda in his expressivist approach, if not his love for abstraction. Born Dennis Lingwood in London in 1925, Sangharakshita founded the Western Buddhist Order and the Friends of the Western Buddhist Order and became one of the most prolific western Buddhists. In a collection of essays entitled *The Religion of Art*, he declares that the functions of Buddhism and art are the same: "the stretching of the mind beyond the limits of understanding, or the expansion of consciousness beyond the boundaries of selfhood," which is the "experience of egolessness" (1973: 34, 81). Art stretches the mind "further than the limits of its own rationality into the 'distance beyond' of Beauty" and into the "super-rational plane" (111–12). This, however, only holds for "true art" or "religious art." The overwhelming bulk of popular and contemporary art—"pseudo-artistic trash"—is "spawned from the slimiest depths of our psychic nature" and narrows rather than expands consciousness by "pandering to our lust for sex and crime" (36). On the other hand, "formally religious art" depicting religious scenes, saints, and devotional figures seldom produces expansion of consciousness so much as a "devotional reflex" (36). The implication is that "formally religious art" is largely Christian art, for the ubiquitous figures of the Buddha, particularly their serene smiles, express "the greatest expansion of consciousness that it is possible for the plastic arts" (37). There is art, however, that is not "formally religious" but is "naturally or essentially" religious and conduces to the experience of egolessness. Chinese landscape painting, Shelley's best poetry, and the music of Beethoven—most western artists to whom he approvingly refers are Romantics or their successors, such as Rilke—are all examples. Finally, there exists art that is both formally and naturally religious, with religious subject matter as well as the capacity to expand consciousness and bring about the experience of egolessness.

Sangharakshita argues that the encounter with truly religious art, whether "formally," "naturally," or both, expands one's wisdom and compassion by deepening experience and widening one's sympathies. Moreover, such art *emerges* from these states. Because Buddhism and "true" art coincide in producing such states, Sangharakshita suggests that there could emerge in the modern world, with its suspicion of institutionalized religion, a "religion of art."[12] This religion, defined primarily by its capacity to induce the same expansion of consciousness and sympathy that Buddhism does, would be centered around *naturally* religious art. The religion of art, in another nod to Platonism, consists in a "conscious surrender to the Beautiful, particularly as manifested in poetry, music, and the visual arts, as a means of breaking up established egocentric patterns of behaviour and protracting one's experience along the line of egolessness into the starry depths of Reality" (1973: 93). Such art not only expands consciousness and leads to sublime experiences of beauty, it naturally leads to moral behavior, insofar as it calls on individuals to transform their lives through surrender to "the demands of the Good" (98). If instead of having a reputation for such surrender, artists often are reputed to indulge in immoral behavior, such a representation is undeserved. Such artists, Sangharakshita insists, are merely purveyors of the lower forms of art, while "true artists" who behave in ways that may be unacceptable to society are, in words he borrows from D. H. Lawrence, substituting a "finer morality for a grosser" (99–100). Indeed, "sometimes it happens that a man may be compelled to shatter moralities out of the sheer intensity of his spiritual life," but this does not mean he is immoral (100). Sangharakshita insists, like many Enlightenment and Romantic thinkers (and quite *unlike* most classical Buddhist writings), that "however useful for practical purposes a moral code may be, the criterion of ethics is, nevertheless, fundamentally not external but internal" (99).

Sangharakshita's religion of art, however, appears at times as morally rigid as the "formal" religions. The adherent must "protect himself from bad art as carefully as he would take precautions against being infected by a particularly dangerous and virulent disease" (1973: 104). Most newspapers, magazines, "tenth rate fiction," bad poetry, "cheap 'religious' lithographs, shoddy reproductions of popular paintings, and badly printed calendars in all their gaudy hideousness, should be ruthlessly banished from the walls of [the devotee's] home. Inartistic furniture, carpets, curtains, and crockery," as well as "factory produced vases," must also be abandoned (104–5). More than just a jeremiad on bad aesthetic tastes, perhaps laced with some hyperbole and humor, Sangharakshita's tirade against popular art, literature, and home furnishings is a part of a larger critique of modern culture that echoes Suzuki's. He decries the ugliness of indistinguishable urban "brick box" homes on identical streets, "with the smell of factory smoke . . . and the noise of traffic" as "offenses against beauty" akin to offenses against morality "and no less deserving of punishment" (105–6). He contrasts such felonious fashions and industrial offenses to the simple, thatched-roof houses of Indian peasants with their beautifully decorated thresholds and mud-plastered walls in the midst of fruit trees and lotus-filled ponds. Clearly his repulsion for modern aesthetic sensibilities is part of a larger aversion to modern life in its industrial, urban, and technological aspects and, conversely, is an idealization of peasant life.

Like Suzuki and Govinda, Sangharakshita embeds his characterization of Buddhism and its relation to art in a discourse derived in part from Romanticism and its successors. This is apparent not only in his explicit estimation of Romantics such as Keats, Shelley, Wordsworth, and Beethoven as representatives of the best of "naturally religious art" but also in the way he attempts to isolate the internal, experiential component as the essential element of religion to which all others are subordinate or of which they are corruptions. The influence of Romanticism is also evident in his critique of industrialism and its aesthetic sensibilities and his approval of the simple beauty of peasant homes. He echoes the Romantics, moreover, in his representation of art as expressive of sublime, interior, and transrational states, as well as his insistence that true art is conducive to morality, which nevertheless might transcend mainstream moral codes.

All of these figures adopted in different ways what Abrams calls the expressivist theory of art: a view of art as an expression of internal states overflowing into concretion. To Buddhist modernists, this may seem self-evidently to be the position of traditional forms of Buddhism. After all, if the essence of Buddhism is meditation, then Buddhist art must be an expression of meditative experiences. However, most conventions of Buddhist art in Asia operate under quite different assumptions. The ubiquitous Buddha-images found in Asian temples that both Govinda and Sangharakshita considered the highest expression of a divine state of consciousness function primarily iconically and ritually rather than as tools for expanding consciousness or expressing and inducing meditative states. That is, temple images are consecrated and considered embodiments of the buddhas and bodhisattvas, serving as focal points for devotion and ritual. Likewise, the stunning Tibetan mandalas now famous in the West are not merely elaborate decorations, nor are they used primarily as focal points for meditation; rather, they serve as material residences for specific buddhas and bodhisattvas who are invoked for merit-making and devotional rituals. These residences must be made to specification to serve such a purpose; hence individual creativity and self-expression are quite limited. Connections could be argued between the Romantic extolling of the imagination and the exercising of the imaginative powers in higher tantric visualization practices based on such mandalas, but these practices, again, have an entirely different function than that of spontaneous creativity. Creative imagination in tantric practice is still iconic, in that it creates an internalized image of a deity—again to pregiven specifications—that the practitioner worships and identifies with. In short, the Romantic interpretation of Buddhist art, emphasizing the expression of interior depths, spontaneity, and individual originality, was something new to Buddhism—the result of placing selected Buddhist themes and cultural products into a distinctively modern context and transposing them to harmonize with the melodies of Romanticism.

Between Romanticism and Modernism

As echoes of Romanticism live on in contemporary culture—in popular entertainment, environmentalism, new spiritualities, the suspicion of technology, and the vocabularies of love, art, honor, spontaneity, and individual identity— echoes of Romanticism also reverberate in twentieth- and twenty-first-century conceptions of Buddhism's relationship to art. The developing art cultures of the twentieth century, however, could not help but nudge the understanding of both Buddhism and art beyond the Romanticist interpretation, even as the echoes remained. Indeed, much twentieth-century art was a reaction against Romanticism and the notion of art as the self-expression of the solitary individual. Yet, as many scholars have observed, twentieth-century Modernism retained themes from Romanticism, though they were often masked (Bayley 1957). While Modernists may have retreated from the Romantic language of self-expression, interior depths, and emotional extremes, they still sought epiphanies within the ordinary and everyday of a fuller and more vibrant life— something they, along with the Romantics before them, feared was rapidly being eroded by the hegemony of the rational-scientific approach to life, the tyranny of work, mechanized labor, alienation, consumerism, and materialism. Figures across a wide spectrum of Modernist art and literature claimed that these elements of modernity had removed people from an authentic experience of life; art, therefore, was a means of recovering the real. Writers like Ezra Pound, T. S. Eliot, and James Joyce emphasized the recovery of experience and the hidden appearance of things, seeking to make their readers see things with a vividness and freshness that the ordinary constraints of habit and routine occlude. Even earlier, the work of realist artists and writers, like Édouard Manet or Gustave Flaubert, suggests that we fail to discern the reality even of the banal elements of life rightly; and for Arthur Rimbaud and, later, Joyce, a radical jolt to our sensibilities may be needed to allow something to present itself in its fullness. What Modernist works often introduced was not the revelation of a deeper *meaning* but the meaninglessness and illusoriness of our usual ways of seeing things—which the work of art was intended to shatter. Charles Baudelaire's and Flaubert's work often exposes the meaninglessness of their subjects' illusions about their lives; this stripping away of meaning, however, holds out the possibility of freedom from illusions. Even when the epiphany is a revelation of meaninglessness, there is a liberative move. In W. Somerset Maugham's novel *Of Human Bondage* (1915) Philip realizes that a person's life is like the intricate patterns of a Persian carpet and has no ultimate significance or purpose beyond the living itself and the creation of one's own pattern. On realizing that his search for ultimate meaning and happiness has been the source of his discontent, Philip becomes happy at the prospect of simply living. In more hard-edged realizations like these, the epiphanic ideal of Romanticism continues among Modernists, even when it entails a rejection of "depths" in a metaphysical or individualistic sense (Abrams 1953; Bayley 1957).

There is a dimension of Buddhism as it emerges in the West that picks up on these themes. The development of modern ideas on Buddhist creativity arose to some extent in the intersection of Modernist and Romantic discourses—between Romantic ideas of persons having "inner depths" from which creativity and art spontaneously emerge and the Modernist artists' attempt to reappropriate the "surfaces" of things in a way that reveals but also takes one beyond the mechanized drudgery of the modern world. Zen modernism especially drew on the common epiphanic element of these two discourses. With its crystalline images in koans and haiku, Zen could appear strikingly similar to the Modernists' effort to recover the surface of things from metaphysical abstraction and thereby direct attention to the more immediate release of the extraordinary pent up within the ordinary. Moreover, Zen literature, with its refusal of cognitive transparency, its paradoxes, its absurdities seemed to engage with what D. H. Lawrence called the "meaninglessness of meaning" haunting western civilization, the lack of inherent meaning in things, and the threat of nihilism (quoted in Taylor 1989: 466). Zen appeared to resonate with modernist skepticism about desire, materialism, progress, social conventions, and even religion itself. Zen's iconoclasm, inscrutability, and refusal of discursive closure, like much of modern art, seemed to drip with ironic detachment and flirt with nihilism. Yet Zen—at the edges of language, at the boundaries of consciousness, in the very depths of meaninglessness—triumphantly claimed it could break through the modern malaise and reaffirm the sacredness of everything through a radical epiphany in which all things became new. Thus William Barrett, in his introduction to Suzuki's *Zen Buddhism*, asserted: "for the march of our own history, as the world of medieval religious images recedes . . . an increasingly secularized society engulfs us, has stripped western man naked and left no rocklike certainty anywhere to lean on. Here there looms before the frightened eyes of the westerner what Buddhism calls the Great Emptiness; but if he does not run away in fear, this great void may bloom with all manner of miracles" (1956: xix). The fact that Barrett misunderstood Buddhism's "Great Emptiness" as having something to do with Tillich's "essential experience of modern man as an encounter with 'meaninglessness'" (x) makes all the more apparent the way Zen was incorporated into western discourses of modernity. Zen in its modernized incarnation could resonate with the dark threat of nihilism and desacralization some Modernist artists—as well as existentialists and, later, postmodernists—expressed yet turn the threat on its head and finally affirm the resacralized Romantic unity of being, the inner depths of the person, and the spontaneous expression of one's true nature through both artistic creation and everyday life in its immediacy. The Zen literature Suzuki introduced to the West, therefore, was placed in between these two epiphanic discourses, one on the depths of things and one on the surfaces. This literature stressed simplicity and ordinariness, emphasizing "immediate experience" of mundane realities, yet also asserted a deeper human nature that promised a rescue from meaninglessness and alienation.

Some twentieth-century visual artists drew on these themes and came to see Zen as a formative influence on their work, and in this way Suzuki's articulation of Zen came to be associated with art movements in the West, including artists such as Marcel Duchamp, Mark Tobey, Robert Beer, Agnes Martin, and Isamu Noguchi. John Cage read Suzuki, attended his lectures at Columbia University in 1950, and saw his own work as deeply informed by Zen. Responding to Suzuki's emphasis on ordinariness and the cognitively disorienting koan, Cage translated these elements into some of the most radical art and music of the twentieth century. He proclaimed that the purpose of art, poetry, and music was "to sober and quiet the mind so that it is in accord with what happens"

(Baas and Jacob 2004: 166). Taking up Suzuki's quest for the "isness" of ordinary things, Cage composed, for example, the (in)famous piece 4'33", in which the pianist sat at the piano for four minutes and thirty-three seconds and played nothing. Against this sonic vacuum, the ambient sounds of the auditorium and audience were the piece itself. Though this work was often considered a joke, Cage intended it to create a space for non-ego-directed, mindful receptivity to whatever happened—a frame in which to experience the simple suchness of sounds arising and passing away in time. Likewise, his experiments with "chance music," for example *Music of Changes*, whose notes were determined by throws of the *Yijing (I Ching)*, were Cage's attempts to remove his "likes and dislikes" from the process of composition and throw it open to the indeterminacy of nature itself (168). His exposure to koans, moreover, gave him a model of utterance and performance not tied to cognitive meaning. As Cage and other twentieth-century artists understood it, the koan could be interpreted as a kind of surreal performance art that could break the mind out of conventional patterns. Koans, like surrealist and other avant-garde art, refused rational analysis, spurned social conventions, and was iconoclastic, spontaneous, irreverent, even brutal. His interest in setting up frames of time and space for events to happen without ego direction led Cage and his colleagues to stage "happenings," minimally scripted theatrical events involving spontaneous and unpredictable interactions between performers and audience. In an attempt to dissolve the boundaries between art and life, performer and audience, in happenings, the events of the performance were responses to contingency and spontaneous impulse. Happenings were considered in their time to be among the most experimental of arts, and few understood their unlikely lineage in Suzuki's presentation of Zen. Cage's work exemplifies a modernist and avant-garde sensibility that was influenced by the Romantic idea of art as facilitating the removal, or the perception of the illusoriness, of the boundary between art and life. The use of commonplace materials like bicycle wheels, linoleum, and newspaper was meant to erode this boundary. Those who brought a Buddhist perspective to this sensibility could style it as nondualism—not just between self and other or divine and human but between art and life, and between high and popular art (Baas and Jacobs 2004).

The Beat writers also worked in this tradition of post-Romantic iconoclasm and spontaneity. As is well known, some of the Beats were among the first American literary figures to explicitly embrace Buddhism and incorporate it in their work. Allen Ginsberg, Jack Kerouac, Philip Whalen, and Gary Snyder were already influenced by Romanticism, especially Blake, and Transcendentalism.[13] They are perhaps the clearest examples of the hybrid lineage of Romanticism, Transcendentalism, Modernism, and Buddhism, as well as sources for the emergence of Buddhism as part of the midcentury countercultural movements. The Beats offered Buddhism as a source not only of spiritual renewal in the "nuclear age" but also of social protest, seeing American triumphalism, consumerism, and militarism not only as structural problems but sicknesses of the soul that Buddhism could help alleviate.

In their writings, the Beats combine the grittiest realism with flashes of Romanticism and sketches of dharma. Here is an example of how these elements were combined. Ginsberg, in a lecture he gave at the Naropa Institute's Jack Kerouac School of Disembodied Poetics, recalled a discussion with Chögyam Trungpa in which Trungpa articulated what would become his often-repeated formula for creativity in art and life: "First thought, best thought" (Tonkinson 1995: 106). It is certainly not an aphorism Trungpa got from his native Tibetan traditions of religious art, in which, as I have pointed out, individual spontaneity and innovation have little place. Yet Trungpa declares "dharma art" to be not "art depicting Buddhist symbols or ideas" but rather "art that springs from . . . the meditative state" (Trungpa 2003–4: 7:13). We would likely search in vain to find any such statement in Tibetan or Sanskrit Buddhist texts, but if we want to find a true kindred spirit to Trungpa, an Oxford-educated Tibetan who spent much of his life in Boulder, Colorado, it would be among Romantics such as Rousseau, who declared: "Let us lay it down as an incontrovertible rule that the first impulses of nature are always right" (1911: 56). Trungpa incorporates the Rousseauian emphasis on following the spontaneous impulses of nature into the Buddhist suspicion of conceptual elaboration: "first thought" is the fresh, spontaneous, "uncensored and unmanipulated" thought that precedes conceptual and "neurotic" elaboration (2003–4, 7: 137–38: 168).

Two points are worth noting here. First, Trungpa's explanation of "first thought, best thought" implies that "dharma" (or in Suzuki's language, "Zen") is associated with—perhaps even a product of—a "state of mind" rather than a historical tradition; it is a kind of free-floating "essence" of religion that precedes conceptual elaboration and imposition of symbols. This is akin to Suzuki's claim that Zen was "the essence of religion" itself—not just Buddhism but all religions. Second, Buddhism is also brought to bear on artistic creation in a way that harmonizes with the Modernist attentiveness to the mundane. Ginsberg thought of poetry as an articulation of the uncensored ordinary movement of the mind, a "spontaneous transcription" of thought in all its particulars (Tonkinson 1995: 103–10). Buddhist meditation, in turn, was a way of accessing that movement. Ginsberg applies mindfulness meditation, in which the meditator simply observes in a detached way all thoughts and feelings, to the creation of poetry as the technique to access poetry's inner source. Because such meditation emphasizes observing *all* activities of the mind as they arise and pass away without judgment or censorship, it becomes for Ginsberg a tool for overcoming the "tendency toward censorship" in the creation of poetry. Modesty, shyness, social conventions, and maintenance of self-image are all obstacles to this creation. The poet must admit into the light of poetry all thoughts, even those that seem "too raw, too naked, too irrelevant, too goofy, too personal, too revealing, too damaging to one's own self-image" (105). Buddhism, therefore, serves a dual function in this respect: first as a means to access what is normally hidden in the mind, and second as a kind of disembodied essence of religion cum creative inspiration itself. Thus we can observe the threads of Romanticism, modernism, psychology, and Buddhism intertwining in Ginsberg's poetry—as well as his spontaneous dancing and other unself-censored behavior.

Contemporary Impulses

There is no shortage of contemporary examples of artists and writers inspired by this articulation of Buddhist-Romantic spontaneity and creativity, and more generally by the practice of meditation as an aid to creativity.[14] The close connection between Buddhist meditation, spontaneity, and art is virtually axiomatic in Buddhist modernism. Countless popular books present Buddhist-inspired art as, in the words of Frederick Franck, art that "rise[s] up from the depth of one's being" (1993: 9). The farthest flung incarnation of the Buddhist-Romantic idea of creativity is the hundreds of books entitled *Zen and the Art of . . .* and *The Zen of . . .* , an entire cottage industry, advising a relaxed but alert approach to golf, finance, and diaper changing. In these productions, the often fatuous spawn of Suzuki's ideas, one can occasionally hear the echo of Takuan's sword swishing and even perceive timid shadows of Suzuki's critique of rationalism, but often in service of either the very capitalist consumerist culture Suzuki critiqued or the quest for temporary escape from it.

There are, however, more serious manifestations of the idea of Zen and Buddhist meditation as a forge for creativity. The prolific novelist and essayist Charles Johnson insists that Buddhist meditation is an essential ingredient in his process of composing his complex and philosophically astute works of fiction. A substantial number of contemporary visual artists, including Marina Abramovic, Nam June Paik, Bill Viola, and Xu Bing, have been have been influenced by modern articulations of Buddhism, especially Suzuki's. A number of contemporary Buddhist or Buddhist-influenced musicians, including Laurie Anderson, Philip Glass, and Meredith Monk, also entwine Buddhism with their work and creative process.

The modern mingling of meditation and art has led, finally, to the develop-ment of programs of instruction in various arts not only at monasteries and meditation centers (mostly in the West) but also at prestigious colleges and uni-versities. One of the largest Zen monasteries in North America—Zen Mountain Monastery in Mt. Tremper, New York—regularly offers classes on "Creativity and the Outsider" (on self-taught art), nature drawing, Japanese flower arrang-ing, sculpture, and poetry. All of these are considered part of "art practice," which is one of the "eight gates of Zen," a special adaptation of Zen teachings to America developed by the abbot John Daido Loori, Rōshi. According to the Zen Mountain Monastery catalogue (winter and spring 2005), art practice em-bodies the assertion that "our creativity and spirituality share a common source" (4). Loori, himself an accomplished photographer, originally established the monastery as a center for meditation and the arts. In a book on Zen and creativity, he encourages students to make use of meditative stillness and non-judgmental attention along with the "uninhibited flow of expression" to create art (90). He emphasizes the need "not to be controlled by convention, prec-edent, or rules, but to express one's creative energy freely and spontaneously" (135). A similar approach guides arts programs at some Buddhist-influenced academic institutions like Naropa University (formerly the Naropa Institute), founded by Trungpa, which offers degrees in the arts that are heavily informed by contemplative practices largely derived from Buddhism.

The University of Michigan offers a bachelor's program in "jazz and contem-plative studies" in which students take "courses which involve meditative prac-tices and other areas related to creative development." In addition to courses in music theory, jazz composition, and improvisation, students take a course called "Creativity and Consciousness" and four terms of "Contemplative Prac-tice Seminar," along with Buddhist studies courses for electives.[15] Brown Uni-versity has recently developed a program in "contemplative studies," which also draws on conceptions introduced in large part by Buddhist modernists. The aim of the initiative is to study the various modes of contemplative states such as "chanting, prayer, ritual performance, and meditation," as well as those in-volving "music, dance, drama, writing poetry or prose, painting, sculpting, and even the intent observation of the natural world." As sources, the project draws on a diverse amalgam of contemplatives and theorists, from "traditional mysti-cal thinkers" of various traditions to William James, Edmund Husserl, and con-temporary thinkers such as Buddhists B. Alan Wallace and Francisco Varela, as well as Mihalyi Csikszentmihalyi, whose concept of the "flow condition" again echoes Suzuki's explication of Zen spontaneity. Incorporating the burgeoning scientific studies of consciousness and meditation, the program explicitly con-nects contemplative states to the arts, and includes in its courses not only the

2

study of meditation but also "engag[ing] directly with these techniques." According to its website, "in addition to being grounded in the philosophy, psychology, and neuroscience of contemplative experience as a *third-person* study, the proposed concentration will emphasize the '*critical first-person*' study that is often found in the musical, dramatic, and visual arts."[16] While such programs are unusual, they show that the modernist Buddhist theme of the relationship between creativity and meditation has strong cultural importance and is finding increasing mainstream acceptance.

The Romantics bequeathed to our age a sense that "what [artists] reveal has great moral and spiritual significance; that in it lies the key to a certain depth, or fullness, or seriousness, or intensity of life, or to a certain wholeness" (Taylor 1989: 422). This entails an "epiphanic" understanding of art "as the locus of a manifestation which brings us into the presence of something which is otherwise inaccessible, and which is of the highest moral or spiritual significance" (419). The very conception of the spontaneous generation of original ideas by the individual artist or author is a theme inherited from Romanticism. This legacy, still quite alive in contemporary culture, is a crucial part of the western understanding of Buddhism, particularly its conceptions of the relation of art and nature. In certain early presentations to the West, Buddhism was tuned to a pitch that resonated with this discourse of modernity. Western culture already gave the artist a quasi-religious standing, as one who accesses the hidden aspects of things. When Sangharakshita suggested that a "religion of art" consonant with the goals of Buddhism might emerge, this was part of Buddhism's bid for participation in western culture by claiming special access to the source of creative epiphany.

Suzuki took the claim further. If Romanticism and post-Romanticism indexed artistic vision to a mediated personal order; if Kant and post-Kantianism insisted on knowledge as mediated through the categories of understanding, thus cutting it off from the thing-in-itself; and if later social theory emphasized the epistemological mediations of culture, language, and society—Suzuki's Zen audaciously held out the possibility of the unmediated access to reality. It thus reasserted not only the Romantic appeal to the interior depths but also the Romantic longing for the premodern, the natural, the uncontrived. It also drew on the Romantic mystification of the East as a place of the imagination, of dreams, of transrational spirituality, primitive authenticity, and artistic vision. But this modernized Zen also associated itself with the post-Romantic themes of Modernism, existentialism, and other currents of twentieth century art and thought, always rhetorically embracing yet claiming to transcend their limitations. This incorporation of modern western themes and then claiming supersession, to be sure, involves ideological claims, rhetorical maneuvers, and "strategies of condescension." But it was also an expression of the ongoing sense, endemic to modernity, of dissatisfaction, lack, and alienation in the modern world and led many intellectuals and artists of the twentieth century who discovered Buddhism to hope that it might provide a way out of Weber's "iron cage." Finally, we see in these artists that just because the idea of a special Buddhist creativity is a hybridized and novel construction of the modern period does not mean it cannot be productive. This idea has, in fact, introduced new ways of thinking about and practicing art that are integral to the work of some of the more interesting artists of the twentieth century.

6

A Brief History
of Interdependence

Everybody might be just a one big soul, well it looks that a-way to
me . . .

—Woody Guthrie, "Tom Joad"

I have on occasion declared to colleagues in academe that my next research project will be to prove that something or other is monolithic.
It is an academic insider's joke; possibly the most fashionable and
stinging critique of a historian, sociologist, or anthropologist today is
that he or she presents something—a culture, a society, a religion, a
practice—as monolithic. As never before, it is now widely recognized
that not only are all of these things internally variegated but also that
nothing can stand on its own; all ideas, social practices, institutions,
and cultural phenomena are the results of a complex multiplicity of
factors that extend out into an ever-widening causal web. Current
studies of natural systems, nations, economies, and cultures see
them as multifaceted, interdependent processes—networks in which
each part both makes up and is made up by larger dynamic systems.
That we live in a radically interconnected world has become a truism.
Indeed, this age of internationalism and the internet might well be
called the age of *inter*: there is nothing that is not interconnected, interdependent, interwoven, interlaced, interactive, or interfacing with
something else to make it what it is. Thus, any religious tradition that
can claim "interdependence" as a central doctrine lays claim to timely
cultural resonance and considerable cultural cachet.

It is not surprising then that this term has been emerging with greater and greater frequency in contemporary Buddhist literature and acquiring increasing consonance with other modern discourses of interdependence. Sometimes used to translate the term *pratītya-samutpāda* (more precisely translated "dependent origination" or "dependent co-arising"), this term's semantic field has now extended to represent what many today see as *the* fundamental outlook of Buddhism—a doctrinal sine qua non with broad-ranging implications on personal, social, and global scales. It is not only a philosophical description of the world but also an idea with powerful ethical and political implications: if we are all part of a vast, interdependent network of being, what we do can have profound effects on others as our actions reverberate throughout it.

As articulated in contemporary Buddhist literature, the concept of interdependence combines empirical description, world-affirming wonder, and an ethical imperative. The empirical description represents the world as a vast, interconnected web of internally related beings—that is, whose identity is not a priori independent of the systems they are a part of but is inseparable from those systems. Description of this web sometimes melds indistinguishably with descriptions of other interrelated processes like communication networks or biological systems. The contemporary Vietnamese Zen master Thich Nhat Hanh has coined the term "interbeing" to capture the idea of the interdependence of all things, presenting it in an accessible and playful style:

> If you are a poet, you will see clearly that there is a cloud floating in
> this sheet of paper. Without a cloud, there will be no rain; without
> rain, the trees cannot grow; and without trees, we cannot make paper.
> The cloud is essential for the paper to exist. . . . So we can say that the
> cloud and the paper *inter-are*.
>
> If we look into this sheet of paper even more deeply, we can see
> the sunshine in it. If the sunshine is not there, the forest cannot
> grow. . . . And if we continue to look, we can see the logger who cut
> the tree and brought it to the mill to be transformed into paper. And
> we see the wheat. We know that the logger cannot exist without his
> daily bread, and therefore the wheat that became his bread is also in
> this sheet of paper. . . . The fact is that this sheet of paper is made up
> only of "non-paper elements." . . . As thin as this sheet of paper is, it
> contains everything in the universe in it. (1988: 3–4)

The doctrine of emptiness (*śūnyatā*) declares all things to lack inherent self-existence (*svabhāva*); therefore, all beings are constituted by their interactions with other beings and have no independent, enduring nature in and of themselves. Interdependence, or interbeing, applies as well to the self: "What we call self is made only of non-self elements" (2000: 87). Because things are empty of a separate self, they live in interdependence with all other things. Some authors use the hologram as a metaphor to suggest that all individual beings contain a miniature cosmos, just as Thich Nhat Hanh's sheet of paper contains the universe. Walt Whitman's statement "I am large, I contain multitudes," as well as William Blake's "To see a world in a grain of sand" are cited regularly in contemporary Buddhist articulations of this microcosm/macrocosm relationship.

Descriptions of interdependence often convey a sense of celebration of this interwoven world, of intimacy and oneness with the great, interconnected, living fabric of life, and an expansion of the sense of selfhood into it. Joan Halifax cites Chinese Buddhists who declare the entire world, including "rock, sea, and flower," to be sentient and presents Buddhism as a matter of connecting deeply with the living "web of creation":

> A thing cannot live in isolation; rather, the condition of being-ness . . . implies a vital and transformative interconnectedness, interdependence. And thus one seemingly separate being cannot be without all other beings, and is therefore not a separate self, but part of a greater Self, an ecological Self that is alive and has awareness within its larger Self. (1990: 23)

This dynamic between the separate self and the larger Self implies a particular interpretation of the Buddhist concept of no-self (*anātman*): once one realizes that one has no fixed, bounded self, one's sense of selfhood expands to include the others in the web of interdependence. According to Jeremy Hayward, "the growing into maturity of a human is experienced as an ever widening sense of self, from identification with the individual bodymind, to self as family, self as circle of friends, as nation, as race, as human race, as all living things, and perhaps finally to self as all that is" (1990: 65).

This idea of interdependence suggests natural alliances with some traditions and critiques of others. Often set up in opposition to the "Cartesian, mechanical, anthropocentric world view," Buddhism, with interdependence as its central feature, is said to conceive of the world as an "interrelated, intercausal universe similar to the world described in Native American wisdom . . . and quantum physics," according to Allan Hunt Badiner (1993: xvi). "Buddhism, shamanism, and deep ecology," asserts Halifax, "are based on the experience of engagement and the mystery of participation" (xxx).

Contemporary descriptions of interdependence, though, do not stop at the celebration of its wonder. They also emphasize the fragility of the interconnected network of beings: because everything depends on everything else, altering the balance of the web of life can be—and has been—catastrophic.

Thus the concept entails strong ecological imperatives. The many Buddhist and Buddhist-inspired groups engaged in environmental activism routinely cite interdependence or interconnectedness as the conceptual rationale for the link between the dharma and environmentalism. Contemporary discourse on interdependence also carries ethical and political imperatives regarding social and economic justice. It recognizes that the interdependencies of the modern world are often sources of suffering. Perceiving interconnectedness may involve tracing a running shoe for sale at the local mall to global warming because of the fuel it took to ship it from China, where it in turn connects to economic injustice, since it is made by women in a sweatshop making barely enough to survive, while a huge percentage of the profit from the shoe goes to corporate executives. It stresses finding root causes and seeking out hidden sources of social problems. The idea of interdependence, therefore, is an essential part of the conceptual arsenal of engaged Buddhism, the contemporary activist movement that strives to relieve suffering by addressing human rights, war, poverty, injustice, and environmental degradation. It is not then just a matter of "experiencing" the world as a part of the self but also a matter of ethical and political commitment.

Interdependence in this sense is often invoked by Americans and Europeans of eclectic spiritual orientation who freely mix Hindu, Daoist, and neo-Pagan traditions with Buddhism. It is not, however, simply a western appropriation. While the poet and essayist Gary Snyder may be the best known American to offer an ecological interpretation of Buddhist interdependence, many of the most prominent Asian leaders of contemporary Buddhism—the Dalai Lama, Thich Nhat Hanh, Daisaku Ikeda, Sulak Sivaraksa, Buddhadasa, and others have made interdependence central to their teachings, explicitly relating it to modern social, political, and ecological realities. The famous Thai reformer Buddhadasa (1906–93), for example, contended that the fundamental truth of nature—and the central doctrine of the dharma—is the dependent arising of things. Seeing this "universal cooperation" of celestial bodies, the elements of the natural world, and the parts of the body leads us to care for nature and others. He insisted that failing to see this mutual dependence has unleashed rampant greed and selfishness, as well as catastrophic social and environmental ills. If we cannot see the world as a "mutual, interdependent, cooperative enterprise," he asserted bluntly, "we'll all perish" (quoted in Swearer 1997: 29).

While modern articulations of interdependence are rooted in the traditional Buddhist concept of *pratītya-samutpāda*, in the last few decades they have taken on meanings, implications, and associations unique to the current era. For the historian of religion, therefore, the contemporary Buddhist concept of interdependence is a fruitful arena for analyzing the processes of conceptual and praxiological change and adaptation to shifting global circumstances. In this chapter I want to show how this concept has developed from both Buddhist and non-Buddhist lineages, including the discourses of Romanticism and scientific thought. It could serve as a paradigm of a hybrid concept. In brief, in some of its current forms, it is a hybrid of indigenous Buddhist concepts—dependent arising, the interpenetration of phenomena in the Huayan school, and various attitudes toward the natural world in East Asian Buddhism—commingled with conceptions of nature deriving from German Romanticism and American Transcendentalism, popular accounts of modern scientific thought, systems theory, and recent ecological thought.

Note that this phenomenon is much more than a disembodied idea. It is the most visible—and therefore most analyzable—aspect of a complex of social practices, attitudes, dispositions, and beliefs very much enmeshed in current social and political worlds. In other words, it is not monolithic! Especially complicating is the fact that early classical formulations took a view of the significance of interdependence that was nearly opposite to that of their contemporary successors. The monks and ascetics who developed the concept of dependent origination and its implications saw the phenomenal world as a binding chain, a web of entanglement, not a web of wonderment. How did this position that took a rather dim view of worldly life develop into the one today that celebrates this-worldly life and promotes activist engagement? Foucault said that "all history is history of the present"—that is, our view of the past is deeply conditioned by the concerns, categories, and assumptions operative in the present (1977: 31). In this respect, I deliberately address in this chapter the concept of interdependence from the perspective of its current transformation.

Classical and Medieval Buddhist Views of Nature

Dependent Origination in Classical Pali Literature

The Buddha, as is often repeated, said he taught only two things: suffering and the end of suffering. No doubt, Buddhists and Buddhist institutions have supported efforts to relieve suffering throughout history. The moral ideal of compassion for all living beings cannot help but harmonize with the various modern efforts to feed the hungry, heal the sick, and promote economic and environmental sustainability for people and animals. The great number of Buddhists around the world active in these efforts are undoubtedly acting in accordance with the basic Buddhist principles of universal compassion and relief of suffering. But the Pali *suttas* do not present temporary relief of suffering as the dharma's ultimate goal. Buddhism has always employed means of such relief, both natural and supernatural, but the "end of suffering" the Buddha declared was to be permanent. The postmortem state of *parinirvāṇa*, or nirvana without the substratum of the five *skandhas*, the aggregates of personal existence, was beyond suffering because it was beyond time and space, beyond becoming, beyond personal existence, beyond all conditioned things. It was by definition nearly unimaginable—everything the phenomenal world of transience and rebirth was not. No doubt the vast majority of Buddhists throughout history have been lay people who did not aspire to such a remote goal. Even most monks, it turns out, have not considered this a realistic aspiration in this lifetime, given the age of decline in which we live. The ideal, however, is at the heart of the symbolic world of Buddhism.

The Pali *suttas* arose out of an ascetic milieu that viewed family, reproduction, physical pleasures, material success, and worldly life as ultimately futile, disappointing, and binding. Dependent origination denotes in early Buddhist literature the chain of causes and conditions that give rise to all phenomenal existence in the world of impermanence, birth, death, and rebirth (samsara). Far from being celebrated as a wondrous web of interconnected life, it is repeatedly referred to as a "mass of suffering" (*duḥkha*). Indeed, it is through the *reversal* of this chain of interdependent causation—not an identification with it—that the Buddha is said to have become awakened. The "world" (*loka*) itself is conceived as a flow of phenomenal events that are dependent on contact between the senses and sense objects, consciousness and objects of consciousness. It does not exist in and of itself but arises with the intertwining of a falsely reified subject and object. The point of the many Pali passages elucidating the relationships between the various kinds of consciousness and its objects—visual consciousness and objects of vision, auditory consciousness and sounds, and so on—is to help the monk learn how to dis-identify with the phenomenal world as it is constituted by this intertwining of consciousness and its objects based on craving, aversion, and delusion (SN 12.44). While modern Buddhists and scholars sometimes present the chain of dependent origination as a kind of empirical theory of causality, it was meant to illuminate not the arising of natural phenomena as much as of the conditions for dissatisfactory life in the cycle of rebirth, so that one could undo them and be released into the liberated state beyond all causes and conditions (see, for instance, DN 15). Rather than celebrating the "experience of engagement and the mystery of participation" in the interconnected "web of life" (Halifax 1993: xxx), Pali literature instead encourages quite the opposite: the *disengagement* from all entanglement in this web.

Many Pali *suttas* attempt to foster this disengagement by emphasizing the impurity and undesirability of physical life. Sense desires are "perilous" and "bring little enjoyment, and much suffering and disappointment" (MN 22). Investigation of the world and worldly life bring about "disgust" (*nibbidā*) with them. In order to cultivate such disgust and to counter lust, some *suttas* spare no detail in describing the unattractive aspects of the body: it oozes secretions from various orifices, is full of foul fluids, slimy organs, bones, and tendons; soon it will decay and become food for jackals, worms, and birds. People in their delusion think it is beautiful; but the monk is to contemplate its foulness and impermanence and become disenchanted of such delusion (e.g., AN 9.15; SN 1.11).

Note, however, that characterizing Buddhism as a whole as "pessimistic" or "life-negating," as many nineteenth-century European writers did, is misleading. Pali Buddhism is in no way thoroughly world-negating: it often tells of the Buddha giving advice on worldly matters and ascribing value to ordinary happiness within the world. The tradition develops positions on family life, work, governing, and other worldly affairs. Very early on, it developed proximate concerns regarding ordinary life, many of which are implicitly life-affirming. But the more remote goal of achieving nirvana and transcending embodied life, beyond rebirth and temporality itself, have always formed at least the symbolic center of the tradition and practitioners' long-term (i.e., multiple-lifetime) goal.[1] Little in early Buddhist literature suggests the contemporary celebration of interdependence.

Nor is today's associated reverence for nature apparent in the Pali canon's attitudes toward the natural world and wilderness, which are ambivalent. Some passages suggest that the best place to practice the dharma is in quiet natural settings, and some do celebrate the beauty of the natural world. In the Theragatha, for instance, Kassapa extols the joys of living and practicing in the wilderness, where "these rocky crags do please me so" (Thag 1062–71). Such early Buddhist ascetics left the burgeoning cities of the time for the relative solitude of the forest, but their primary aim is not usually expressed in terms of appreciation of the beauties of nature or enjoying the rewards of living close to it. Some Indian Buddhist literature suggests that the forest was considered a place of fear and danger from animals, insects, and bandits (Lancaster 1997: 10). More important, there is no sense in the Pali literature that nature is sacred or that the feeling of merging with the natural world is synonymous with or even conducive to achieving awakening.

However, more general values that feed into the contemporary conception of interdependence and its ethical implications can be found in Pali literature. The canon emphasizes a universal moral imperative to preserve the lives and well-being of all sentient beings and to practice unselfish acts for the widest possible circle of living things, including animals and even insects.

Metta meditations in a number of early *suttas* and commentaries are designed to train the mind to cultivate this compassion and loving-kindness toward all beings. This universal ethic does not depend on any idea of the dense interconnectedness of beings such that the actions of one reverberate throughout the cosmos to affect all but rather on the moral law of karma, the high value placed on compassion, and the fact that rebirth in various orders of beings provides a continuity between humans and animals—they could be one's own relatives and friends from the past. While this moral imperative encourages empathetic identification with all sentient beings, this does not imply expanding the subjective sense of *selfhood* to include other beings—any sense of selfhood, limited or encompassing, is ultimately rejected in this early literature.

The early concept of dependent origination, therefore, cannot fully account for the contemporary concept of Buddhist interdependence and its implications. In some ways, the early view looks quite contrary to the contemporary one.

Interdependence and Interpenetration in Mahayana Buddhism

EMPTINESS AND DEPENDENT ORIGINATION. A number of South Asian Mahayana texts, however, introduced ways of thinking about dependent origination that allowed for a tilt toward a more affirmative view of the phenomenal world, and these have proven to be important sources for the modern versions of interdependence. They include the ideal of the bodhisattva who remains in samsara until all beings are saved, as well as new conceptions of the goal of the path as Buddha-hood within the world rather than a wholly transcendent nirvana. These are prominent themes, for example, in the highly influential *Lotus (Saddharmapuṇḍarika) Sutra* and *Perfection of Wisdom (Prajñāpāramitā) Sutras*.

Another important source for rethinking the valuation of dependent origination is Nāgārjuna's *Fundamentals of the Middle Way (Mūlamadhyamakakārikā)*, one of the most influential texts of Mahayana Buddhism. The basic thrust of the text is a development of the idea that all things lack, or are empty (*śūnya*) of, inherent self-existence (*svabhāva*)—a fixed, substantial, independent, and permanent nature. They consist instead of a multiplicity of causes and conditions. In asserting that both samsara and nirvana are empty of inherent self-existence, Nāgārjuna declares there is "not the slightest difference between the two" (MMK 25: 19–20). Since all things lack inherent self-existence, any conceptual construction, including even the difference between samsara and nirvana, is merely a conventional truth (*saṃvṛtti-sātya*). Nāgārjuna also identifies emptiness (*śūnyatā*), the ultimate truth of this lack of inherent self-existence of things, with dependent origination: "That which is dependent origination is emptiness / It is a convenient designation, and is itself the middle way" (MMK 24:18). This suggests that samsara be viewed not as something inherently binding—for lacking inherent self-existence, it cannot be *inherently* anything. Rather samsara, since it is itself empty, is from the highest level of understanding just like nirvana. As a Perfection of Wisdom text puts it, all dharmas are "limitless" and "boundless" (*ananta* and *aparyanta*) (Conze 1973; 207; Aṣṭa 103). That is, if we correctly "see" all of the elements of existence (dharmas) that make up dependent origination, we see them as empty and therefore of the nature of awakening itself. I have argued elsewhere that this reconfigures the relationship between nirvana and samsara, the unconditioned and the conditioned, presented in the Pali literature (2002a: 25–33). Rather than attempting to attain nirvana and reject samsara, Nāgārjuna and the Perfection of Wisdom literature suggest that what is important is stopping the conceptual reification of any dharma at all, thus seeing all of them as empty. Apprehending the true empty nature of the dharmas that make up dependent origination, therefore, can be the occasion for liberation, for their nature is ultimately the same as that of nirvana itself.

Seeing dependent origination, therefore, is awakening. This is not a new idea: Pali *suttas* claim that on the night of his awakening, Śākyamuni Buddha "saw" dependent origination, beholding the causes and conditions that produce both suffering and its cessation. Through this sweeping vision of all causes and conditions, he was able to enact his own liberation (Ud 1.3). There is a subtle difference, however, between the emerging Mahayana understanding of "seeing" dependent origination and that of the Pali traditions. The biographies of the Buddha present him as seeing dependent origination first in the specific case of the trajectory of his own karma extending back into the infinite past, thus apprehending all of the causes and conditions that have brought him to the brink of awakening. This vision then expands to encompass the causes and conditions of all sentient beings and the karmic trajectories by which they have come to be what they are. The seeing of dependent origination, therefore, is not in itself liberative; it is not a becoming one with the world, merging with the infinite web of existence, in fact, the Buddha becomes "disjoined" from the world (Iti 112). This, *in turn,* gives him a thorough understanding of the entire process of dependent origination, that is, the factors that give rise to dissatisfaction. His vision was a kind of map or instruction manual of the way of their undoing, leading to liberation (see e.g. Ud 1.3).

It is possible to read Nāgārjuna, however, as abandoning this interpretation of "seeing dependent origination" as a map in favor of simply seeing any dharma in its emptiness as sufficient for apprehending the highest truth. Seeing the emptiness of all dharmas renders one liberated in this world. Revulsion for dependent origination is no better than clinging to it; the important thing is not so much transcending it altogether as seeing into its true nature.

THE VISIONARY COSMOS. This reading of Nāgārjuna is supported by quite a few Mahayana sutras that reinterpret the ultimate goal of Buddhism, shifting the focus from transcending samsara to various conceptions of awakened life in the midst of the world. Subsequently, tendencies emerge toward a view of this "seeing" of dependent origination as a kind of vision of the cosmos that is itself liberative, aside from any "instructive" elements showing the causes and conditions of both bondage and liberation.

The *Avataṃsaka Sutra*, which epitomizes this visionary tradition, is one of the most important sources for the contemporary interpretation of interdependence. Here, especially in the *Gaṇḍavyūha* section, the idea of emptiness is transposed into visual imagery in which each individual thing and all things in the universe interpenetrate yet retain their distinctiveness.[2] The fact that all individual things in some sense contain or reflect all others corresponds to Nāgārjuna's "truth in the highest sense" (*paramārtha-sātya*), the emptiness of inherent self-existence—everything consists in other things. The fact that things, despite this, maintain their individual distinctiveness corresponds to the conventional truth (*saṃvṛtti-sātya*). In the Chinese Huayan school of Buddhism, which takes the *Avataṃsaka* (Chin. *Huayan*) as its main text, this interpenetration is symbolized by the jeweled net of Indra: an immense net with multifaceted jewels at each juncture, each of which both reflects and is reflected by all of the others. This powerful image has become a standard symbol for interdependence in its contemporary sense, and the Perfection of Wisdom literature and the *Avataṃsaka* are the sources for Thich Nhat Hanh's idea of "interbeing."

The *Avataṃsaka* also contains numerous visionary episodes culminating in one in which the hero, Sudhana, has a vision of the entire cosmos within the body of the Buddha Mahāvairocana. This vision, in which Sudhana becomes one with Mahāvairocana, enacting in a moment all of his eons of wondrous deeds as a bodhisattva, reveals the world as a resplendent, radically interpenetrating cosmos in which the ordinary categories of time and space are collapsed. Here we have an example of a motif important to the modern articulation of interdependence: the identification of a person with a being who is the universe itself or with the underlying reality of things. Moreover, the world into which Sudhana merges is not permeated with foulness and suffering but shot through with countless Buddhas and bodhisattvas, some in resplendent garb, some in the guise of fishermen, children, and all manner of seemingly ordinary people, some in the pores of a Buddha's skin and in the land itself. It is a transfigured world of magic and wonder, quite distant, it would seem, from the binding chains of dependent origination in the Pali literature. We have, therefore, three more ingredients of the contemporary conception of interdependence: the identification of the individual with the cosmos or a cosmic being; the radical interpenetration and interreflectivity of all things; and a more affirmative, wonder-inducing view of the world of phenomena.

The visionary strains of the Mahayana, however, cannot be interpreted as wholly world-affirming. For instance, Pure Land sutras may at first seem to depict the possibility of a fully affirmative view of phenomenality. Like the *Avataṃsaka*, they describe the pure land as filled with jeweled trees, sweet-smelling, golden earth and air, immaculately clear waters, and birds that sing utterances of the dharma. Ornaments and jewels are strewn everywhere. There are no death or disease, no briars or rough ground. While such descriptions clearly offer a positive view of *another* world, merely to reside in which is at least a penultimate form of liberation, they reinforce the dissatisfactoriness of the "ordinary" world (Eckel 1997). The idea of the pure land, rather than celebrating nature, improves on it. These lavish descriptions suggest the ideal not of undisturbed nature but of a tamed and cultivated land with gardens and splendid buildings. The pure land is an inverse reflection of the "flaws" of nature experienced by sentient beings in "our" world and is thus largely in continuity with the earlier literature's assessment of life in the realm of rebirth.

Some South Asian Mahayana texts, then, marking a rethinking, hold that seeing dependent origination—that is, seeing all things as empty of inherent self-existence—itself is awakening. This is then developed into a conception of a liberative vision of the totality and of the world as manifestation of a cosmic reality: Vairocana, *dharma-kāya*, or Buddha-nature—the hidden "Buddha-ness" or Buddha potential of all things.

Nature and Buddha-Nature in East Asia

While the ideas of the emptiness of all phenomena, liberation within the world, the interpenetration of all phenomena, and identification of the individual with a cosmic reality all provide important resources for the contemporary conception of interdependence, they were not associated with reverence for the natural world until they became transformed in East Asia.

When Buddhists came to China, they encountered views of the natural world quite alien to those of South Asia. Chinese literature shows little of the distaste for embodiment and everyday life found in Indian ascetic traditions. At the time Buddhism was becoming established in China, China already had an indigenous literature of reverence for mountains, rivers, and uncultivated forests, as well as the concept of an underlying force, the Dao, that coursed through humanity and the natural world.[3] The Chinese sages' views of nature created conditions for a revaluation of the phenomenal world within Buddhist traditions. As noted, some Indic Mahayana traditions characterized awakening as identification with this larger reality of buddha-nature, or what was sometimes called the "womb" or "matrix" of the Buddha (*tathāgata-garbha*). In contrast to the earlier emphasis on no-self (*anātman*), texts such as the *Mahāparinirvāṇa Sutra* affirmed a "great self" that was hidden in all people. The Buddha became a transcendent and eternal cosmic being with which the individual was seen to be ultimately identical.

In China, this buddha-nature came to be mapped more explicitly onto the natural world, and the natural world to be reenvisioned as both symbol and manifestation of this cosmic reality rather than a continuing cycle of dissatisfaction to be transcended. Some Chinese Buddhist thinkers contended that all beings, even grasses, rocks, and rivers, contained Buddha-nature. Such ideas suggest a different relationship emerging within the Buddhist tradition between humanity and nature, one of mutuality and harmony rather than ambivalence and suspicion.

A number of the philosophical writings of East Asian schools of Buddhism support both a more positive view of the conditioned, dependently originated world and the idea of awakening as identification with this larger cosmos. Fazang, the most prominent thinker of the Huayan school, developed the implications of the *Avataṃsaka Sutra* in ways that essentially overturn the Pali conception of dependent origination and the distinction between the conditioned and the unconditioned. For Fazang, since all entities interpenetrate each other, the distinction between samsara and nirvana ultimately breaks down in a more radical way than for Nāgārjuna. The universe is the body and mind of the cosmic Buddha Mahāvairocana, which pervades all things equally, essentially sacralizing all things. There is no need to escape from the process of dependent origination, only to see it aright as the marvelous manifestation of the cosmic Buddha. Like most Chinese Buddhist thinkers, Fazang rejects the idea of transcending the realm of the conditioned and instead suggests attunement to the world and seeing it as the wonder that it is. It is not surprising that some modern ideas of Buddhist interdependence draw heavily from this school.[4]

The work of famous East Asian Buddhist poets, such as China's Hanshan and Japan's Bashō, combines in unprecedented ways Buddhist teachings with a keen appreciation of the objects and processes of the natural world. In Hanshan's poems, Cold Mountain—his recluse home as well as the name he took for himself—is a symbol of awakening, and the abundant images of clouds, towering mountains, and wind-blown trees are all fashioned into metaphors of the path to awakening. Yet Hanshan has more than a merely metaphorical interest in nature and clearly revels in the beauty of his natural surroundings. It is no wonder that the contemporary American Buddhist poet Gary Snyder, also a reverent disciple of the natural world, translated many of Hanshan's poems about freely wondering in wilderness, seeing traces of buddha-nature in the crags and streams, and spurning affluence and reputation (1999: 524):

> In a tangle of cliffs I chose a place—
> Bird-paths, but no trails for men.
> What's beyond the yard?
> White clouds clinging to vague rocks.
> Now I've lived here—how many years—
> Again and again, spring and winter pass.
> Go tell families with silverware and cars
> "What's the use of all that noise and money?"

The last lines are Snyder's obvious smuggling of Hanshan's spirit into the modern world, playfully rendering what is more precisely translated "I send this message to families of wealth / An empty name will do you no good" (Henricks 1990: 32). The intent in both versions is clear: to sketch the contrast between civilization, with its demands for money and reputation, and the unencumbered sacredness of the wilderness. This contrast is easily translated into nineteenth- and twentieth-century American sensibilities, and the mingling of Chinese and American versions of this opposition was highly productive for modern Buddhism.

Buddhistic attention to the natural world continued and developed in Japan as well. Saigyō, the twelfth-century Japanese Buddhist thinker and poet, reflected on the natural world as a locus for awakening, partly in view of the fact that plants were conceived as having buddha-nature. Encounters with the vast variety of sentient and even nonsentient beings could be occasions for perceiving this hidden, sacred reality within all things (LaFleur 1998). Dōgen, the prolific thirteenth-century founder of the Sōtō school of Zen, likewise discussed the nonduality of humanity and nature in a number of his writings. In the "Mountains and Rivers Sutra," of which Snyder has written an ecological interpretation, Dōgen puts the matter vividly:

> The mountains and rivers of this moment are the actualization of the way of the ancient Buddhas. Each, abiding in its own phenomenal expression, realizes completeness. Because mountains and waters have been active since before the eon of emptiness, they are alive at this moment. Because they have been the self since before form arose, they are liberated and realized. (quoted in Snyder 1990: 97)

A brief passage from Dōgen has also become a standard citation for modern Buddhist expressions of the widening sense of selfhood that encompasses all beings: "We study the self to forget the self. When you forget the self you become one with the ten thousand things" (Snyder 2006: 17).[5] The verse in a stroke erases what for many Buddhists are the "Mārās" of the present age: the erroneous belief in the isolated Cartesian ego, the mechanistic view of the natural world, and the disenchantment and desacralization of the world with the accompanying materialism, overconsumption, and environmental degradation. But in order for thinkers such as Dōgen to be called forth from their own time to speak to such issues, a variety of western ideas and practices had to prepare the ground. The various pictures of dependent origination, samsara, and the natural world that emerge from South and East Asian canonical texts do not themselves provide sufficient material to account for the ways the concept of Buddhist interdependence has developed in recent decades. In the West, a parallel genealogy of this concept existed that did not join the one just discussed until well into the twentieth century.

Western Sources of Buddhist Interdependence

Between Rationalism and Romanticism . . . Again

For the Buddhist conception of interdependence to attain the significance it has today, it had to acquire ingredients from a variety of sources and situate itself within the broad tensions, already described, between rationalist and Romantic orientations. The western lines of influence that eventually fed the contemporary conception can be traced back to the eighteenth century. The modern age in Europe, going back as far the Deists, produced a number of philosophies depicting the universe as a vast "interlocking order"—to use Taylor's phrase—with beings of various natures and purposes organically connected and unified into a total system (Taylor 1989: 266–84). It is a view of a cosmos in which all the various functions and purposes of individual things work together in a harmonious order for the ultimate good of all. This view affirms the goodness of nature and asserts that human beings must act in accordance with it. We find an early articulation in Alexander Pope's *Essay on Man* (3, ll. 7–26.), where he describes nature as an interconnected whole pervaded by one spirit:

> Look round our world; behold the chain of love
> Combining all below and all above.
> See plastic Nature working to this end,
> The single atoms each to other tend,

Attract, attracted to, the next in place,
Form'd and impell'd its neighbour to embrace.
See matter next, with various life endued,
Press to one centre still, the gen'ral good;
See dying vegetables life sustain,
See life dissolving vegetate again.
All forms that perish other forms supply
(By turns we catch the vital breath, and die),
Like bubbles on the sea of Matter borne,
They rise, they break, and to that sea return.
Nothing is foreign; parts relate to whole;
One all-extending, all-preserving, soul
Connects each being, greatest with the least;
Made beast in aid of man, and man of beast;
All serv'd all serving: nothing stands alone;
The chain holds on, and where it ends unknown.

In the Romantic tradition, the German idealists, as we have already seen, also developed various iterations of the organic wholeness of nature and our inseparability from it, as well as conceptions of the absolute as nature itself, endowed with subjectivity and coming to individual consciousness in human beings. They described a human ego that was separated from nature and longed to return to the primordial unity with the larger whole that connects everyone and everything. This ego, according to Schelling, could be reunited, at least in part, with the absolute from which it "fell" when it took on existence as a seemingly separate subject. The way to this harmony, Schelling and Schiller asserted, was through aesthetic appreciation and serene reflection.

The English Romantics maintained that feeling and internal impulse provided more profound access to nature than did the dissecting blade of rational analysis. As noted, this was connected to an antimechanistic critique of the Newtonian cosmology and Cartesian dualism, as well as the exclusive epistemological reliance on instrumental reason. Such reliance, the Romantics argued, fragmented the wholeness of nature, cutting us off from its vital force. Coleridge, for example, praised the "intuition of things which arises when we possess ourselves, as one with the whole," while characterizing as "mere understanding" the perception that occurs when "we think of ourselves as separated beings, and place nature in antithesis to the mind, as object to subject, thing to thought, death to life" (2004 [1818], 261–62). This sense of the wholeness of life, its organic unity and interrelatedness, was for the Romantics also a powerful source of the sublime, a feeling of awe and reverence.

All these themes worked their way into Buddhist modernism. The idea of the separate ego that finds its way back to wholeness in expanding its boundaries to identify with the vast interrelated cosmos and all its inhabitants, giving up its separate, egocentric existence, is clearly a key conception in the contemporary understanding of Buddhism, especially in the West. Moreover, the sense of an animate universe, of a life-force flowing through all things and offering an inner access to the spiritual essence of the whole, appears in various ways in modern and contemporary Buddhism. Clearly, there are indigenous Buddhist sources for similar ideas, which I have just identified—*tathāgata-gārbha*, the identification of the individual with the cosmic Buddha, dependent origination, and the interpenetration of phenomena. However, the way they were appropriated in a modern, western context was a hybrid process that also drew on a western lineage extending back to the Deists and Romantics.

Buddhist ideas were used to augment the Romantic critique of Enlightenment rationalism and its descendants. Descartes and Bacon are often identified as the starting point for the desacralized view of nature, and authors discussing Buddhist interdependence today often evoke Cartesian dualism as the quintessential orientation against which this conception contends. One of the key consequences of Descartes's reenvisioning of the self as "unextended substance" distinct from the extended substances (material things) was the view of the world as a mechanism or machine and the concomitant emergence of an attitude of disengagement toward and objectification of the "not-I." The world as a machine could no longer be understood, as the ancients had done, as the embodiment of a meaningful order with spiritual and moral ramifications. All meaning was now located in the mind itself and its private representations of external objects. This marks an important phase of the "disenchantment" of the world. Because all meaning now was "in" the mind, what was "outside" the mind was disinvested of intrinsic meaning or value. Nature was neutralized. On this view—quite different from the view of things as having meaning and value in and of themselves, that is, ontologically residing in them (Taylor 1989: 187–88)—the mind's primary orientation toward the world is that of instrumental control. Descartes said that knowledge of the physical world is "very useful in life," and by knowing the various principles by which nature operates "we can . . . employ [objects of nature] in all those uses to which they are adapted, and thus render ourselves the masters and possessors of nature" (1982: 1: 119). Rational understanding of nature—developing clear and distinct ideas of its many facets—was inseparable from the mastering of nature as a collection of objects to be used for our purposes.

To be fair, the founders of this instrumentalist orientation did not conceive of it as inviting the plundering of the natural world in hedonistic pursuit of pleasure and power, nor could they have imagined the ramifications of this conceptual neutralization of nature when later it was combined with innumerable other social and material factors that have contributed to the current ecological crisis. It is too simplistic to attribute to Cartesian dualism the tremendous causal power that some have given it, drawing a nearly direct line from Descartes's *Meditations* to Chernobyl. Descartes's and Bacon's attitudes toward the natural world were part of larger cultural forces already in play. Moreover, notwithstanding Bacon's famously crass characterization of science as putting nature on the rack and extracting "her" secrets, like a judge interrogating a witch, his emphasis on disengaged rational control of nature was not purely materialistic and instrumentalist. His interpretation of such control was part of his vision of the biblical injunction to humanity to be stewards of creation, which he interpreted as laboring to foster the usefulness of things to the good of humankind and the alleviation of suffering (Taylor 1991: 104–5). Nonetheless, this orientation toward the mind and natural world was a part—though not the sole cause—of the long, complex processes that led to the objectification and commodification of the things of the world that served as the rationale for the unrestrained exploitation of natural resources.

In attempting to stem this exploitation, contemporary societies across the globe have searched for conceptual and religious resources for reenvisioning and respiritualizing nature, as well as for practical solutions. It is, in part, this effort that has prompted late modern Buddhists (as well as followers of other historical religions and new religious movements) to try to revivify a sense of the intrinsic worth and spiritual significance in nature, resacralizing and revalorizing it, and bridging the Cartesian split between the mind and the material.

Transcendentalism and the Reenchantment of the World

As noted, some elements of Asian Buddhism, particularly certain strains of East Asian traditions, early on developed rationales for the intrinsic religious value of the natural world. As with many important developments in Buddhist modernism, Transcendentalists and their kindred spirits shaped the particular way this reverence for nature was taken up in the West. I have discussed already some of the ways Emerson brought romantic metaphysics into an American framework that provided the vocabulary for D. T. Suzuki's translation of Zen into Western categories. Nineteenth- and early-twentieth-century America also inaugurated new ways of valuing the natural world that would later contribute to the development of the contemporary concept of Buddhist interdependence, especially with regard to its implications for environmental valuation and protection.

The period of the Transcendentalists saw a revolution in ways of under-standing nature. Departing from the earlier Puritan sense of it as a place of dan-ger, evil, testing, and purification, the Transcendentalists voiced a full-throated affirmation of the sacredness of the natural world. This affirmation was also tinged with philosophical idealism; like their predecessors, the German ideal-ists, some American Transcendentalists saw the natural world not just as a part of God's creation but as a part of God. This was one source of the American idea that undeveloped wilderness had an intrinsic, not just utilitarian, value. Sometimes connected to ideologies of American nationalism and sometimes suspicious of them, the romance of the wilderness was a prominent feature of American literature at this time. The sense of nature as a place of spiritual repose and rejuvenation, of awe and wonder, became widespread, stripping away the grotesque and macabre aspects of the sublime of the Romantics and leaving just the wonderment and awe (Albanese 1991).

The famous naturalist John Muir, a pivotal figure in the American concep-tion of wilderness and its spiritual value, as well as the development of the ethic of preservation, embodied this new perception of nature. Muir's writings brought to an apotheosis the Transcendentalist reverence for wilderness as a place of wonder and sacredness as well as renewal and refuge from the harsh conditions of modernity. His articulation of the significance of the natural became ensconced in American consciousness and remains quite palpable today. Having studied both Emerson and Thoreau, Muir imbibed the vitalistic and holistic tendencies that they in turn had appropriated from the Romantics: nature, he declared, was "one soul" and wilderness a "unity in interrelation" that is "alive and familiar" (quoted in Albanese 1991: 99). "When we try to pick out anything by itself," he declared, "we find it hitched to everything in the universe" (1988 [1911]: 95). Retuning Christian language to the key of the earthy paradise of the mountains, forests, and lakes, Muir wrote of nature itself as an incarnation of divinity, its individual things "portions of God" (Al-banese 1991: 99–100). Communing with nature was a kind of earthly sacra-ment in which "you lose consciousness of your own separate existence: you blend with the landscape, and become part and parcel of nature" (Muir 1988 [1991]: 120). There was a contemplative element to Muir's appreciations as well; both he and Thoreau suggested that a disciplined purification of the body and senses was necessary in order to properly access nature and allow its holiness to present itself. In contrast to Emerson, who even as he revered the natural world asserted that human mastery over it was a part of the divine and lordly quality of human beings, Muir complemented his rapturous contemplations of nature with the development of an activist preservationist ethic, inspiring the development of the national park at Yosemite and founding the Sierra Club

(Albanese 1991: 82–87). Muir fiercely criticized unrestrained commercialism as dangerous to not only the natural world but the soul: "These temple destroyers, devotees of ravaging commercialism, seem to have a perfect contempt for Nature, and, instead of lifting their eyes to the God of the mountains, lift them to the Almighty Dollar" (1912: 261–62). Muir knew little of Buddhism, but the most important expositors of late twentieth-century ecological interpretations of Buddhism have undeniably incorporated his sensibilities into their perspective. The most articulate of the contemporary expositors of Buddhist interdependence regularly reference his emphasis on direct experience and reverence of nature, as well as his biocentric view of a deeply interconnected world, his rejection of mechanistic conceptions, and his contempt for modern commercialism and materialism.

Elements of this American reverence for nature went hand in hand with a new valuation of solitude, especially solitude in the woods and the feelings of connection to nature that it could bring. Thoreau is of course the paradigmatic example, though he was just the most visible of those who placed a high spiritual value on the solitary contemplation of nature. The writings of a lesser known Transcendentalist, William Rounseville Alger, show that this perspective was a response to a increasing crowdedness of cities and the stress of modern bureaucratic and industrial work. Tapping into a wider anxiety among nineteenth-century progressives about urban life—its vice and materialism, its overcrowdedness alongside its alienation and isolation, as well as its masses of threatening immigrants—Alger saw the wilderness as a wholesome spiritual refuge. Praising solitude, he declared that society is "full of multiplicity and change, is in every way finite, wasting its force in incessant throbs; solitude, an unfaltering unity, is allied to the infinite" (2003 [1867]: 170–71). Modern society for Alger was a cauldron of narcissism, anxiety, and greed, while solitude was the antidote to the "overtaxed . . . weary, uneasy, and ambitious" condition and to a market-driven world that thrived on competition and ego assertion (168).

The first entry of this nineteenth-century combination of disenchantment, love of solitude, and reverence for nature into the interpretation of Buddhism came through the dichotomous representations of East and West in currency at the time. It is no coincidence that Alger published, in addition to *The Solitudes of Nature and of Man* (in which he lists the Buddha as an example of the solitary life), a volume entitled *The Poetry of the East*, in which he reiterates the familiar representation of the spiritual, contemplative "East" as a necessary balance to the materialist, competitive, money-driven "West." Here again we see Asia portrayed as the Other as against that which is disturbing about modernity in the West. This Other comes to be associated with solitude, asceticism, interiority, and, most important here, nature. "The East" was seen as a place that was still enchanted, populated by sages who themselves retired to the forest in search of spiritual wisdom offered by the natural world. Thoreau in fact drew parallels between his own retreat to Walden Pond and the asceticism of the "Hindoos" (1997 [1845]: 184).

The internalization of religion, the attribution of religious significance to the natural world, the emphasis on solitary contemplation of nature, and the view of such contemplation as a remedy for the excessive materialism of the modern world all served as essential ingredients in the interpretation of Buddhism in the West, particularly North America. The explicit connection made in the Transcendentalist period between nature and what many considered a universal mystical experience provided a hermeneutical context in which Hanshan, Bashō, Dōgen, and others were later understood. We have seen how D. T. Suzuki deployed the Transcendentalist image of the nature-loving mystic to portray the Zen hermit. The Transcendentalist category of "Universal Religion"—which was believed to transcend the bounds of time and place and to consist of personal experience rather than dogma, ritual, and the specificities of culture—provided a vast arena into which promoters of Buddhism could easily introduce its ascetic, hermitic, and meditative traditions, along with the East Asian reverence for nature. These factors influenced how westerners understood Buddhism, as well as the shape it would take in the modern world. These influences allowed the sketch of Buddhist attitudes toward the natural world to be crosshatched with American reverence for wilderness, as well as with the social and political concerns of the time.

Interdependence and Eco-Buddhism

The Romantic-Transcendentalist line of thinking supplied a ready array of motifs useful for hybridizing and transposing into the key of modern discourse the Buddhist concepts of dependent origination, assertions of nondualism, universalist ethics, and East Asian affinities with the natural world. These themes were not, however, sufficient to produce the synthesis that has emerged in today's conception of interdependence. The final element was the infusion of recent theoretical approaches in the social and physical sciences, along with contemporary ecological thought. The synthesis of all of these elements did not in fact take place in a systematic way until quite recently.

If there is an overarching theoretical paradigm lurking in the background of this development, it is probably systems theory, a broad-ranging, multidisciplinary theoretical paradigm that focuses on various kinds of systems—economic, biological, physiological, psychological, and social—that form wholes having qualities different from their constituent parts. Widely applicable, systems theory can in principle address any network of relationships whose constituents act as a whole and create emergent properties that cannot be accounted for by analysis of the parts in isolation. A figure who was very influential to the contemporary Buddhist concept of interdependence is Gregory Bateson (1904–80), who argued that the mind was in many respects similar to other kinds of living, dynamic systems like cells, rainforests, and communities. He insisted that minds should not be seen as either separate from their physiological substrata or as isolated from other minds. The basic unit, for Bateson, is not the individual entity but the system of which entities are a part. Individuals must be understood as organisms in symbiotic relationships with their environments (1979).

Arne Naess, a Norwegian philosopher and mountaineer, was the first to explicitly interpret Buddhist dependent origination in terms of systems theory. Naess began to bring together Spinoza with Mahayana Buddhism in the 1970s, ruminating on the Buddhistic implications of meditation in terms of Spinoza's notion of freedom (Naess 1978). Spinoza was an important influence on the Romantics; he came up with the pantheistic (or panentheistic) metaphysic adopted by the German idealists, as well as the most comprehensive early challenge to Cartesian dualism. Employing systems theory seasoned by Spinozistic and Buddhist metaphysics as his guiding theoretical framework, Naess founded the deep ecology movement, which rejects the "man-in-environment image in favor of the relational, total-field image" and sees "organisms as knots in the biospherical net or field of intrinsic relations" (1973: 95). Deep ecology asserts a symbiotic relationship between the individual and environment in which each reciprocally constitutes the other. Individuals are seen as open-ended nodes in larger networks of activity rather than bounded, atomistic entities. This conception of the relationship between the self and the wider network of humans, animals, and plants also finds a deep kinship with James Lovelock's famous Gaia hypothesis. Often cited by deep ecologists and ecologically minded Buddhists, this hypothesis proposes that the biosphere is a self-regulating organism. Naess and Lovelock's approaches are also kin to some extent with process philosophy/theology, which began with Alfred North Whitehead and has been an important force in the contemporary interpretation of Buddhist dependent origination and emptiness (Inada 1984; Odin 1982).

Popular accounts of recent scientific theories have also made a significant contribution. As noted, the discourse of scientific Buddhism lay largely at the level of rhetoric until the 1970s, when a number of popular books attempted to draw explicit parallels between recent scientific developments and Buddhism, as well as other Asian religions. Fritjof Capra, in his best-selling book *The Tao of Physics* (1975), argued for correlations between recent findings in quantum physics and ideas of the "universal interwovenness" of self and other in Buddhism and other forms of "Eastern mysticism." Such conceptions, he claimed, were similar to ideas in quantum physics of the "universe as an interconnected web of physical and mental relations whose parts are defined only through their connections to the whole" (1975: 129). His later work, including a book significantly entitled *The Web of Life*, criticizes Cartesian mechanistic and "linear" thinking, associating it with a host of contemporary evils and urging that not only quantum mechanics but also complexity theory and systems theory show the way to a more integrative, holistic understanding that reveals underlying connections between biological, psychological, social, and ecological systems. As noted, a voluminous literature has followed *The Tao of Physics* in exploring the putative parallels between Buddhism and various sciences. Scientists and Buddhists alike in recent decades have debated the value of such studies for understanding Buddhism. Whatever their limitations, what is important here is that they have not only imbued dependent origination with the scent of scientific theory but also influenced the reconfiguration of the concept itself in modern scientific terms.

Joanna Macy has been as important as any contemporary author in assembling all of the components I have been discussing and forging them into the contemporary conception of interdependence. A knowledgeable, charismatic, and popular writer in the world of contemporary western Buddhism, Macy explicitly articulates dependent origination in terms of systems theory and deep ecology, applying it to various social and ecological problems. Seeing these problems as manifestations of the "rampant, pathological individualism" that is a dominant feature of modern life, she takes it as a matter of urgency to show that the separate, isolated self is an illusion (1991b: 185). She hopes that the traditional way of viewing the self as a "skin-encapsulated ego" is being replaced by "wider constructs of self-identity and self-interest—by what you might call the ecological self or eco-self, co-extensive with the other beings and the life of our planet" (183). With Macy we come to the full articulation of the contemporary Buddhist conception of interdependence:

> Contemporary science, and systems theory in particular, goes
> farther in challenging old assumptions about a distinct, separate,
> continuous self, by showing that there is no logical or scientific basis
> for construing one part of the experienced world as "me" and the
> rest as "other." That is so because as open, self-organizing systems,
> our very breathing, acting and thinking arise in interaction with our
> shared world through the currents of matter, energy, and information
> that move through us and sustain us. In the web of relationships that

sustain these activities there is no clear line demarcating a separate, continuous self. (187–88)

She then incorporates these claims into the doctrines of *anātman* and dependent origination:

In much the same way as systems theory does, Buddhism undermines categorical distinctions between self and other and belies the concept of a continuous, self-existing entity. It then goes farther than systems theory in showing the pathogenic character of any reifications of the self. What the Buddha woke up to under the Bodhi tree was the paticca samuppada, the dependent co-arising of phenomena, in which you cannot isolate a separate, continuous self. (189)

Dependent origination is then turned into a mandate for an active—indeed activist—life, fully engaged in the world: "Far from the nihilism and escapism that is often imputed to the Buddhist path, this liberation, this awakening puts one *into* the world with a livelier, more caring sense of social engagement" (190). Such a view of the self, Macy asserts, "helps us recognize our imbeddedness in nature, overcomes our alienation from the rest of creation, and changes the way we can experience our self through an ever-widening process of identification," to the point where (quoting Naess) "the self [is] widened and deepened so that the protection of nature [is] felt and perceived as protection of our very selves" (191).

Macy not only sees the "ego-self" as an illusory product of the modern age, she sees it in terms of a universal process illustrated by a retelling of a narrative that might seem surprising coming from a Buddhist: the fall of man. In the early stages of our species, she says, human beings lived in womb-like "primal intimacy" with trees, rocks, and plants. From this came "the fall out of the Garden of Eden," the emergence of self-consciousness, individuality, and free will, and thus began the "lonely and heroic journey of the ego." The "distanced and observing eye" brought about science and systems of governance based on individual rights. Thus enriched, we can now "turn and recognize what we have been all along . . . we are our world knowing itself. . . . We can come home again—and participate in our world in a richer, more responsible and poignantly beautiful way than before, in our infancy" (1991b: 13–14). What is important in the historical lineages of Buddhist modernism is not that Macy would draw on a story from a tradition she has rejected but that this reimagining of the Genesis narrative is straight from the Romantics. Schelling, recall, glossed the fall of man as a separation from primordial unity with the absolute into individuated self-consciousness and the spiritual journey as a higher reintegration with it (1978 [1800]). Blake offers a similar view of the fall: man lived in perfect unity and brotherhood until the original sin, which is none other than the descent into individual selfhood, and entails fragmentation and alienation from other people and from nature. Redemption is the resurrection of humanity out of its solitary and dissatisfied state into unity—not the return to the oneness of humankind's infancy but a return that retains individuality while harmonizing with the whole.

Macy's recapitulation of this narrative suggests the importance to contemporary Buddhism in the West of the Weberian dynamics of disenchantment/ reenchantment of the world, which are here reconfigured into a universalized narrative. In addition to a Rousseauian longing for return to nature, community, and innocence, the implication is that the rationalizing, market-driven, differentiating processes of disenchanted modernity are a stage—the outer boundary—in the individuation and self-consciousness of humanity. We have now reached the juncture, the narrative suggests, where this individuation has become so self-destructive and fragmenting that it is suicidal, and now we must reintegrate, rediscovering our more primal, unitive relationship with the world. This formulation of Buddhist interdependence, therefore, is framed not just within the modern narrative of disenchantment but also within the wider Romantic narrative of the emergence and transcendence of self-consciousness, which is itself a reconfiguration of the biblical narrative of the fall of man.

Like Romanticism, the late modern Buddhist articulation of interdependence gravitates toward the large-scale questions that science asks while maintaining a suspicion of "reductive," as well as militarily or commercially driven, science. It continues the Romantics' scientific passion for discovering the "vital powers" that animate everything, as well as their critique of instrumental reason. It resists Cartesian dualism and its divesting the world of inherent meaning and attempts to resacralize the world by envisioning it as coextensive with human consciousness or animated by a universal consciousness. But it is also very much a product of the late modern world, drawing together a bricolage of resources, ancient and modern, to address current social and ecological issues. And its solution to all of them is to reperceive and reembrace the world as an interconnected web of life rather than a collection of isolated egos within a neutral environment. Thus interdependence in this iteration assumes a significance nearly opposite to that of the early Pali account. Far from a chain of causes and effects binding beings to rebirth in a world of suffering, today's interdependence implies a sacred matrix of mutual communality and coparticipation, the extended body of all beings. And, most significant here, this shift in meaning and valuation developed not only out of the Mahayana tradition's rethinking of Buddhahood and the infusion of East Asian sensibilities into Buddhism but also out of some of the fundamental dynamics of modernity.

Implications of Interdependence

Reenvisioning Karma and Rebirth

The implications of the contemporary Buddhist articulation of interdependence can sometimes be striking. It not only takes on new political and ethical significance in the modern world but also can shift the meanings of associated Buddhist doctrines—for example, karma and rebirth, two fundamental ones.

In classical portrayals of karma, nature responds to the individual's actions to produce circumstances resulting from those actions. Disease, floods, injury—or in contrast, a narrow escape from such things—may all be interpreted as the results (*phala*) of the individual's actions (karma). Variations on this view that nature responds directly to human action are pervasive in ancient and medieval worlds. Broadly construed, this understanding of the dialectic between humanity and nature is not limited to Asia but also manifests itself in countless examples in literature, for instance, earthquakes in response to tremendous events (the Buddha's awakening, Jesus' death). We may dismiss such things today as symbolic, but we cannot dismiss their important part in the way many people have understood their lives. The idea of random chance, while perhaps not unique to the modern period, is atypical in nonmodern societies. Solar eclipses, thunderstorms, illnesses, and coincidences have *meant* things, on a personal or communal level, that they have tended not to mean to those who subscribe to a scientific worldview. They were warnings, signs, or consequences.

The classical idea of karma is more a systematic regularization of nature's supposed responses to human action than a "natural law," as it has often been called. The underlying idea is that moral responses are intertwined with natural processes, and that they shape individuals' circumstances in direct response to their morally significant actions. There are indeed multiple causes and conditions that bring about particular fortunate or unfortunate circumstances in one's life; not all experiences are the result of prior karma. Some may be the result of particular physiologic conditions that are not karmic results of previous actions (SN 36.21). Karmic results, however, do directly shape a great deal of one's life. They determine the realm of life one will be reborn in, whether one is born into high or low social standing, and whether as an animal, human, or other order of life. And there are more specific correspondences between particular actions and characteristics a person acquires as a result. People who harm other creatures tend to be sickly in this or future lives, while those who do not are healthy. Those who are irritable tend to be ugly, while those who are not are handsome. Jealous people tend to be weak, while those free from jealousy are strong (MN 35). The early understanding of dependent origination was of a piece with this doctrine of karma, in that it described not so much how natural phenomena in the world arise but rather how beings have come to be born and reborn in various circumstances through their own karma.

The idea that the circumstances in one's life are primarily determined by one's past actions is obviously more difficult to accept today. The modern view of causality supposes that any event comes about through a multiplicity of causal trajectories that cannot be understood as governed primarily by an individual's morally significant actions. It may well be that a one's excessive drinking causes one to crash his car, and a modern Buddhist might use the language of karma to describe this. It is more difficult, however, to make a causal connection between one's excessive drinking and, say, getting hit by a bus after one has been sober for fifteen years. The traditional view of karma would have no trouble making this connection, while a modern scientific view would see the causal trajectory of the bus as unrelated to that of the person—until impact. One just happened to be at the wrong place at the wrong time. To bridge the gap between these two views, Buddhist modernists have often referred to karma in terms compatible with modern ideas of causality: she is abrasive, therefore people tend not to like her; he eats too much meat, therefore the heart attack was his karma. The Buddhist modernist, however, would not tend to think one's physical ugliness is the direct result of one's past irritability.

Some modern Buddhist thinkers appear largely to have abandoned traditional views of karma and rebirth in light of the contemporary transformation of the conception of interdependence. Thich Nhat Hanh offers surprising views of moral responsibility and rebirth in relation to "interbeing." Recall Nhat Hanh's formula for interbeing: any X is made of wholly of non-X elements. In his discussion of the *Heart Sutra* and interbeing, he offers the example of a prostitute in Manila. She is young, poor, and taken advantage of by many people. As a result, she feels shameful and wretched. But if she were to look at her "whole situation," she would see that she is the way she is because others—those who created her poverty, those who sold her into prostitution, those who hire her, we who ignore the problem—have all contributed to making her that way. "No one among us has clean hands. No one can claim it is not our responsibility. The girl in Manila is that way because of the way we are. Looking into the life of that young prostitute, we see the non-prostitute people" (1988: 33). Now a response of compassion rather than condemnation of the prostitute would be wholly justified within traditional Buddhist ethical frameworks. Moreover, we can obviously see the empirical truth of Nhat Hanh's contention that her situation is brought about by multiple causes and conditions that go beyond her personal responsibility. In effect, he points out the *systemic* causes of her circumstance. Clearly his intention is to employ the doctrine of interbeing to encourage society to take responsibility for the plight of the disadvantaged, not to reformulate the doctrine of karma. (Nhat Hanh is, after all, one of the founders of engaged Buddhism and one of the world's most prominent Buddhist activists.) A more traditional Buddhist analysis, however, would eventually have to come around to ascribing ultimate responsibility to the prostitute herself, for the doctrine of karma must affirm that people's circumstances are ultimately the results of their own past actions, even if the vehicles of bringing those circumstances about might be the unmeritorious actions of others. Through the doctrine of interbeing, moral responsibility is decentered from the solitary individual and spread throughout the entire social system. This is an important element of engaged Buddhism, which again emphasizes systemic and not just individual causes of suffering.

Nhat Hanh reenvisions another key doctrine in light of interbeing: "in our former lives, we were rocks, clouds, and trees. . . . This is not just Buddhist; it is scientific. We humans are a young species. We were plants, we were trees, and now we have become humans. . . . We are continually arising from Mother Earth, being nurtured by her, and then returning to her" (2000: 85–86). This account makes no mention of rebirth in the traditional Buddhist sense, and "former lives" here assume a metaphorical meaning. In discussing the "no birth and no death" doctrine of the *Heart Sutra*, he says:

> We cannot conceive of the birth of anything. There is only continuation. . . . Look back further and you will see that you not only exist in your father and mother, but you also exist in your grandparents and in your great grandparents. . . . I know in the past I have been a cloud, a river, and the air. . . . This is the history of life on earth. We have been gas, sunshine, water, fungi, and plants. . . . Nothing can be born and also nothing can die. (1988: 21)

Interbeing means that everything—humans, rocks, water—is dependent on nonhuman, nonrock, nonwater elements. All of these elements combine into protean forms that then dissipate and become something else, and every being is just one of an infinite number of forms the universe takes in its endless manifestations, like waves on the water. Our true life, though, is that of the water—the living cosmos as a whole—not the waves, its transient forms. Death, therefore, is not to be feared, for all of the elements of which we are made will after our death continue to exist in other forms—trees, flowers, rocks, other people, etc. Again the "I" expands to include everything. Even though what we transform into may be dust, every dust speck reflects the whole cosmos, and the cosmos is reflected in every dust speck. Here the traditional idea of the continuity of a karmically constituted life-trajectory from birth to death to rebirth is replaced by the dispersion of a being at death into the vast, interrelated cosmos to be "reborn" as any (and all) of the other forms while at the same time being one with the whole.

These ideas of the dispersion of karmic responsibility into the social system and the dispersion of the individual at death into all of the universe are significant innovations in Buddhist thought by one of the most influential contemporary Buddhists. This demythologization of karma is perfectly intelligible in terms of modern social analysis, and this vision of "rebirth" is amenable to a scientific view of the universe. The latter vision also recalls nineteenth-century Romanticism. William Cullen Bryant (1794–1878), a Massachusetts lawyer and poet reputed for his knowledge of science who is often considered a "prototranscendentalist," wrote a poem, "Thanatopsis," that is considered emblematic of the emerging nineteenth-century view of nature. In it he vividly portrays death as a merging with the elements of the natural world, rejoining all who have gone before in a fusion of human, animal, plant, and rock (ll. 22–33):

> Earth, that nourished thee, shall claim
> Thy growth, to be resolved to earth again,
> And, lost each human trace, surrendering up
> Thine individual being, shalt thou go
> To mix forever with the elements,
> To be a brother to the insensible rock
> And to the sluggish clod, which the rude swain
> Turns with his share, and treads upon. The oak
> Shall send his roots abroad, and pierce thy mould.
>
> Yet not to thine eternal resting-place
> Shalt thou retire alone, nor couldst thou wish
> Couch more magnificent.

The poem proffers no notion of an individual afterlife but rather a postmortem kinship with all of nature and with the living beings that have gone before. Therefore, he advises, "approach thy grave / Like one who wraps the drapery of his couch / About him, and lies down to pleasant dreams" (ll. 79–81). The likeness to Nhat Hanh's mingling of entities in an all-encompassing life shared by all things, such that death is simply the transformation of one manifestation of life into another, is clear.

Many Buddhist modernists do maintain more traditional views of karma and rebirth. Nevertheless, modernity often opens a space for radical reinterpretation and for a wider continuum of hermeneutic options regarding key doctrines. Nhat Hanh's rethinking of karma and rebirth shows how the elaboration of one concept—interdependence—can exert a magnetic pull on others, reconfiguring the significance of a whole cluster of ideas and practices.

Is It Buddhist?

Developing a vision that works to address the myriad social and environmental problems of our time is of course a more urgent endeavor than tracing that vision's history. Yet the historian must still ask whether this Buddhism-inspired articulation of interdependence—in its contemporary forms, with its infusion of western ideas and practices and its sometimes radical reinterpretations of traditional doctrine—is really Buddhist. Some scholars, in fact, have argued that the environmentalist strains of contemporary Buddhism are not ultimately compatible with traditional doctrine (Blum 2005; Harris 1991, 1997).

I will look briefly at two issues in this regard, one having to do with ethics and the other with the sacrality of the natural world. First, is the idea of an artificially bounded ego that can, through meditation and cultivation of compassion, expand its boundaries to include a wider and wider sphere of entities, not only in its ethical scope but in its feeling of selfhood a specifically Buddhist idea? Buddhist ethics clearly mandate compassion for all sentient beings bound together in a chain of conditioned dependence. It is not at all clear, however, that dependent origination in premodern traditions is the basis for the modern concept that the reason for ethical behavior is because the boundaries of self and other are ultimately artificial—hurting you is essentially hurting myself (and everything else), therefore I should not hurt you. It is not present in the Pali canon or South Asian Mahayana literature, which often discusses ethics but never, as far as I have found, bases ethics on interdependence in this manner. Eighth-century philosopher Śāntideva's exposition of altruism through empathetic identification with others is probably the closest we find: "Just as the body, which has many parts owing to its division into arms and so forth, should be protected as a whole, so should this entire world, which is differentiated and yet has the nature of the same suffering and happiness" (1997: 100). The point, though, seems to be that one should identify with others' suffering *as if* it were one's own. The metaphor of the body here is not based on an assertion of the ontological unity with others or with the cosmos.

In East Asian thought, however, particularly in Huayan and Huayan-influenced Buddhism, we occasionally find passages like this one by the Korean monk Gihwa (1376–1433): "Humaneness implies the interpenetration of heaven and earth and the myriad things into a single body, wherein there is no gap whatsoever. If you deeply embody this principle, then there cannot be a justification for inflicting harm on even the most insignificant of creatures."[6] Here is an explicit assertion of ethical obligation based on the underlying unity of things in a single "body." Such an explicit link between the ontology of interdependence (or interpenetration) and ethics, is far as I have found, rare (and even this passage is so far unpublished). This sentiment, however, bears a striking resemblance to some found in nineteenth-century American thought—for example: "We find that we are all members of the one great body, and that no portion of the body can be harmed without all the other portions suffering thereby." This passage, which would be quite at home in contemporary Zen or engaged Buddhist writings, comes from the 1897 bestseller *In Tune with the Infinite,* by Ralph Waldo Trine (1995: 169–70). His influences were leftist, spiritualist, and Transcendentalist; he brought Emerson's pantheistic tendencies, New Thought, Christian social gospel, and a hodgepodge of eclectic spiritualities of his day to bear not only on finding inner peace but also on serving his fellow human beings (as well as nonhuman ones—he was active in the Society for Prevention of Cruelty to Animals). This specific assertion of his rationale for ethics is clearly rooted in the Romantic-Transcendentalist cosmologies I have discussed (combined with neo-Vedantic nondualism).[7] What is noteworthy is that it was almost certainly *not* influenced by Huayan or other Mahayana thought, which was not widely understood by American thinkers of his time. The influence, rather, was the other way around. The contemporary Buddhist ethic of interdependence, though it had occasional precedents in pre-modern Asian Buddhism, likely worked its way into contemporary Buddhist thought through remnants of the Romantic-Transcendentalist line of thinking that resonated with similar ideas in Huayen and Zen thought. In other words, this ethic was largely a *potential implication* of the traditional Buddhist doctrines of interdependence—an implication that was only developed into a fully articulated ethic in combination with the modern discourses of Romanticism-Transcendentalism and systems theory.

Second, there is debate on whether canonical texts refer to this wider identification of self and other as identification with the Earth or with the natural world per se. Mark Blum insists that there is no notion of "the expansion of self through a process of identification with the world" in traditional forms of Asian Buddhism. To the contrary, liberation is articulated in terms of a "rhetoric of nonidentification" with any form whatsoever, including those of nature. "Even Dōgen's statements about the self and object merging are not specific to merging with nature or natural objects but with any object of attention. The point, therefore, is one about the mind rather than about mountains and rivers" (30–31). There is room for debate here regarding interpretation of Dōgen. Certainly there is a dialectic in Zen thought between disidentifying with constructed conceptions of things and reidentifying with a larger, all-encompassing unity, Buddha-nature. Yet Blum is right to question whether Buddha-nature, despite the Chinese inclusion of grasses and rocks within its scope, should be seen as the natural world per se. And the idea of identifying with an all-encompassing, ultimate reality is simply not operative in certain forms of Indic Mahayana or in any forms of Theravada. In fact, one of its main sources is neo-Vedanta thought and perennial philosophy, which, as noted, have often been amalgamated with Buddhism in the modern period.

My point here is not to make claims about authenticity or inauthenticity but to recognize that whatever its various components, there is something *new* in the contemporary articulation of interdependence, something emerging in response to the unique circumstances of the modern world and attempting to answer questions that simply could not have arisen in the time of the Buddha, Nāgārjuna, or Dōgen. Let us reask the question, then. Is the contemporary articulation of interdependence an unalloyed rendition of canonical and classical understandings? Harris and Blum are generally correct in saying that it is not. It is something unique to this age—a hybrid construction that draws on Asian and western sources, synthesizing them into a novel conception. So one might be tempted to argue that it is "inauthentic." But this would be to grant a static, essentialized meaning to canonical texts, to the normative interpretation of one school or another, or to a particular moment in the history of Asian forms of Buddhism. The historian of religion, qua historian, should not merely recapitulate sectarian or even canonical rhetorics of authenticity but examine what practitioners *do* with the texts and other elements of the tradition. The reconfiguration of traditional doctrine and practice in response to novel historical circumstances is the norm in the development of religions. Texts and doctrines are never static but are repeatedly reappropriated to deal with changing situations. Certain themes fall away into irrelevance, others emerge as salient, and both are given new meanings that arise in a dialectical relationship with changing political, economic, social, and material realities, as well as other traditions. The text or doctrine, then, is not a static reference point but a dynamic process whose meanings are always being reconstituted. This dynamic process of tradition-in-change establishes what Buddhism *is* empirically.

There are limits, of course. Texts have built-in boundaries for plausible interpretation: no informed person will ever try to argue that Buddhism espouses the doctrines that everything is permanent, that there is an individual and eternal soul, or that there are no causes and effects. Moreover, if interdependence in the most novel senses were only embraced by Californian Buddhists while all other Buddhists espoused conservative views, we might see it as a peripheral development insignificant to the main thrust of Buddhism in the modern world. But when leading Buddhist figures, along with a mass of laity and sympathizers, begin to embrace a novel interpretation, practice, or idea, it should alert the scholar that an important reconstruction of doctrine is underway and that a new normativity could be emerging. And if the most prominent Buddhists in the world seem to be embracing a reconception of interdependence, it would seem inevitably to be—or at least *becoming*—Buddhist.

Simply to dismiss the current environmental and ethical discourse of Buddhist interdependence as an inadequate representation of historical Buddhism, therefore, would fail to take seriously the process of modernity as it manifests on the ground, in Buddhism or any historical religion. Although the late modern Buddhist discourse inevitably draws on historical sources, its starting point is the pressing environmental crisis of the present. Like virtually all normative religious reflection, this discourse is practitioners' constructive response to an unprecedented situation, not a historiographical endeavor. Pointing out the incongruities between ancient and modern cosmologies, while crucial, is not more historically important than showing how the often radical reconstitution of doctrine in terms of present circumstances has attempted to bridge these incongruities. The history of religions is precisely the history of such reconstitutions of doctrine and practice, which are themselves reconstitutions of prior versions.

Cultural Currency and Contestation

"So it's like another whole take on interconnectedness?" American *vipassanā* teacher Sharon Salzberg asked Daniel Goleman in response to his description of "mirror neurons" in the brain that attune individuals' emotional states to those of others (Salzberg 2006: 67). It is a question that has been asked of countless recent theories and findings in sociology, economics, quantum physics, and life sciences, all of which seem to confirm the central insight of Buddhism—interdependence. To see these new theories merely as confirming the traditional understanding, though, would be anachronistic, for the harmony between ancient Buddhist interdependence and modern interdependencies is produced in part by the way the former has been elaborated in terms of the latter. Contemporary Buddhism has reached out to embrace multiple late modern interdependencies, claiming them for its own and synergistically weaving its own insights into countless contemporary ideas and realities, like mirror neurons tuning themselves to the emotional ambience of a crowded room. The currency the Buddhist concept of interdependence enjoys today comes not only from its intermixing with explicitly theoretical frameworks like systems theory but also from the term's more amorphous resonance with a central fact of our time: the interconnectedness of the various natural, national, corporate, and biological entities throughout the world. The fact that in recent decades "interdependence" has come to stand for the Buddhist position on virtually everything (I have not found this term used in such a way before the 1960s) reflects the currency of similar concepts in contemporary discourse on many other subjects. In the age of the web, the network, the matrix, the nexus, the system, and the complex, the thing-in-isolation, it seems, is a thing of the past.

As has been the case with most hybrid elements of Buddhist modernism, however, the adaptation of interdependence to the conditions of late modernity has not been a matter of unidirectional accommodation to the times. Buddhism also contributes unique elements to the discourses of modernity that may challenge or augment western approaches to interdependence. It brings, for example, rich resources for a critique of the definition of human well-being in terms of fulfillment of desires through the buying and consuming of products. Buddhism also offers a view of ethical responsibility toward all orders of life. Buddhists today are attempting to bring such contributions to bear on contemporary realities. The degree to which they will have an impact on the discourses of modernity is as not yet clear.

For all of the concept's cultural cachet, however, the late modern interpretation of interdependence is not universally accepted in the Buddhist world and is subject to contestation, even in North America, where it is perhaps most widely accepted. Some contemporary Buddhists, especially from the Theravada tradition, have criticized the contemporary interpretation of interdependence, through appealing to more traditional doctrines in Pali literature. In a popular Buddhist periodical, an essay displaying impressive historical acumen by the American-born Theravada monk Bhikkhu Thanissaro has traced the popular ideas of "interconnectedness, wholeness, and ego-transcendence" from the German Romantics (especially Schiller and Schleiermacher) through Emerson, William James, Jung, and Abraham Maslow. Many popular ideas about Buddhism, Thanissaro argues, come from these figures and are quite different from some of the "original principles of the dharma" (2002: 109). "Buddhist Romanticism," he argues, masks the Buddhist teaching that "all interconnectedness is essentially unstable, and any happiness based on this instability is an invitation to suffering. True happiness has to go beyond interdependence and interconnectedness to the unconditioned" (112). Similarly, Andrew Olendzki, director of the Barre Center for Buddhist Studies in Massachusetts and editor of *Insight Journal*, cautions that "the more interconnected we become, the more bound in the net of conditioned phenomena we may find ourselves. I think the Buddha was pointing a way out of all this, but it is not through getting further connected. It has more to do with getting less connected, less entangled, and less attached" (2005: 3).

Moreover, while some Asian teachers embrace the contemporary, world-affirming view of interdependence, many insist on more traditional interpretations of samsara and dependent origination. Andrew Cohen quotes the contemporary Tibetan teacher Chatrul Rinpoche as saying: "the world has no real essence; it's meaningless, the whole of *samsara* is just meaningless. In fact, if you have complete realization of the faults of *samsara,* that *is* realization. That means you have gone beyond *samsara* to understanding that this world has no ultimate meaning" (Cohen 2000). Similarly, Mahāsi Sayādaw, as we have seen, gives a traditional exposition of life in the wheel of rebirth as "dreadful": "Every effort should therefore be made to acquaint oneself with the miserable conditions of *Samsara* and then to work for an escape from this incessant cycle, and for the attainment of Nirvana" (quoted in Fronsdal 1998: 171). This is clearly far from Macy's seeing the world as "lover" and as "self."

Such fissures in the interpretation of the meaning and significance of interdependence highlight tensions between traditional and modernist iterations of Buddhism. They also recapitulate differences between the Theravada and Mahayana traditions, as the Mahayana is more amenable to idealist interpretations, and between various traditions unique to geographical areas within Asia, as the East Asian traditions are more affirming of positive conceptions of the natural world than the Indian and Tibetan ones. Such tensions suggest that the meanings of interdependence and the valuation of the phenomenal world will continue to shift and change in the contestations and negotiations between tradition and modernity that continue to shape Buddhism today.

7

Meditation and Modernity

Nowhere, beloved, can world exist but within.
Life passes in transformation. And, ever diminishing,
vanishes what's outside. Where once was a lasting house,
up starts some invented structure across our vision, as fully
at home among concepts as though it still stood in a brain. . . .
Temples he knows no longer. We're now more secretly saving
such lavish expenses of the heart. Nay, even where one survives,
one single thing once prayed or tended or knelt to,
it's reaching, just as it is, into the unseen world.
Many perceive it no more, but neglect the advantage
of building it grandlier now, with pillars and statues, *within!*
          —Rainer Maria Rilke, *Duino Elegies* (Seventh Elegy)

Modern Transformations of Meditation

Most casual observers and many ardent practitioners of Buddhism,
particularly in the West, would identify meditation as the essential
Buddhist practice. Yet, as noted, while meditation has always been
considered necessary to achieving awakening, only a small minority
of Buddhists actually practice it in any serious way. The vast majority
of Asian Buddhists have practiced the dharma through ethics, ritual,
and service to the *sangha*. Although provisions have sometimes been
made for laity to practice meditation—and some important figures

have explicitly advocated it—it has generally been considered an arduous endeavor taken up by small number of monastics who specialize in contemplative practice.

Today, however, throughout Asia as well as the West, many lay Buddhists and Buddhist sympathizers—not to mention Christians, Jews, Hindus, and secular people—now practice various forms of Buddhist meditation and mindfulness techniques. While the practices of most Buddhists throughout the world still consist primarily of following its ethical precepts and performing rituals for gaining karmic merit, a growing number of educated, middle-class men and women in Asia and the West now consider meditation essential to their practice of Buddhism. Contemporary dharma teachers routinely invite people of all religious traditions and none to practice meditation and mindfulness for a wide variety of purposes, including increasing awareness, compassion, peace of mind, and even enhancing their practice of other faiths. Western Buddhists and Buddhist sympathizers have often been the most eager to extract meditation from the larger doctrinal and praxiological frameworks of Buddhism, yet widespread lay meditation is also an important phenomenon in modernized strata of Asian Buddhism—indeed, modern lay meditation movements originated there before being exported to the West. Monasteries in Japan, Taiwan, Sri Lanka, and across much of the Buddhist world now offer meditation instruction to laypeople, while uniquely modern "meditation centers," where people can take classes and attend retreats, have sprung up all over the world.

Contemporary literature geared toward laity and Buddhist sympathizers often presents meditation as a mode of internal observation and analysis akin to empirical science and not bound by authority and tradition. Closely allied with modern psychology, it is sometimes described as a psychological method for accessing deeper, unconscious recesses of the mind in order to expose unconscious constraints and negative dispositions so that they may be transformed or released to allow creative and compassionate forces naturally residing in the mind to flow forth unimpeded. This transformation of internal dispositions, rather than the following of externally imposed rules, is the root of ethical behavior, according to many contemporary Buddhist teachers. No longer just a technique of transcendence for ascetics who have renounced the worldly life, meditation has acquired the purpose of fostering deeper appreciation of everyday activities and of cultivating skillful, robust, and mindful engagement in life. Rather than exclusively a means of achieving awakening in a traditional sense, it has in some cases been reconfigured as a technique for self-discovery, self-discipline, self-transformation, and physical and mental health outside of doctrinal and sectarian formulations. Meditation has also become democratized and individualized in a way quite foreign to all but the recent history of Buddhism.[1] Book culture and widespread literacy have a great deal to do with this. When meditation manuals were written in ancient India and medieval Tibet, the only ones with access to them were a small number of literate, educated elites, again usually monastics. Now, despite the frequent assertions that one must ultimately learn from an experienced teacher, a plethora of how-to books on meditation offering step-by-step instructions with diagrams illustrating correct postures and mudras rests on the shelves of most bookstores, inviting housewives, professionals, laborers, and college students to cross their legs, straighten their spines, and follow their breath.

Paradoxically, while meditation is often considered the heart of Buddhism, it is also deemed the element most detachable from the tradition itself. It has in some sectors become disembedded from the Buddhist tradition and rearticulated as a technique of self-investigation, awareness, personal satisfaction, and ethical reflection, taking on a life of its own, in some cases altogether outside of Buddhist communities. Psychotherapists and physicians prescribe Buddhist-derived meditation and mindfulness practices for stress reduction, lowering of blood pressure, and pain management. Buddhist meditation is taught in prisons, hospitals, and schools, and consultants integrate mindfulness practice into programs for increasing worker productivity and decreasing job-related stress. More than any other facet of Buddhism, meditation and mindfulness are presented as psychological, spiritual, or scientific techniques rather than as *religious* practices.

This way of thinking about meditation as a technique detachable from the wider ethical, social, and cosmological contexts of Buddhism is implicit in the nineteenth century and becomes explicit in some of the earlier western discussions of meditation that began to be written in the mid–twentieth century. Rear Admiral E. H. Shattock, a British naval officer who studied meditation in a Theravada monastery near Rangoon, wrote: "Meditation . . . is a really practical occupation: it is in no sense necessarily a religious one, though it is usually thought of as such. It is itself basically academic, practical, and profitable" (1960: 17). More recently, Jon Kabat-Zinn, a psychotherapist whose Mindfulness-Based Stress Reduction program has adapted Buddhist meditation to a variety of medical and psychological applications, echoes this view, contending that "[mindfulness] has nothing to do with Buddhism per se or with becoming a Buddhist, but it has everything to do with waking up and living in harmony with the world. It has to do with examining who we are, with questioning our view of the world and our place in it, and with cultivating some appreciation for the fullness of each moment we are alive" (1994: 3). This detraditionalization of meditation is not exclusive to western interpreters: S. N. Goenka, a well-known Indian Burmese lay teacher of *vipassanā* meditation, insists that

what he teaches is "universal." The Buddha, he argues, did not teach a sectarian doctrine or a "religion," did not in fact teach "Buddhism," but rather "an
art of living." "He never established or taught any religion, any 'ism.' He never
instructed his followers to practice any rites or rituals, any blind or empty formalities. Instead, he taught just to observe nature as it is, by observing reality
inside" (2007). "The day 'Buddhism' happened," he insists, "it devalued the
teachings of the Buddha. It was a universal teaching and that made it sectarian"
(2000: 49–50). While not all meditation teachers today share Goenka's explicit
antitraditionalism, many present meditation as a freestanding way of discovering things as they are, more an "interior science" than a religious practice.

The renewed emphasis on meditation, the bringing of meditation to the
laity, and the insistence on mindfulness as universal and nonsectarian have
been central in a number of reform movements and trends in twentieth-century
Buddhism. Most of these have taken place within established traditions, but
the insight meditation (*vipassanā*) movement, emerging from the Theravada
traditions of Burma (Myanmar), Thailand, and Sri Lanka, has become a kind
of modern meditation tradition of its own. It takes the *Sutta on the Foundations
of Mindfulness* (*Satipaṭṭhāna Sutta*) as its central text, and it has become an increasingly independent movement in which meditation is offered absent the
ritual, liturgical, and merit-making elements integral to Theravada Buddhism,
with which westerners often consider it synonymous. Joseph Goldstein, Jack
Kornfield, and Sharon Salzberg, and other American teachers who studied with
Burmese and other Southeast Asian teachers have made *vipassanā* especially
popular in North America. The American *vipassanā* movement is largely independent of ties to Asian institutions, and there is no national body that certifies
teachers, making the movement, as scholar and *vipassanā* teacher Gil Fronsdal
puts it, "inherently open, amorphous, and arbitrarily defined" (1998: 165).

This elevation of the role of meditation over merit making, chanting, ritual, and devotion is, again, not a simply a western product. One of the most
important founders of the modern *vipassanā* movement, the Burmese monk
Mahāsi Sayādaw (1904–82), like many modern meditation teachers, focused
almost exclusively on the practice of meditation and the goal of awakening,
deemphasizing ritual and monasticism.

Likewise, Zen meditation (*zazen*) has in some cases become disembedded
from its traditional institutional context of the Japanese, Chinese, Vietnamese,
or Korean monastery. Popular accounts of Zen have adopted a similarly univer-
salistic tone, presenting meditation as a way not just of achieving a uniquely
Buddhist goal but of realizing a universal reality to which all religions, along
with some secular philosophies, aspire. D. T. Suzuki, as noted, insisted that
this reality transcended all cultural specificity and therefore was not uniquely

Buddhist, although he suggested that it achieved its highest expression in Japanese Zen culture. The idea that the goal of meditation is not specifically Buddhist, and that "Zen" itself is common to all religions, has encouraged the understanding of *zazen* as detachable from the complex traditions of ritual, liturgy, priesthood, and hierarchy common in institutional Zen settings. Today, while many traditional Zen monasteries around the globe still hold to largely traditional structures of doctrine and practice, *zazen* also floats freely across a number of cultures and subcultures, particularly in the West, where grassroots Zen groups with little or no institutional affiliation meet in homes, colleges, and churches.

Tibetan traditions have tended to be more conservative, insisting on initiation into the more complex forms of meditation, but laicization and detraditionalization of meditation are in no way absent. Tibetan forms of meditation have gone rather abruptly from being the province of a small number of specialist monks in Himalayan hermitages to being offered widely to the public in countries all over the globe. Numerous diaspora teachers in India, Europe, and North America now teach meditation to monks and laity alike. Some Tibetan teachers in exile have also been innovators in adapting meditation to modern, secular lifestyles. Chögyam Trungpa's Shambhala training, for example, offers methods of mind training stripped of traditional rituals and requiring minimal doctrinal commitment. The Dalai Lama also encourages non-Buddhists to practice meditation, offering it as a Buddhist contribution to a turbulent world, one that cultivates peace of mind, compassion, and ethical responsibility in anyone, regardless of religious commitments.[2]

This privatization, deinstitutionalization, and detraditionalization of meditation is a significant development in the history of Buddhism. While meditation, or the lack of it, continues as it has for centuries within many institutional contexts around the globe, its place and significance beyond the monastery has changed considerably in the modern era. There are a number of prima facie reasons for the growing prominence of Buddhist and other kinds of meditation among middle-class professionals around the world. Popular literature widely attests to its bid to be an ancient antidote to the new kinds of stresses in the modern workplace and to the frenetic pace of modern life. Perhaps it is not surprising that people of Asia taking on such stresses would turn to their own cultural and religious resources for assistance. But what is it in the cultural resources of Europe and North America that has made meditation viable? I have explored a number of preunderstandings that disposed westerners to receptivity toward Buddhism as well as particular reinterpretations of it. Scholars have also explored the meditation-friendly environment created by the culture of nineteenth- and early twentieth-century eclectic spiritualities in North America and Europe—Swedenborgianism, New Thought, neo-Vedanta, transcendentalism, and Theosophy (Albanese 2007; Almond 1988; Schmidt 2005; Tweed 2000). In the rest of this chapter, I will explore how Buddhism—and especially meditation—is placed within what social thinkers have sometimes called the "subjective turn" of modernity, that is, a shift in western consciousness across a number of cultural spheres toward greater attention to the interior life and personal experience and away from institutions and external authority. This shift is implicit in the rise of western individualism, with its suspicion of authority and institutions, and provides, I will argue, part of both the tacit and explicit ideological structure within which Buddhist meditation has been reimagined and transformed. It has created spaces for Buddhist meditation to be interpreted across three important discourses of modernity: Romanticism, psychology, and scientific rationalism. Examining how these discourses have informed the modern interpretation of meditation will help to illuminate how Buddhist meditation has assumed unprecedented functions, meanings, and purposes in the modern world.

The Subjective Turn

Despite the assertion that we have come across repeatedly that "the East" is spiritual, subjective, and intuitive, while "the West" is materialistic, rational, and extraverted, many recent thinkers have elucidated a shift inherent in western modernity toward an increased attention to subjectivity, selfhood, and the mind. Alongside, indeed in reaction to, the West's extraordinary industrial and technological development and its explosion in scientific knowledge, we find also what Taylor has called a "massive subjective turn" that begins in earnest in the seventeenth and eighteenth centuries. Theorists of modernity have declared this turn toward interiority a new thematization of subjectivity, even the making of a new kind of selfhood, constituted by increased self-reflexivity—making one's own experience an explicit object of reflection and becoming aware of self-awareness itself.[3] While some claims about the radical novelty of the modern self are perhaps exaggerated, no doubt something new has developed in this age. If this new sense of selfhood consists in a turn toward the subject and increased reflexivity, surely this is an important site at which to understand the meeting of modernity and meditation—itself a realm of intensive subjective scrutiny.

The subjective turn has taken place in Romantic, psychological, and rationalist modalities, and Buddhist modernism draws on all of them. First, some elements of the subjective turn that have roots in Romanticism. These are manifest, for instance, in the nineteenth-century esoteric movements that were so crucial to the development of Buddhist modernism and continue today in the New Age movement, "spiritualities of life," neo-paganism, and some loose articulations of Buddhism and Hinduism. All of these movements embody Romanticism's tension between fierce individualism and cosmic unity. They see the ego as a lower form of selfhood and posit higher forms of cosmic identity in unity or interrelation with all things. They contain echoes of some Romantics' suspicion of religious and political institutions and their claims to authority, placing ultimate authority instead in individual intuition. Inner freedom and self-expression are paramount: one must find one's authentic voice, one's own inner truth, and express it freely in art and everyday life. This perspective also embraces perennialist assumptions: all religions are different paths to the same ultimate reality; therefore, adherence to particular traditions is looser and more eclectic. One can select elements of different traditions and patch them together according to one's individual needs. In the 1930s, Ernst Troeltsch identified this orientation as "religious romanticism" and saw it at work in the interiorization of Christianity. He understood this phenomenon to be a bricolage of Christian and Romantic ideas under the influence of the "Naturalistic Monism of the nature philosophers, and Brahmanic and Buddhist ideas." Religious romanticism, he said, consisted in "the coalescence of the fully developed religious 'inwardness' and individuality with the aestheticism of individuality, with the differentiation of the altogether individual artistic feeling." This he saw as the "secret religion of the educated classes" (1931: 793–95).

Sociologists have often tied this interior turn to the confrontation with pluralism and the loss of faith in public institutions, be they religious, social, or political. Even a century ago, sociologist Goerg Simmel saw this trend toward inwardness and posited its source in the increasing instability of the modern world: "The subjectivism of modern personal life . . . is merely the expression of [the fact that] . . . the vast, intricate, sophisticated culture of things, of institutions, of objectified ideas robs the individual of any consistent inner relationship to culture as a whole, and casts him back again on his own resources" (1976 [1909]: 251). Peter Berger discussed this trend when it was perhaps at its peak in the counterculture of the 1960s in North America and Europe; not coincidentally, Buddhist and Hindu meditation was attaining unprecedented attention in the West at the time. Berger argued that in frustration about the state of the world and with a sense of impotence regarding the course of global events, many rejected the institutional and communal facets of religion, turning from public to privatized spirituality and developing individualized forms of religious practice tailored to personal desires and market-driven forces. With the relativization of orthodoxy, the breakdown of unquestioned normativity and structures of authority, and the proliferation of worldviews and ways of being, modern individuals were thrown back on their own personal experiences and decisions, with the internal becoming the primary locus of significance.

> The modern individual's experience of a plurality of social worlds relativizes every one of them. Consequently the institutional order undergoes a certain loss of reality. The "accent of reality" consequently shifts from the objective order of institutions to the realm of subjectivity. Put differently, the individual's experience of himself becomes more real to him than his experience of the objective social world. Therefore, the individual seeks to find his "foothold" in reality in himself rather than outside himself. . . . Subjectivity acquires previously unconceived "depths." (Berger et al. 1973: 77–78)

While such accounts often underestimate the degree to which modern individuals are still subject to various kinds of authority, institutional mandates, communal norms, and traditional cosmologies, they do highlight the importance of the modern self-perception among certain populations—specifically, Troeltsch's liberal "educated classes" (those most responsible for the construction of Buddhist modernism)—of the individual as autonomous and guided morally and behaviorally by internal sources.

Taylor sees this modern individualism as rooted in the "eighteenth-century notion that all human beings are endowed with an innate moral sense, an intuitive feeling for what is right and wrong" (1991: 14). This idea, he argues, is essential to the development of an individualism that sees "self-determining freedom" as the goal: the idea that I must decide for myself what is good, important, and of value, independent of external influence. One must be "true to oneself" and seek one's own fulfillment by discovering meaning within oneself. Robert Bellah, Christopher Lasch, and others have famously critiqued this orientation as narcissistic and conducive to social and political apathy, while both Taylor and Leigh Schmidt argue that there are redeeming social and political values inherent in it, however much they may have become obscured (Bellah et al. 1985; Lasch 1991 [1979]; Schmidt 2005; Taylor 1991). What is important here is simply to note that Bellah's argument that the mandate declaring that "each individual must work out his own ultimate solutions" without churches "imposing on him a prefabricated set of answers," as well as the implicit notion that "culture and personality themselves have come to be viewed as endlessly revisable," is clearly important to understanding the integration of Buddhism into modernity (Bellah 1963: 374, quoted in Woodhead and Heelas 2000: 349). Buddhism, according to many modernist interpretations, imposes no answers but invites self-discovery, interior exploration, and inner freedom.

And since individuals are free to collect and assimilate their own resources in their autonomous pursuit of truth—to construct what Durkheim called "a free private, optional religion, fashioned according to one's own needs"—not only they themselves but the traditions from which they collect ideas and practices are "endlessly revisable": one can take what is of use in a tradition (in this case, meditation) and disregard the rest (institutions, rituals, explicit ethical rules, etc.).

Under such conditions, meditation could be extracted from its cultural and religious contexts and seen as a matter of subjective personal development. Contemporary representations of Buddhism are often pressed into this mold. Sheldon Kopp's popular 1972 book *If You Meet the Buddha on the Road, Kill Him!* interprets a famous Zen koan along these lines:

> The Zen Master warns: "If you meet the Buddha on the road, kill him!" This admonition points up that no meaning that comes from outside of ourselves is real. The Buddhahood of each of us has already been obtained. We need only recognize it. Philosophy, religion, patriotism, all are empty idols. The only meaning in our lives is what we each bring to them. Killing the Buddha on the road means destroying the hope that anything outside of ourselves can be our master (1972: 140).

This interpretation has become normative in Buddhist modernism. The nonconformist antics of the Zen masters in the canonical literature, the Buddha's injunction to his disciples to "be lamps unto yourselves," his warning to the Kālāmas not to accept teachings without personal verification, his rejection of his own birth tradition in favor of seeking individual awakening alone at the foot of a tree—all of these elements of Buddhism are magnetically drawn into the modern narrative of self-determining individualism, lifted out of their broader cultural and communal contexts.

Despite the examples of individualistic impulses just listed, numerous ethnographic and historical studies suggest that Buddhism—even Buddhist meditation—has always been a communal as well as individual endeavor. There are strong bonds of support within the *sangha*, which is itself embedded in the wider community of laity. Even when Buddhism has functioned as a countercultural movement, it has seldom resembled the free-form, private spiritualities of today. Modernist interpretations of meditation are nestled within a network of tacit attitudes and assumptions derived from modern western individualism. Thus meditation comes to be seen as a species of individual spiritual exploration, open-ended interior probing, and psychological and physiological self-maintenance rather than as a means to the traditional goal of achieving nirvana and transcending the realms of rebirth. Meditation is sometimes described as a technique to foster the kinds of autonomy implicit in modern, western notions of the individual (more on this later). This articulation of the purposes, significance, and application of meditation is a new and important development in the history of Buddhism, one that has brought it decisively into one of the most visible modern discourses of interiority—as well as one of the most influential models for interpreting Buddhism: that of psychology.[4]

Meditation and Psychoanalysis

The school of western psychological thought that was the first and most important to enfold Buddhism within its hermeneutic milieu was psychoanalysis. As noted, Buddhist modernism deploys analytic psychology to demythologize deities, reconceiving them as archetypes in the mind. Another way psychoanalysis meets Buddhism is through an interpretation of meditation and its relation to the unconscious. One of the most influential views of meditation to emerge from the psychoanalytic tradition is that, like psychoanalysis itself, it opens up the unconscious to consciousness and in doing so frees the individual from destructive habits and repressed contents of mind. This psychological model of liberation, as noted, commences with D. T. Suzuki's assertion that the way toward liberation is into the unconscious, which he presents as a kind of portal leading eventually to the free space of awakening. Erich Fromm expanded on this idea, solidifying the psychoanalytic interpretation of Buddhism, especially Zen, in his book *Zen Buddhism and Psychoanalysis*, coauthored by Suzuki. Fromm offered the hypothesis that Zen enables the "full recovery of the unconscious," unlike psychoanalysis, which only seeks to recover sectors of the unconscious that are the basis of symptoms. Freud believed the best that psychoanalysis can do is make people somewhat less neurotic by revealing the unconscious bases for particular symptoms; Fromm saw Zen as pushing further, toward the clearing away of all unconscious conditioning, allowing the emergence of the truly free individual. "If one carries Freud's principle of the transformation of unconsciousness into consciousness to its ultimate consequences, one approaches the concept of enlightenment" (Suzuki et al. 1960: 139). Fromm recast this process of enlightenment in largely psychological terms:

> The aim becomes that of overcoming alienation, and of the subject-
> object split in perceiving the world; then the uncovering of the
> unconscious means the overcoming of affective contamination and
> cerebration; it means the de-repression, the abolition of the split

within myself between the universal man and the social man; it
means the disappearance of the polarity of conscious vs. unconscious; it means arriving at the state of the immediate grasp of reality,
without distortion and without interference by intellectual reflection;
it means overcoming of the craving to hold on to the ego, to worship
it; it means giving up the illusion of an indestructible ego . . . [and] to
be open, responding, to *have* nothing and to *be*. (135–36)

Fromm also touches on a theme prominent in both Enlightenment rationalism and Romanticism and magnified in the more recent manifestations of the
subjective turn: that freedom of the mind is inextricable from freedom from
authority. Thus he asserts that this expunging of the unconscious involves overcoming the "desire to submit to an authority who solves one's own problem of
existence" (137).

Under the influence of Jung and Fromm, the articulation of meditation in
terms of analytic psychology has become a staple of popular Buddhist literature
in the West. For instance, Douglas Burns, in his book *Buddhist Meditation and
Depth Psychology*, identifies the traditional Buddhist mental defilements (*kleśas*)
with repressed emotions, and insight (*vipassanā*) with their de-repression:

In its psychiatric usage insight means gaining awareness of those
feelings, motives, and values which have previously been unconscious. Repressed feelings of guilt, fear, lust, and hatred may lurk in
the hidden recesses of our minds and unconsciously shape our lives
until such time as they are brought into awareness. And unless they
are brought into awareness, we cannot effectively deal with them.
(1994)

The interpretation of meditation as probing the unconscious is not limited
to the idea of revealing unconscious "negative" states, however; its goal, according to influential popular book *Mindfulness in Plain English*, by Sri Lankan
monk Henepola Gunaratana, "is to reach the perfection of all the noble and
wholesome qualities latent in our subconscious mind" (2002 [1993]: 50).

The idea of meditation as derepression, making the unconscious conscious, also entails enlisting Buddhism's assent to a nearly axiomatic claim of
the psychological era: that one must not suppress negative emotions—a claim
numerous modern authors on Buddhism feel compelled to make. Burns insists:
*"Neither in the Satipatthana Sutta nor in any of the other seven steps of the Eightfold
Path is advocated the denial or suppression of feelings.* It is a widely spread and
inaccurate belief that Theravada Buddhism attempts to destroy evil thoughts
by forcing them from the mind" (1994; italics original). Although this is not an

unfair interpretation of many meditation practices, it was clearly not the issue for the ancients that it is for us. Otherwise, we would not have such counter-evidence as we find, for example, in the *Vitakkasanthana Sutta* (MN 20):

> If evil, unskillful thoughts continue to arise in a bhikkhu in spite of his reflection on the removal of a source of unskillful thoughts, he should with clenched teeth and the tongue pressing on the palate, restrain, subdue and beat down the (evil) mind by the (good) mind. Then the evil, unskillful thoughts connected with desire, hate and delusion are eliminated; they disappear. . . . Like a strong man holding a weaker man by the head or shoulders and restraining, subduing and beating him down, should the bhikkhu in whom evil, unskillful thoughts continue to arise in spite of his reflection on the source of unskillful thoughts, restrain, subdue and beat down the (evil) mind by the (good) mind. (Soma Thera 1981)

Burns's italicized adamance on this point suggests that the psychological commandment "Do not repress" is a virtually nonnegotiable element of modern culture. A surviving mandate of Romantic expressivism, it insisted on the expression of the deep interior of the psyche and developed later into the maxim of psychoanalytic theory that declares that repressed emotions haunting the unconscious are dangerous.[5]

The psychoanalytic interpretation also asserts that meditation, particularly "nonjudgmental awareness," is akin to free-association techniques for excavating contents of the unconscious. Fromm saw free association, like Zen, as a means to "by-pass logical, conscious, conventional thought" and thus transcend the hyperrationalism he considered characteristic of the West (Suzuki et al. 1960: 83). Mark Epstein, in his influential book *Thoughts without a Thinker*, points out Freud's insistence that for psychoanalysis to work, the therapist must temporarily suspend his or her "critical faculty" and attend to his or her own thoughts as well as the patient's. The therapist must "give himself over completely to his unconscious memory" and listen to the patient with "evenly suspended attention," not judging or evaluating but allowing for "impartial attention to everything there is to observe. He should simply listen, and not bother about whether he is keeping anything in mind" (quoted in Epstein 1995: 114–15). Epstein concludes that Freud "apparently taught himself without knowing that this was precisely the attentional stance that Buddhist meditators had been invoking for millennia" (114). Following these and similar reflections, a great deal of contemporary Buddhist literature sees meditation and psychoanalysis as two varieties of essentially the same activity, meditation being a more radical and thoroughgoing version of psychoanalysis.

Meditation, Conditioning, and Western Individualism

This model of meditation entails another important psychological conception about meditation: that the purpose of meditation is a *deconditioning* of the mind; that is, to strip a person of all psychological, social, and cultural conditioning—the false ego. This ego is an artificial sense of selfhood constructed from cravings and delusions based on the often unconscious residue of past impressions, thoughts, feelings, social roles, and self-images, as well as cultural assumptions and presuppositions. This is a radicalization of Freud's position that cultural values are inherently oppressive to individuals, force them to repress their instincts and thus give rise to psychological symptoms. Theorist of psychoanalysis Philip Reiff saw psychoanalysis purely as a mode of liberating the individual, who was "buried alive, as it were, in the culture. To be thus free from the tyrannical super-ego is to be properly bedded in the present world" (1966: 77). Buddhist modernist literature, especially of the 1960s and 1970s, commonly interprets Buddhist awakening as an overcoming of all "conditioning." Midcentury French Zen author Robert Linssen characterized it this way:

> When the illusion of the "I-process" is unmasked all our desires,
> mental routines and memory-automatisms disappear. We are re-
> newed from instant to instant. Each day is veritable re-birth to us, for
> every morning we awaken freed from the grip of the innumerable
> yesterdays of our existence. We begin again at zero, and we leave
> behind all danger of mental fossilization. (185)

Alan Watts posited a distinction between the "acquired self" and "your genuine, deepest self, not the self which depends on family and conditioning, on learning and experience, or any kind of artifice" but Buddha-nature, or the "original face" of the famous Zen koan (1973 [1958]: 69). For Watts, Zen requires a person to realize that the "ego, the self which he has believed himself to be, is nothing but a pattern of habits or artificial reactions." As long as a person is responding to the affairs of life "not spontaneously but by socially conditioned habit," he is "just unconsciously acting his role, and still not showing his original face" (70). Meditation on these accounts is a way of dissolving the ego so that one is eventually emancipated from all conditioning derived from family, society, and institutions and can live, moment by moment, in a state of authenticity, spontaneity, and inner freedom. Freud would have denied the possibility of such radical deconditioning, as well as the existence of some spontaneous deeper authentic and moral self beyond the ego. Yet the idea has roots in his own culture—in the Romantic ideals of the deep interior and of liberal individualism.

This now standard western interpretation of Buddhist meditation is informed by a cluster of emancipatory aspirations deeply rooted in western modernity, including not only Romanticism-inflected subjectivism and psychoanalysis but also the ever-present, tacit assumptions of liberal social and political theory and its emphasis on the freedom of the individual from external constraints. One of the central convictions of modern liberalism is the right of individuals not to be unduly coerced by others, particularly their rulers. Locke, for example, extolled the ideal of people living in "a *State of perfect Freedom* to order their Actions . . . as they think fit . . . without asking leave, or depending on the Will of any other Man" (1979 [1706]). Liberal social theory conceives of a social order that assures individuals the freedom to pursue their own self-directed and individually chosen ends. It entails a deep suspicion of the collective, often seeing society as at least potentially, if not inherently, oppressive of these individual interests and ends. Liberalism asserts that free persons act according to their own inner mandates, critically reflect on their own ideals, and resist blindly following social custom. Rousseau's assertion of the source of true morality and wisdom as the human heart rather than the rules imposed by society informed this discourse. Later, analytic psychology in turn tacitly incorporated it: psychoanalysis became a technique for freeing oneself from the neuroses that inevitably arise from one's repression of desires in order to manage in society. Protestantism's emphasis on the individual whose personal and intimate relationship with God is unmediated by institutional structures also played a role. All of these conceptions envision individuals as distinct entities, ontologically prior to social groups and relations, and society as an a posteriori way of attempting to harmonize individual wills and assure that each person has the right to actualization.

Drawing on, and indeed radicalizing, this discourse of freedom, individualism, and self-transformation, the American and European alternative spiritualities within which Buddhism was often interpreted tilted heavily toward this individualist model of spiritual fulfillment and liberation. These movements often cast the social, communal, and institutional as oppressive, not just in terms of overtly political power but also in terms of the mental and spiritual freedom of the individual, insofar as the restrictive powers of society were seen to condition not only social behavior but consciousness and the spirit itself. Emerson, in his famous Harvard Divinity School address, admonished graduates to shun traditional authority in matters religious: "Let me admonish you, first of all to go alone; to refuse the good models, even those which are sacred in the imagination of men, and dare to love God without mediator or veil" (1974: 64). Edward Shils claims that this spiritual individualism as it develops in the twentieth century includes "the metaphysical dread of being encumbered by something alien to oneself." As Buddhism has been enfolded into western spiritual eclecticism and individualism, it has often operated on some version of the idea that

> within each human being there is an individuality lying in potentiality, which seeks an occasion for realization but is held in the toils of the rules, beliefs, and roles which society imposes . . . that the real state of the self is very different from the acquired baggage which institutions like families, schools, and universities impose. To be "true to oneself" means . . . discovering what is contained in the uncontaminated self, the self which has been freed from the encumbrance of accumulated knowledge, norms, and ideals handed down by previous generations. (Shils 1981: 10–11)

Shils traces this view directly to Romanticism and the late nineteenth-century "affirmation of life" against the constraints of Victorian morality, giving rise to the "release of the novelist's imagination," particularly in Joyce and D. H. Lawrence (more on this in the next chapter).

The Buddhist rejection of the substantial, permanent self has in some cases not been sufficient to discourage such a conception of the spontaneous, uncontaminated self. To the contrary, the conceptions of "Buddha-nature" or "self-nature" in Zen and other Mahayana traditions have often been articulated explicitly in these terms, as I have shown in Suzuki's work and in Kopps's and Watts's comments here. I do not mean to suggest that the idea of a pure, uncontaminated identity within is a wholly western invention. Indeed, Buddhist conceptions of Buddha-nature, as well as the Vedantic idea of atman, likely had a substantial *impact* on the very idea of this "uncontaminated self" to which Shils refers; thus we cannot see this merely as an imposition of western thought on Buddhist thought. Rather this is, again, a hybrid formation that draws on both, intermingling them and bringing Buddhist conceptions of a pure inner identity into the orbit of various western conceptions of freedom and the individual, especially the romantic ideal of the deep inner self beyond the ego, the source of creativity and true morality.

What, then, *are* the western elements in this hybrid construction? One is this assertion that this inner self comes forth as a result of the deconditioning of the mind—the uprooting of conditioned neuroses deep in the unconscious and the casting off or seeing through of the "social self." Why should we consider this deconditioning a specifically western contribution? There is substantial discussion in canonical Buddhist texts of what could quite justifiably be called "conditioning" and the attempt to get free from it. Nevertheless, these discussions lack the implication that the conditioning that is to be cast off is the psychological and social conditioning imposed by cultural institutions or that the transcendence of social and cultural conditioning is the sine qua non of awakening.

In Pali accounts, the emphasis is on the conditioning powers of one's own actions (karma), not the imposition of cultural and social factors from outside. Habitual actions of mind, body, and speech establish karmic formations (*vāsanās*), which condition one's interpretation of present events, shape future actions, and create conditions for future rebirths. While these could reasonably be interpreted as unconscious tendencies, and while it is certainly a desideratum of Buddhism to get free of these conditioning processes, early texts give us little reason to interpret "conditioning" as the infusion into the psyche of external social norms, or of awakening as simply transcending all psychological conditioning and social roles. Karmic conditioning drifts semantically toward "cultural conditioning" under the influence of western discourses that elevate the individual over the social, cultural, and institutional. The traditional import of the karmic conditioning process, however, is primarily ethical and soteriological—actions condition circumstances in this and future lives. "Conditioning" thus serves to explain fortunate or unfortunate situations as well as to inspire moral actions to create good rebirths. Breaking through such conditioning to awakening in traditional accounts is not throwing off the yoke of social norms, childhood traumas, and cultural limitations ensconced in the deep recesses of the psyche but rather the disciplined overcoming of one's own karmic tendencies that keep one bound to the cycle of rebirth. (Here is Buddhism's own kind of radical individualism!)

In fact, the conceptions of personhood in the Asian cultures in which Buddhism has developed are quite divergent from those in the modern West. Clearly, the explicit doctrines of the western autonomous self and *anātman* are quite disparate, but there is perhaps an even more important divergence on a sociological level. In traditional Asian cultures, the person is not an individual prior to the network of social relationships; personal identity is determined by one's position in the family, community, and society. Victor Sōgen Hori puts it well:

> In the West, the person is an independent being, who exists autonomous from social roles and relations. For most societies outside the influence of the European Enlightenment, however, a person is not an independent being . . . ; quite the opposite, a person has identity and uniqueness only because of his or her social relationships. In answer to the question, "Who are you?" one does not answer with just one's name, but rather, "I am the son or daughter (gender makes a difference) of so-and-so, father or mother to so-and-so, husband or wife

to so-and-so, member of such-and-such, resident of such-and-such, etc." My identity as a person depends on my relationships with other persons, and, ultimately, with place, land and nation, with history and time. Rights and responsibilities accrue to me in virtue of the social roles and relationships in which I am involved. Not merely personal identity, but also my very nature as a human being is dependent and social. (1994: 49)

Despite the centrality of monasticism, the goal of individual awakening, and the presence of isolated hermits, as well as scriptural injunctions to be "lamps unto yourself," most cultures of Buddhism have been deeply embedded in these familial and civic relationships and have not in fact stressed transcending social conditioning in the modern western sense. Buddhism does contain a particular kind of individualist impulse in its ascetic orientation; the act of joining the monastic order entails a radical break with traditional social roles. But the *sangha* has always maintained close relations with the community as a whole, and the rationale for leaving society was never expressed in terms of release from social and psychological conditioning in order to bring about the spontaneous freedom of the individual. Monasticism, in fact, entails far greater degree of social control than that of lay life. The rationale, instead, was rather expressed in terms of karma, ethics, and the difficulties of focusing exclusively on the path while maintaining work and family life. Moreover, monasticism in most countries has become quite domesticated—with Thais taking temporary ordination to bring their parents merit, Japanese monks serving as temple priests, Tibetan monks serving as ritualists for their lay communities. The monastic vocation is, and perhaps has always been, a collective endeavor and the individual seeker—the *pratyeka-buddha*—the exception. Perhaps the western interpretation of meditation as attaining freedom from social and cultural conditioning is partly a function of the fact that many western Buddhist converts from Christianity and Judaism have cast off their own traditions, attempting to overcome their cultural norms and start anew. Yet escape is not so easy. In fact the leaving of one's "home" and striking out on one's own as the lonely individual spiritual seeker is itself a Protestant theme (Bellah et al. 1985).

Rationalism and Reflexivity

While its fullest implications and most radical manifestations came to fruition in the nineteenth and twentieth centuries, the inward turn began even earlier. Taylor argues that it was Augustine who introduced into western thought *radical reflexivity*—the focus on being present to oneself and making one's own experience an explicit object of reflection. Augustine believed that God was accessed through the inner light of the self. He introduced the language of inwardness into the discussion of the spiritual life and thus made the self a resource for morality and access to holiness. He was, Taylor claims, "the originator of that strand of western spirituality which has sought the certainty of God within" (1989: 140). Other Catholic monastics have left rich records of interior probing and analysis of the workings of the God's will in the human mind, and many have asserted the relevance of Christian mystics like Meister Eckhart and St. John of the Cross to Buddhist meditation traditions. Although hardly an overt influence on the interpretation of meditation, the Puritans, who interrogated their thoughts and feelings to discern signs of grace and bring the dispositions in line with God's will, also played an important part of the inward turn's history. From a more secular perspective, Montaigne also inaugurated a kind of self-exploration, not to find the divine but to discern what is unique to the individual and to try and penetrate the illusions erected by religion, society, and pride.

There are, therefore, different sides to the subjective turn: the religious/mystical, the Romantic, the psychological, and a strain of thinking that comes from rationalist Enlightenment thinkers and works its way into contemporary psychology, where it meets Buddhist meditation head on. This strain, which developed in the early phases of the modern period, was a particular mode of disengaged reflexivity—a standing apart from one's own thoughts and feelings in order to analyze and control them. It continues to this day. It may not have directly influenced the explicit conceptions of Buddhist meditation in the West, but it has been an important part of the tacit modern understanding of the mind. It formed part of the preunderstanding of Buddhist meditation, and was an important precursor to the contemporary scientific approaches to cognition that are currently playing an important role in the developing conceptions of Buddhist meditation.

To understand this element of the subjective turn, we must return to an unlikely source. As noted, Descartes is often held up as the foil of Buddhism modernism, the arch-dualist whose conceptions of the disengaged, autonomous self set the foundations for the mechanization of the world and the alienation of humanity from nature. Indeed Descartes's cogito has largely (and anachronistically) replaced the atman in modern Buddhist discourse as that which the doctrine of *anātman* refutes. In many respects, the Cartesian account of the subject clearly is the antithesis of Buddhist thought on the self. However, another element in Descartes's and other Enlightenment thinkers' stance toward subjectivity helped clear a space within the modern West for the practice of meditation. Descartes, along with other early modern philosophers, under-stood "the disengaged self" as "capable of objectifying not only the surrounding world but also his own emotions and inclinations, fears and compulsions, and achieving thereby a kind of distance and self-possession which allow him to act 'rationally'" (Taylor 1989: 21). As Foucault, Taylor, and others have pointed out, Enlightenment thought produced a "growing ideal of a human agent who is able to remake himself by methodical and disciplined action. What this calls for is the ability to take an instrumental stance to one's given properties, de-sires, inclinations, tendencies, habits of thought and feeling, so that they can by *worked on*" (159–60). Thus, Descartes's disengagement is turned not only toward the objects of the world but toward the subject itself. Taylor again:

> Instead of being swept along by error by the ordinary bent of experi-ence, we stand back from it, withdraw from it, reconstrue it objec-tively, and then learn to draw defensible conclusions from it. To wrest control from "our appetites and our preceptors," we have to practise a kind of radical reflexivity. We fix experience in order to deprive it of its power, a source of bewitchment and error. (163)

This view also entails freedom from not only external authority but also from the coercive power of one's own compulsions, passions, and cravings that prevent autonomous self-direction. Essential to this individual freedom is the notion that one who is controlled by impulse or craving, according to nineteenth-century political theorist Thomas Green, is "in the condition of a bondsman who is carrying out the will of another, not his own" (1986 [1895]: 228). The ability to stand back from spontaneous opinion, emotion, and desire and subject them to observation and scrutiny is thus another important facet of western individualism. Locke conceives of this capacity as the independent use of reason, which allows one to rise above the clamor of received custom and opinion and think for oneself. Acquiring knowledge, for Locke, is thus an intensely individual process involving autonomous reasoning, self-reflection, self-reconstruction, and self-liberation. The Enlightenment's contribution to the subjective turn introduced to the West the possibility of standing back from experience, analyzing it, and thereby potentially bringing it under one's con-trol. The idea that all reality is mediated, ordered, and reflected by the mind—*in* the mind—gave unprecedented power to the mind. Through the powers of observation come powers of control, and through powers of control comes the possibility of self-transformation, through which one is free to pursue the truth on the basis of one's own reasoning rather than of received authority or tradi-tion. This idea of distancing oneself from one's own thoughts, beliefs, emo-tions, and desires opened up, if not an altogether new, at least an intensified, modality of self-observation in western thought. The self became, in effect, a new object of systematic inquiry.

Descartes and other rationalists and empiricists, came to see this self-observation and self-objectification as a means for *happiness*, conceived as the fulfillment of one's potentials and natural capacities in this life. In the oeuvres of the great rationalists—Descartes, Locke, Kant, and so on—one inevitably encounters densely systematized accounts of the various functions of the soul, including "the passions," ultimately with a view to taming them and subordinating them to reason. Amid long enumerations and descriptions of the passions (esteem, generosity, pride, love, hatred, desire, etc.) in his "The Passions of the Soul," Descartes explains the point of the systematic attempt to isolate, clarify, and define them: "even those who have the feeblest souls can acquire a very absolute dominion over all their passions if sufficient industry is applied in training and guiding them" (1982: 1:356). Descartes's treatise has the feel of Abhidharma texts, deeply informed by Buddhist meditation traditions, that attempt to carve up the world of experience into neat and discrete chunks, isolable and identifiable, therefore controllable. Both embrace this radical disengagement from the mind's manifestations for the purpose of observation, analysis, control, and ultimately transformation.

The differences between the two approaches and their conclusions are obvious. Buddhist meditation isolates thoughts, emotions, and sensations not to establish their place in a fixed jigsaw puzzle of being but to reveal their very lack of fixity (especially in Mahayana thought, where dharmas are declared empty). In contrast to the isolated cogito, in Buddhism the subject identifying these phenomena is itself one of the phenomena; there is no transcendent or fixed "I" that stands outside the flow of experience. Indeed, the insight into this lack of a fixed "I" is precisely the point. Like the rationalist reflexivity, the Buddhist mode involves an initial disengagement from thoughts, feelings, and so on and a corresponding establishment of an "observer" of them; but the observer is not to be construed as a fixed reference point, a permanent and independent "I"; rather, it too is observed and given over to the continuum of experience, excavated from its seemingly solid ground to become a part of the flow of consciousness. Self-discovery, therefore, does not uncover an independent, rational self but rather finds that there is no self, no subjectivity outside the flow of events.

Yet, while the doctrinal elements of western rationalism and Buddhism diverge in many ways, the issue of the empowerment of the mind through disengagement from and observation and ultimately control of its contents is a theme that could be—and I believe has been—implicitly brought to the interpretation of Buddhist meditation. Consider *vipassanā* meditation as it is commonly presented in modern Buddhism: one first observes the mind in a detached way, noting and sometimes labeling thoughts as they arise; then, through gaining greater familiarity with the mind's patterns, beliefs, and habitual emotional responses, one can gain control over the process and acquire insight into the true nature of the process itself, thereby transforming it. Cartesian thinking's emphasis on reason and mind-body dualism were not what allowed it to become a part of the preunderstanding of Buddhism in the West, but rather radical reflexivity, along with the instrumental stance toward the desires, appetites, habits of thought and feeling, and so on such that they can be "worked on" and transformed.

This reflexivity is the great-grandfather of today's neurobiological and cognitive psychologies that have recently become important in the study of meditation. It worked its way into western interpretations of Buddhism first in the nineteenth- and early twentieth-century conceptions of Buddhism as a "rational religion" compatible with science (see chapter 4). Buddhism gained entry into modern western culture in part by being represented as a path of human development that accorded with western conceptions of the perfectibility of man through rational action, moral reflection, disengaged self-observation, and the attainment of control over the passions. Some Buddhists and Buddhist sympathizers saw meditation and mind training as a uniquely practical technique for accomplishing these aims—or at least Buddhist-influenced reformulations of them. This conviction remained largely theoretical for most westerners in the Victorian era; few Victorians actually took up the practice of Buddhist meditation in a serious way, largely because access to Buddhism was mainly through texts, and the wave of Asian meditation teachers appearing in Europe and the United States did not arrive until later (Tweed 2000: 159). The rationalistic interpretation of meditation remained in the background until it came to fruition in the twentieth century.

In the Victorian era, the central elements in western conceptions of Buddhism were its rational philosophy, ethics, and emphasis on compassion; by the mid- to late twentieth century, meditation had attained a paramount place. Only then did the wide range of contemplative techniques become a subject of systematic consideration. Since then, the general picture of meditation has become a microcosm of the West's picture of Buddhism: meditation, in implicit contrast to Christian faith, is a practical spiritual technique that requires neither belief nor a particular worldview but is a means for acquiring understanding of oneself and the world through personal experience and investigation of the mind. In this "empirical" and pragmatic aspect, meditation has been considered akin to the sciences yet not shackled by the assumptions of "materialistic science" and more open to "spiritual" discoveries. Buddhist modernism therefore took the Enlightenment rationalist aspiration to human perfectibility through self-observation, discipline, and control of the passions and not only added a practical element—a systematic discipline of mind training—but also promised to challenge the purely materialistic approach to science itself. This general picture of Buddhist meditation has implicitly guided the contemporary meeting of science and meditation. Indeed Alan Wallace, one of the most prolific and thoughtful participants in this meeting, interprets Buddhist meditation as a further development of the tradition of self-reflexive rationalism: "René Descartes and John Locke were both deeply committed to the introspective examination of the mind, but like their Greek and Christian predecessors, they did not devise means to refine the attention so that the mind could reliably be used to observe mental events" (2007: 53). Buddhism, he argues, has.

Meditation as an Object of Science—and as Science Itself

Meditation as Object of Science

The rationalist conception of the human being as something to be worked on through self-observation and disciplined ordering of the elements of the psyche was a necessary preunderstanding for a new approach to Buddhist meditation. Yet it remained largely in the background until the recent empirical studies of meditation in the lab. While the psychoanalytic interpretation of Buddhism is still prominent in the West, a new psychological understanding has emerged in the last couple of decades from the neurosciences—an understanding informed by empirical studies analyzing the effects of meditation on the brain and nervous system. These studies have brought an increased rigor to the scientific investigation of meditation, going well beyond the vagaries of earlier attempts to ally Buddhism and science on the basis of "natural laws," or "causality" and instead subjecting meditators to controlled experiments.

Scientific studies of meditation began in the 1960s, when Japanese researchers conducted extensive electroencephalographic studies of Zen meditators, recording changes in alpha and theta waves and testing reactions to external stimuli. Their studies suggested that *zazen* promotes a quiescent but alert state in which the mind is calm but also responsive to various stimuli (Kasamatsu and Hirai: 1963). Since then, a spate of studies has measured changes in brain waves, hormonal levels, and heart rate using the increasingly sophisticated technology available for observing and measuring physiological functioning. Such research has assessed the effects of meditation on attention, perceptual sensitivity, anxiety, regulation of emotional states, neurophysiological responses to stressful stimuli, immune system functioning, central nervous system activity, and specific neurological structures.

Some studies have not only have shed further light on what the brain and nervous system do during meditation but also contributed more generally to the understanding of certain characteristics of the brain. Richard Davidson's studies of experienced meditators in the Tibetan Buddhist tradition, for example, have helped lead to the growing awareness among neuroscientists of brain plasticity—the brain's ability to change in response to repeated activity or training. According to his research, meditation shows considerable promise for possibilities of retraining the brain to manage destructive emotions and activate neurological centers associated with happiness, well-being, and compassion. Considerable evidence gathered in the last couple of decades also suggests potential uses for Buddhist and other meditation techniques in therapeutic contexts, be it for stress reduction, pain management, cardiovascular disease, or simply as an aid to greater contentment and well-being.[6]

Meditation as *Science*

The representation of Buddhism as generally compatible with science was an important part of its entry into the discourses of modernity. The conception of meditation as itself a species of scientific activity has attained increased visibility in contemporary Buddhist literature.

This representation has roots in nineteenth-century metaphysical movements, which saw the contemplative elements of all major religions as an interior science parallel to—and in some ways superseding—empirical science, with both of them reaching beyond specific claims of religious traditions to verifiable knowledge. The popular distinction between "religion" and "spirituality" inherits one way of talking about this distinction: religions have to do with belief, ritual, hierarchy, and maintenance of community, while spirituality and mysticism have to do with the direct, unmediated, and individual experience of the divine, an experience that transcends religion's "external" forms. Meditative inquiry, on this model, aims not to reinforce traditional beliefs bound to parochial religious traditions but to discern the reality of things through *experience*. To recall the opposition put forth by Rahula and numerous other modern authors between the terms *belief* and *experience*: belief is a matter of "religion" (i.e., Christianity) while experience is the province of Buddhism, which invites one to "come and see," to verify for oneself, much like scientific inquiry. Meditation is thus conceived not as a "religious" activity but as a method for empirically investigating reality—not that of rocks and stars and quarks but rather laws of nature as manifested in the activities of consciousness. As science explores the external world, meditation probes the internal world, discovering truths about the mind that are neither bound by nor the property of any religion.

Thus Goenka has said that the Buddha was not the founder of a "religion" but an intrepid interior explorer who discovered truths about the mind that anticipate truths only recently discovered in the West. Lama Govinda says of this relationship between science and mysticism:

> this common basis [of all schools of Buddhism] rests on experience, that is, on that area where science and mysticism meet. The only difference between those two fields of experience is that the truth of science—being directed toward external objects—is "objectively" provable or, better, demonstrable, whereas mysticism, being directed toward the subject, rests on "subjective" experience. (1989: 51)

Both, according to this narrative, serve to establish truths irrespective of sectarian identities. Although they may seem science's opposite, these universalist articulations of mysticism and spirituality—standard from the nineteenth century until the present—stem from the same desire as the sciences to establish universal truth by direct encounter, thereby establishing a language of truth that transcends the plural and parochial truth claims of the religions. As the motto of Theosophy asserted: "There is no religion higher than truth." This interpretation not only construes meditation as a discipline paralleling the physical sciences but also conduces to decontextualizing meditation from Buddhism as a religion.

In the mid–twentieth century, Nyanaponika Thera called Buddhist meditation a "science of mind," drawing from earlier spiritualist terminology, and presented the method of "bare attention" as essentially the same as that of the scientist: "unprejudiced receptivity" to things, reduction of the subjective element in judgment, and "deferring judgment until a careful examination of the facts has been made." This is the "genuine spirit of the research worker," though Buddhist meditation goes beyond "explanation of facts" and a "theoretical *knowledge* of the mind" to an attempt to shape the mind itself (1954: 42). K. N. Jayatilleke and David Kalupahana and other scholars developed this line of thinking in detail, presenting Buddhism as a kind of "radical empiricism" akin to that of David Hume and William James (Jayatilleke 1963; Kalupahana 1975).[7] Contemporary scholars, dharma teachers, and popular writers have in turn popularized the conception of Buddhist meditation as an internal science. Contemporary Tibetan teacher Dzogchen Ponlop Rinpoche, for instance, presents Buddhism itself as a kind of science, highlighting the distinction between religion and spirituality as well as the blending of spirituality and science:

> Buddhist spiritual teachings present a genuine science of mind that allows one to uncover . . . the nature of the mind and the phenomena

that our mind experiences. When we say that Buddhism is a "science," we do not mean the dry science of analyzing material things. We are talking about something much deeper. We are talking about going into the depths of the reality of our inner world. . . . In this sense, Buddhist spirituality is not what is ordinarily meant by the term "religion" (Ponlop n.d.)

Similarly, Goenka often refers to *vipassanā* meditation as a scientific method of investigating consciousness. Jeremy Hayward contends that Buddhist meditation is essentially a scientific endeavor, because its findings can be experientially confirmed or refuted by other meditators (1987). Alan Wallace is most explicit in elucidating meditation in scientific terms:

Buddhism, like science, presents itself as a body of systematic knowledge about the natural world, and it posits a wide array of testable hypotheses and theories concerning the nature of the mind and its relation to the physical environment. These theories have allegedly been tested and experientially confirmed numerous times over the past twenty-five hundred years, by means of duplicable meditative techniques (2003: 8)

He characterizes advanced meditators as investigators performing repeatable experiments, making "discoveries . . . based on firsthand experience," then subjecting them to "peer review by their fellow contemplatives, who may debate the merits or defects of the reported findings" (9).

As noted, Buddhist modernism attempts to embrace science while distancing itself from strict materialism. Meditation often serves as a focal point of this stance, as some authors construe it as both a scientific endeavor and a corrective to what they consider the excessive rationalism, materialism, and reductionism of mainstream science. Contemporary Tibetan author Geshe Kelsang Gyatso of the New Kadampa school asserts that scientists "have specialized in knowing about external elements, have learnt how to manipulate the material world, make great technological advances, and produce many wonderful things" but the dharma as an "inner science" allows us to "know subtle elements precisely" (502).[8] Advocates often view this inner science as a benign corrective to the dangers of "external" science, which for all its benefits has also brought many of the horrors of the modern age, such as nuclear weapons and environmental destruction. They assert that Buddhism not only has just as sophisticated a rational psychology as any in the West but also has something western science has lost in its drive to reduce all phenomena to measurable data: a more direct, intuitive, experiential apprehension of things, particularly things of the mind.

The general idea is not new; Lama Govinda contrasted "theoretical" and "hypothetical (western) psychology, which relies heavily upon logical operations and abstracts principles," to Buddhist "practical psychology," which is "based on experience" (1961: 35–36). Chögyam Trungpa claimed that "traditional Buddhist psychology emphasizes the importance of direct experience" of the mind, which is developed through meditation, and notes that "if one relies on theory alone, then something basic is lost" (1983: 1). The implication is clearly that western psychology does just this. Buddhist psychology, according to these and many other contemporary authors, does not get caught up in the endless ratiocination common to the habits of western thought and therefore maintains a more direct, unmediated access to its subject matter: the mind itself.

Contemporary iterations of this argument often take aim at today's increasingly sophisticated materialist models for understanding consciousness. Robert Thurman, for example, criticizes western psychology for abdicating its ground to strictly physicalistic neuroscience, while at the same time adopting the latter's mind-as-computer metaphor (1991: 57–61). In contrast to western psychology's increasing emphasis on the "hardware" of the mind, Thurman sees Tibetan Buddhist psychology, and meditation in particular, as an "inner science" (a gloss of the Sanskrit term *adhyātmavidyā*) with "sophisticated methods of software analysis and modification [that] can help with the individual's inner reprogramming. . . . There is a vast array of mental technologies, modification techniques that enable individuals to incorporate and integrate the improved software" (64). This inner science is not just another avenue of exploration that can increase scientific knowledge but is also a correction to the "dogmatism" of western "scientific materialism" (59). Thurman admits that this materialist approach has helped humanity develop an excellent understanding of the environment, cured diseases, and improved some conditions of life, but maintains that it has also produced unprecedented means of self-destruction. Western science in fact has taken a wrong turn, in that "our powers to effect the outer reality have outstripped our powers over ourselves" (56). Many contemporary Buddhists, including sympathetic scientists, hope that Buddhist contemplative methods can introduce into scientific disciplines a more balanced, humanizing view of the mind, over against the strictly materialist view of contemporary science, along with its associated social, geopolitical, and environmental consequences (see for example Hayward 1987; Varela et al. 1991).

A Brief Critique of Meditation as a Science

Contemporary scientific studies of Buddhist meditation practices do indeed suggest their potential value, both in psychotherapy and medical applications.[9]

These studies also appear to have potential to contribute to wider discussions about the nature of the brain and its functions. More broadly, the possibilities for meditation to help assuage a variety of problems rooted not only in the modern world but in the human condition more generally are, I believe, great. Crossing over from meditation as an *object* of scientific investigation to characterizing it as *itself* a science, however, is not without problems.

For one thing, descriptions of meditation from this perspective often neglect its purposes and functions in its traditional social, ethical, institutional, and cosmological contexts. They often present meditation as a freestanding mode of inquiry, analysis, and transformation. This is, perhaps, what meditation has *become* in some modern contexts, but it is not an adequate *description* of meditation in its more traditional settings, for it neglects the ritual, social, even magical functions of meditation as it is practiced throughout Asia. For the ancients, and in more traditional contexts today, meditation was not so much a method of self-discovery but a tool for reversing the causal processes of birth and rebirth in order to bring about a complete cessation of suffering and attain full awakening. It also generated supernatural capabilities, as well as good karma, propelling the practitioner toward better rebirths. More than just a solitary practice, as noted, it is usually tied to the social system. Monks in Sri Lanka, for example, who have meditated intensively throughout the three-month rains retreat generate "power" that the laity can then access during the ritual presentation of gifts at the end of the retreat. The power generated from the monks' concentration (*jhāna*), it is believed, may allow them to tell the future and generate miraculous healings. Both Tibetan and Zen meditation have also traditionally been inseparable from, and sometimes subordinate to, ritual and devotional elements. For instance, meditation sometimes helps create a sacred space (*bodhimaṇḍa*) for the devotional evocation of Buddhas and bodhisattvas. Some have argued that Sōtō Zen meditation itself is less a matter of internal investigation than a ritual re-creation of the awakening of the Buddha, hence the exacting requirements for posture and physical performance (Faure 1996: 217). Such examples suggest how meditation is traditionally embedded in the social, ethical, and cosmological orders. This does not mean that meditation has no legitimate place outside of such traditional contexts or that modernist meditators are somehow inauthentic if their practice fails to include these elements; it does mean, however, that *descriptions* of the traditional functions of meditation as scientific experiments ignore these contexts and neglect the variety of functions that meditation is called on to fulfill.

Further, the interpretation of meditation as a science overestimates the degree to which it can be considered an empirical and open-ended inquiry, unbounded by the claims of tradition and unconditioned by social, doctrinal, and ritual factors. How do we distinguish a Buddhist meditator's "discoveries based on firsthand experience," in Wallace's sense, from those of Christian or Hindu contemplatives who through repeated "experiments" have confirmed and had verified by their peers—and superiors—that there *is*, in fact, an eternal soul beneath the fleeting apparitions of the personality? If I am doing Buddhist meditation and make such a discovery, what then? There is no scientific way to adjudicate between Buddhist doctrine and my conclusion. This does not mean that there can be no personal grounds for one or the other conclusion; it simply means that it is not publicly verifiable, as scientific experiments must be. This example suggests that Buddhist meditation in its traditional contexts, rather than being an open-ended "scientific" experiment, is bounded by Buddhist suppositions that guide the practitioner toward certain experiences and conclusions. It is a method less of open-ended inquiry than of discovering for oneself the truths of the dharma that the Buddha put forth, that is, those authorized by the tradition. That does not mean there is no room for novel ideas or experiences to arise; the very history of Buddhism suggests that the dharma is constantly being reformulated. Nor am I insisting that leaping beyond the bounds of cultural conditioning through meditation is impossible. But, parallel to Georges Dreyfus's claims about Tibetan debate, meditation's "open-endedness is partial and often actively limited by the tradition" (2003: 274). It therefore operates within the constraints of tradition and the authority of the past in ways that science *in theory* does not.[10]

Another question is whether meditation can, as Thurman, Wallace, Hayward, and others suggest, "spiritualize" science or whether it risks being coopted by the very scientific materialism it hopes to mitigate. As I have noted repeatedly, since its introduction to the West Buddhism has met modernity with the promise of embracing its fundamental tenets yet ameliorating its materialistic excesses. Critics often cite science—or at least scientism—as an enabler, if not a source, of these excesses. At a lecture I attended by an enthusiastic and articulate participant in the dialogue between Buddhism and science, he suggested the possibility of using biofeedback machines in meditation centers for practitioners to monitor their brain activities during sitting. Is the evocative image of robed meditators in lotus position hooked up to their individual biofeedback machines one of seamless confluence between science and meditation, the rehumanization of science, or contrariwise, the mechanization of meditation and the acquiescing of Buddhism to the very scientific materialism it has hoped to transform? Further, while Buddhists happily draw on the prestige scientific attention brings, what if further scientific studies show that meditation is actually not nearly as effective in diminishing destructive emotions as, say, cognitive behavioral therapy or psychotropic medications? Such considerations suggest that meditation need not necessarily be construed as a science in order to be beneficial and that the enfolding of meditation within the discourses of scientific rationalism may leave some of its possibilities undisclosed.

For the historian, though, the representation of meditation as a science says a great deal about how it has come to be situated within the discourses and practices of modernity. Meditation in the modern context is detraditionalized precisely at the point where it can now *become* a mode of open-ended inquiry, a tool of self-investigation that may lead to any conclusion whatever. Here is where it has become disembedded from the traditional worlds of Buddhist practice and has taken up residence in an entirely new realm as one among other tools of psychology and self-exploration. In this context, its ends are no longer determined solely by the authority of Buddhist tradition but also by modern psychology, which in turn is embedded in the broader discourses of modernity that stress autonomy, self-direction, and self-discovery. Meditation, thus, has entered an entirely unprecedented arena in which its benefits, purposes, and even methods are open to question and revision not only by meditation masters but by neuroscientists, psychologists, and the public at large. It is not that meditation within more traditional contexts has disappeared; it is rather that it has overflowed its traditional containment within the borders of the monastery and now contends in the postmodern marketplace of ideas and practices.[11]

Detraditionalization, Accommodation, and Cultural Critique

The meaning, purpose, and social significance of Buddhist meditation has changed in important ways as a result of its encounter with modernity. It has in some contexts come to be seen as the central practice of Buddhism and at the same time become detraditionalized, privatized, and unmoored from institutional authority and its traditional soteriological significance—in some cases even taking on a life independent of Buddhism altogether. This transformation is largely due to its encounter with the aforementioned discourses and practices of western modernity, whether in the West or in Asia.

It has claimed a place within these discourses and practices in particular ways. As a spiritual-mystical technique that aspires to a universal truth transcending religious dogma, in some cases it breaks away from the "religion" of Buddhism and is seen as a path, transcending all religions, to an alleged truth at their core. As an instrument for ascertaining "natural laws" within the mind, it becomes a technique for empirical inquiry. As a tool of taming negative emotions and gaining control over the mind, it is a therapeutic tool and a means for the enhancement of the individual's freedom to choose his or her own destiny. As a method for excavating the unconscious, it is a means for extracting the individual from internalized social and cultural constraints that prevent self-actualization. And as a means to health and relaxation, it becomes a globalized medical and psychological practice for the benefit of all humankind.

These are all forms of Buddhist meditation's detraditionalization, part of which, as noted, entails a shift of authority from without to within. Underlying all of these novel approaches is a tendency to grant considerable—indeed nearly absolute—authority to individual meditative experience. It may seem strange to suggest that this is a shift at all—after all, is not the goal of meditation the discovery of reality through personal experience? The answer is yes and no. In traditional contexts, personal meditative experience is generally not considered authoritative on its own; it is always checked, tested, and confirmed by the teacher and the tradition. As Robert Sharf points out, "the legitimacy and authority of Buddhist *mārga* [path] narratives lie precisely in their filiality to the canon"—rather than appeal to practitioners' individual meditative experiences (1995a: 239). The heightened authority of individual experience is largely a modern development.

As noted, not all of Buddhist meditation practice across the world is detraditionalized. Meditation in many monasteries proceeds in very traditional ways, and detraditionalized meditation coexists, sometimes even in the same institutions, with traditional approaches. Yet the image of meditation as a noninstitutionalized, nontraditionalized practice, along with the virtual identification of Buddhism with meditation, has made Buddhism itself appear in some western representations as a species of free-form, individual spirituality. This is especially true of western representations of Zen. Alan Watts insists that "if there is anything in the world that can overcome cultural conditioning, it is Zen," because Zen is not "institutionalized" and its "ancient exponents were 'universal individualists'" who were neither members of an organization nor relied on formal authority (Watts 1989 [1957]: xii). These assertions about the adherents of Zen are highly dubious—Zen monks have always functioned within highly institutionalized structures and have relied on the strict and highly formal authority of the Zen master. My point, however, is not that Watts was inaccurate but that his inaccuracy was clearly guided by the modernist ideal of the unaffiliated "universal individualist" who is free from institutions and under the authority of no one. To whatever extent similar ideals exist in East Asian Daoist-inflected Buddhism, Watts is clearly ringing tones that resonate with the western individualistic ideals we have discussed. Hubert Benoit strikes a similar chord: "Zen is not a church of which one is or is not a member. It is a universal point of view, offered to everyone, imposed on no one; it is not like a political party which one has to enroll in and commit oneself to. I can make use of the Zen approach in my search for truth without arraying myself, literally or metaphorically, in Chinese or Japanese garments" (2004: 7). Meditation, on this model, becomes one tool among others from which one can choose in fashioning one's own individual religious practice without having to commit to an institutional structure. It is in this sense that it has become privatized, individualized, and detraditionalized.

It might be tempting here to conclude that the integration of Buddhist meditation into the various discourses and practices of modernity is always a one-way assimilation, an appropriation of a specific element of Buddhism as a tool for achieving ends for human well-being defined solely in western terms. While examples exist in which meditation would indeed seem wholly co-opted by decidedly non-Buddhist interests—meditation for increasing worker productivity or improving one's golf game—this integration also brings Buddhist values into these modern contexts and carries the potential to transform them just as meditation has been transformed by them. Meditation, even in such radically new settings as the conference room, the doctor's office, and the health club, *does* contribute something new to modern psychology, medicine, and other aspects of modern western culture. Something of Buddhist values and ideas survives the transmutation into western idioms; while meditation is changed by the West, it also changes the West. Buddhist meditation has, in fact, contributed unique things to modern culture, in spite of—or perhaps *because* of—the fact that it has been changed and adapted to the West. It is probably too early to see what kind of impact meditation will have on western culture—or indeed on Asian Buddhist cultures, in which it is now widespread among the laity.

In trying to discern such changes, though, we can see certain aspirations that are by now familiar in modern (and not just western) approaches to Buddhist meditation. The meeting of Buddhism and modernity is suffused with a hope that the dharma can reform, repair, or develop further some of the modernity's dominant paradigms and practices. The idea of meditation as an science of the internal realm, for example, implies a general acceptance of science but also a dissatisfaction with some of its "materialistic" implications. Thurman is quite explicit, for example, in his hopes for a Buddhist rehumanizing of the sciences. Likewise, Fromm hoped that meditation could push psychoanalysis further. To whatever extent these hopes are based on adequate representations of meditation and Buddhism, they complicate the view that they have simply been brought on board the modern project to further modernity's ends. Although the foregoing examples show how Buddhist meditation has been infused into modernity's individualistic tendencies, the function to which it has been called is not merely to reinforce those tendencies. Rather, Buddhism—in this case meditation—has infused itself into the modern conversation with the hope that it can ameliorate some of modernity's malignant aspects. Buddhism has been asked to work within the western traditions of radical reflexivity and in-dividualistic spirituality not just to perpetuate them but to reform them. Some scholars have rightly pointed out that this hope for Buddhist solutions to non-Buddhist problems often has had much to do with western fantasies of rescue by the "mysterious East." But surely not all attempts to engage with Buddhist ideas and practices can be reduced to this. Some in fact have been serious at-tempts to find new ways out of some of modernity's entrenched problems. For all its accommodation to modern life, meditation still has been enlisted as an implicit critique and an antidote to some of the destructive elements of that life: its frenetic pace, its materialistic nihilism, its consumption-driven ethos, its convulsive violence. Many of the things contemporary meditation teachers invite students to use meditation to "see through" are none other than these ill-nesses of modernity—including its excessive individualism itself. Thus medi-tation's adaptation to western modes of individualism has not been complete. In this very adaptation it has acquired a new vocabulary for cultural critique (a subject I will address in chapter 9).

8

Mindfulness, Literature, and the Affirmation of Ordinary Life

But they beckoned; leaves were alive; trees were alive. And the leaves being connected by millions of fibres with his own body, there on the seat, fanned it up and down; when the branch stretched he, too, made that statement. The sparrows fluttering, rising, and falling in jagged fountains were part of the pattern; the white and blue, barred with black branches. Sounds made harmonies with premeditation; the spaces between them as significant as the sounds. A child cried. Rightly far away a horn sounded. All taken together meant the birth of a new religion.

—Virginia Woolf, *Mrs. Dalloway*

William Perkins was a drunk before he became an esteemed English Puritan minister and well-known scholarly exponent of Calvinism. He died in 1602, shortly before the end of Queen Elizabeth's reign and a few years before Galileo made his famous observations of the moons of Jupiter, confirming the heliocentric view of the solar system. Perkins, though, was quite down-to-earth. Belying the ascetic image of the Puritan preacher, he insisted that Christians should feel free to employ material goods not only for pragmatic purposes but also "for honest delight," as long as it was in accord with biblical principles. He declared in one of his works that even activities like doing the dishes and wiping one's shoes, "so long as they are done within the lawes of God . . . howsoever grosse they appear outwardly, yet are they sanctified" (quoted in George 1961: 139).

Today such an idea might seem more familiar to Buddhists than to Christians. It is commonplace, in fact, to find exhortations in contemporary Buddhist literature to perform the tasks of life with mindfulness and care. In doing so, countless books, articles, and dharma talks urge, one can realize something extraordinary, even sacred, in the most mundane things and activities. Thich Nhat Hanh's often-cited recipes for mindfulness in the midst of ordinary activity include, "taking my time with each dish, being fully aware of the dish, the water, and each movement of my hands." Hurrying through the task mindlessly, he insists, "would be a pity, for each minute, each second of life is a miracle" (1991: 26). His recommendations for mindful housework, walking, and eating—tasting each bite of the food, noting its texture, contemplating its sources and relationships to other things—have become staples of the contemporary practice of Buddhism in the West. Mindfulness is ideally to be brought into every facet of life so that the alert quiescence of the meditative mind pervades all activities. The practitioner is advised to bring calm, alert, and non-evaluative attention to the flow of present moments, letting go of thoughts, memories, and anxieties about the past and future. The objects of mindfulness can be one's own thoughts and feelings, sensations, bodily states, memories, physical objects one encounters—indeed anything and everything that makes up the experience of the present moment in its continual flowing from future to past. There is a certain sensuality to some modern descriptions of mindfulness. Lama Surya Das (Jeffery Miller) recommends mindfully walking barefoot on grass or the beach, or treading slowly on autumn leaves, appreciating each sensation, "attending to the crackle of each step" (1997: 71–72). The insight meditation teachers Joseph Goldstein and Jack Kornfield describe one aspect of mindfulness as "opening what is closed," particularly opening the senses: mindfulness cultivates a "much greater sensitivity and refinement in our sense impressions" as the mind lets go of concepts and experiences things more immediately (1987: 15). In *vipassanā* meditation, the practitioner attends to all experiences, precisely noting and sometimes labeling them—"thinking, breathing, remembering"—but not grasping at them. In letting go of the usual concepts, attachments, aversions, and associations connected to any given object of attention, the simple wonder of things "as they are" comes into awareness; released from egocentric appropriation, they can be seen as a "miracle."

In this chapter, I will shift the focus a bit from meditation to the more general category of mindfulness, which includes formal meditation practices but also extends to include meditative attentiveness to any activity at all. In today's lay-oriented Buddhist environments, mindfulness is a tool for bringing greater awareness, skill, and appreciation to every aspect of life, not only personal but also family, public, and political life. Mindfulness, say countless modern

Buddhist texts, contributes to heightened sensitivity to the beauties of life, as well as cultivating skill in addressing its painful elements. It is conducive not only to personal well-being but also to the cultivation of ethical responsibility, as one becomes more aware of the implications of one's actions for one's family, community, and the world as a whole. Among many lay Buddhists and Buddhist sympathizers in North America, Europe, and Asia, mindfulness has become a way of negotiating the fast-paced complexities of modern life with its seemingly endless stream of tasks and obligations; of transmuting its frenetically banal activity into a spiritual exercise—a moment-by-moment, vividly quiescent appreciation of things in their ordinariness.

To explain the recent centrality of mindfulness practice in Buddhist modernism, especially among laity, many practitioners and analysts point to the frenziedness of late modernity: meditation in activity, the focus on the moment, the appreciation of the ordinary are antidotes to both the petty anxieties and deep spiritual illnesses of the consumer-oriented, psychically fragmented, and hypertensively stressful lifestyles of the global middle class. Certainly there is truth to this assessment. But I shall attempt to elucidate a few more elusive historical and cultural factors that have come together both to create a place for and to transform Buddhist mindfulness practice in such a way that it could be understood and employed as such an antidote. Perkins's and Thich Nhat Hanh's respective sanctifications of the commonplace form parentheses around the modern period, the first occurring at its beginning, when Puritanism in England still had an air of the radical about it, and the second occurring amid the full flowering of multicultural late modernity, when Buddhists and Muslims live next to Baptists and atheists. Can these two superficially similar sentiments from utterly different traditions really have anything to do with each other? Can they be placed in a relationship that illuminates how Buddhism has taken its place in the modern world? Comparative religionists of the past might have seen the resemblance as pointing to a deep commonality in these two approaches to life on an experiential level, despite the vast differences in their respective cultures and doctrines. Approaching the issue more historically, I will ask if there is in fact a wider context, even a common milieu or novel cultural formation—though occupying opposite poles, both temporally and culturally—in which these two sanctifications of ordinary facets of life come to make sense.

And in this chapter I will suggest that yes, a particular sort of world-affirmation has been a constituent of modernity and created an ecology of ideas and practices in which a new interpretation of Buddhist mindfulness could find a niche. I will sketch a few of the broad elements of this facet of modernity, and then focus on the ways modern literary sensibilities have helped to shape the interpretation of Buddhist mindfulness practices and the kinds of experiences they are understood to facilitate. I intend to examine, in other words, the conditions under which mindfulness practices have come to take their place in the modern context. I will develop three points to illustrate these conditions, as follows. First, Buddhist mindfulness has taken on a new significance within the context of modernity's broad world-affirming attitude. Second, its recent articulation is informed by modern literature's valorization of the details of everyday life, its finely tuned descriptions of the flow of consciousness, and its new reverence for ordinary objects and their capacity to reflect the universal. And third, this articulation provides a distinctively modern way of resacralizing the world without resort to the supernatural.

Modernity and the Affirmation of Ordinary Life

What is ironic about the use of Buddhist mindfulness techniques to approach more skillfully the complex vicissitudes of modern life—work, family, social, and political life—is that these techniques were originally developed by monks who had ostensibly renounced these very things. Indeed, the early formulations of such practices seem to have little to do with "opening to the world" or "appreciating everyday life," much less being more productive and efficient in the workplace (another current application of mindfulness). They were designed, first, to bring heightened awareness of various states of mind and free the practitioner from entanglement in them, with the ultimate end of achieving nirvana, overcoming suffering, and ending the cycle of rebirth. As I have suggested, the early Buddhist monastic ethos, at least insofar as it is represented in the Pali canon, is not one of encouraging deeper engagement, participation, and connectedness with the world.[1] Like the concept of interdependence, however, mindfulness practices had a long history of interpretation, reinterpretation, and transformation in Asia as well as in the West. Some Mahayana texts tend to insist less on ascetic detachment and deemphasize the goal of ending rebirth, preferring a model of this-worldly Buddhahood. Yet little evidence exists, either from historical records or from contemporary ethnography, that mindfulness and meditation in traditional contexts have been key components in the ways ordinary people have typically lived the dharma. The application of mindfulness to finding more appreciative and skillful approaches to work, family, and all of the hectic activities of life is a phenomenon of the current age.

What is it about the modern period that has provided an arena for mindfulness to emerge as central to the practice of Buddhism among the laity? To first sketch the answer in the broadest possible terms: one of the constituent features of modernity—so deeply ingrained in modern cultures that it is in fact hard to see—is a new kind of world-affirming attitude that began with the Reformation and continues to our time. Taylor contrasts this attitude—which he calls "affirmation of ordinary life"—to premodern ones such as the medieval warrior ethic of honor and glory, the monastic ethic of self-denial and asceticism, and the Platonic view of the forms, all of which saw the ordinary life of work and family as profane. Modernity, he suggests, inaugurated a new valuation of ordinary life, an ethic that saw production, family, work, and reproduction as the loci of a good life. This world-affirmation entails the idea that human dignity, even sacrality, is not found outside the ordinary life but rather in the particular manner of living it (1989: 211–304). One need not become a great warrior or live solely for the next world for life to have meaning and dignity; one can instead embrace the possibilities and potentials afforded by whatever circumstances one's life offers. There is a nobility to ordinary life here that is absent in previous eras of western culture, as well as a critique of previous ideals for their implied elitism.

Reformation theologies put forward the early versions of this affirmation—hence Perkins's sacralization of shoe-wiping and dish-washing—and Enlightenment thinkers pushed it further into the secular realm, relating it both to cosmology and the pursuit of happiness. Deists insisted that human happiness entails the fulfillment of natural desires. God built into humanity natural needs and wants, and their satisfaction is not only acceptable, it is the rational fulfillment of God's laws. They interpreted God's providence as granting the means for human happiness on earth, an end they unapologetically embraced as noble and elevated. It is not that these thinkers stopped believing in an afterlife (though a few did), but rather that life here on Earth was no longer seen merely as something to endure until one could enjoy the rewards of Heaven, or natural desires only as temptations to be avoided. In the Deistic conception, to fulfill our natural desires and sentiments rationally and morally was itself the good God intends for human beings on Earth. Happiness here and now, then, became a rational way of using one's God-given abilities to conform to the natural order of things. This contrasted starkly to medieval religious conceptions of fulfilling God's will, which placed little value on happiness per se, except as a by-product of obedience to God's will. Medieval theologians often portrayed life on Earth as something to be endured and with little value in itself except as a preparation for eternity. The Enlightenment thinkers largely rejected ascetic moralities and introduced respect for what they considered a healthy self-love. In this way, human happiness and the proper means to it became a dominant theme in Enlightenment and post-Enlightenment discourse.

The history of this affirmation of ordinary life in the West is also pertinent to the desacralization of materiality that the Protestant Reformation brought about. Protestant thinkers, like William Perkins, largely rejected localized, material sacrality—sacred objects, relics, places—which had the effect of leveling the spiritual landscape of the world. In the new Protestant order, no place or object was inherently more sacred than another. This began with the Reformers' assertion that each individual could have unmediated access to God and hence had no need for special places, priests, icons, or rituals. Sacredness began to withdraw from things—relics, pilgrimage places, the sacraments—and to be pushed to two poles: God himself, beyond the world, and the individual in his or her own faith. This aspect of the desacralization or disenchantment of the world was then pushed further by scientific rationalism. With the rejection of the "material sacred" and the suspicion of the various mediators of sacrality, more room was made for the purely instrumental valuation of everyday things.

This increasing instrumentalization of things, though, produced a tension between broadly rationalist and Romantic views. The rationalist tendency was to instrumentalize the things of ordinary life—to appreciate more fully the commonplace objects of the world, but to see them primarily in terms of their capacity to serve human needs. This further contributed to the sense that the world had become disenchanted, which in turn produced a response, first from the Romantics and later from a variety of twentieth-century artists, writers, and thinkers who tried to recover a sense of lost meaning in these things. Tennyson's "Flower in a Crannied Wall" exemplifies the romantic tendency: if I could understand what the flower truly is, "root and all," he opines, "I should know what God and man is." The instrumentalizing of ordinary things, therefore, produced a corresponding sense of hiddenness and mystery about them; a sense that there must be "something more" to them than just their utility. In the twentieth century, phenomenologists took up the effort to reclaim things from their merely instrumental value in a different way: they attempted to reestablish the primordial intimacy between persons and objects in their everyday interactions. Heidegger's explication of things as "ready-to-hand" and Merleau-Ponty's explications of the body's relationship to objects both were attempts to recover the prereflective experience of the physical world from the representational model of consciousness by asserting a subpersonal and tacit intertwining of consciousness and objects.

Clearly, many other powerful cultural forces—political, economic, commercial, and social—for the revaluation and affirmation of the ordinary have been at work during the modern period. But this very broad characterization will suffice to make some initial suggestions about the context in which modernist Buddhist concepts of meditation and mindfulness have emerged. The affirmation of everyday life in the modern West is one of modernity's pervasive cultural attitudes. It embodies both the aforementioned tensions between rationalistic, Enlightenment-dominated thinking about the status of minds and things and the resistance to the purely instrumentalist and rationalist approach that Romanticism inaugurated and various twentieth-century movements then developed. This world-affirmation, as well as the tensions between its various modes, created a space for Buddhist mindfulness practices and transformed them from monastic disciplines into techniques of happiness and self-cultivation often serving this-worldly ends. Specifically, the new world-affirmation made room for various attempts to resacralize the everyday world without a return to premodern modes of sacralization, such as the veneration of relics common to both Christianity and Buddhism. The contemporary adaptations of mindfulness practices became possible only because of the space opened for them by the distinctively modern valuation of ordinary life as itself the location of sacrality. It was through this facet of modernity that Buddhism came to be understood today not as a way to an otherworldly nirvana or heavenly realm but as, in the words of modern Japanese Zen teacher Maezumi Rōshi, a way to "appreciate your life" or, in Thich Nhat Hanh's, "a clever way to enjoy life" (Maezumi 2002; Nhat Hanh 1988: ix).

With the foregoing account as a backdrop, I shall now focus on certain twentieth-century literary forms that were important in enabling Buddhism's embrace of modernity's world-affirmation, as they established practices of attentiveness to the everyday and pointed to the possibility of the extraordinary, even the transcendent, enfolded within the commonplace.

Literary Epiphanies

Henry Perowne wakes in his bed to the sound of his wife's hair dryer in the bathroom. A phrase from Darwin—"There is grandeur in this view of life"— echoes from the previous night's reading. He hears her wardrobe door opening and pictures its interior lacquered veneer. The sounds of her bare feet and the rustle of her robe on the floor reach his ears, and then the "businesslike tapping of her boot heels" across the tiles. He recalls a conversation about a poem with his daughter during a walk by a river with a light dusting of snow and briefly considers that there is, in fact, a kind of religious grandeur in the theory of evolution. He then remembers his plan to make fish stew for a family gathering that evening and rises to use the toilet, feeling a vague memory of some past shame or embarrassment that he can't quite place. As he flushes, he recalls with some skepticism an article that he read claiming that at least one molecule of his waste will one day fall on him as rain. He begins humming a wartime tune: "We'll meet again, don't know where, don't know when."

Perowne is a fictional character in Ian McEwan's novel *Saturday*, a work having nothing whatsoever to do with Buddhism.[2] This kind of narrative, how- ever, is one of countless examples in modern and contemporary literature of two themes relevant to my subject: the self-reflexive inward turn toward an examination of consciousness itself and the attention to the details of the ordi- nary lives of human beings in particular contexts. *Saturday* is a finely wrought, densely textured, and precisely rendered account of the thought and world of its main character through the course of a single day. It is, as a review in the *Nation* said, "a novel about consciousness" (Siegel 2005). The reason it is relevant to the examination of modern and contemporary forms of Buddhism is that works of this genre constitute not only an important literary development but also a broader sensibility characteristic of the modern and late modern age that, I want to argue, is crucial to understanding the contemporary adaptation of Bud- dhist mindfulness practice: the meticulous attending to the quotidian objects of everyday life and the precise interactions of consciousness with them.

Such minutiae in most eras would have been considered unworthy of notice, much less art. It is unthinkable that the rustle of Perowne's wife's robe, the random phrases and memories of songs and conversations, not to mention the act of relieving himself, would have found a place in, say, Greek or Indian epic narratives or European crusade literature. They simply would not have been considered significant to the story. The details of everyday life are invested with an unprecedented importance in the modern novel, rising from obscurity to claim the attention of the reader and demand recognition. Part of this is due to the increased sophistication in the use of symbol—rings, vases, rain, and rivers in modern novels and poems are impregnated with meaning that evokes major themes of the narrative. This attention to the pedestrian elements of life, however, invites more than just the discerning of symbolic significance: we are asked to look at the most ordinary objects, events, thoughts, and feelings as important in their own right, simply because they make up the dense fabric of human life itself. In defining the task of the modern novelist, Virginia Woolf implores the reader to "look within" and "examine for a moment an ordinary mind on an ordinary day":

> The mind receives a myriad impressions—trivial, fantastic,
> evanescent, or engraved with the sharpness of steel. From all sides
> they come, an incessant shower of innumerable atoms; and as they
> fall, as they shape themselves into the life of Monday or Tuesday,
> the accent falls differently from of old; the moment of importance
> came not here but there. . . . Is it not the task of the novelist to convey
> this varying, this unknown and uncircumscribed spirit, whatever

aberration or complexity it may display, with as little mixture of the
alien and external as possible? (1984b: 150)

This approach, rather than filtering out the infinite minutiae that might dis-
tract a reader from the movement of the plot, opens the attention to "whatever
aberration or complexity" arises. Not only does such promiscuity call attention to previously unconsidered objects—the "furniture of the world," as Hegel
derisively called it—it draws forth the most intimate movements of thinking,
feeling, and sensing. For Woolf, along with many other Modernists and contemporary writers, "the external event is significant primarily for the way it
triggers and releases the inner life" (Showalter 2000: xx).

The modern novel demonstrates an unprecedented attention to the details of ordinary life, as does modern visual art's depiction of commonplace
scenes rather than heroic battles, biblical stories, or medieval visions of the
afterlife. This orientation goes back at least to the Romantic period, with its impulse to transform the ordinary through art. According to Coleridge, genius
is the ability to place "things in a new light." Wordsworth likewise imagines
seeing things entirely anew: "You look round on your mother earth . . . As if
you were her first-born birth, / And none had lived before you!" (quoted in
Perry 2005: 596). For the Romantics, this had to do with a closeness to nature
over against the contrivances of society, an attentiveness to the stirrings of the
soul that could pierce through convention to see things as a child might and
thereby reenchant things that had been mechanized, reimbuing them with a
sense of mystery. The post-Romantic afterlife of this aesthetic presents itself in
a number of nineteenth-century novelists, such as Flaubert, Balzac, and Zola;
but literary Modernism took up the emphasis on making an ordinary thing
or situation extraordinary in an entirely new key. Even as Modernists overtly
rejected much in Romanticism—its emphasis on feelings, the individual, the
transcendent, its often overheated and ostentatious language—many reframed
the emphasis on a deep intuition of nature in terms of a wresting of something
extraordinary from the mundane elements of life.[3] The descriptive power to
re-create the familiar so that its banality becomes remarkable, and the recovery
of the immediacy, freshness, and vividness of things obscured by habit and
fixed conceptions, have been crucial to the literary and artistic sensibilities of
the twentieth century. They suggest the need not only to recover things themselves from their increasing engulfment in the rationalized, bureaucraticized,
and mechanized world but also to free the mind to apprehend things in ways
not determined and prescribed by such a world. According to Frederic Jameson, "The most influential formal impulses of canonical modernism have been
strategies of inwardness, which set out to reappropriate an alienated universe

by transforming it into personal styles and private languages" (1979: 2). Part of the Modernist impulse is to break free from the stultifying perceptions foisted on the mind by the modern world, even when such freedom entails looking unflinchingly at its horrors.

Joyce's stream-of-consciousness novels are perhaps the most ready examples of this new transfiguration of the ordinary: indeed the publication of *Ulysses* heralded what Henri LeFebvre called the "momentous eruption of everyday life into literature" (1971: 2). Joyce's work elucidates the moment-by-moment passage of human experience in its uncensored density and ambiguity, shining light on the commonplace and transforming it in a poetic presentation of the often cacophonous interplay of internal and external voices. Traditional considerations of plot, narrative, and point of view are cast aside to reveal the constantly shifting, complexly layered interweaving of internal dialogue with physical realities. The traditional unified protagonist gives way to a protean subjectivity that unfurls in a continuously transforming array of voices, positions, and perceptions. *Ulysses* and countless other novels and poems since not only illuminate the most mundane physical realities, they render the operations of the psyche in unprecedented detail and nuance. Joyce called such literary revelations of the extraordinary in the ordinary "epiphanies," which meant for him "'the sudden revelation of the whatness of a thing,' the moment in which 'the soul of the commonest object . . . seems to us radiant.'" For Joyce, these "sudden spiritual manifestation[s]" might be found "in casual, unostentatious, even unpleasant moments" (Ellman 1959: 87).

Likewise, in his *Remembrance of Things Past*, Marcel Proust's narratives of involuntary memory triggered by the encounter with some ordinary object reach the pitch of secular religiosity. His celebrated description of the arising of an old memory when his protagonist tastes a cookie and tea is a classic Modernist eruption of the astonishing from the utterly mundane:

> No sooner had the warm liquid mixed with the crumbs touched my
> palate than a shudder ran through me and I stopped, intent upon
> the extraordinary thing that was happening to me. An exquisite
> pleasure had invaded my senses, something isolated, detached,
> with no suggestion of its origin. And at once the vicissitudes of life
> had become indifferent to me, its disasters innocuous, its brevity
> illusory—this new sensation having had on me the effect which love
> has of filling me with a precious essence; or rather this essence was
> not in me, it *was* me. I had ceased now to feel mediocre, contingent,
> mortal. Whence could it have come to me, this all-powerful joy?
> I sensed that it was connected with the taste of the tea and the cake,

but that it infinitely transcended those savours, could, no, indeed, be of the same nature. Whence did it come? What did it mean? How could I seize and apprehend it? (1981: 48–50)

Discussing another kind of secular revelation in a Jane Austen novel in which a couple converses on the stairs before dinner, Woolf notes Austen's ability to wrest a character's self-revelation out of ordinary moments: "But, from triviality, from commonplace, their words become suddenly full of meaning, and the moment for both one of the most memorable in their lives. It fills itself; it shines; it glows; it hangs before us, deep, trembling, serene for a second; next, the housemaid passes, and this drop, in which all the happiness of life has collected, gently subsides again to become part of the ebb and flow of ordinary existence" (1984a: 142.)

Although it is safe to assume that there are many contemporary Buddhists who have not read Joyce, Woolf, or Proust, the sensibilities of literary Modernism and its successors introduced an element into modern culture, within the larger context of the affirmation of the ordinary, that informed and provided a preunderstanding for the way Buddhist mindfulness is understood today. My point is not simply that they, or any other modern novelist, may have "influenced" the shape of Buddhism in the West; it is that such literary works have informed, and also illustrate, the conditions under which Buddhism could be made sense of and transformed in modern, western contexts. The idea that heightened awareness of the details and textures of ordinary life and the suggestion that everyday things, events, and thoughts could be transfigured through art to reveal something profound—Joyce's "epiphany," Pound's "magic moment," or Proust's flood of memories on tasting a cookie—illustrate a dialectical interweaving of the prosaic and the profound—of what Woolf called "the cotton wool of everyday life" and "moments of being," memorable and ecstatic experiences prompted by ordinary things like the sound of waves crashing on the shore (1985: 69–70). This interweaving of the ordinary and extraordinary articulated a particular language into which Buddhist mindfulness has been translated, providing a new context in which such practices make sense and directing the expectations of what the practitioner is supposed to derive from them.

Modern Buddhist Epiphanies

A number of modern Buddhists and commentators on Buddhism have explicitly attempted to connect the dharma—and meditation especially—with Modernist and contemporary literature. In his introduction to D. T. Suzuki's *Zen*

Buddhism, philosopher William Barrett called Joyce's *Ulysses* a "profoundly Oriental . . . book" since it, "like the Oriental mind, succeed[s] in holding the opposites together: light and dark, beautiful and ugly, sublime and banal" (1956: xiii). Barrett also saw D. H. Lawrence, in his "preaching against the bloodless rationalism of his culture" and his interest in becoming "mindless," as "a groping intuition after the doctrine of 'no-mind'" of Zen (xii–xiii). Barrett discerned in Zen, Lawrence, and Joyce, as well as Heidegger, possibilities for overcoming failed western abstraction and dualism and a redirection of attention to the concrete.

Contemporary scholar and Zen teacher Taigen Dan Leighton goes beyond such generalities and makes more precisely the connection I am interested in, asserting that *Ulysses*, in its "detailed depictions of its main characters' consciousnesses during their activities and convergences," exemplifies the Buddhist adept's "penetrating insight into the essence of everyday, mundane awareness" (2003: 129). Contemporary Indian writer Pankaj Mishra connects the passage by Proust quoted earlier with the Buddhist doctrine of *anātman*, claiming that both suggest epiphanies in which the self is seen as a fictional unity covering a wide-ranging continuity of experiences held together by memory (2004: 259–61). Natalie Goldberg, an American student of Zen and author of *Writing Down the Bones: Freeing the Writer Within*, similarly suggests connections between meditation, world-affirmation, and the precise rendering of detail in writing. She insists that a writer "must say yes to life, to all of life: the water glasses, the Kemp's half-and-half, the ketchup on the counter." Writers must "accept things as they are, come to love the details, and step forward with a yes on our lips" (1986: 44). Goldberg ties this affirmation of worldly particulars directly to Zen meditation and its effacement of the ego: "Katagiri Roshi said: 'When you do zazen, you should be gone. So zazen does zazen. Not Steve or Barbara does zazen.' This is also how you should be when you write: writing does writing. You disappear: you are simply recording the thoughts that are streaming through you" (45–46). Similarly, as noted, some of the Buddhist-influenced Beat writers, Ginsberg especially, saw mindfulness practice as a way of opening up the mind to itself in an uncensored stream that was the very stuff of their literature. Other writers have seen mindfulness as a prerequisite to writing, as well as other activities. Charles Johnson, the celebrated African American novelist and Buddhist, writes that mindful concentration is

> required for the doing well of any worldly activity, including the
> lifelong labor of writing. . . . Yet it matters not at all if the activity
> we're talking about is writing a novel, preparing dinner, teaching a
> class, serving tea, or simply walking, the spiritual point is everywhere
> and always the same: Any action is performed best and most

beautifully, especially unpleasant tasks, when the actor practices what
Buddhists call "mindfulness"; when he is wholly and selflessly aware
of every nuance in the activity and immersed in it. (2003: 34–35)

Mindfulness here is asserted to be more than an effective way of inspiring writing; it has become a specific *technique* for attending to the details of the world
and the nuances of the mind in ways that bring about epiphanies similar to
those the Modernist novelists have attempted to render in literature.

This modern Buddhist affirmation of the ordinary is in tension with the
more traditional Buddhist suspicion of the things of the world and their ability
to mesmerize the mind and enchain it to suffering. Buddhist modernist literature, in fact, does not just "step forward with a yes on [its] lips" in an unqualified
way: often the epiphanic insight into the ordinary is a realization of the impermanence or insubstantiality of things, their inability to satisfy completely. In
his poem "What would you do if you lost it?" Ginsberg weaves Buddhist allu-
sions together with an inventory of the contents of his apartment and his mind,
realizing that each one will vanish on his death (Tomkinson 1995: 101):

> Teachings, Tantras, Haggadahs, Zohar, Revelations, poetries,
> > Koans
> Forgotten with the snowy world, forgotten
> With generations of icicles crashing to white gullies by roadside,
> Dharmakaya forgot, Nirmanakaya shoved in coffin,
> > Sambhogakaya eclipsed in candle-light snuffed by the
> > > playful cat—
> Goodbye my own treasures, bodies adored to the nipple,
> old souls worshipped flower-eye or imaginary auditory
> > panoramic skull—
> goodbye old socks washed over & over, blue boxer shorts, subzero
> > longies,
> new Ball Boots black hiplength for snowdrifts near the farm
> > mailbox. . . .
>
> notebooks untranscribed, hundreds of little poems & prose my
> > own hand, newspaper interviews, assemblaged archives, useless
> > paperworks surrounding me imperfectly chronologic, humorous
> > later in eternity, reflective of Cities' particular streets studios and
> > boudoirs. . . .
>
> Goodbye America you hope you prayer you tenderness, you
> > IBM 135-35 Electronic Automated Battlefield Igloo White
> > > Dragon-tooth Fuel-Air Bomb over Indochina

Goodbye Heaven, farewell Nirvana, sad Paradise adieu, adios all
    angels and archangels, devas & devakis, Bodhisattvas, Buddhas,
    rings of Seraphim, Constellations of elect souls weeping singing
    in the golden Bhumi Rungs, goodbye High Throne, High Central
    Plane, Alleluiah Light beyond Light, a wave of the hand to Thee
    Central Golden Rose. . . .

None left standing! No tears left for eyes, no eyes for weeping,
        no mouth for singing, no song for the hearer, no more words for
        any mind.

Here the teachings of impermanence and an intertwining of attentive engagement and Buddhist detachment are at play. One attends to things, seeing their
hidden miraculousness; yet clinging to them as if they will endure only brings
more frustration and suffering. These two insights are often quite closely entwined in Buddhist thought. In fact, Ginsberg's poem is not as sorrowful as
it might first appear: the last lines playfully allude to the *Heart Sutra*, which
hammers home with its negations piled upon negations the lack of inherent
self-existence in all things—their impermanence, dependence, and lack of
fixity—but celebrates this realization as awakening itself, ending with an ex-
clamation of joy: *Svahā*! Part of the miraculousness of things, then, is their
very ephemerality. With the intertwining of the ordinary and profound is also
the intertwining of affirmation and negation: the details of life can only be affirmed when they are accepted as fleeting, interdependent, and insubstantial.
Moreover, they can only be affirmed when they are disentangled from personal
cravings and aversions, from their purely instrumental relationship to the "I."

Hermann Hesse's Ancient-Modern Buddha

Not only Modernist or Beat writers' work embodies this dialectic of the prosaic
and the profound. Hermann Hesse's novel *Siddhartha* relates this dialectic in
a kind of neo-Romantic fable set in India at the time of the Buddha. Still frequently used in college courses to represent the world of ancient India, this
book has had an enduring influence on the western understanding of South
Asian religion since its publication in 1922. The novel tells of a man whose life
parallels that of Siddhartha Gautama (even sharing the Buddha's given name).
Despite his placement in ancient India, Hesse's protagonist embodies many of
the themes I have been discussing—individualism, world-affirmation, suspicion of institutional religion—and the novel itself both reflects and has shaped
the modern western conceptions of Asian enlightenment.

The story takes place in India at the time of the Buddha. The protagonist, a Brahmin, is restless and dissatisfied with his life among the priests, suspecting that their rites, lore, chants, and supplications to the gods are all of limited value. To Siddhartha's devoted friend Govinda, who also shares his restlessness, the typical Brahmin is a "lazy sacrificial official, an avaricious dealer in magical sayings, a conceited worthless orator, a wicked sly priest, or just a good stupid sheep amongst a large herd" (1951 [1922]: 4). When the two friends encounter the Buddha, Siddhartha can find no fault with his doctrines and recognizes him as one who has found the truth. Unlike Govinda, however, he does not deign to join the *sangha*, for, as he points out to Gautama, "you have [achieved awakening] by your own seeking, in your own way." Siddhartha insists he must do the same: "that is why I am going my own way—not to seek another and better doctrine, for I know there is none, but to leave all doctrines and all teachers and to reach my goal alone—or die" (33–34). Like the young Gautama, he joins a band of ascetics (shramanas), but after mastering their ways, abandons them, finding that radical asceticism leaves him short of his goal. He resolves to reenter the world to "gain experience himself," deciding that "he would only strive after whatever the inward voice commanded him, not tarry anywhere but where the voice advised him," for Gautama himself had obeyed "the voice in his own heart" to sit under the bo tree when he gained awakening (47–48).

In apparent contradiction to that voice, though, Siddhartha then becomes involved with a courtesan and a businessman and learns the arts of love and money making. In the ensuing years he becomes a rich man, until finally, in his forties, having become accustomed to rich foods and comforts, he becomes disgusted by his life of meaningless indulgence, leaves his property, servants, and lover behind, and sets out again into the forest. Like the Buddha, he has drunk deeply of both indulgence and asceticism and found both wanting. On the verge of suicide, he comes to the river where he had once met a ferryman, Vasudeva, years earlier. Looking into the river, for a moment he "remembered all that he had forgotten, all that was divine" (1951 [1922]: 90). He had to put an end to this "foolish, empty life" of riches and appetites, his "soft, well-upholstered hell" (97–98), to realize that his inner voice was still alive.

Siddhartha now begins a new life as a ferryman with the wise but unlearned Vasudeva. While doing so, he learns to listen to the river and hear its many voices: "Has it not the voice of a king, of a warrior, of a bull, of a nightbird, of a pregnant woman and a singing man, and a thousand other voices?" he asks Vasudeva. All of these mingle and become "the voice of life, the voice of Being, the voice of perpetual Becoming" (107–8). The peace arising from the river's "teaching" is interrupted, however, by the sudden appearance of his young son, of whom he was previously unaware. Siddhartha takes him into his care, but the son is spiteful toward his father and his simple life and eventually runs away. The pain of this loss serves to identify Siddhartha—who previously had a tendency toward aloofness and superiority toward common people—with their troubles, desires, and anxieties. Seeing that Siddhartha is deeply wounded by the loss of his son, Vasudeva takes him to the river again and urges him to listen closely. Concentrating fiercely, Siddhartha now sees pictures of his past floating by in the water: his father, his childhood, his time as an ascetic and as a businessman; he hears again in the river the countless voices of happiness and sorrow, good and evil, gain and loss, until he can no longer distinguish between them: "They all belonged to each other. . . . They were all interwoven and interlocked, entwined in a thousand ways," and together they formed a perfect harmony. Siddhartha finds himself finally at peace, "surrendering himself to the stream, belonging to the unity of all things" (135–36).

In the final chapter, Govinda, who joined the Buddha's order many years before but has failed to find realization, encounters his childhood friend Siddhartha one last time. Recognizing that Siddhartha has found enlightenment, he presses him for a "doctrine" or "certain knowledge." Siddhartha again expresses his distrust of doctrines and teachings but offers some ideas to his old friend: that the world is "perfect at every moment"; that "everything that exists is good; death as well as life, sin as well as holiness, wisdom as well as folly." In fact, he has *needed* lust, money, wretchedness, he explains, to "learn to love the world" (1951 [1922]: 144). He then picks up a stone and discusses it with Govinda:

> This stone is stone; it is also animal, God and Buddha. I do not
> respect and love it because it was one thing and will become something
> else, but because it has already long been everything and always is
> everything. I love it just because it is a stone, because today and now
> it appears to me as a stone. I see value and meaning in its fine
> markings and cavities, in the yellow, in the gray, in the hardness and
> the sound of it when I knock it, in the dryness or dampness of its
> surface. . . . Each [stone] is Brahman. At the same time it is very much
> stone, oily or soapy, and that is just what pleases me and seems
> wonderful and worthy of worship. (145)

Words and even thoughts are unimportant, he insists, but *things* are of value. "Every wind, every cloud, every bird, every beetle is equally divine and knows and can teach just as well as the esteemed river" (146).

Govinda questions this unqualified affirmation of the world, noting that the Buddha, while admonishing his disciples to compassion and forbearance, "forbade us to bind ourselves to earthly love." Siddhartha, however, assures his friend that the "apparent contradiction" between his and Gautama's teaching is a product of the "maze of meanings, within the conflict of words"; he insists, "I know I am at one with Gotama" (1951 [1922]: 147–48). This accord is confirmed when Govinda then has his own sweeping vision of unity in diversity and the profound in the ordinary, gazing not at the river but at Siddhartha's face. Within his friend's visage, Govinda beholds a stream of faces: people, animals, fishes, gods, some being born, some dying, some in agony, some committing violence, some in sexual ecstasy, all in flux, all passing away yet continuously coming to be again, transforming over and over endlessly. Encompassing all of these manifestations is Siddhartha's smiling face. "And Govinda saw that this mask-like smile, this smile of unity over the flowing forms, this smile of simultaneousness over the thousands of births and deaths—this smile of Siddhartha—was exactly the same as the calm, delicate, impenetrable, perhaps gracious, perhaps mocking, wise, thousand-fold smile of Gotama, the Buddha" (151).

The biographical note on Hesse on the last page of the Bantam English translation of *Siddhartha* calls it a "novel about the Buddha." No doubt this is simply a careless oversight based on the fact that Hesse gives his protagonist the same name as the Buddha. (The cover illustration perpetuates this confusion, showing a bronze Buddha-figure.) Yet it inadvertently signals Hesse's own identification of his Siddhartha with Siddhartha Gautama. The identification is part of the narrative itself—Siddhartha ultimately achieves the same goal as Gautama (indeed their shared name, in Sanskrit, means "one who has accomplished his aim"), the same blessed state of peace and happiness, the same enigmatic smile.

The two are identified on another level as well. Hesse's Siddhartha is the Buddha reconceived for the twentieth century, perhaps the Buddha Hesse *wished* the historical Buddha was: an awakened one with no baggage of centuries of accumulated tradition, who embodies not just the spiritual concerns of ancient India but those of modern Europe and America. Hesse's Siddhartha is the model of the Emersonian self-reliant spiritual seeker: antiauthoritarian, skeptical of rites and devotionalism, and fiercely individualist. Like the Romantics, he makes much of the unassailable authority of the "inner voice." His disgust at the urban world of business, hedonism, and acquisitiveness (the "well-upholstered hell") that stifled his inner voice, and the idealization of the simple, unlearned ferryman's life surely is a condemnation of the ills of modernity and the idealization of the peasant like that of Romantic-influenced Buddhist modernists. The book's harsh treatment of brahmanical priestcraft similarly reflects the anticlericism and growing dissatisfaction Hesse and many of his contemporaries felt toward the Christian church and "organized religion." His mistrust of words, teachings, and the "maze of meanings," moreover, embodies more than the traditional cautions in Indian thought about the limitations of language; it is also a response to modern pluralism and expresses the desire to find commonality between traditions, just as Siddhartha insists there is commonality between Gautama and himself. Indeed, Siddhartha's insistence that he is "at one with Gotama" is Hesse's insistence that his own uniquely modern conceptions are in accord with ancient Buddhism, despite their apparent differences. Echoing the perennialists, Hesse suggests that such accord cannot be reached at the level of doctrine but might be reached by a common *experience*, an experience of unity prompted not so much by teachings but by attention to *things*—a river, a face, a stone. In a Romanticism- and Vedanta-inflected instantiation of the dialectic of prosaic and profound, Siddhartha's rapt attention to one thing gives way to a flood of awareness of all things, which then resolve again into one as each takes its place in a unified cosmic harmony. In this case, the dialectic yields an unqualified affirmation of the world, a valuing of all things—even evil, death, and decay—as necessary parts of the cosmic accord, which is in its totality holy and good. Such an affirmation of the particulars of the world is largely foreign to the early Buddhist context Hesse evokes and is instead a product of the modern age and its affirmation of the world. Siddhartha's assertion of unity between his radically world-affirming insights and the spirit of the Buddha's teachings is Hesse's own attempt to build a bridge between the modern affirmation of the ordinary and the Buddhism of Indian history. The ancient Buddha of the modern age must, again, say yes to the world; the net of interdependence is not a binding chain but a harmonious web.

Hesse's depiction of the epiphanies of the ordinary is clearly different from that of the literary Modernists. His epiphanies are more cosmological, more transcendental, more optimistic than the often resolutely secular epiphanies of the Modernists, who, despite their "moments of being," are seldom interested in resolving all particulars into a glowing cosmic whole. This just demonstrates, however, the development of the experiential, epiphanic ethos across a number of literary subcultures, as well as different worldviews. What matters here is not that Joyce and Hesse shared the same vision of the world but that despite their differences they both saw something of ultimate significance in the transfigurational apprehension of the banal. Both the Modernist and the neo-Romantic assert that an ultimate significance dwells in the quotidian particulars and events that we experience every day. Both embody the modern dialectic of the prosaic and profound that became a way of understanding Buddhism and, more broadly, informed the very conception in the twentieth century of "religious experience."

Interweavings of the Prosaic and Profound,
Buddhist and Western

Some of the specific Buddhist sources, ideas, and practices that have become
interlinked with this modern, epiphanic, dialectical interweaving of the prosaic
and the profound are as follows. They include, first, the methods of mindfulness
found in Pali *suttas* and meditation texts. The *Larger Scripture on the Foundations of Mindfulness* (*Mahāsatipaṭṭhāna Sutta* [DN 22]) and the *Scripture on the
Mindfulness of Breathing* (*Anapanasati Sutta* [MN 118]) are the most frequently
cited of the Pali meditation texts.[4] They are the core texts of the contemporary
mindfulness movement and have been used to introduce mindfulness to countless monks and laypeople alike throughout the world. They give explicit instructions on establishing mindfulness in relation to various human activities and
faculties. The core practice is observation of the breath. "Breathing in long, [the
monk] knows 'I am breathing in long'; or breathing out long, he knows, 'I am
breathing out long.' Or breathing in short, he knows, 'I am breathing in short'; or
breathing out short, he knows, 'I am breathing out short.'" In the *Mahāsatipaṭṭhāna*, mindfulness is extended to various activities and carried out within particular frames of reference or foundations (*paṭṭhāna*): mindfulness of the body
(*kāya*), feelings (*vedanā*), thoughts (*citta*), and objects of thought (*dharmas*) (DN
2: 290). In the mindfulness of the body, for example, the practitioner extends
this alert attentiveness to a wide variety of physical activities: walking, sitting,
standing, lying down, going forward, returning, bending, stretching, carrying
one's robe, eating, chewing, excreting, speaking, and remaining silent (DN 2:
292). The text further recommends rigorous analysis of the body: "just as a
skilled butcher or his apprentice, having killed a cow, would sit at a crossroads
cutting it up into pieces, the monk contemplates this very body." Within each
frame of reference, the meditator observes the various components: within "feelings" one observes pleasant, unpleasant, or neutral feelings; within "mind," one
notes anger, greed, delusion, thoughts that are restricted, scattered, expansive,
concentrated, and so on. All of these the practitioner observes while remaining
"unattached, not clinging to anything in the world." The purpose of mindfulness as promoting detachment from the world is reinforced in the Vinaya, the
large compendium of rules for monks and nuns. Here every detail of life is
examined not for the purpose of appreciation of its hidden depths and nuances
but for disciplined regulation of every aspect of the monastic life.

   It is important to note that there is no hint here of the loving attentiveness,
the openness and communion with all things, one often comes across in some
modern dharma literature. The attitude is far from celebratory of the things

contemplated. Things of the world are often deemed deceptive, useless, and conducive to suffering. All craving and aversion to things is to be overcome, and through this dispassionate observation things are to be seen outside the usual networks of personal intentions. As noted in chapter 5, more positive valuations of the phenomenal world emerge in some Mahayana writings, where detachment is not necessarily the prime object of meditation and the passions are identified with awakening. The doctrine of emptiness, the insistence on the lack of distinction between samsara and nirvana, Huayen's interpenetration of all phenomena, and the Mahayana assertion of an all-pervasive buddha-nature infuse a nirvanic element into all dharmas, affirming the sacrality of all things. This allows the apprehension of a thing—any thing—in its "suchness" (*tath-atā*) to reveal the truth in the highest sense (*paramārtha-sātya*). Likewise, in *tathāgata-garbha* thought, if everything has buddha-nature, truly apprehending even the most mundane thing can provoke a realization. These developments never completely abandon the original desideratum to detach from worldly phenomena, but they add complexity to the earlier, more world-renouncing, goals of mindfulness. One withdraws from things, or from one's habitual reactions to things, but in such withdrawal lies the possibility of apprehending a deeper mystery lying within them.

This approach is perhaps best represented in Zen literature, and it is no surprise that Zen is the tradition that most commonly becomes interlaced with the modern dialectic of the prosaic and profound. The cypress tree in the courtyard, six pounds of flax, the dried shit-stick, the Dao as everyday mind, the Buddha holding up a flower for Kāśyapa, the chopping of wood and carrying of water, Bashō's frog plopping into the pond, and countless other crystalline images of the highly specific and utterly mundane pervade canonical Chan/ Zen literature and are frequently cited in modern Zen as illustrations of the sacred-everyday. Each of these examples is said to have prompted a monk to a profound realization of the dharma. The images, which are often masters' replies to questions in koans, snap erring disciples' minds back to the ordinary, concrete, and specific when they expect something abstract, metaphysical, or theoretical. Thwarting such expectations, the masters galvanize their students to apprehend the ultimate in the commonplace features of life, cutting off metaphysical speculation and abstract rumination.

In addition to these often-cited literary expressions of the profoundly ordinary, Zen monastic practice ritualized everyday activity. Extending the logic of the Mahayana doctrine of the inseparability of samsara and nirvana, every act and thing became an expression of ultimate reality. As Dōgen asserts: "There is no gap between practice and enlightenment or zazen and daily life" (Yokoi 1976: 47). In contrast to contemporary interpretations of Zen spontaneity, however, this meant an intensive formalization of every activity, from medi-tation to eating to using the bathroom. True spontaneity, on this model, was not doing whatever one wanted; it could only come about when the extremely formal gestures and acts that made up the monastic life became "natural" and effortless. Then they could be understood as expressions of buddha-nature.

Attentiveness to the everyday in twentieth-century art and literature, within the broader context of the turn toward affirming ordinary life, provided part of the framework through which this sacralization of the mundane in traditional Buddhist contexts could be reconceived. D. T. Suzuki was again one of the most influential sources of this interpretation. His description of satori, which has become normative in modernist Zen, contends that it "finds a meaning hith-erto hidden in our daily concrete particular experiences, such as eating, drink-ing, or business of all kinds," which is "reality in its isness" (1959: 16). Robert Linssen adds: "Zen asks us to bring to bear the intensity of an extraordinary attention in the midst of all so-called 'ordinary circumstances.' . . . Each inci-dent of daily life, each perception of the concrete world, can be an occasion for 'Satori'" (1988 [1958]: 174). Here the suchness (*tathatā*) of the Mahayana, along with the Zen notion of sudden awakening, is allowed to resonate with the liter-ary epiphanies of the ordinary: Joyce's revelation of the "whatness" of a thing and Woolf's "moments of being." Sokei-an Sasaki (1882–1945), often cited as the first Japanese Zen priest to take up residence in the United States, asserted that for the legendary founder of the Chan/Zen school, Bodhidharma, "every act from morning to evening was religion—swallowing water, eating food, sleeping, tending shop, talking to one's neighbor" (Ross 1960: 35). And yet what makes the minutiae of everyday life religious, according to Alan Watts, is a state of mind in which "we are simply aware of what is without distorting it by the complexities of self-consciousness." Such states, according to Watts, attend to the utter ordinariness of things, yet to see ordinary things in this undistorted way, we must, like the haiku poet, have a "moment of intense perception" in which "we are aware of being alive in an unusually vivid way" (1960: 124–25).

There is here another dialectic: Watts and Suzuki encourage the reader on the one hand to eschew the search for deeper meaning in these ordinary things yet on the other to transform the perception of things in such a way that, even in their unelaborated banality, they attain ultimate and sacred significance. The language Watts and many other modern interpreters of Zen use to describe this sacralization of the everyday is quite foreign to canonical Chan/Zen texts. Yet it is nearly identical to the language that twentieth-century novelists (as well as poets and visual artists) have used to describe the significance of the extraor-dinary within the everyday. Consciously or not, modern Zen apologists high-lighted this aspect of Zen and expressed it in ways that would resonate with the attention to things in their ordinariness that was already at issue in western art and literature. This, in turn, has had an impact not only on how Zen has been represented but on what it has become in the modern world.

Miracles of Modernity

Mindfulness, as the attentive appreciation of the everyday world, has assumed its place in the late modern world in another way: it has become a way of reenchanting the world that accords with the naturalistic tenets of modernity. To return to Thich Nhat Hanh's "miracle of mindfulness": the evocation of this most antimodern of terms—"miracle"—may seem an odd choice for a contemporary author trying to reach a modern, educated, and often secular, audience. Clearly it is intended as metaphorical. More than that, though, it seamlessly draws together lineaments of Buddhism and western thought that could only become entwined in the modern "postmiraculous" era. Miracles, while not banished from the world of modernity and late modernity, are largely excluded from public discourse and are, among educated elites (including—even especially— religious elites) often viewed with suspicion and embarrassment. The fact that many people still believe in them does not mitigate their marginalized place with respect to the way they were viewed in other eras. Buddhist modernism, as I have argued already, has had a particular investment in minimizing appeals to the miraculous because of its self-conscious attempt to ally itself with science and naturalism over against Christianity, with its explicit appeals to the supernatural. It has found itself, therefore, in a similar position to that of a number of traditions in the West that have attempted to find ways of respecting the Enlightenment's divesting the world of contraventions of natural law while at the same time not divesting the world of sacred significance.

In Europe, Schleiermacher provided one solution, in *On Religion* (1799)— a solution the Transcendentalists adopted and various religious and secular modernisms still widely deploy. Keen to press on his audience of "cultured despisers of religion" that religion in its essence is not really about ceremonies, hierarchies, and supernatural wonders but rather an *experience*, an intuition of the infinite within the finite, he insists that "miracles" are not singular events that transgress natural laws; rather all things are miraculous in that they are manifestations of the infinite. "For me," he declares, "everything is a miracle. . . . The more religious you would be, the more you would see miracles everywhere (1988: 133). This move dismisses the singular miraculous event— walking on water or through walls—and diffuses the miraculous throughout the entire creation, reinvesting it with sacredness on naturalistic terms.

Thich Nhat Hanh's miracle of mindfulness echoes not only the classic Zen masters but also Schleiermacher's diffusion of sacrality. "I think the real miracle is not to walk either on water or in thin air, but to walk on earth. Every day we are engaged in a miracle which we don't even recognize: a blue sky, white clouds, green leaves, the black, curious eyes of a child—our own two eyes. All is a miracle" (1976: 12). This declaration of the "real" miracle of everyday life not only evokes the emphasis on the concrete in Zen but also signals assurances to the modern reader that Buddhism is precisely *not* about "miracles" in the traditional sense of which moderns have grown skeptical. And in his implicit contrast of the miracle of mindfully walking on the earth with Jesus' walking on water, we cannot help but hear a gentle displacing of traditional Christianity's emphasis on supernatural miracles in favor of Buddhist modernism's appreciation of the miracle that things simply *are* in their utter ordinariness.

This "concreteness" of Buddhism (especially Zen) in contrast to the abstractions, dogmas, and supernaturalism of traditional Christianity signals the struggle many in the West have had with Christianity, as well as the frequent hopes of Buddhist converts that they have found a rational religion. It is no coincidence that out of the many koans, one of the best known in the West is one entitled (by the compiler Paul Reps, in his famous *Zen Flesh, Zen Bones*) "The Real Miracle." It tells of a Shinshu priest who "believed in salvation through the repetition of the name of the Buddha of Love" (Amitabha) and was jealous of Zen master Bankei's large audience.

> "The founder of our sect," boasted the priest, "had such miraculous powers that he held a brush in his hand on one bank of the river, his attendant held up a paper on the other bank, and the teacher wrote the holy name of Amida through the air. Can you do such a wonderful thing?"
>
> Bankei replied lightly: "Perhaps your fox can perform that trick, but that is not the manner of Zen. My miracle is that when I feel hungry I eat, and when I feel thirsty I drink." (Reps 1987 [1957]: 68)

The easy assumption by the modern interpreter is that this passage proves once again the rationality of Buddhism—Bankei rejects supernatural displays in favor of a naturalistic beholding of the sacrality of every act and every thing. Indeed, the reading of this story in modernist terms is nearly irresistible to the westerner; and for this reason it has acquired of a number of coded messages in the process of translation. In a modern western reading, the Shinshu priest easily stands for the traditionally religious who profess dogmatic adherence to their own views and rely on ostentatious displays of supernatural prowess to score points with crowds (faith healers and televangelists come to mind). The use of the term "priest" invites us further to imagine a parallel between Shin-shu and the Catholic cleric, often cast in modernist discourse as the benighted, tradition-bound believer. In contrast, the Zen master (much like the Deist) follows his healthy, natural desires to eat and drink in moderation. Eschewing the contravention of natural law, he resacralizes the world (much like the Romantic or Modernist) through the fulfillment of the simple acts that, when done with mindfulness, are miracles. The attentiveness that transforms the quotidian into the miraculous is thus more astounding than the priest's miracle, for it re-infuses sacrality into the modern world, which had previously banished it. Thus the sectarian polemic between two rival schools of Buddhism is reconfigured as a story of a modern, free-spirited, earthy mystic trumping the antics of a dogmatic, superstitious, tradition-bound cleric. Indeed the modern interpretation of Zen, as noted, draws considerable capital from the image of the Zen master (not the far more common Zen "priest") as a freelance mystic unencumbered by institutional ties, superstitious beliefs, or slippery metaphysics. It is an image, however, that is largely modern, drawn from Suzuki, Hesse, and others who have infused Buddhism with the western image of the radical individualist who encounters the sacred outside of all conventions, rejecting the benighted ritualists and institutionalized dogmatists so as to find their own unique revelation of things.

All of this suggests that recent configurations of Buddhist modernism have depended on a very particular combination of historical and cultural conditions. If the almost uncannily elevated significance that Zen literature ascribes to the commonplace had encountered the world of, say, thirteenth-century England, no remotely hospitable framework could have existed for trying to make sense of it. Not that the Brits could not have understood the sacralization of material objects; anyone looking for affinities between Buddhism and Christianity could have noted their common reverence for relics associated with their respective founders and their disciples. For despite its iconoclastic reputation, and after all of modernist Zen's emphasis on the naturalized miraculous, Zen in its more traditional forms has never repudiated the miraculous power of relics. This, however, is a completely different kind of elevation of objects—the reverence for *particular* objects of power. But modernism, in its broad sense, has little tolerance for such *selective* sacralization. It does not ask of objects that they heal us of bodily ailments or protect us from evil spirits but that they give us insight into the human experience. We may see "infinity in a grain of sand" but not curative powers in a bone. Thus the widespread veneration of relics in Buddhism is nearly invisible in Buddhist modernism, except for its occasional denunciation as a superstitious cultural accretion, while the literature of paradox, in which all is one and one is all, the ordinary profound and the profound ordinary, is central. Here the specific is the doorway to the universal, and the very randomness of the particular object or act that opens that door—the cypress tree in the courtyard or the ketchup bottle on the table—is testimony to the expulsion of *particular* powers in *particular* material objects from the world of the modernist. The combing of the mundane particulars of the world for elevated significance or sudden revelation, whether in modern literature or Buddhist meditation, entails a *revalorization* of materiality that could be aspired to only after Protestantism and rationalist instrumentalism divested particulars of their supernatural powers—after the desacralization of the world.

The miracle of modernism, then, is not walking on water, just as modernist enlightenment is not the beholding of one's past lives, all others' past lives, and the discerning of the eightfold path, as the early Buddhist texts define it. Modernist enlightenment is instead more like the literary Modernist's epiphany, the moment of being that reveals the ordinary in a new light as the fullness of being itself. It is not that similar epiphanies are wholly unknown to traditional Buddhism, but their interfusion with the Modernist dialectic of the prosaic and profound leaves much that is specific to traditional Buddhism behind and creates a unique space in the modern world for mindfulness techniques that explicitly cultivate such experiences.

Modernist iterations of mindfulness, like many other aspects of Buddhist modernism, negotiate between the rationalist imperative to avoid supernaturalism and the Romantic longing for the reenchantment of the world. Their placement within the field of this tension has allowed ancient practices designed to extract consciousness from entanglement in the world to become enfolded within modern modalities of world-affirmation, including the dialectic of the prosaic and profound in modern literature. Epiphanies like those found in Modernist works, along with world-affirming mystical experiences like those in Hesse's *Siddhartha*, have become interpretive frameworks for Buddhist mindfulness practices and have informed modern conceptions of Buddhist insight and enlightenment and more generally of "religious experience" itself. Buddhist modernists have often contended that such experiences are more primary than teachings and doctrines, and this has provided a way of negotiating pluralism—it is experience that matters, not dogma, institutions, and concepts. This understanding has contributed to what Robert Sharf has called the "rhetoric of experience" in Buddhist modernism—the tendency to see Buddhism as concerned almost exclusively with individual experience (1995a).

The desire to see something deeper in the stone, the river, or the ketchup bottle is of course not solely a product of modernity; traditional Mahayana conceptions of Buddha nature have long sent people on quests to plumb the hidden depths of ordinary things. But modernity has imbued this desire with a particular significance: it is the modern period that has neutralized, objectified, and commodified the stone and thus invited the question of whether there is in fact anything *more* to it. Works of modern literature have provided one way of investigating this question and attempting to rescue the things of the world from this kind of objectification by making them come alive in the minds of their characters, in the rich, dense detailing of the way the world comes into being within the experience of a particular subject. Buddhist modernism has allied itself closely with this project of recovery of ordinary things and events, reconstituting itself as a specific discipline for such nuanced attending to the flow of experience. Thus mindfulness has re-created itself as a Buddhist contribution to the cultural forces that seek the revivification of the mundane elements of life, whose sacrality the rationalizing, mechanizing forces of modernity threaten to banish.

9

From Modern
to Postmodern?

Positing a heterogeneous continuum between Buddhist traditionalists and modernists, I have attempted here to analyze some of the
ways Buddhism has cross-pollinated with modernity. I have suggested the roles of detraditionalization, demythologization, and
psychologization in this adaptation. I have also attempted to demonstrate how the development of Buddhist modernism placed Buddhism in particular relationships to three overlapping constitutive
discourses of modernity: western theism (mainly Protestant Christianity), scientific rationalism, and Romanticism and its successors.
These themes—which in no way address the entire range of Buddhist
modernism and its sources—serve to illustrate the historicity and
hybridity of the movement, as well as the wide variety of resources it
has drawn on in Asia, Europe, and North America.

The formations of Buddhist modernism I have been using as
case studies are ones that, even when they have been constructed by
Japanese, Sri Lankans, Thais, or Tibetans, have tended to draw Buddhism into the orbit of western thought, rather than vice versa. Their
particular kind of hybridity is often like that of Henry Steel Olcott's,
which, in Stephen Prothero's interpretation, was a "creolization" that
assimilated Buddhism to largely Protestant categories, assumptions,
and logic. Like a creole dialect, its lexicon was Buddhist, while its
grammar was largely Protestant (1996: 9). While making the point
that much of Buddhist modernism in the West is rooted not just in
Protestantism but also in scientific rationalism and Romanticism,

I have also hinted that other, often Asian, Buddhist modernisms, like other modernities, may reverse this situation, assimilating the lexicon of modernity to the grammar of Buddhism.

Having looked at the present in order to understand the past, I shall now look at some themes in the present with a glance toward the future. Once again, I will not attempt to give a comprehensive overview but will look at a few developments that seem important and clearly emerge out of the history and themes I have been discussing. If, as it is rumored, the modern age is giving way to late, radical, or postmodernity, is there a corresponding shift in Buddhist modernism as it enters this era? How viable is Buddhist modernism in the late modern world? Is there something like a postmodern Buddhism emerging from the strains of Buddhist modernism I have been discussing? And does the accommodation of Buddhism to modern, western, and postmodern cultures render it less able to provide challenges, critiques, and alternatives to these cultures?

Democratization, Feminization, and Hybridity

In my primary geographical case, North America, one finds a great deal of democratization, feminization, and increasing hybridity, as others have ably pointed out (Prebish 1999; Prebish and Tanaka 1998; Seager 1999). In the last few decades, these trends have now gone beyond rhetorical claims of earlier Buddhist modernism, when the insistence that Buddhism was democratic, espoused the equality of men and women, and was compatible with western religious traditions was made in virtually complete disregard of the actual situations of living Buddhists. "Buddhism" was defined by classical texts, and passages amenable to women's equality and democracy could be found in such texts; hence "Buddhism" was in line with these values, no matter what the conditions on the ground among actual Buddhists might have been. Today, Buddhists themselves address these issues not just as matters of textual hermeneutics but at the social and institutional level.

In the United States, there has been a push for democratization at some of the most visible Buddhist institutions. For example, since scandal rocked it in the 1980s, the San Francisco Zen Center, founded by Shunryu Suzuki Rōshi and one of the most prominent Zen centers in the country, has explored ways of democratizing the leadership and ensuring that no one will have too much power. When Richard Baker Rōshi resigned after admitting to an affair with a married student, his dharma-heir, Reb Anderson, was hired for a four-year term, and a system of electing rather than appointing board members was instituted

(Fields 1992: 362–64). Another innovation came in the 1990s: an experiment in shared leadership between Zoketsu Norman Fischer and Zenkai Blanche Hartman. The changes were made to discourage a concentration of power and to shift to what Fischer calls a "student centered" rather than "teacher-centered" organization of the *zendo* (quoted in Tworkov 1994: 245–46).

Socially engaged modes of Buddhism have also begun to reform the roles of women within modernist Buddhist settings, sometimes leading to radical departures from traditional roles and opportunities. For instance, women have taken on unprecedented leadership roles in western Buddhist settings. They are among the most prominent Buddhist teachers in the United States, and female teachers routinely instruct male students—something extremely rare in Asian settings. Modernist trends in Asia, moreover, have contributed to efforts to revive the *bhikṣuni sangha*—the order of nuns—and incorporate women into public life and leadership roles.[1] Such efforts are aided by recent global organizations such as Sakyadita International, a network of international Buddhist women that promotes female teachers of Buddhism and encourages the establishment of communities of fully ordained nuns. Such experiments in leadership and institutional organization, along with the way women around the world are increasingly shaping their traditions, promises to have a profound effect on the future of Buddhism.

Much of the hybridity I have discussed in this book has come about without conscious intention, as the result of inevitable transformations that occur when one cultural formation is translated into the terms of another. While many struggled with how to adapt Buddhism to the modern world, Victorians who depicted the Buddha as a model Victorian gentleman were often simply viewing him through their available categories and conceptions. As noted, the Victorian interpretation of Buddhism also was often governed by the logic of colonialism and postcolonialism and its inherently unequal relations of power; Europeans pressed Buddhism into the mold of their own thought, and Asian Buddhists themselves took up such forms both to increase Buddhism's prestige and to turn it back on colonial powers in forms of resistance.

While this colonial logic persists in the contemporary period, it is not the primary force governing new forms of hybridity. Today more conscious efforts are being made to amalgamate Buddhism and other traditions, not just in representation and theory but in practice. This endeavor is made possible by particular modernist constructions of Buddhism as a "technique" or "way of life" that holds to no particular dogmas or beliefs and thus is unusually compatible with other religious traditions. Perennialism has again played a part: if all paths are different ways to the same mystical experience or ultimate reality, their distinctiveness is less important than their common goal. But so has the view that Buddhist meditation can be an aid to Christian worship: thus the concept of *Zen Meditation for Christians* (Lassalle 1974). Inspired primarily by Thomas Merton's amalgamation of Christian and Zen contemplative practice, a number of Catholic contemplatives have attempted to crossbreed the traditions. Robert Kennedy, for example, an American Jesuit priest and Zen teacher in the While Plum lineage, established by Maezumi Rōshi, has written *Zen Gifts to Christians* and *Zen Spirit, Christian Spirit* and has a number of dharma heirs who are both Catholic nuns and ordained Zen priests. There are now not only dozens of popular books in print on combining Buddhist and Christian, as well as Buddhist and Jewish, practice but also dozens of communities engaging in this experimental religious hybridity.

This selective combination of elements of Buddhism with non-Buddhist traditions is creating tensions that are important to the shape of contemporary Buddhist modernism: tensions between radically detraditionalized and retraditionalized Buddhism, between Buddhism as privatized spirituality and engaged social activism, and between localized and globalizing forms of the dharma.

Posttraditionalism and Postmodern Buddhism

In addition to such interreligious hybrids, certain facets of Buddhist modernism, especially in North America, have become more and more hybridized with secular culture in a radicalization of the demythologizating and detraditionalizing tendencies I have already described. This movement shows a decidedly western inclination to dispense with authority, hierarchy, ritual, and "religious" aspects of Buddhism, usually making meditation the central if not sole practice. An increasingly popular and global movement, Chögyam Trungpa's Shambhala Training, and the variety of adaptations of meditation to secular settings I have discussed represent a movement toward the secularization and detraditionalization of Buddhism that sees Buddhist techniques, attitudes, and ideas as part of a semisecular "spiritual" approach to life with a minimum of institutional, ritual, and liturgical elements (Baumann 2001). British dharma teacher and scholar Stephen Batchelor, for instance, uses selected readings from classical Buddhist scriptures and commentaries to advocate a "Buddhism without beliefs," grounded in what he believes to be the Buddha's own original exposition of the dharma—an "existential, therapeutic, and liberating agnosticism." Like many modernists, he claims to return to the original, ancient source of Buddhism—his own awakening, before the dharma became "institutionalized as a religion (i.e., a revered belief system valid for all time, controlled by an elite body of priests)" (1997: 15–16).

While some contemporary detraditionalizers see their renditions of the dharma as rooted in the "original teachings," others have quite consciously distanced themselves from tradition and admitted they are developing something new. An advertisement for Open Mind Zen, a Zen center in Florida, offers "a new way to practice Zen" with "no monks, no magic, no mumbo jumbo." Open Mind Zen eschews a "priestly class, medieval oriental clothing . . . golden throne, guru worship or inner circle," as well as "chanting in foreign tongues, bowing, and posturing."[2] Manfred B. Steger and Perle Besserman, founders of the Princeton Area Zen group in New Jersey, tell (in a bit more nuanced way) of finding themselves disillusioned with trying to fit their practice into Japanese cultural modalities:

> we could no longer avoid the fact that we were Westerners living in
> the late twentieth century. As humanists and "progressives," we were
> concerned with civil rights, racial equality, economic justice, nonvio-
> lence, ecology, and feminism. We were bothered by the patriarchal
> and hierarchical nature of traditional Japanese Zen, its militarism,
> and its distance from social action and "real world" concerns. As wit-
> ness to our genocidal century, we could no longer close our eyes and
> ears to the violent racism of some of our most revered Zen masters.
> (2001: 4)

Steger and Besserman, therefore, began to form out of more American cloth a kind of "grassroots Zen" that consciously dispensed with vestiges of Japanese tradition they could no longer abide—patriarchy, hierarchy, emphasis on lineage—while retaining what they believed were the essential elements: *zazen, sesshin* (meditation retreats), dharma talks, koans, and *dokusan* (private student-teacher interviews) (4–5).

German-American teacher Toni Packer is the most detraditionalized example of this trend. She was Phillip Kapleau Rōshi's successor at the Rochester Zen Center in New York but left and formed her own *sangha* after becoming disillusioned with traditional forms and hierarchy. She now runs the Springwater Center for Meditative Inquiry and Retreats, which holds meditation workshops and retreats influenced by Zen, but with no overt affiliation and few of the standard formalities of the tradition. In her teachings and books, she dismisses the value of transmitting a lineage and ensuring the transition of teachings from one generation to the next. Instead, she insists on the importance of being present in the moment, openly investigating the network of conditioned thoughts, and allowing the mind to move beyond that network. The only authority is the authority of one's own experience. Chanting, bells, bowing, and, most important, the traditional master-disciple relationship are all seen as inessential and even deleterious to the possibility of awakening (1995a, 1995b).

Few Buddhist teachers have gone as far as Packer in abandoning traditional beliefs, practices, and social institutions. Most Buddhist institutions in the West, including those catering mainly to converts, follow some degree of traditional protocol; they still maintain the importance of the teacher, though not in the sense of an absolute authority; Zen and Tibetan institutions still hold to the significance of lineage; and they still observe some of the rituals and use many of the material implements of traditional Buddhism. In dismissing most of these, Packer admits that she is no longer really practicing Buddhism, even while still emphasizing the importance of "meditative inquiry." In this sense, Packer's is a kind of "post-Zen" that represents the extremity, yet in some ways the logical conclusion, of an important underlying theme in Buddhist modernism, and particularly Zen, that can be traced back to Suzuki—the idea that Zen is more an inner process or experience than a historical tradition or institution. Packer, in distancing herself from Zen as the latter, has said that the word "Zen," as she understands it, "is descriptive of a mind that understands itself clearly and wholly from instant to instant" and that it "suggests a way of seeing and responding freely, without the limitations of the self" (quoted in Friedman 1987: 60). And it is this idea of Zen as essentially a condition of mind separable from historical tradition and East Asian cultural forms that has been one of the prime movers in the development of the unique character of modernist Zen and Buddhist modernism in the West.

Retraditionalization

Although extreme detraditionalization has gained some currency in the West, it in no way exhausts the main trends in the postmodern condition of Buddhism. In fact, we see across the globe a number of movements attempting to reappropriate tradition, to cast off some of the staples of Buddhist modernism, and to reassert more conventional views of the dharma. Such "returns" are themselves products of modernity: they reconstruct tradition in response to some of modernity's dominant themes, attempting to imagine their opposites in the ancient past. Some are not simply traditional forms of Buddhism but retraditionalized forms. They do not necessarily attempt abandon modernity in toto—they often use modern technologies and may draw upon the language of Buddhist modernism—but they have rejected some of its innovations in favor of attempting to reconstruct more orthodox aspects of Buddhism.

We see a number of such attempts to reclaim tradition in Asia. These include Burma's reforms of the *sangha* in the 1980s, which restored its hierarchical structure and curbed freedom to innovate doctrinally. Sri Lanka and Southeast Asia have also seen a renewal of the tradition of forest-dwelling monks. Tibetan Buddhism, having been thrust into abrupt confrontation with modernity by the Chinese annexation of the country in 1950, has maintained more traditional elements than other modernizing forms. This more conservative tendency is partly a result of Tibetans' culture and religion being under threat; they have an urgent interest in maintaining tradition while at the same time making it viable in the context of late modernity. In addition, the niche created in the West for Tibetan Buddhism has been cultivated for over a century by western Romanticization of Tibet as an isolated pocket of ancient wisdom untainted by modernity (Lopez 1998). To the West, Tibetan Buddhism has represented both the typical modernist hope for a rational religion and, conversely, the longing for "magic and mystery" in a still enchanted region of the world.[3] It has also embodied a powerful narrative of the desperate struggle for survival of this enchantment in the face of modern powers of brute military force and imperial aggression.

These factors have created a place for Tibetan Buddhism in the West that has perhaps allowed for more traditionalism. Despite the fact that the public face of Tibetan Buddhism is the Fourteenth Dalai Lama, who is in many respects the quintessential modernizer, some strains of Tibetan Buddhism have not been as quick to embrace the world-affirming, egalitarian, and democratic reinterpretations of the path as have other forms of Buddhism catering to western converts. In an interview with Penor Rinpoche (His Holiness Drubwang Pema Norbu Rinpoche), the head of the Palyul lineage of the Nyingma tradition, Andrew Cohen asked for his response to a quotation from Elizabeth Lesser claiming that the "unique and most positive aspect of the new American spirituality is its emphasis on self-authority. . . . With democratic spirituality it no longer makes sense for an [external] authority to describe to you the sacred truth and the path to discover it. In [new American spirituality], *you* map the journey" (emphasis and brackets original; Lesser, quoted in Cohen 2000). Penor Rinpoche responded flatly: "There is no benefit to following the democratic spiritual path. . . . They are just wasting time." For any chance of success on the path, he insisted, there must be "transmissions and blessings from a lama, the master," who is from a "very pure lineage" (Cohen 2000). The term "pure," in fact, comes up often in contemporary Tibetan teachings, no doubt in acknowledgment of the degree to which Buddhist teachings around the world have been hybridized and, in the traditionalist view, compromised.

Tibetans and traditionalist Asian Buddhists are not the only ones with a renewed interest in conserving traditional aspects of Buddhism in the face of modernism. Some western monks in the Theravada traditions have leveled some incisive critiques at various facets of Buddhist modernism. Bhikkhu Bodhi, a prolific contemporary American-born monk, translator, and commentator on Pali texts, has expressed skepticism about modernist construals of Buddhism based on the *Kālāma Sutta*, that most central of *suttas* in the modernist canon, in which the Buddha encourages a group of seekers to test teachings for themselves rather than accept them on faith. Bodhi asserts: "on the basis of a single passage, quoted out of context, the Buddha has been made out to be a pragmatic empiricist who dismisses all doctrine and faith, and whose Dhamma is simply a freethinker's kit to truth which invites each one to accept and reject whatever he likes." Bodhi insists that the Buddha in this *sutta* was encouraging skepticism among people not yet committed to the dharma, but never recommended such an attitude for those already on the Buddha's path. He rejects the idea that "a follower of the Buddhist path can dispense with all faith and doctrine, that he should make his own personal experience the criterion for judging the Buddha's utterances and for rejecting what cannot be squared with it." Rather, while testing those elements of the dharma that fall within the purview of their experience, Buddhists must, having verified these, place faith in the Buddha's doctrines that are beyond their current ability to verify personally (1998).

Thanissaro Bhikkhu, as noted (chapter 6), has leveled criticism at "Buddhist Romanticism," sharply contrasting the traditional teachings of the Pali canon with the contemporary Buddhism that is infused with talk of interconnectedness, wholeness, self-fulfillment, spontaneity, and transcendence of the ego, which he claims are derived from the influence of Romanticism, transcendentalism, and western psychology. In contrast to the modernist emphasis on intense "peak experiences," Thanissaro insists, the early teachings see religious experience as knowledge of the principles of causality, as well as the "dimension beyond causality where all suffering stops." He also rejects the idea of suffering as rooted in a "divided self" that expands into the infinite self of the cosmos. Instead, suffering is rooted in clinging, especially clinging to *any* sense of self, "whether finite or infinite." And instead of the cure for suffering as an "ongoing process of personal integration," Buddhism, he insists, offers awakening as a "total cure, opening to the unconditioned beyond space and time" (2002: 108–11).

Western lineages of Chinese (Taiwanese) Buddhism in the United States also show far less accommodation to modernity than their modernist predecessors. Monastics at the City of Ten Thousand Buddhas in northern California, for example, eat only one meal a day, sleep sitting up all night, and live in sex-segregated quarters. Such rigorous monastic standards, along with critiques of

Buddhist modernism by prominent dharma teachers in the West, suggest that more options are now available for practice in the West that do not conform to the "standard" modernist forms I have been discussing. Such critiques suggest a reevaluation and reassertion of traditional elements of Buddhism and a greater sense of confidence that tradition can hold its own against modernity. In Asia, such reassertions no doubt have much to do with the rise of identity politics, as traditions around the globe in the latter part of the twentieth century have been newly emboldened to assert their distinctiveness and unique value, even—and perhaps especially—if they do not conform wholly to the cultures of the modern West. They are sometimes imbued with nationalism, as in Sri Lanka and Burma, and often exhibit a sense of anxiety about the rapid pace of modernization in Asian nations.

The success of more conservative and traditional teachers and institutions in North America indicates not only that Asian immigrant Buddhists have increasing visibility and power in shaping Buddhism in the West but also that not all westerners desire a thoroughly modernized version of Buddhism. As western and immigrant communities intermingle, westerners are exposed to more traditional models of being Buddhist, and some adopt them. As serious practitioners learn more about the traditions they practice, due to the increasing numbers of available texts and teachers, they may become more steeped in the tradition, habituated to less modernized versions of it, and more willing to take a variety of positions along the traditionalist-modernist spectrum. And as more teachers come from Asia to the West and set up monasteries and dharma centers, more people in the West get involved with particular traditions with specific lineages, thus mitigating the universalist tendencies of Buddhist modernism.

These are all signs of the emergence of conditions more associated with late modernity or postmodernity: multiple interpretations of tradition, increasing pluralism, and heterogeneous combining of various modernities and traditions. The postmodern situation makes it more feasible to live in various "lifestyle enclaves," and traditionalist forms of Buddhism sometimes make up such enclaves.[4] The image, therefore, of western Buddhism as largely free of ritual, dogma, nonscientific worldviews, and belief in supernatural beings is becoming less adequate than it was a few decades ago. The coexistence of very detraditionalized "post-Buddhism" with moves toward a reclaiming of tradition as well as the existence of various combinations of tradition and innovation within particular schools of the dharma suggest an increasing variegation and heterogeneity in Buddhism today.

Important to this heterogeneity, and no doubt to the future development of Buddhist modernism (or postmodernism), is the role now being played by schools that were not as prominent in the early formation of Buddhist modernism, such as Pure Land, Nichiren schools, Chinese and Taiwanese schools, and organizations such as the Dharma Realm Buddhist Association. These groups grapple with questions of modernity and attract a more ethnically diverse population than those I have addressed, something that increases their range of activities, interpretations, and orientations. They often bridge the gap between western converts and immigrants, developing forms that appeal to both western spiritual seekers and ethnic Asians whose Buddhism is more deeply embedded in their cultural formations. As modernist forms of these traditions continue to gain prominence, they will surely change the face of Buddhist modernism and further increase the number of ways one can be Buddhist.

Privatized Spirituality and Social Engagement

We can map the detraditionalization of Buddhism along other coordinates as well. Alongside the variegated continuum between tradition and modernity, another continuum has become prominent in recent decades—between Buddhism as an inward-directed, detraditionalized "spirituality" and socially engaged Buddhism, which emphasizes social, political, and environmental activism as well as medition. In some instances, the former represents the merging of Buddhist meditative traditions into various eclectic alternative religious orientations, often classed under New Age spirituality, the great-grandchild of nineteenth-century metaphysical movements, as well as psychotherapy, the human potential movement, and self-help trends. The latter descends from the political engagement of some of the early Buddhist modernists like Anagarika Dharmapala and Ambedkar and, more recently, the tremendous social and political upheaval and wars that have plagued Buddhist countries like Vietnam, Cambodia, Laos, and Tibet, along with movements of the political left in western countries. Certainly Buddhism throughout its history has carried forth various programs of both introspective contemplation and sociopolitical engagement—forest monks and ascetics in mountain caves as well as Dalai Lamas as political leaders and monks as advisors to kings. But the conditions that have produced the contemporary spectrum of personal spirituality and socially engaged Buddhism are uniquely formed by the crossfertilizations between Buddhism and the discourses of modernity, along with their late modern articulations.

The interpretation of Buddhism as a form of spirituality directed toward integration of mind, body, and spirit, personal development, facilitation of religious experience, psychological health, healing, and inner transformation draws on the ascetic aspects of Buddhism, as well as the Protestant, Enlightenment, and Romanticist traditions of interiority and reflexivity. This approach embodies ideas of spirituality as an inner experience in a private, personal realm, and a corresponding suspicion of institutional religion, ritual, and priesthoods. I have discussed some of the history of how Buddhism came to be interpreted as a free-form spirituality and of how meditation has been drawn into the discourses and practice of psychotherapy, health, education, and even consumer and corporate culture. The appropriation of Buddhist meditation and analysis of mind by New Age spirituality and psychotherapy is one example of the relative privatization of religion in the West and is a significant part of the contemporary interpretation of Buddhism in Europe and North America. While this has increased the cultural capital of Buddhism in certain western circles, it has also radically decontextualized particular elements of the tradition, sundered them from traditional goals and social contexts, and reembedded Buddhism in wholly novel contexts. The most extreme expressions of this tendency are the presentations of Buddhism as one among "techniques" for providing personal meaning, blissful experiences, self-improvement, and private solace in a harsh world. In a great deal of popular literature, "Buddhism" in this sense is marketed, like many other products, as a quick remedy for a wide variety of problems, from difficulty with relationships to workplace stress, promising to improve one's performance of a plethora of activities, including sex, financial planning, and sports. Popular books promise, as does the back cover of *The Complete Idiot's Guide to Understanding Buddhism*, "Enlightenment has never been easier." A British system of recordings called "Pearls of Zen" promises to "meditate you": "Within minutes you will be meditating like a Zen Master, without the need for years of training or practice, and also get all the benefits of meditation." Among other things, those purchasing this system can expect it to "make your brain healthier and more powerful, enhance creativity, accelerate learning, improve memory, enhance your motivation, concentration and creativity, alleviate pain, [improve] self confidence and self esteem, [and] boost the immune system."[5]

The explosion of socially engaged Buddhism onto the international scene—one of the most important recent developments in Buddhism in the late twentieth century—stands in stark contrast to such privatized, commercialized interpretations and appropriations. This transnational movement combines the traditional language of Buddhism on suffering, compassion, and liberation with that of emancipatory strains of modern western thought: human rights, social justice, equality, and women's rights. In its multiple forms throughout the world, socially engaged Buddhism heads up peace activism, advocates for the homeless and disenfranchised, promotes environmental causes, and works with rural villages to establish sustainable economic independence (see Queen 1999, 2003; Queen and King 1996).

Engaged Buddhism expands the meanings of Buddhist terminology to address systemic suffering and liberation in this-worldly terms. Clearly this is an extension of some of the tendencies I have already described in Buddhist modernism: the reinterpretation and demythologization of traditional doctrines, vigorous world-affirmation, and hybridity with western discourses of emancipation. In many respects, engaged Buddhism resembles certain liberation movements in the West, particularly liberation theology, articulating many of the same commitments by extrapolating from traditional Buddhist concepts. Kenneth Kraft summarizes some of these extrapolations with regard to the precepts:

> The precepts, originally a code of conduct for individual monks, are now being applied to global concerns. Thus "do not kill" has been extended to include resistance to war and militarism. "Do not steal" proscribes exploitive economic systems; and "do not lie" becomes an injunction to speak truth to those in power. Thich Nhat Hanh's "diet for a mindful society," an interpretation of the precept that restricts intoxicants, highlights the social grounds of individual conduct. . . . Buddhism classically analyzed suffering in psychological and spiritual terms (desire is the principal cause of suffering). Present-day Buddhist thinkers maintain that social conditions and political institutions also affect suffering in crucial ways, exacerbating it or easing it. The same forces that were underscored in early Buddhism—desire, greed, anger, ignorance—must be dealt with socially and politically as well as individually. For example, runaway consumerism makes individuals anxious, widens the gap between rich and poor nationally and internationally, and wrecks the environment. Sulak Sivaraksa bluntly declares: "Consumer culture works hand-in-glove with greed and lust, arising out of delusion and ignorance." (Kraft 1999: 53)

Engaged Buddhism, therefore, insists on addressing systemic in addition to personal causes of suffering.

That there is tension between privatized and engaged modes of Buddhism does not mean that the latter dispenses with the traditional concern for meditation and mindfulness. To the contrary, many authors consider these activities essential to the practice of political activism, combining them with social activism. Thich Nhat Hanh, as noted, is among the prominent Buddhist advocates of mindfulness in everyday life. Eating, washing dishes, and countless other activities can be occasions for appreciating the wonder of the everyday. As I have described it so far, it would seem a wholly personal practice, one that could take its place firmly within the most privatized spiritualities of personal experience; but Thich Nhat Hanh, who coined the term "engaged Buddhism" as a young monk in Vietnam to describe his order's peace activism and social programs during the war there, extends its implications to wider spheres. To eat mindfully, for example, one must be aware not only of the flavors and textures of the food but also of the network of causes and conditions that has brought it to the table, which might include hard-working, underpaid farmers, exploited laborers in poor countries, and the considerable amount of fossil fuels used and greenhouse gases emitted in importing it to wealthy countries. Eating is an occasion to be mindful of the people who die of hunger every day or who are too poor to eat the fine foods that are exported from their countries to wealthy ones (1991, 1998). Cultivating this kind of awareness, he maintains, is an important stimulus to social action, as cultivating inner peace is important to bringing peace to the world.

The continuum between Buddhist modernism as a personal spirituality and as a socially and politically active force for social and environmental justice, like the other continua I have described, is a variegated one. At the one extreme are iterations of Buddhism that are nearly thoroughly accommodated to the consumerist, materialist, capitalist culture of globalized postmodernism. Their main goal is personal peace of mind in a complex and stressful world, and they largely leave out traditional ethical concerns as well as larger social issues. They require no commitment to the social or institutional aspects of Buddhism and are highly selective in their adaptation of Buddhist teachings and techniques. It is difficult, however, to find such a thoroughly privatized Buddhism without any ethical or social relevance except in the most uninformed presentations of Buddhism. Buddhism's traditional stress on moral life is difficult to excise, even from the most individualized forms of spirituality. Most popular books on Buddhism at least gesture toward the idea that meditation is meant to bring about not only personal peace of mind but also a transformation of one's ethical stance toward others.

On the other end of the continuum is the socially engaged Buddhist who sees carrying out the mandate for universal loving-kindness (*metta*) or the bodhisattva path of saving all sentient beings as necessitating social and political activism. Buddhism, on this model, is of little use if it is only for finding personal solace in a world filled with suffering and injustice. Compassion for all sentient beings means confronting militarism, racism, inequality, poverty, and environmental degradation head on, challenging not only the personal but also the systemic causes of these phenomena. A number of ways of being Buddhist lie between these starkly contrasting poles; indeed most varieties of Buddhist modernism today combine the two orientations. Still, they suggest a tension in contemporary Buddhist modernism, one that will likely pull the tradition one way or the other in years to come.

Globalization and the Decentering of Legitimacy

The hybridity of Buddhist modernism, its protean nature, its discarding of much that is traditional, and its often radical reworking of doctrine and practice naturally invite questions of authenticity, legitimacy, and definition. What is a Buddhist? What is the boundary between Buddhism and non-Buddhism? At what point is Buddhism so thoroughly modernized, westernized, detraditional-ized, and adapted that it simply no longer can be considered Buddhism?

We can surely dispense with the myth of the pure original to which every adaptation must conform. If "true Buddhism" is only one that is unalloyed by novel cultural elements, no forms of Buddhism existing today qualify. To say that western Buddhisms must adhere rigidly to their Asian predecessors would still be arbitrary, since they, too, are hybrids embracing numerous cultural adapta-tions. Every extant form of Buddhism has been shaped and reconfigured by the great diversity of cultural and historical circumstances it has inhabited in its long and varied existence. Buddhist traditions—indeed all traditions—have constantly re-created themselves in response to unique historical and cultural conditions, amalgamating elements of new cultures, jettisoning those no longer viable in a new context, and asking questions that previous incarnations of Bud-dhism could not possibly have asked.

I have been concerned in this book not with establishing authenticity and inauthenticity—terms that may have some empirical applications but more often entail normative and polemical claims—but with tracing some threads in the unique fabric of Buddhist modernism. Nevertheless, the questions of definition, legitimacy, and authenticityhave become important to practitioners in the contemporary period because of its unprecedented rapidity of change and proliferation of new forms of Buddhism. And as the voices speaking for and about Buddhism multiply beyond the boundaries of the traditional *sangha*, discussions of what Buddhism is become more complex for scholars and prac-titioners alike. As Stephen Berkwitz points out, "it becomes ever more impor-tant for scholars to recognize that totalizing and essentializing claims made on what constitutes Buddhist identity and tradition are, at root, historically contin-gent and differently authorized within the shifting grounds of contemporary debates over issues such as politics and religion" (2006: 7).

In one respect, to ask if any of the various forms of, or developments within, Buddhist modernism are legitimate is to ask whether there are communities of practice that have been convinced of its legitimacy. Certainly the answer here, for many of these forms, is yes. But the rapid globalization of Buddhist modernism in recent decades has made this issue more complex. According to Anthony Giddens, late modernity and globalization entail a reconfiguration of social space—it is no longer mapped just in terms of physical territories and national boundaries. Social relations are now disembedded, lifted out of "local contexts of interaction and . . . restructur[ed] across indefinite spans of space-time" (1990: 21). Globalization entails the "intensification of worldwide social relations which link distant localities in such a way that local happenings are shaped by events occurring many miles away and vice versa" (64). David Held and his colleagues (1999: 16) define globalization similarly as a "process (or set of processes) which embodies a transformation in the spatial organization of social relations and transactions—assessed in terms of their extensity, intensity, velocity and impact-generating transcontinental or inter-regional flows and networks of activity." In this situation, massive population shifts and mass media thrust systems of thought and practice into unprecedented relationships with other systems. Since various schools and geographically particular forms of Buddhism have become internationalized, Buddhist traditions now function within multiple systems—ideological, political, social, and commercial. It is no longer sufficient for the *sangha* simply to have the allegiance of the laity and the sanction of the kingdom or state. The postmodern situation has multiplied the systems within which the legitimacy and cultural capital of any form of tradition or any novel development within a tradition can be—and often must be—granted and contested.

For example, Tibetan Buddhists, having been thrust into abrupt confrontation with modernity, find themselves in an unprecedented multiplicity of discursive contexts in which they must redefine and reinterpret their tradition and generate legitimacy and cultural capital. Tibetan Buddhism now must address and adapt to the needs and desires of western enthusiasts in order to gain worldwide support for its struggle with the government of the People's Republic of China; it must assert its right to exist as a religious tradition within a communist government; it must debate internally the degree to which tradition can and must adapt to the radically new situation of a Chinese-occupied Tibet, a substantial exile community, and a new global population of non-Tibetan practitioners of Tibetan Buddhism; and it must negotiate fidelity to the dharma with the desire to share teachings with non-Tibetans and adapt these teachings to their cultures. The Dalai Lama may get expansive global recognition and press coverage for promoting modernized articulations of Buddhism, and such legitimation in the popular press may reverberate back not only to the Tibetan community but to other Buddhist communities. Yet he is subject to criticism from more traditionalist Buddhists within his own Gelukpa school and must convince them that his adapting teachings to the modern world is not a fatal compromise of the dharma. Tibetan Buddhism, moreover, has become popular not only in the United States and Europe but also Singapore, Taiwan, New Zealand, Brazil, and other nations and must think about how to present itself in each of these cultural contexts.

The situation demands more than just adaptation to different cultures. The decentering tendencies of postmodern globalization disembed Buddhist discourse from its traditional sites and reembed it in a wide variety of discourses—not only those of the environmental movement, for instance, or the recent dialogues between "world religions" but also in the ubiquitous expressions of the market, in which Buddhist books, CDs, and ritual performances compete with novels, music, and theater. Prominent teachers must now also consider things like the market for books, venues for speaking, how to interact with the press and politicians, whether and how to participate in Hollywood movies and, yes, even rock concerts.[6] The contexts in which this tradition must adapt its teachings and practices and generate legitimacy and prestige, therefore, are multiplied beyond those of different sects or geographical areas, and the need to adapt and tailor messages to these multiple contexts often serves as an engine for rapid change.

Certainly there have been other times in Buddhist history when rhetorics of legitimacy and contexts of cultural capital were spread among different constituencies, but never before have they been spread throughout the globe, across manifold cultural, religious, and ideological lines. This disembedding of the dharma from traditional social networks and its new participation in multiple discourses and cultural contexts multiplies the circumstances in which Buddhists must develop adaptations and strategies of legitimation. This in turn tends to spawn new interpretations, new practices, and new hybrids, as different forms of Buddhism seek ecological niches within the ever-increasing diversity of cultures, discourses, ideologies, print cultures, electronic media venues, and communities, both local and international.

In such contexts, the idiom of Buddhist modernism often comes into play as a kind of de facto international language of multiple Buddhist traditions when they address a transnational, cosmopolitan audience. The popular tours of Tibetan monks creating sand mandalas and performing chants, dances, and rituals on stages around the world are a specific example of the postmodern disembedding of traditional Buddhist cultures and of Buddhism's participation in multiple contexts, as well as the use of Buddhist modernism as an international Buddhist language.

In an American tour called "The Mystical Arts of Tibet," monks of the Drepulng Loseling monastery perform, on stages in concert halls and college auditoriums, a mix of rituals normally performed in monasteries, popular dances traditionally performed at seasonal festivals, and a sample of debate that forms a part of the monk's traditional education. The language of the pamphlet distributed at these performances is neither that of traditional philosophical, ritual, or tantric texts nor the language in which the common laity observing these rituals would understand them.[7] I mean this, of course, in more than the obvious sense, that it is a pamphlet in English rather than Tibetan. Rather, some of the meanings and implications in the pamphlet are unique to this utterly novel context and might be only dimly recognized by many Tibetan Buddhists. Descriptions of specific rituals include one that "invoke[s] creative awareness within themselves [the monks] and the audience" and "enhance[s] the spirit of goodness in the environment." The construction of a small mandala is said to "create a world as seen through the eyes of inner perfection. This is sent forth as an offering for world healing." The description of the "dance of the black hat masters" (sha-nak gar-cham) calls it an "ancient dance for the elimination of neg- ative energies and hindrances . . . in the style known as drak-po, or 'wrathful.'" References to "creativity" pepper the pamphlet: songs inspire "ways of creative living," rituals bring forth "creative energy," and chants for "world peace" invoke a "subliminal force invoking peace, harmony and the ways of creative living."

The pamphlet illustrates some of the ways Buddhist practices and ideas have been translated into the language of Buddhist modernism. The dance of the black hat masters, for instance, in its traditional context, is a play in which lamas subdue malevolent demons by transforming the redeemable among them into guardians of the dharma and destroying the rest. It is popularly as- sociated with a story of a monk who killed Langdarma, a ninth-century king of Tibet and persecutor of Buddhism. Also notable is that the descriptions of the beautifully intricate sand mandalas that the monks often construct in days leading up to these performances lack any reference to the fact that mandalas, traditionally, while they may represent the "world as seen through the eyes of inner perfection" are meant to embody *particular* deities often evoked for particular purposes (seldom just an "offering for world healing"). A mandala represents the palace of a specific buddha or bodhisattva. After a consecration ceremony inviting the divine being to take up residence in it, the image serves as temporary residence for him or her, and it is thus treated as an object of ven- eration. All language relating to the specificity of deities and their habitation of the mandala is eliminated from the pamphlet. It would also be difficult to find a Tibetan term corresponding to the frequently used "creativity," at least one that would convey the implications inevitable to a western audience.

Geoffrey Samuel has analyzed two orientations in Tibetan Buddhism, the *bodhi* and the pragmatic orientations (1993). The latter has to do largely with the controlling of unseen beings for protection from evil and the creation of better life-circumstances; and the former has to do with attaining awakening (*bodhi*). Buddhist modernism, as noted, nearly always occludes this pragmatic element, emphasizing a modernized version of the *bodhi* orientation. When such rituals are presented in the West, the language of Buddhist modernism mediates between the pragmatic orientation and the modernist *bodhi* orientation. Part of this involves a depersonalizing of particular actors in the drama: benevolent deities in the Buddhist pantheon become "the spirit of goodness" or altruistic motivations within oneself, and demons likewise become wrathful forces within the psyche. As with many instances of modernization, this internalization and pscyhologization of unseen beings is not purely a western invention but rather an elaboration on interpretations already in the Buddhist tradition. Demons, bodhisattvas, dharma protectors, and other unseen beings *do* in fact correlate with qualities of mind in Tibetan Buddhist philosophical thought. In order to resonate with the West's subjective turn and the modernist tendency to psychologize such things, the "Mystical Arts of Tibet" pamphlet offers a somewhat esoteric interpretation—one that might not be familiar to most lay Buddhists in Tibet but would be understood by educated monks. There is an important difference, however, between the elite Tibetan symbolic internalization of unseen beings and the western psychologization of them: the former admits a correlation between, for instance, demons as external beings and internal negative psychological states but does not *reduce* the former to the latter. As already noted, Tibetans consider these beings really to exist, even though they also symbolize elements of mind. In the presentation to the West, however, supernatural beings fall away and are reduced to symbols of psychological states or impersonal spiritual "energies."

I have examined such instances of demythologization many times in this study already. What is noteworthy about this one is that it illustrates how a previously highly localized form of Buddhism employs the language of Buddhist modernism to translate something of its culture to a western, cosmopolitan audience. It is not meant to convey the complex ritual cosmology of Tibetan Buddhism but to translate—and thus transform—it into a preexisting idiom for use within novel settings: the stage presentation, the touring theater group, the art exhibition, the CD recording.

This translation of Tibetan ritual into the language of Buddhist modernism illustrates a way that globalization multiplies the contexts in which formerly localized traditions operate, and how such multiplication can generate novel iterations of the dharma. Descriptions like the one in the "Mystical Arts of Tibet" pamphlet, while meant to be quick, thumbnail sketches for a wide, largely non-Buddhist audience, both arise from and become cues for popular authors (both western and Tibetan) who present Buddhism in still popular but more in-depth ways. And dozens of popular books psychologize and modernize Tibetan Buddhist teachings in language similar to that of the pamphlet, and these writings become authoritative representations of Buddhism in the West. More than just representations, however, they are, in effect, new subtraditions within Buddhism, insofar as they generate not only new interpretations but also new communities of practice. Further, these modernized articulations of Tibetan doctrines and practices, as they attain a degree of global currency among powerful elite populations with social prestige, political influence, and access to media, in turn influence more localized Buddhist populations, inducing some to adopt these modern interpretations and provoking traditionalist backlash among others. Globalization, therefore, creates conditions for rapid innovation, the multiplication of novel subtraditions, retraditionalization, and contestation over authenticity and legitimacy.

By suggesting that Buddhist modernism is becoming the lingua franca of Buddhism as it is presented in transnational, cosmopolitan contexts, I do not mean to that it necessarily replaces the central common elements of the various Buddhist traditions. The four noble truths, the eightfold path, the practice of taking refuge: these remain common features of Buddhism across the globe, modern or not, and it is these that we hear Buddhist teachers discussing around the globe. We might say rather that the language of Buddhist modernism is a metalanguage, one that suggests how to interpret these fundamental elements and situate them in modern social, political, and cultural contexts. The metalanguage suggests what we should attend to and ignore, what is central and peripheral. As the languages and practices of western modernity become more globalized, the language of Buddhist modernism increasingly becomes the language of cosmopolitan dharma.

Global Buddhism: Adaptation and Challenge

Buddhist modernism's departures from tradition and hybridization with western thought and practice invite questions not only of adaptation and authenticity but also of Buddhism's capacity to challenge the normative cultural values of modernity and the West. As noted, one recurring theme in the interaction of Buddhism and the West is the hope that Buddhism might have solutions to the formidable problems of modernity—solutions that the West has missed in its drive to technological development and material well-being. While many such hopes have been rooted in orientalist fantasies and romantic exoticism, it would be cultural arrogance to think that Buddhism cannot offer the West—and more broadly, the contemporary world—new perspectives, insights, and critiques. Buddhist modernism, as we have seen, has accommodated itself in many ways to western thought, culture, and social practice. This reformulation of Buddhism in the languages of western modernity could have two potential and opposite effects. It could position Buddhism to bring novel conceptual resources to the West and the modern world that might indeed offer new perspectives on some of modernity's personal, social, political, and environmental ills. Indeed, if it does not speak the language of modernity, it cannot address these ills. The second possibility, however, is that it could accommodate itself so completely to mainstream western values and assumptions that it no longer is an alternative to them and thus accedes the resources it has for critiquing them.

What, then, is the capacity for Buddhist modernism, now entering a postmodern, global phase, to challenge, critique, augment, and offer alternatives to modern, western ideas, social practices, and ethical values? An adequate answer might require another book, but here is a sketch of some implications of the question. Buddhist modernism would appear to have ample resources for such challenges, critiques, and contributions. The Buddhist analysis of the relationship between craving (*tṛṣṇa*) and dissatisfaction (*duḥkha*), for example, as well as its ascetic tendencies, can be fashioned into a formidable critique of the very foundations of consumerism, materialism, and the pathological aspects of capitalism (see, for example, Loy 2003; Kaza 2005). Buddhism's sophisticated techniques of meditation combined with its vigorous ethical reflection offer forms of psychological and spiritual self-cultivation that can transcend the self-absorption and social irrelevance that has beset some modern psychotherapies and New Age spiritualities (Carrette and King 2005). Engaged Buddhism, furthermore, brings a unique perspective and a new vocabulary to the discourses of human rights, war and peace, environmentalism, and other pressing social and political concerns, expanding their conceptual resources.

Buddhist modernism can be mapped along yet another continuum, one gauging the capacity to challenge (post)modernity's status quo and offer novel insights. At one end are various reconfigurations of Buddhism that address such issues and develop such critiques, whether they be modern modes of monasticism or socially engaged Buddhism. Many of the most renowned contemporary Buddhists, such as the Dalai Lama, Thich Nhat Hanh, and Buddhadasa, along with the many who expand on their teachings, occupy this end of the continuum. A great deal has been written on such globally influential figures, and I hardly need expand further on the ways they have both drawn upon and offered challenges to modernity.

At the opposite end of this continuum are forms and fragments of Buddhism that have been absorbed into western culture so thoroughly that they lose any potential to offer any real alternative to or critique of its values and assumptions or offer anything new. This is where Buddhism fades into vague New Age spiritualities, self-help therapies, and purely personal paths of self-improvement. While there may indeed be personal benefits to such approaches, they are largely subservient to popular values and often merely instrumental to their ends: making money, working efficiently at the office, having a rich and satisfying private life. At the continuum's furthest extremes, these fragments fade into pop culture, splintering into shards of Buddhist imagery that become tropes for countless commercial products: Zen popcorn, Zen tea, Buddha bikinis, and Buddha bars.[8] Here Buddhist modernism dissipates into the immense machinery of media-driven consumption, becoming not only a means for selling products but a product itself. From the point on the continuum where Buddhism becomes a purely personalized mode of self-help with scant ethical ramifications to where it becomes a mere commercial trope, it is accommodated so thoroughly to the values of western (and increasingly globalizing) popular culture and its consumerism and commercialism that its capacity to critique these elements of contemporary culture—for which Buddhism has such ample resources—is neutralized.

Global Folk Buddhism

Toward this end of the continuum, we have a new development, which I will call *global folk Buddhism*—the emerging "popular religion" within Buddhist modernism. It is an admittedly ironic category that confounds the usual taxonomies of "great" and "little" traditions and "elite" and "popular" or "folk" traditions. Scholars often describe popular traditions as the relatively unsophisticated local religion of the common people. They contain more ritual than complex doctrine, blend traditions liberally, and employ magic and the manipulation of material objects for protection and other this-worldly benefits. They may include fetishism and witchcraft and are often disruptive of orthodoxy. Popular traditions tend to be local, rooted in particular places, versus elite traditions with their universalizing impetus. The latter are sophisticated, textual, philosophical, normative, and often imperial. They belong to the higher social classes and offer themselves as universal, true for all times and places.

Global folk Buddhism inverts certain staples of the popular/elite distinction: its appeal is often to the affluent; it is increasingly global, not tied to a particular locality; and it tends to dismiss local, cultural, and ethnic difference, instead privileging unity. Rather than being embedded in a particular cultural context, it is disembedded, merging into the currents of global discourse, commercial venues, popular culture, and social practices of the electronic age. This postmodern global folk Buddhism is a unique form of lay Buddhism that has emerged with the rise of globalization. It intermingles with continually emerging and expanding transnational popular culture, circulating primarily through television, print, and the internet. When elite Buddhist modernists, be they performing Tibetan monks or international Buddhist authors, work within the systems of significance, cultural practices, and commercial venues of this globalizing popular culture, they enact a variation of what Buddhist traditions have always done when bringing the dharma to a new place: they selectively and creatively re-present elements of Buddhism using the local vernacular, sometimes diluting it with local custom, accommodating it to local dialects, adapting it to local practices, and co-opting local deities—while often themselves, in turn, being shaped by all of these.

What is unique to the postmodern situation is that the local vernacular, customs, dialects, and practices of global folk Buddhism are *not* local—they are instead bound up with global systems of media, commerce, and international popular cultures. Their venues are the popular book, lecture tour, concert stage, website, and CD. Practitioners of global folk Buddhism, like those of local folk Buddhisms, do not have a sophisticated understanding of their own tradition and liberally mingle it with their "native" customs—in this case, various forms of self-help, sports, commerce, entertainment, drug use, fashion, corporate culture, and other religious traditions and subcultures (e.g., the "Dead Buddhist Society," for fans of Buddhism and the Grateful Dead; *Zen Management* for corporate heads). Rather than the elite occupation of dismantling the self through rigorous meditation, global folk Buddhism becomes an aid in the ever-ongoing process of reflexive self-making and remaking that, according to Giddens, constitutes self-identity in the contemporary world (1991). This Buddhism produces a unique material culture of Buddhist paraphernalia—beads, statues, exotic clothing—as practitioners fashion a Buddhist identity by imbibing popularized Buddhist teachings and practices, as well as consuming within a niche market of consumer goods and services. Buddha images multiply endlessly, not only in stone and metal but in printed and electronic images, no longer embodiments of buddhas themselves but advertisements for particular products, accessories to a particular lifestyle. They manifest not to answer prayers, grant wishes, and bestow good merit, as in local popular Buddhism, but to project cultural capital and, particularly in the current vogue for using Buddhism in advertising, draw actual capital.

Should we be horrified by this picture? In an article in *Salon*, Stephen Prothero decries American "boomer Buddhism"—not all of which is so crassly commercialized as the foregoing description—as a domesticated flattening of the truly radical ideas of Buddhism, a watered-down dharma that "soothes rather than upsets, smoothing out the palpable friction between Buddhist practice and the banalities of contemporary American life" (2001). He compares this quite unfavorably with the robust traditional monasticism of American monk Bhikkhu Thanissaro. And in many respects he is right. Yet from a historian's perspective, we should not be surprised by the routinization of Buddhist charisma and the accommodation to popular cultures. After all, the vast majority of Buddhists in Asia are not monks like Thanissaro but laity whose practice of Buddhism is similarly soothing, offering comfort and accommodation to cultural norms rather than radical transformative challenge. Such laypeople blend Buddhism liberally with local spirit and amulet cults just as Americans and Europeans blend it with their cults of consumerism and commodity fetishism. The difference is that the global postmodern popular culture of which global folk Buddhism is a part, with its tendency to assimilate all elements of culture to its banality, is imperialistic. Globalizing cultures tend to insert themselves into local cultures in ways that aspire to occupy all social space, while local popular cultures are less mobile, have less transnational appeal, and therefore are more vulnerable to being displaced by globalizing cultures. For this reason, global folk Buddhism may in fact represent a danger to local Buddhisms. Conversely, if the accommodation of Buddhist modernism to western modernities has diminished its ability to challenge and critique them, such more drastic accommodations further diminish its capacity to offer any alternative to mainstream American and globalizing culture.

In threatening to colonize the space that has opened up in popular culture for Buddhist modernism, global folk Buddhism nevertheless must compete with some of the more serious forms of Buddhist modernism that have taken root. Traditionalist monastics and politically engaged Buddhists have obvious conceptual resources with which to challenge the axioms of globalized American and European culture and thus further the inaugural hopes of Buddhist modernism. The forms of Buddhist modernism that combine aspects of both of these, as well as both selective accommodation and critique of mainstream culture, may have the greatest viability. There are uniquely modern Buddhist organizations that unite rootedness in tradition with media savvy, broad cultural knowledge, and efforts to engage contemporary culture and thought both critically and openly. Crucially, they also involve lay Buddhists and sympathizers at different levels of participation in the dharma and in different areas of their lives. Perhaps these modernizers, rather than ardent traditionalists, are the ones who will be able to develop a Buddhist modernism (or postmodernism) that can form viable Buddhist responses to the problems of (post)modern culture—its narcissism, consumerism, militarism, and so on—as well as of traditionalism: its sexism, hierarchism, and dogmatism.

In the United States, John Daido Loori Rōshi's Zen Mountain Monastery in Mt. Tremper, New York, offers an example of such a balance between tradition and adaptation that has had considerable success. Despite the central focus on meditation, Zen Mountain Monastery's programs extend into all areas of lay life in a way that does not dilute the identity of the organization as a Zen Buddhist institution. Its adherence to traditional lineage and institutional affiliation gives it credibility with serious Buddhists as well as sympathizers who may come occasionally to participate in short retreats or workshops. This combination of a strong traditional identity, a charismatic leader, and the developing of innovative ways of reaching out to the general public has made the monastery one of the most successful American Buddhist organizations. It offers formal and rather traditional instruction in Zen monastic training and houses a number of ordained monastics. It offers extended residential meditation retreats as well as short weekend sessions to the general public. It also offers thematic retreats centered on various arts, wilderness meditation, youth programs, text study, family relationships, psychological issues, work issues, and political activism. The monastery has various outreach programs; its prison program teaches meditation in prisons, and its Zen Environmental Institute sponsors nature retreats, research opportunities, and programs of ecological activism. Its outreach nonprofit, Dharma Communications, has an online radio station, a monthly print journal, an online art gallery, and a gift shop (both through a catalogue and online) that sells books, art, meditation cushions, bells, and statues. It also produces videos, podcasts, tapes, and interactive multimedia.

What makes this organization a possible model for a viable adaptation of Buddhism in postmodern America is not the extensiveness of its activities but the way it adapts to currents of American culture and adjusts its teachings and methods to the discourses of modernity while maintaining central elements of tradition—monasticism, liturgy, meditation, and emphasis on lineage. This monastery effectively combines adaptation to selective elements of modernity and mainstream culture with a critical stance toward them.[9]

Many successful iterations of Buddhist modernism have a similar mixture of tradition and innovation, contemplation and social engagement, commercial entrepreneurship and cultural critique. Certainly Soka Gakkai, a more recent Buddhist modernism, has mastered these. This relatively young movement has had tremendous success attracting new adherents from a wide variety of social, economic, and ethnic backgrounds, something that cannot be said for the many meditative forms of Buddhist modernism that appeal mostly to the white, educated, and relatively affluent in the West and largely the middle and upper classes in Asia. The central practice of Soka Gakkai is chanting rather than meditation. The organization has been adept at raising funds and spreading its message worldwide, becoming a truly transnational movement in just a few decades. It has been unapologetically political, even messianic, with its members hoping for nothing less than to transform the world. Its political mission has aligned itself in many respects with those of other engaged Buddhists, advocating peace and nonviolence, economic justice, and human rights. Soka Gakkai represents, therefore, another model that combines successful adaptation to modern culture with a vigorous ethic and a critical stance toward contemporary culture.

Although it is fairly clear which end of the continuum of global Buddhism I have mapped here has the most potential to challenge and critically engage western and modern problems, values, and tacit assumptions, it is not clear which will ultimately be most influential. Global folk Buddhism, precisely because it has accommodated itself so well to western ways of being, may ultimately be quite successful. Like certain forms of New Age religion, however, its inability to speak to issues beyond the personal may severely limit its development, while a more socially engaged Buddhism has the capacity to draw wide interest through its combination of interior cultivation with social/ethical conceptions.

Perhaps the question of which genre of globalized postmodern Buddhism will have the day, however, is misleading and too dichotomous to address the increasing complexity and heterogeneity of the subject. As noted, many forms of contemporary Buddhism combine elements from across this continuum. The Dalai Lama and Thich Nhat Hanh, for example, often intermingle complex Buddhist teachings liberally with vaguely New Age spirituality. Perhaps the question therefore is: What particular combinations of features on the continuum will produce new formations that compellingly address the needs of contemporary individuals and societies? The answer will appear not only in the monasteries but on the internet, on television, in bookstores, in blogs, and in auditoriums. Thus the dharma that emerged from Kyoto and Colombo over a century ago returns, through transnational flows of culture, in new clothing, wearing different jewels, on invisible airwaves and in books of a foreign tongue, confirming the age-old teachings of impermanence, incessant change, and things arising from a vast multiplicity of causes and conditions.

Notes

CHAPTER 1

1. "The dharma" refers to the teachings of Buddhism.

2. I use the term "monastics" to refer both to monks and nuns. More recently, the term *sangha* has expanded to include lay practitioners and even informal meditation groups.

3. I mean the term "discourses" to signify not only explicitly linguistic elements but the sociocultural practices, tacit assumptions, and pretheoretical forms of life particular to a place and age.

4. For more on the concept of "multiple modernities," see Eisenstadt 2002.

5. Gergen also says that these languages are giving way to postmodern modes of structuring the self.

6. I am not proposing here that these elite ideas "cause" these tacit understandings and dispositions. How such things come to be is a complicated issue that I have little room to address here, but I suggest that explicit ideas are often part of larger cultural forces already in play. They are articulated explicitly at an elite level, and this articulation then refracts back to the popular level, especially in the modern era of mass education and literacy. The tacit and theoretical are, therefore, interimplicated.

7. The fact that one can be "into" Buddhism in a way it is impossible to be "into" Presbyterianism says something about its cultural location in the West.

8. For a discussion of the role of the West in the modernization of Tibetan Buddhism, see Dreyfus 2005.

CHAPTER 2

1. The term "Buddhist sympathizer" was coined by Thomas Tweed and refers to "those who have some sympathy for [Buddhism] but do not embrace it exclusively or in full" (1999: 74; see also Tweed 2000).

2. The Soka Gakkai tradition, on the other hand, has attracted a much more diverse array of adherents, especially in the United States. See Seager 2006.

3. The Vinaya does not require meditation as an ethical obligation, though it is seen as soteriologically necessary.

4. We need not be detained here to justify the use of the term "self" with regard to Buddhism, which advocates the doctrine of "no-self" (*anātman*). "Self," in the more sociological sense used here, refers not to a fixed, permanent soul—an *atman*—but to a fluid agent operating within a particular social context.

5. Bultmann's insistence that such things are no longer relevant suggests that his circle of acquaintances was rather limited. In light of the contemporary resurgence of more traditional religious beliefs and practices, it is tempting to think that his "modern man" is a rarer species than he thought. Yet it is just this species—the elite, educated, and modern person—that has been most responsible for the construction of Buddhist, as well as Christian, modernism.

6. The term implies an appearance that is phenomenal rather than absolute and that is dependent in some respect on the perceiver, without a substantial object behind it. In Evans-Wentz, it is translated "thought-form." Francesca Fremantle's and Chögyam Trungpa's translation renders it "projection."

7. Often protector deities are thought to be indigenous Tibetan demons that were converted to protect the dharma when Padmasambhāva brought Buddhism to Tibet.

8. For more detailed accounts of the controversy and its implications, see Lopez 1998: 188; Dreyfus 2003: ch. 13; and "Deity or Demon" 1998.

9. See *Journal of Transpersonal Psychology*, www.atpweb.org/journal.asp.

CHAPTER 3

1. The motto stressed the society's commitment to the discovery of truth through experimentation rather than reliance on authority.

2. A few modern commentators have expressed skepticism about the common modernist interpretation of this text: see chapter 9 for Bhikkhu Bodhi's reservations.

3. Stephen Batchelor's *Buddhism without Beliefs* (1997) is a contemporary example of a highly rationalist presentation of Buddhism that appeals to the idea of an early "pre-religious," empirically minded, verification-based, and agnostic worldview at the core of Buddhism. Since Buddhism becomes an institution, however, he says, it "has tended to lapse into religiosity" (1997: 3).

4. See, for example, *Aṅguttara Nikāya* IV, 7:62; X, 10: 91; V, 4:41.

5. In identifying Buddhism as "panentheism," the idea that the universe is a part of God but does not exhaust God's being, he refers to an unnamed "modern German scholar" who coined the term (1993 [1913]: 26). He may be referring to Karl Krause, one of the German Romantic idealists who studied with Fichte and Schelling and who

likely coined the term "panentheism" to suggest that all things are in God but that the manifest universe does not exhaust God's being. The reference is significant because it suggests some familiarity with the Romantic line of thinking, which became crucial to the early metaphysics of Buddhist modernism.

6. This is one of many of Sōen's themes that his student, D. T. Suzuki, developed in his discussions of Christian mysticism in relation to Zen (Suzuki 1979 [1957]).

7. Roger-Pol Droit interprets this horror of "Buddhist nothingness" as a projection onto Buddhism of the encroaching threat of nihilism emerging in nineteenth-century European culture: "In their reference to Asia, to the Buddha's confrontation with the traditional Brahmanic hierarchy, to the place of nothingness in his teaching, or to this atheism, Europeans were really talking about themselves, about the old power structure that was now on shaky ground, about the breaking up of metaphysical systems, about the death of God—about the nihilism that was to come" (2003: 5).

8. The most influential early formulations include James Freeman Clarke's *Ten Great Religions* (1871) and Samuel Johnson's *Oriental Religions and Their Relation to Universal Religion* (1872).

9. Though largely dismissed by scholars, perennialism has lost none of its popularity in the twentieth and twenty-first centuries as pluralism and the conflicts between worldviews have become increasingly prominent as awareness of how much individuals are conditioned by culture becomes more pervasive. Perennialism has offered (I will argue later) a kind of parallel to science: the possibility of an internalized "view from nowhere" above the conflicting claims of various religions and secular philosophies in a purified experiential realm. The conclusions of perennialism are hard to defend today in light of heightened awareness of cultural and religious diversity, not to mention its imperial implications. Yet perennialism underscores two genuine and inescapable modern concerns that have been a constant companion of Buddhist modernism: (1) the relation of different cultures and worldviews to each other and the often well-intentioned attempt to find common ground among them in a world perceived as increasingly dangerous, and (2) the impulse toward freedom from the bondage of cultural conditioning in a mechanized and bureaucratized world. The aspirations and failures of this movement invite one of the most important questions of the day: whether there is a way of conceiving of our common humanity without essentialism or covert cultural imperialism.

10. For a critique of Suzuki, see Faure 1993: 53–74.

11. Sōen again serves as an example. He seldom credits any western thinkers with "influencing" his presentation of Buddhism to the West, but a number of Romantics and Transcendentalists pepper his presentations. He mentions, for example, Emerson (1993 [1913]: 84), Goethe (169), Schleiermacher (176) and deploys tropes derived from the Romantics, including that of the dichotomy between a deep inner self and the "ego": "The heart essentially free and pure becomes contaminated as soon as it is caught in the meshes of egoism" (119).

12. Like many other "isms" that promise to bring order by imposing a singular term on an untidy profusion of phenomena, "Romanticism" is a term that cannot help but belie the complexity of what it refers to and, as many scholars have pointed out, is variegated enough to best be rendered in the plural (Romanticisms). What is most important here is to highlight certain features that worked their way into Buddhist modernism.

13. See Payne 2006 for a discussion of the Romanticist interpretation of the fall in Buddhist modernism.

CHAPTER 4

1. In classical literature, the most extensive description of such phenomena is found in Buddhaghosa's *Visuddhimagga (Path of Purification)* (2003).

2. Taking refuge in the three jewels—the Buddha, dharma, and sangha—is the most common way to identify oneself as a Buddhist.

3. At the forefront of these studies is the Mind and Life Institute, which hosts conferences and sponsors empirical research on the scientifically discernible effects of Buddhist meditation and contemplative practices. Participants have published a number of books on the institute's conferences with the Dalai Lama and on the results of empirical research. See Davidson and Harrington 2001; Goleman 1997, 2003a; Hayward and Varela 1992; Houshmand, Livingston, and Wallace 1999; and Varela 1997.

4. The issue of epistemic authority in Buddhism is complex and variegated. The *Kālāma Sutta*, again the central text on whose basis Buddhist modernists argue for the compatibility of Buddhism with modern scientific and rationalist modes of inquiry, presents the Buddha telling his disciples to accept his teachings only when they have verified them personally. Yet some schools have accepted the "reliable testimony" (*śabda*) of the Buddha as a means of valid knowledge (*pramāṇa*), making the words of the Buddha as authoritative as perception and inference, the other two universally accepted *pramāṇ as*. Even among those who rejected reliable testimony, it is difficult to find evidence that the word of the Buddha was not held supremely authoritative, both in the texts and certainly on the ground. Dignāga, the sixth-century master of Buddhist epistemology, rejected reliable testimony as a *pramāṇa*, not because he held the words of the Buddha as less than authoritative but because, he argued, they themselves were based on the Buddha's perception and inference; adding reliable testimony to the list of *pramāṇa* as acceptable to the Buddhist, therefore, was redundant. I believe one would be hard pressed to find a "nonmodern" Asian Buddhist, living or in the ancient texts, who did not consider the words of the sutras all but supremely authoritative. For further discussion of Buddhist *pramāṇas*, see Mohanty 1992; Hattori 1968; McMahan 2002a: 47–51.

CHAPTER 5

1. For representations in film, see *Principles and Practices of Zen Buddhism*, 1992, Films for the Humanities, Princeton, N.J.; *The Long Search: Land of the Disappearing Buddha* (dir. Peter Montagnon), 2001 (1970), Ambrose Video, New York.

2. Enthusiasts have declared his work to have had an impact similar to that of the translation of Plato into Latin, Commodore Perry's opening of trade between the United States and Japan, the work of Einstein and Gandhi, and the discovery of nuclear energy (Faure 1993: 53).

3. The exact western sources of his ideas are varied and often difficult to trace. He refers in various works to Emerson, Thoreau, and Schopenhauer, from whom he

likely derived Romantic and idealist philosophical terminology, as well as Romantics themselves, including Goethe, Wordsworth, and Alfred Lord Tennyson, from whom he gleaned the poetic sensibilities of the movement. Other important influences on his thought, particularly his metaphysics, included Swedenborg, Theosophy, and William James. Later in life, he also engaged existentialism to some extent. But his essential interest in the reconciliation of humanity and nature most resembles the concerns of the German Romantic philosophers, for example Schelling. Whether he actually read them is uncertain, but it is also unnecessary to establish this; their ideas were present in the works he clearly did read, and it is possible he picked them up secondhand. It is notable that scholars of the Kyoto School, with whom Suzuki was intimately involved, engaged with the German idealists. Nishida Kitarō taught the German Idealist philosophers in classes and demonstrates familiarity with them in his own work; see Yusa 2002. Nishitani Keiji (1900–1990) wrote on Schelling early in his career. See Hanaoka 2005.

4. For some of the religious influences on the Beats, see Lardas 2001.

5. He relies especially on koan collection *The Transmission of the Lamp*. A great deal of research has been done on koans since Suzuki's, much of which calls his interpretation into question. See Heine and Wright 2000; Heine 2004; Hori 2003.

6. It might be tempting here to assert that, since many Romantics had a fascination with Asian—especially Indian—philosophy and mythology, we are observing here a double appropriation, i.e., Suzuki reappropriating concepts that the Romantics like Schelling, Herder, Schlegel, and others got from reading Indian literature. While these and other Romantic thinkers did absorb various elements of Asian thought into their own, those who have studied this issue in depth generally conclude that the Asian influence was more a matter of confirming ideas they had already developed rather than being formative in that development. See Halbfass 1988, Clarke 1997.

7. Suzuki here translates the term *mushin* (Chin. *wuxin*), often rendered "no-mind" or "no-thought," as the unconscious, a problematic and potentially misleading translation that shows, perhaps, an overeagerness to assimilate psychoanalytic theory to Zen.

8. See Faure 1991 for a relevant discussion of Zen's "rhetoric of immediacy," which has a long history in the tradition; also Hori 2003 for a critique of the anticonceptualist interpretation of Zen literature, especially koans.

9. Although we must also keep in mind the often-neglected self-transcending elements of some Romantic conceptions of art and expression.

10. This essay was later incorporated into his *Creative Meditation and Multi-Dimensional Consciousness* (1976).

11. I shall use "Modernist" and "Modernism," capitalized, to refer not to modernism in the generic sense but to the multifarious early twentieth-century movement in literature, music, and visual art.

12. He likely derived this idea from Ernest Fenellosa (1853–1908), an earlier Buddhist who was also overtly influenced by Romanticism and Transcendentalism, who declared that art would replace religion in the new age (Harris 2002: 374–75).

13. Tonkinson (1995) details the ways these and like-minded writers entwined the dharma into their work.

14. For more examples (some convincingly influenced by Buddhism, others only tendentiously related), see Baas and Jacob 2004; Baas 2005.

15. See the program's website, www.music.umich.edu/departments/jazz_improv/bfa_jazz_contemplative.htm.

16. See the program's website, www.brown.edu/Faculty/Contemplative_Studies_Initiative/rationale.html.

CHAPTER 6

1. The interpretation I have offered of nirvana as transcendence of the phenomenal world is disputed by some who claim that nirvana is simply the overcoming of psychomoral afflictions (*kleśas*) and attaining a state of peace and internal freedom within this world. See, for example, Kalupahana 1992. I see this interpretation itself as a form of demythologization that, while a viable reinterpretation for modern practitioners, is unacceptable as a *historical* account. For a critique of Kalupahana's general approach to interpreting Indic Buddhist texts, see McMahan 2004a.

2. The *Avataṃsaka* as a whole is compilation of sutras, some of which may have been composed in central Asia or China. The *Gaṇḍavyūha* is the last section and was composed in Sanskrit in India, circa the second century CE.

3. Lewis Lancaster suggests that one factor in the divergent orientations was that India was at the time a large forest with islands of urban centers, while China was mostly deforested with islands of mountain forest. It is not, therefore, that the Chinese had a uniformly positive valuation of uncultivated wilderness; rather, some intellectuals and sages began to appreciate the remnants of wilderness in part because it was disappearing, giving way to cities and cultivated fields (Lancaster 1997).

4. Some process philosophers and theologians, drawing on the thought of Alfred North Whitehead, have taken a systematic interest in Huayan thought, on the basis of its resemblance to Whitehead's highly nuanced cosmology of interdependence. Though not widely read outside academic circles, process thought has likely had an impact on the contemporary Buddhist idea of interdependence (Odin 1982).

5. This is a loose translation that is popular in the West; significantly, it lends itself to being interpreted as the self expanding into all things. More precise translations of the whole passage include this one: "to study the Way is to study the self. To study the self is to forget the self. To forget the self is to be enlightened by all things of the universe. To be enlightened by all things of the universe is to cast off the body and mind of the self as well as those of others. Even the traces of enlightenment are wiped out, and life with traceless enlightenment goes on forever and ever" (Kim 2004: 125).

6. Gihwa, exact date of text uncertain. I am grateful to Professor Charles Muller for informing me of this text.

7. NeoVedanta is a modern articulation of the ancient Hindu school of Vedanta. In many ways parallel to Buddhist modernism, it is a reformulation of one strand of Hindu thought that, under the guidance of figures like Swami Vivekananda (1863–1902), became popular among nineteenth- and twentieth-century progressives in the West.

CHAPTER 7

1. It is tempting to see the current revival of meditation as a return to the "original" teachings and practices of Buddhism, where it was central. The Pali *suttas* clearly assert the importance of meditation and its indispensability to awakening, and most Buddhist schools since have agreed. In this sense, the modern centralization of meditation could be considered a kind of revival of ancient teachings and practices that have become occluded, especially as the *sangha* has been called on to fulfill the roles of priest and ritualist. Yet in the Pali canon, as well as most Buddhist literature since, meditation has been considered a monastic practice and difficult under the conditions of typical lay life. Buddhist teachings for the laity generally were not aimed at the far goal of nirvana but at the more proximate goals of ethical cultivation and a favorable rebirth. A number of Mahayana sutras complicate this picture, depicting laypeople as meditating and attaining full awakening within the conditions of ordinary life. Dōgen also affirmed the primacy of meditation among monastics and laity alike. Little evidence exists, however, that the ideal of meditation in the pursuit of full awakening has been commonly undertaken in most lay Buddhist contexts until recently. For some references regarding the Pali texts addressing this issue, see Gombrich 1988: 73–74.

2. Parts of the preceding is adapted from McMahan 2007.

3. For an annotated discussion of this idea of the turn toward the self, see Woodhead and Heelas 2000: 342–73, to which I am indebted for pointing me toward some of the sources referenced in this section. For more detailed explorations, see Taylor 1989 and Giddens 1991.

4. For an overview of the interactions between Buddhism and western psychology, see Metcalf 2002.

5. For a discussion of the close connections between Romanticism, psychoanalysis, and Buddhist modernism, see Payne 2006.

6. For a summary of recent meditation research, see Cahn and Polich 2006. See also Austin 1998, 2006; Begley 2007; Davidson and Harrington 2001; Goleman 2003.

7. This, as so many modern interpretations of Buddhism, may well have its origins with D. T. Suzuki, who calls Buddhism "radical empiricism" in his first series of *Essays in Zen Buddhism* (1949: 140).

8. The reference here is specifically to the eighteen elements (*dhātus*).

9. For a bibliography of both scholarly studies and popular books and articles, see the Center for Mindfulness's website at the University of Massachusetts Medical School website, www.umassmed.edu/cfm/index.aspx.

10. The claim of science that it is truly open to any conclusion to which evidence leads is itself, of course, debatable. The history of science shows how social, institutional, and ideological constraints operate in scientific endeavor—it has its own boundaries of tradition. The point here is that at least *in theory*, science is an open-ended inquiry without predetermined doctrinal bounds, whereas it is more problematic to make such a claim for Buddhist meditative inquiry, which has a predetermined end established by tradition.

11. It is worth noting that this situation has produced debate within traditional communities of meditators. The Dalai Lama has generated great enthusiasm for

scientific research on meditation, encouraging broad dialogues between Buddhism and science through the Mind and Life Institute, with its regular conferences and publications. Nevertheless, José Cabezón reports "widespread skepticism among [Tibetan] meditator monks as regards the exploding interest in the neuroscientific study of meditative states and the long-term effects of meditative practice," not so much because they worry about acceding too much authority to scientists but because of their doubts about studying "nonphysical states of mind" by physical means, as well as the value of doing so (2003: 42). This new arena, therefore, opens up a realm of tension not only between Asian and western approaches to meditation but also among those within more traditional communities, as they must now renegotiate the place of meditation in their traditions and beyond.

CHAPTER 8

1. The exception is the development of empathetic compassion, which virtually all forms of Buddhism unambiguously recommend.

2. The passage described is from McEwan 2005: 51–53.

3. For a discussion of surviving Romantic elements in modernist literature, see Bayley 1957.

4. The *Mahāsatipaṭṭhāna Sutta* (DN 22) and the *Satipaṭṭhāna Sutta* (MN 10) are largely identical; the former includes a discussion of the four noble truths omitted in the latter.

CHAPTER 9

1. For an overview, see Findly 2000.

2. In *Buddhadharma: The Practitioner's Quarterly.* Spring 2007, p. 84. See also www.openmindzen.com.

3. Alexandra David-Neel's book *Magic and Mystery in Tibet* (1971 [1932]) solidified the image, already in play in, for example, Blavatsky's Theosophy, of Tibet as a place where magic still existed.

4. With the ease of instantaneous communication, moreover, such enclaves are not bound to specific places. Various "cyber-sanghas" now connect Buddhists of many varieties across the globe, so one's enclave need not be based on geography (Prebish 1999).

5. At www.pearlsofzen.com/index.htm.

6. In the 1990s, three major Hollywood films featured Tibetan Buddhism: *Little Buddha, Seven Years in Tibet*, and *Kundun*. All included real Tibetan monks. In the 1990s, the Tibet Freedom concert series featured Tibetan monks chanting on stage in between popular music acts such as the Beastie Boys, Red Hot Chili Peppers, Björk, and John Lee Hooker. The Gyuto monks, who specialize in polyphonic chanting, have been featured in a number of CD releases, including *Freedom Chants from the Roof of the World*, which also features a track with Mickey Hart (of the Grateful Dead), Phillip Glass, and Kitaro.

7. The pamphlet is available at www.mysticalartsoftibet.org/.

8. Zen Popcorn is a product of Robert's American Gourmet. Zen Tea is a product of Tazo. The Buddha bikini, which featured Buddha-images on revealing swimwear—including Śākyamuni centrally located on the crotch—was marketed by Victoria's Secret until it was withdrawn after protests by Buddhists. The Buddha Bar is a high-end restaurant and bar in Paris, with locations now in Manhattan, Beirut, Dubai, Amman, and Lisbon. It features Asian cuisine and décor, down-tempo world-beat music, and large Buddha-statues.

9. For a more detailed description of Zen Mountain Monastery and its activities, see Prebish 1999: 96–107 and the Mountains and Rivers Order website, http://www.mro.org/mro.html.

Bibliography

ABBREVIATIONS

AN   *Aṅguttara Nikāya*
Aṣṭa   *Aṣṭasāhasrikā Prajñāpāramitā Sūtra*
DN   *Dīgha Nikāya*
Iti   *Itivuttaka*
MMK   *Mūlamadhyamaka-kārikā*
MN   *Majjhima Nikāya*
SN   *Saṃyutta Nikāya*
Thag   *Theragāthā*
Ud   *Udāna*

WORKS CITED

Abrams, Meyer. *The Mirror and the Lamp: Romantic Theory and the Critical Tradition.* New York: Oxford University Press, 1953.
———. *The Correspondent Breeze: Essays in English Romanticism.* New York: Norton, 1984.
Albanese, Catherine L. *The Spirituality of the American Transcendentalists.* Macon, Ga.: Mercer University Press, 1988.
———. *Nature Religion in America: From the Algonkian Indians to the New Age.* Chicago: University of Chicago Press, 1991.
———. *A Republic of Mind and Spirit: A Cultural History of American Metaphysical Religion.* New Haven: Yale University Press, 2007.
Alger, William Rounseville. *The Solitudes of Nature and of Man or The Loneliness of Human Life.* 1867. Reprint, Whitefish, Mont.: Kessinger, 2003.

Almond, Philip C. *The British Discovery of Buddhism*. Cambridge: Cambridge University Press, 1988.

Austin, James H. *Zen and the Brain: Toward an Understanding of Meditation and Consciousness*. Cambridge, Mass.: MIT Press, 1998.

———. *Zen-Brain Reflections: Reviewing Recent Developments in Meditation and States of Consciousness*. Cambridge, Mass.: MIT Press, 2006.

Baas, Jacquelynn. *Smile of the Buddha: Eastern Philosophy and Western Art from Monet to Today*. Berkeley: University of California Press, 2005.

Baas, Jacquelynn, and Mary Jane Jacob, eds. *Buddha Mind in Contemporary Art*. Berkeley: University of California Press, 2004.

Badiner, Allan Hunt, ed. *Dharma Gaia: A Harvest of Essays in Buddhism and Ecology*. Berkeley: Parallax Press, 1990.

———. "Introduction." In *Dharma Gaia: A Harvest of Essays in Buddhism and Ecology*, ed. Allan Hunt Badiner, xiii–xviii. Berkeley: Parallax Press, 1990.

Barbour, Ian G. *Religion and Science: Historical and Contemporary Issues*. San Francisco: HarperSanFrancisco, 1997.

Barrett, William. "Zen for the West." In Daisetz T. Suzuki, *Zen Buddhism: Selected Writings of D. T. Suzuki*. Edited by William Barrett, vii–xx. Garden City, N.Y.: Anchor, 1956.

Barrows, John Henry, ed. *The World's Parliament of Religions: An Illustrated and Popular Story of the World's First Parliament of Religions, held in Chicago in connection with the Columbian exposition of 1893*. Chicago: Parliament, 1893.

Barthélemy Saint Hilaire, Jules. *The Buddha and His Religion*. London: Routledge, 1895.

Batchelor, Stephen. *The Awakening of the West: The Encounter of Buddhism and Western Culture*. Berkeley: Parallax Press, 1994.

———. *Buddhism without Beliefs: A Contemporary Guide to Awakening*. New York: Riverhead Books, 1997.

———. "Letting Daylight into Magic." *Tricycle* 7, no. 3 (spring 1998): 60–66.

Bateson, Gregory. *Mind and Nature: A Necessary Unity*. New York: Dutton, 1979.

Baumann, Martin. "Global Buddhism: Developmental Periods, Regional Histories, and a New Analytic Perspective." *Journal of Global Buddhism* 2 (2001): 1–43. www.globalbuddhism.org/2/baumann001.html.

Bayley, John. *The Romantic Survival: A Study in Poetic Evolution*. London: Constable, 1957.

Bechert, Heinz. *Buddhismus, Staat und Geselschaft in den Ländern des Theravada Buddhismus*. Vol. 1. Berlin: Alfred Metzner, 1966. Vol. 2. Wiesbaden: O. Harrassowitz, 1967. Vol. 3. Wiesbaden: O. Harrassowitz, 1973.

———. "Buddhist Revival in East and West." In *The World of Buddhism*, ed. Heinz Bechert and Richard Gombrich, 273–85. London: Thames and Hudson, 1984.

———. "Buddhistic Modernism: Present Situation and Current Trends." In *Buddhism into the Year 2000: International Conference Proceedings*, 251–60. Bangkok: Dhammakaya Foundation, 1994.

Begley, Sharon. *Train Your Mind, Change Your Brain: How a New Science Reveals Our Extraordinary Potential to Transform Ourselves*. New York: Ballantine, 2007.

Bellah, Robert N. "Religious Evolution." *American Sociological Review* 29, no. 3 (1963): 358–74.

Bellah, Robert, et al. *Habits of the Heart: Individualism and Commitment in American Life.* Berkeley: University of California Press, 1985.

Bennett, Andrew. "The Idea of the Author." In Roe, *Romanticism,* 654–64.

Benoit, Hubert. *The Light of Zen in the West.* Portland, Ore.: Sussex Academic Press, 2004.

Berger, Peter L. *The Social Reality of Religion.* London: Faber and Faber, 1969.

Berger, Peter L., Brigitte Berger, and Hansfried Kellner. *The Homeless Mind: Modernization and Consciousness.* New York: Random House, 1973.

Berkwitz, Stephen C. "The History of Buddhism in Retrospect." In *Budddhism in World Cultures: Comparative Perspectives.* ed. Stephen Berkwitz, 1–44. Santa Barbara, Calif.: ABC-CLIO, 2006.

Berman, Marshall. *All That's Solid Melts into Air: The Experience of Modernity.* New York: Simon and Schuster, 1982.

Bhabha, Homi. *The Location of Culture.* London: Routledge, 1994.

Blake, William. *The Poetry and Prose of William Blake.* Edited by David Erdman. New York: Doubleday, 1965.

Blum, Mark L. "Baptizing Nature: Environmentalism, Buddhism, and Transcendentalism." In *Bukkyo to Shizen* [Buddhism and nature], 133–63. Kyoto: Research Institute of Bukkyo University, 2005.

Blyth, Robert. *Zen in English Literature and Oriental Classics.* Tokyo: Hokuseido Press, 1942.

Bodhi, Bhikkhu. "A Look at the Kalama Sutta." *Buddhist Publication Society Newsletter* 9 (spring 1988). www.accesstoinsight.org/lib/authors/bodhi/bps-essay_09.html.

Bond, George Doherty. *The Buddhist Revival in Sri Lanka: Religious Tradition, Reinterpretation and Response.* Chapel Hill: University of North Carolina Press, 1988.

Brahmavamso, Ajahn. "Buddhism, the Only Real Science." *Daily News* (Sri Lanka), February 23, 2005. www.tipitaka.net/community/news.php?page=050227b.

Bryant, William Cullen. *Poems by William Cullen Bryant.* Whitefish, Mont.: Kessinger, 2004.

Buddhaghosa. *Path of Purification (Visuddhamagga).* Translated by Bhikkhu Ñāṇamoli. Seattle, Wash.: BPS Pariyatti Editions, 2003.

Bultmann, Rudolf. *Jesus Christ and Mythology.* New York: Scribner's, 1958.

Burns, Douglas M. *Buddhist Meditation and Depth Psychology.* The *Wheel* publication no. 88/89. Kandy, Sri Lanka: Buddhist Publication Society, 1994. www.accesstoinsight.org/lib/authors/burns/wheel088.html.

Cabezón, José. "Buddhism and Science: On the Nature of the Dialogue." In *Buddhism and Science: Breaking New Ground,* ed. B. Alan Wallace, 35–68. New York: Columbia University Press, 2003.

Cahn, B. Rael, and John Polich. "Meditation States and Traits: EEG, ERP, and Neuroimaging Studies." *Psychological Bulletin* 132, no. 2 (2006): 180–211.

Capra, Fritjof. *The Tao of Physics: An Exploration of the Parallels Between Modern Physics and Eastern Mysticism.* New York: Bantam, 1975.

Carrette, J., and Richard King. *Selling Spirituality: The Silent Takeover of Religion.* London: Routledge, 2005.

Carus, Paul. *Homilies of Science.* Chicago: Open Court, 1892.

———. *The Religion of Science.* [1893] Reprint, Chicago: Open Court, 1896.

———. *Buddhism and Its Christian Critics.* Chicago: Open Court, 1897.

———. *The Gospel of Buddhism, Compiled from Ancient Records.* Chicago: Open Court, 1915.

———. *The Dawn of a New Religious Era and Other Essays.* Chicago and London: Open Court, 1916.

Clarke, James Freeman. *Ten Great Religions.* Boston: Osgood, 1871.

Clarke, J. J. *Oriental Enlightenment: The Encounter between Asian and Western Thought.* London: Routledge, 1997.

Cleary, Thomas F., trans. *The Flower Ornament Scripture: a Translation of the Avatam-saka Sutra.* 3 vols. Boulder, Colo.: Shambhala, 1984–87.

———. *Entry into the Realm of Reality: The Text.* Boston: Shambala, 1989.

Cohen, Andrew. "The World Is Unreliable: An Interview with His Holiness Penor Rinpoche." *What Is Enlightenment?* 18 (fall–winter 2000). www.wie.org/j18/penor.asp.

Coleridge, Samuel Taylor. *The Friend.* 3 vols. 1818. Reprint, Whitefish, Mont.: Kessinger, 2004.

Conze, Edward. *The Perfection of Wisdom in Eight Thousand Lines and Its Verse Summary.* San Francisco: Four Seasons Foundation, 1973.

Coleman, James William. *The New Buddhism: The Western Transformation of an Ancient Tradition.* New York: Oxford University Press, 2001.

Cuevas, Bryan J. *The Hidden History of the Tibetan Book of the Dead.* New York: Oxford University Press, 2006.

Dalai Lama, His Holiness the Fourteenth [Bstan-'dzin-gyat-mtsho]. *The Way to Freedom.* Edited by Donald S. Lopez. San Francisco: HarperSanFrancisco, 1994.

———. *Ethics for the New Millennium.* New York: Riverhead Books, 1999.

———. *The Universe in a Single Atom: The Convergence of Science and Spirituality.* New York: Morgan Road Books, 2005.

Das, Lama Surya. *Awakening the Buddha Within: Tibetan Wisdom for the Western World.* New York: Broadway Books, 1997.

Alexandra David-Neel. *Magic and Mystery in Tibet.* 1932. Reprint, New York: Dover, 1971.

Davidson, Richard J., and Anne Harrington, eds. *Visions of Compassion: Western Scientists and Tibetan Buddhists Examine Human Nature.* Oxford: Oxford University Press, 2001.

DeCharms, C. *Two Views of the Mind: Abhidharma and Brain Science.* Ithaca, N.Y.: Snow Lion, 1998.

"Deity or Demon? The Controversy over Tibet's Dorje Shugden." Series of articles. *Tricycle* 7, no. 3 (spring 1998): 58–82.

Descartes, René. *The Philosophical Works of Descartes.* 2 vols. Translated by Elizabeth S. Haldine and G. R. T. Ross. Cambridge: Cambridge University Press, 1982.

Dharmapala, Anagarika. *Return to Righteousness: A Collection of Speeches, Essays and Letters of the Anagarika Dharmapala.* Ceylon: Government Press, 1965.

Dreyfus, Georges B. J. *The Sound of Two Hands Clapping: The Education of a Tibetan Buddhist Monk.* Berkeley: University of California Press, 2003.

———. "Are We Prisoners of Shangri-la?" *Journal of the International Association of Tibetan Studies* 1 (October 2005): 1–21. www.thdl.org/collections/journal/jiats/index.php?doc=dreyfus01.xml.

Droit, Roger-Pol. *The Cult of Nothingness: The Philosophers and the Buddha.* Translated from the French by David Streight and Pamela Vohnson. Chapel Hill: University of North Carolina Press, 2003.

Eckel, Malcolm David. "Is There a Buddhist Philosophy of Nature?" In *Buddhism and Ecology: The Interconnection of Dharma and Deeds,* ed. Mary Evelyn Tucker and Duncan Ryūkan Williams, 327–50. Cambridge, Mass.: Harvard University Center for the Study of World Religions Publications, 1997.

Eisenstadt, Shmuel N. *Multiple Modernities.* New Brunswick, N.J.: Transaction, 2002.

Ellmann, Richard. *James Joyce.* New York: Oxford University Press, 1959.

Emerson, Ralph Waldo. *The Portable Emerson.*

Edited by Mark Van Doren. New York: Viking Press, 1974.

Epstein, Mark. *Thoughts without a Thinker: Psychotherapy from a Buddhist Perspective.* New York: Basic Books, 1995.

Evans-Wentz, W. Y., ed. *The Tibetan Book of the Dead or The After-Death Experiences on the Bardo Plane, according to Lāma Kazi Dawa-Samdup's English Rendering.* 1927. Reprint, London: Oxford University Press, 1960.

Faure, Bernard. *The Rhetoric of Immediacy: A Cultural Critique of Chan/Zen Buddhism.* Princeton: Princeton University Press, 1991.

———. *Chan Insights and Oversights: An Epistemological Critique of the Chan Tradition.* Princeton: Princeton University Press, 1993.

———. *Visions of Power: Imagining Medieval Japanese Buddhism.* Princeton: Princeton University Press, 1996.

———. *Double Exposure: Cutting across Buddhist and Western Discourses.* Palo Alto: Stanford University Press, 2003.

Fields, Rick. *How the Swans Came to the Lake: A Narrative History of Buddhism in America.* 3rd ed. Boston: Shambala, 1992.

Findly, Ellison Banks, ed. *Women's Buddhism, Buddhism's Women: Tradition, Revision, Renewal.* Somerville, Mass.: Wisdom, 2000.

Foucault, Michel. *Discipline and Punish: The Birth of the Prison.* New York: Pantheon Books, 1977.

Franck, Frederick. *Zen Seeing, Zen Drawing.* New York: Bantam, 1993.

Freund, Julien. *The Sociology of Max Weber.* New York: Pantheon, 1968.

Friedman, Lenore. *Meetings with Remarkable Women: Buddhist Teachers in America.* Boston: Shambhala, 1987.

Fronsdal, Gil. "Insight Meditation in the United States: Life, Liberty, and the Pursuit of Happiness." In *The Faces of Buddhism in America,* ed. Charles Prebish and Kenneth Tanaka, 163–80. Berkeley: University of California Press, 1998.

Fulford, Tim. "Science." In *Romanticism: An Oxford Guide*, ed. Nicholas Roe, 90–101. Oxford: Oxford University Press, 2005.

Garfield, Jay. "Translation as Transmission and as Transformation." In *TransBuddhism: Translation, Transmission and Transformation*, ed. Nalini Bhushan, Jay Garfield, and Abraham Zablocki. Amherst: University of Massachusetts Press, forthcoming.

Gate of Sweet Nectar: Feeding the Hungry Spirits in an American Zen Community. Dir. Peter N. Gregory and Lesley J. Weaver. DVD. 2004.

George, Charles H. *The Protestant Mind of the English Reformation*. Princeton: Princeton University Press, 1961.

Gergen, Kenneth J. *The Saturated Self: Dilemmas of Identity in Contemporary Life*. 1990. 2nd ed. New York: Basic Books, 2000.

Giddens, Anthony. *The Consequences of Modernity*. Stanford: Stanford University Press, 1990.

———. *Modernity and Self-Identity: Self and Society in the Late Modern Age*. Cambridge: Polity Press, 1991.

Gihwa. "The Exposition of the Correct" *Hyeonjeong non* 顯正論 By 己和 (Hamheo Deuktong 涵虛 得通), chapter 7. Translated from the Hanmun Text by Charles Muller. Unpublished. Available online at: *http://www.acmuller.net/jeong-gihwa/hyeonjeong non.html#refpoint-6-33*.

Goddard, Dwight. *The Buddha's Golden Path: A Manual of Practical Buddhism Based on the Teachings and Practices of the Zen Sect, but Interpreted and Adapted to Meet Modern Conditions*. Whitefish, Mt.: Kessinger Publications, 2004 (1930).

Goenka, S. N. "The Art of Living: Vipassana Meditation." *Vipassana Meditation* web site. http://www.dhamma.org/.5/11/08

———. "Superscience: An Interview by Helen Tworkov." *Tricycle* 10, no. 2 (2000): 44–50.

Goldberg, Natalie. *Writing Down the Bones: Freeing the Writer Within*. Boston: Shambhala, 1986.

Goldstein, Joseph, and Jack Kornfield. *Seeking the Heart of Wisdom: The Path of Insight Meditation*. Boston: Shambhala, 1987.

Goleman, Daniel. *Destructive Emotions: Psychology and Psychiatry*. New York: Bantam, 2003a.

———. "Taming Destructive Emotions." *Tricycle* 47 (spring 2003b): 75–78.

———, ed. *Healing Emotions: Conversations with the Dalai Lama on Mindfulness, Emotions, and Health*. Boston: Shambhala, 1997.

Gombrich, Richard. *Theravada Buddhism: A Social History from Ancient Benares to Modern Colombo*. London: Routledge and Kegan Paul, 1988.

Gombrich, Richard, and Gananath Obeyesekere. *Buddhism Transformed: Religious Change in Sri Lanka*. Princeton: Princeton University Press, 1988.

Govinda, Anagarika. *The Psychological Attitude of Early Buddhist Philosophy and Its Systematization According to the Abhidharma Tradition*. London: Rider, 1961.

———. *Creative Meditation and Multi-dimensional Consciousness*. Wheaton, Ill.: Theosophical, 1976.

———. *A Living Buddhism for the West*. Boston: Shambhala Press, 1989.

————. *Art and Meditation: An Introduction and Twelve Abstract Paintings.* 1936. Reprint, Delhi: Book Faith India, 1999.

Green, Thomas Hill. *Lectures on the Principles of Political Obligation and Other Essays.* Edited by Paul Harris and John Morrow. 1895. Reprint, Cambridge: Cambridge University Press, 1986.

Gunaratana, Henepola. *Mindfulness in Plain English.* 1993. Reprint, Boston: Wisdom, 2002.

Gyatso, Geshe Kelsang. *The Joyful Path of Good Fortune: The Complete Guide to the Buddhist Path to Enlightenment.* 1990. Reprint, Glen Sprey, N.Y.: Tharpa, 2003.

Halbfass, Wilhelm. *India and Europe: An Essay on Understanding.* Albany: State University of New York Press, 1988.

Halifax, Joan. "The Third Body: Buddhism, Shamanism and Deep Ecology." In *Dharma Gaia: A Harvest of Essays in Buddhism and Ecology,* ed. Allan Hunt Badiner, 20–38. Berkeley: Parallax Press, 1990.

————. *The Fruitful Darkness: Reconnecting with the Body of the Earth.* San Francisco: HarperCollins, 1993.

Hanaoka, Eiko. "The Problem of Evil and Difference: A Report on Nishitani's Relationship to Schelling." In *Schelling Now: Contemporary Readings,* ed. Jason M. Wirth, 238–46. Bloomington: University of Indiana Press, 2005.

Hardy, Robert Spense. *A Manual of Buddhism.* 1853. Reprint, Varanasi: Chowkhamba Sanskrit Series Office, 1967.

Harris, Ian. "How Environmentalist Is Buddhism?" *Religion* 21 (1991): 101–14.

————. "Buddhist Environmental Ethics and Detraditionalization: The Case of Eco-Buddhism." *Religion* 25 (1995): 199–211.

————. "Buddhism and the Discourse of Environmental Concern: Some Methodological Problems." In *Buddhism and Ecology: The Interconnection of Dharma and Deeds,* ed. Mary Evelyn Tucker and Duncan Ryuken Williams, 377–402. Cambridge, Mass.: Harvard University Press, 1997.

————. "'A Commodius Vicas of Recirculation': Buddhism, Art, and Modernity." In *Westward Dharma: Buddhism beyond Asia,* ed. Charles S. Prebish and Martin Buamann, 365–82. Berkeley and Los Angeles: University of California Press, 2002.

Hattori, Masaki. *Dignāga, On Perception, Being the Pratyakṣapariccheda of Dignāga's Pramāṇasamuccaya.* Cambridge, Mass.: Harvard University Press, 1968.

Hayward, Jeremy. "Ecology and the Experience of Sacredness." In *Dharma Gaia: A Harvest of Essays in Buddhism and Ecology,* ed. Allan Hunt Badiner, 64–74. Berkeley: Parallax Press, 1990.

————. *Shifting Worlds, Changing Minds: Where the Sciences and Buddhism Meet.* Boston: Shambhala, 1987.

Hayward, Jeremy W., and Francisco J. Varela, eds. *Gentle Bridges: Converstions with the Dalai Lama on the Sciences of Mind.* Boston: Shambhala, 1992.

Heelas, Paul. "Introduction: Detraditionalization and Its Rivals." In *Detraditionalization,* ed. Paul Heelas, Scott Lasch, and Paul Morris, 1–20. Cambridge: Blackwell, 1996.

Hegel, Georg Friedrich Wilhelm. *Introduction: Reason in History*, in *Lectures on the Philosophy of World History*. Translated by H. B. Nisbet. Cambridge: Cambridge University Press, 1975.

Heine, Steven. *Opening a Mountain: Kōans of the Zen Masters*. New York: Oxford University Press, 2004.

Heine, Steven, and Dale Wright. *The Kōan: Texts and Context in Zen Buddhism*. New York: Oxford University Press, 2000.

Held, David, et al. *Global Transformations: Politics, Economics, and Culture*. Stanford: Stanford University Press, 1999.

Helmstadter, Richard J., and Bernard Lightman, eds. *Victorian Faith in Crisis: Essays on Continuity and Change in Nineteenth-Century Religious Belief*. Stanford: Stanford University Press, 1991.

Henricks, Robert G. *The Poetry of Han-shan: A Complete, Annotated Translation of Cold Mountain*. Albany: State University of New York Press, 1990.

Hesse, Hermann. *Siddhartha*. 1922. Reprint, New York: Bantam, 1951.

Hori, Victor Sōgen. "Sweet-and-Sour Buddhism." *Tricycle* 4, no. 1 (fall 1994): 48–52.

———. *Zen Sand: The Book of Capping Phrases for Koan Practice*. Honolulu: University of Hawaii Press, 2003.

Houshmand, Zara, Robert B. Livingston, and B. Alan Wallace, eds. *Consciousness at the Crossroads: Conversations with the Dalai Lama on Brain Science and Buddhism*. Ithaca, N.Y.: Snow Lion, 1999.

Huxley, Aldous. *The Perennial Philosophy*. 1949. Reprint, New York: Harper, 1970.

Inada, Kenneth. *Buddhism and American Thinkers*. Albany: State University of New York Press, 1984.

Jameson, Frederick. *Fables of Aggression*. University of California Press, 1979.

Jayatilleke, K. N. *Early Buddhist Theory of Knowledge*. London: Allen and Unwin, 1963.

Jensen, Lin. "An Ear to the Ground." *Tricycle* 15, no. 4 (summer 2006): 34–37.

Johnson, Charles. *Turning the Wheel: Essays on Buddhism and Writing*. New York: Scribner's, 2003.

Johnson, Samuel. *Oriental Religions and Their Relation to Universal Religion*. Boston: Osgood, 1872.

Jones, Sir William. *Works of Sir William Jones*. Edited by Lord Teignmouth. 1799. Reprint, London: John Stockdale, 1807.

Jung, Carl G. "Psychological Commentary." In W. Y. Evans-Wentz, *The Tibetan Book of the Dead, or, The After-death Experiences on the Bardo Plane, According to Lama Kazi Dawa-Samdup's English Rendering*, xxxv–lii. Oxford: Oxford University Press, 1960.

Kabat-Zinn, Jon. *Wherever You Go, There You Are: Mindfulness Meditation in Everyday Life*. New York: Hyperion, 1994.

Kalupahana, David J. *Buddhist Philosophy: A Historical Analysis*. Honolulu: University of Hawai'i Press, 1975.

———. *A History of Buddhist Philosophy: Continuities and Discontinuities*. Honolulu: University of Hawaii Press, 1992.

Kandinsky, Wassily. *Concerning the Spiritual in Art.* 1914. Reprint, New York: Dover, 1977.

Kasamatsu, A., and T. Hirai. "Science of Zazen." *Psychologia* 6 (1963): 86–91.

Kaza, Stephanie, ed. *Hooked! Buddhist Writings on Greed, Desire, and the Urge to Consume.* Boston: Shambhala, 2005.

Kaza, Stephanie, and Kenneth Kraft, eds. *Dharma Rain: Sources of Buddhist Environmentalism.* London: Shambhala, 2000.

Ketelaar, James E. "Strategic Occidentalism: Meiji Buddhists as the World's Parliament of Religions." *Buddhist-Christian Studies* 11 (1991): 37–56.

Kim, Hee-jin. *Eihei Dogen, Mystical Realist.* Sommerville, Mass: Wisdom, 2004.

King, Richard. *Orientalism and Religion: Postcolonial Theory, India and the "Mystic East."* London: Routledge, 1999.

Knight, David. *The Age of Science: The Scientific World-View in the Nineteenth Century.* Oxford: Blackwell, 1986.

Kopp, Sheldon. *If You Meet the Buddha on the Road, Kill Him! The Pilgrimage of Psychotherapy Patients.* 1972. Reprint, New York: Bantam, 1976.

Kraft, Kenneth. *The Wheel of Engaged Buddhism: A New Map of the Path.* New York: Weatherhill, 1999.

Kwee, Maurits G. T., Kenneth J. Gergen, and Fusako Koshikawa. *Horizons in Buddhist Psychology: Practice, Research and Theory.* Chagrin Falls, Ohio: Taos Institute, 2006.

LaFleur, William. "Enlightenment for Plants and Trees." In Tucker and Williams, *Buddhism and Ecology,* 109–16.

Lai, Whalen, and Michael von Brück. *Christianity and Buddhism: A Multicultural History of Their Dialogue.* Maryknoll, N.Y.: Orbis, 2001.

Lamotte, Etienne. "The Assessment of Textual Interpretation in Buddhism." In *Buddhist Hermeneutics,* transl. Sara Boin-Webb and ed. Donald S. Lopez Jr. Honolulu: University of Hawaii Press, 1988.

Lancaster, Lewis. "Buddhism and Ecology: Collective Cultural Perceptions." In *Buddhism and Ecology: The Interconnection of Dharma and Deeds,* ed. Mary Evelyn Tucker and Duncan Ryūkan Williams, 3–20. Cambridge, Mass.: Harvard University Center for the Study of World Religions, 1997.

Lardas, John. *The Bop Apocalypse: The Religious Visions of Kerouac, Ginsberg, and Burroughs.* Urbana: University of Illinois Press, 2001.

Lasch, Christopher. *The Culture of Narcissism: American Life in an Age of Diminishing Expectations.* 1979. Reprint, New York: Norton, 1991.

Lassalle, H. M. Enomiya. *Zen Meditation for Christians.* LaSalle, Ill.: Open Court, 1974.

Lefebvre, Henri. *Everyday Life in the Modern World.* Trans. Sacha Rabinovitch. New York: Harper and Row, 1971.

Leighton, Taigen Daniel. *Faces of Compassion: Classic Bodhisattva Archetypes and Their Modern Expression.* Boston: Wisdom, 2003.

Linssen, Robert. *Living Zen.* Translated by Diana Abrahams-Curiel. 1958. Reprint, New York: Grove, 1988.

Locke, John. *An Essay Concerning Human Understanding* (1706). Edited by Peter H. Nidditch. New York: Oxford University Press, 1979.

Lopez, Donald S., Jr. *Prisoners of Shangri–La: Tibetan Buddhism and the West*. Chicago: University of Chicago Press, 1998.

———, ed. *A Modern Buddhist Bible: Essential Readings from East and West*. Boston: Beacon Press, 2002.

Loy, David. *The Great Awakening: A Buddhist Social Theory*. Boston: Wisdom, 2003.

Macy, Joanna. *Mutual Causality in Buddhism and General Systems Theory: The Dharma of Natural Systems*. Albany: State University of New York Press, 1991a.

———. *World as Lover, World as Self*. Parallax Press, 1991b.

Maezumi, Taizan Rōshi. *Appreciate Your Life: The Essence of Zen Practice*. Boston: Shambhala, 2002.

Marx, Werner. *The Philosophy of F. W. J. Schelling: History, System, and Freedom*. Bloomington: Indiana University Press, 1984.

Maugham, W. Somerset. *Of Human Bondage*. New York: Viking Penguin, 1915.

McEwan, Ian. *Saturday*. New York: Doubleday, 2005.

McMahan, David L. *Empty Vision: Metaphor and Visionary Imagery in Mahāyāna Buddhism*. London: RoutledgeCurzon, 2002a.

———. "Repackaging Zen for the West." In *Westward Dharma: Buddhism beyond Asia*, ed.Charles S. Prebish and Martin Baumann, 218–29. Berkeley: University of California Press, 2002b.

———. "Demythologization and the Core-versus-Accretions Model of Buddhism." *Indian International Journal of Buddhism* 10, no. 5 (2004a): 63–99.

———. "Modernity and the Discourse of Scientific Buddhism." *Journal of the American Academy of Religion* 72, no. 4 (2004b): 897–933.

———. "Meditation, Modern Movements." In *The Encyclopedia of Buddhism*, ed. Charles S. Prebish and Damien Keown, 502–505. London: Routledge, 2007.

Metcalf, Franz Aubrey. "The Encounter of Buddhism and Psychology." In *Westward Dharma: Buddhism beyond Asia*, ed. Charles S. Prebish and Martin Buamann, 348–64. Berkeley and Los Angeles: University of California Press, 2002.

Mishra, Pankaj. *An End to Suffering: The Buddha in the World*. New York: Picador, 2004.

Moacanin, Radmila. *The Essence of Jung's Psychology and Tibetan Buddhism: Eastern and Western Paths to the Heart*. Boston: Wisdom, 2003.

Mohanty, Jitendra Nath. *Reason and Tradition in India Thought: An Essay on the Nature of Indian Philosophical Thinking*. Oxford: Clarendon Press, 1992.

Muir, John. *The Yosemite*. New York: Century Company, 1912.

———. *My First Summer in the Sierra*. 1911. Reprint, San Francisco: Sierra Club Books, 1988.

Naess, Arne. "The Shallow and the Deep: Long Range Ecology Movements." *Inquiry* 16 (1973): 95–100.

———. "Through Spinoza to Mahāyāna Buddhism or through Mahāyāna Buddhism to Spinoza?" In *Spinoza's Philosophy of Man: Proceedings of the Scandinavian Spinoza Symposium 1977*, ed. Jon Wetlesen, 136–58. Oslo: Universeitetsforlaget, 1978.

Nauriyal, D. K., Michael S. Drummond, and Y. B. Lal. *Buddhist Thought and Applied Psychological Research: Transcending the Boundaries.* London: Routledge, 2006.

Nhat Hanh, Thich. *The Miracle of Mindfulness! A Manual of Meditation.* Boston: Beacon Press, 1976.

———. *The Heart of Understanding: Commentaries on the Prajñaparamita Heart Sutra.* Edited by Peter Levitt. Berkeley: Parallax Press, 1988.

———. *Peace Is Every Step: The Path of Mindfulness in Everyday Life.* New York: Bantam, 1991.

———. *Interbeing: Fourteen Guidelines for Engaged Buddhism.* Edited by Fred Eppsteiner. Berkeley: Parallax Press, 1998.

———. "The Sun in My Heart." In *Dharma Rain: Sources of Buddhist Environmentalism,* ed. Stephanie Kaza and Kenneth Kraft, 83–91. Boston: Shambhala, 2000.

Nicol, Caitrin. "Brave New World at 75." *New Atlantis* 16 (spring 2007).41–54. www.thenewatlantis.com:80/archive/16/nicolprint.htm.

Numrich, Paul David. *Old Wisdom in the New World: Americanization in Two Immigrant Theravada Buddhist Temples.* Knoxville: University of Tennessee Press, 1996.

Nyanaponika Thera. *The Heart of Buddhist Meditation.* Kandy, Sri Lanka: Buddhist Meditation Society, 1954.

Nyanaponika, Thera, and Bhikku Bodhi, trans. *Numerical Discourses of the Buddha: An Anthology of Suttas from the Aṅguttara Nikāya.* New York: Altamira Press, 1999.

Obeyesekere, Gannanath. "Personal Identity and Cultural Crisis: The Case of Anagarika Dharmapala of Sri Lanka." In *The Biographical Process: Studies in the History and Psychology of Religion,* ed. Frank Reynolds and Donald Capps, 221–52. Paris: Mouton, 1976.

Odin, Steve. *Process Metaphysics and Hua-yen Buddhism.* Albany: State University of New York Press, 1982.

Olcott, Henry Steel. *A Collection of Lectures on Theosophy and Archaic Religions, Delivered in India and Ceylon by Colonel H. S. Olcott, President of the Theosophical Society.* Madras, India: A Theyagar Rajier, 1883.

———. *A Buddhist Catechism, According to the Canon of the Southern Church.* Colombo, Ceylon: Theosophical Society, Buddhist Sections, 1881. Rev. 47th ed. Adyar, India: Theosophical, 1947.

———. *Old Diary Leaves: The History of the Theosophical Society.* 6 vols. 1895–1935. Reprint, Adyar, India: Theosophical, 1974–75.

Olendzki, Andrew. "Interconnected . . . Or Not?" *Insight Journal* 24 (Spring 2005): 3.

Packer, Toni. *The Light of Discovery.* Rutland, Vt.: Tuttle, 1995a.

———. *The Work of This Moment.* Rutland, Vt.: Tuttle, 1995b.

Payne, Richard. "Individuation and Awakening: Romantic Narrative and the Psychological Interpretation of Buddhism." In *Buddhism and Psychotherapy across Cultures: Essays on Theories and Practices,* ed. Mark Unno, 31–52. Boston: Wisdom, 2006.

Perry, Seamus. "Literary Criticism and Theory." In *Romanticism: An Oxford Guide,* ed. Nicholas Roe, 594–606. New York: Oxford University Press, 2005.

Preece, Rob. *The Psychology of Buddhist Tantra.* Ithaca, N.Y.: Snow Lion, 2006.

Ponlop Rinpoche, Dzogchen. "A Science of Mind." www.nalandabodhi.org/science_of_
mind.html.

Prebish, Charles S. *Luminous Passage: The Practice and Study of Buddhism in America.*
Berkeley: University of California Press, 1999.

Prebish, Charles S., and Kenneth Tanaka, eds. *The Faces of Buddhism in America.* Berkeley: University of California Press, 1998.

Prothero, Stephen. *The White Buddhist: The Asian Odyssey of Henry Steel Olcott.* Bloomington: Indiana University Press, 1996.

———. "Boomer Buddhism," *Salon.com,* February 2001. http://archive.salon.com/
books/feature/2001/02/26/buddhism/print.html.

Proust, Marcel. *Remembrance of Things Past.* Vol. 1. *Swan's Way: Within a Budding
Grove.* Translated by C. K. Scott Moncrieff and Terence Kilmartin. New York:
Vintage, 1981.

Queen, Christopher, ed. *Engaged Buddhism in the West.* Wisdom, 1999.

———. *Action Dharma: New Studies in Engaged Buddhism.* London:
RoutledgeCurzon, 2003.

Queen, Christopher S., and Sallie B. King. *Engaged Buddhism: Buddhist Liberation
Movements in Asia.* Albany: State University of New York Press, 1996.

Rahula, Walpola. *What the Buddha Taught.* 1959. Reprint, New York: Grove Press, 1974.

Reiff, P. *The Triumph of the Therapeutic: Uses of Faith after Freud.* Chicago: University of
Chicago Press, 1966.

Reps, Paul. *Zen Flesh, Zen Bones: A Collection of Zen and Pre-Zen Writings.* 1957. Reprint,
Rutland, Vt.: Tuttle, 1987.

Rhys Davids, Caroline A. F. *Buddhism: A Study of the Buddhist Norm.* London: Williams
and Norgate, 1912.

Rhys Davids, Thomas W. *Lectures on the Origin and Growth of Religion as Illustrated
by some Points in the History of Indian Buddhism.* Hibbert Lectures. New York:
Putnam, 1882.

Rilke, Rainer Maria. *Duino Elegies.* Translated by J. B. Leishman and Stephen Spender.
New York, London: Norton, 1939.

Ross, Nancy Wilson, ed. *The World of Zen: An East-West Anthology.* New York: Random
House, 1960.

Rousseau, Jean-Jacques. *Emile.* Translated by Barbara Foxley. London: Dent, 1911.

———. *The Social Contract and Discourse on the Origins of Inequality.* Edited by Lester G.
Crocker. New York: Simon and Schuster, 1967,

Rydell, Robert. *All the World's a Fair: Vision of Empire at American International Exhibitions, 1876–1916.* Chicago: University of Chicago Press, 1984.

Safran, Jeremy, ed. *Psychoanalysis and Buddhism: An Unfolding Dialogue.* Boston:
Wisdom, 2003.

Salzberg, Sharon. "I Feel Your Brain." *Tricycle* 62, no. 2 (Winter 2006): 67–69,
188–89.

Samuel, Geoffrey. *Civilized Shamans: Buddhism in Tibetan Societies.* Washington, D.C.:
Smithsonian Institution Press, 1993.

Sangharakshita. *The Religion of Art.* Glasgow, UK: Windhorse Publications, 1973.

Śāntideva. *A Guide to the Bodhisattva's Way of Life.* Translated by Alan Wallace and Vesna Wallace. Ithaca, NY: Snow Lion, 1997.

Schelling, Friedrich Wilhelm Joseph von. *Friedrich Wilhelm Joseph Schelling's Sämmtliche Werke.* Edited by K. F. A. Schelling, Pt. I, vols. 1–10. Pt. II, vols. 1–4, Stuttgart: Cotta, 1856–61.

———. *System of Transcendental Idealism* (1800). Translated by Peter Heath. Charlottesville: University Press of Virginia, 1978.

———. *Philosophy of Art.* Translated and edited by Douglas W. Stott. Minneapolis: University of Minnesota Press, 1989.

Schiller, Friedrich. *On the Aesthetic Education of Man, in a Series of Letters.* Translated by Elizabeth M. Wilkinson and L. A. Willoughby. Oxford: Oxford University Press, 1967.

Schleiermacher, Friedrich. *On Religion: Speeches to Its Cultured Despisers.* Translated and edited by Richard Crouter. Cambridge: Cambridge University Press, 1988.

Schmidt, Leigh Eric. "The Making of Modern Mysticism." *Journal of the American Academy of Religion* 71, no. 2 (June 2003): 273–302.

———. *Restless Souls: The Making of American Spirituality.* New York: HarperCollins, 2005.

Schopenhauer, Arthur. *The World as Will and Representation.* Translated by E. F. J. Payne. New York: Dover, 1969.

Schwab, Raymond. *Oriental Renaissance: Europe's Rediscovery of India and the East, 1680–1880.* New York: Columbia University Press, 1987.

Seager, Richard Hughs. *The World's Parliament of Religions: The East/West Encounter, Chicago, 1893.* Bloomington: Indiana University Press, 1995.

———. *Buddhism in America.* New York: Columbia University Press, 1999.

———. *Encountering the Dharma: Daisaku Ikeda, Soka Gakkai, and the Globalization of Buddhist Humanism.* Berkeley: University of California Press, 2006.

Sharf, Robert H. "Buddhist Modernism and the Rhetoric of Meditative Experience." *Numen* 42, no. 3 (October 1995a): 228–83.

———. "The Religion of Science: Paul Carus and the *Gospel of Buddha*." *Tricycle* 4, no. 4 (summer 1995b): 12–15.

———. "The Zen of Japanese Nationalism." In *Curators of the Buddha: The Study of Buddhism Under Colonialism,* ed. Donald S. Lopez Jr., 107–60. Chicago: University of Chicago Press, 1995c.

———. *Coming to Terms with Chinese Buddhism: A Reading of the Treasure Store Treatise.* Honolulu: University of Hawaii Press, 2001.

Shattock, E. H. *An Experiment in Mindfulness.* New York: Dutton, 1960.

Shils, Edward. *Tradition.* Chicago: University of Chicago Press, 1981.

Showalter, Elaine. Introduction to Virginia Woolf, *Mrs. Dalloway,* xi–xlix. New York: Penguin Books, 2000.

Siegel, Lee. "The Imagination of Disaster." *Nation,* April 11, 2005. www.thenation.com/doc/20050411/siegel.

Singh, Nagendra Kumar, ed. *International Encyclopedia of Buddhism.* New Delhi: Anmol, 1996.

Simmel, Goerg. "The Future in Our Culture." In *Georg Simmel: Sociologist and European.* 1909. Reprint, Middlesex, England: Thomas Nelson, 1976.

Snodgrass, Judith. *Presenting Japanese Buddhism to the West: Orientalism, Occidental-ism, and the Columbian Exposition*. Chapel Hill: University of North Carolina Press, 2003.

Snyder, Gary. *The Practice of the Wild: Essays*. San Francisco: North Point Press, 1990.

———. *The Gary Snyder Reader: Prose, Poetry and Translations, 1952–1998*. Washington, D.C.: Counterpoint, 1999.

———. "Writers and the War against Nature." *Resurgence* 239 (2006):12–17. http://www.resurgence.org/magazine/article291-WRITERS-AND-THE-WAR-AGAINST-NATURE.html.

Sōen (Soyen) Shaku. *Zen for Americans: Including the Sutra of Forty-two Chapters*. 1913. Reprint, New York: Barnes and Noble Books, 1993.

Soma Thera. *The Removal of Distracting Thoughts: A Discourse of the Buddha*. Kandy, Sri Lanka: Buddhist Publication Society, 1981. www.accesstoinsight.org/lib/authors/soma/wheel021.html.

Steger, Manfred B., and Perle Besserman. *Grassroots Zen*. Rutland, Vt.: Tuttle, 2001.

Strauss, C. T. *The Buddha and His Doctrine*. Port Washington, N.Y.: Kennikat Press, 1922.

Suzuki, Daisetz Teitarō. *Essays in Zen Buddhism*. First series. New York: Grove Press, 1949.

———. *Zen Buddhism: Selected Writings of D. T. Suzuki*. Edited by William Barrett. Garden City, N.Y.: Anchor, 1956.

———. *Zen and Japanese Culture*. Princeton: Princeton University Press, 1959.

———. "Lectures on Zen Buddhism." In *Zen Buddhism and Psychoanalysis*, ed. D. T. Suzuki, Erich Fromm, and Richard De Martino, 1–76. New York: Grove Press, 1960.

———. *Mysticism Christian and Buddhist*. 1957. Reprint, London: Allen and Unwin, 1979.

Suzuki, D. T., Erich Fromm, and Richard De Martino, ed. *Zen Buddhism and Psychoa-nalysis*. New York: Grove Press, 1960.

Swearer, Donald K. *The Buddhist World of Southeast Asia*. Albany: State University of New York Press, 1995.

———. "The Hermeneutics of Buddhist Ecology in Contemporary Thailand: Buddhadāsa and Dhammapiṭaka." In *Buddhism and Ecology: The Interconnection of Dharma and Deeds*, ed. Mary Evelyn Tucker and Duncan Ryūkan Williams, 21–44. Cambridge, Mass.: Harvard University Center for the Study of World Religions, 1997.

———. "Aniconism versus Iconism in Thai Buddhism." In *Buddhism in the Mod-ern World: Adaptations of the Ancient Tradition*, ed. Steven Heine and Charles S. Prebish, 9–26. New York: Oxford University Press, 2003.

T'ai hsu [Taixu]. *Lectures in Buddhism*. Paris, 1928.

Tambiah, Stanley J. *Buddhism and the Spirit Cults in North-East Thailand*. Cambridge: Cambridge University Press, 1987.

Taylor, Charles. *Sources of the Self: The Making of Modern Identity*. Cambridge: Harvard University Press, 1989.

————. *The Ethics of Authenticity.* Cambridge: Harvard University Press, 1991.

Thanissaro Bhikkhu. "Romancing the Buddha." *Tricycle* 12, no. 2 (Winter 2002): 45–47, 106–12.

Thoreau, Henry David. *Walden.* New York: Quality Paperback, 1997.

Thurman, Robert. "Tibetan Psychology: Sophisticated Software for the Human Brain." In Herbert Benson et al., eds., *Mindscience: An East-West Dialogue.* Somerville, Mass.: Wisdom, 1991.

————, trans. *The Tibetan Book of the Dead: The Great Book of Natural Liberation through Understanding in the In-Between.* New York: Bantam, 1994.

————. Interview. *Pulse of the Planet,* program 2971, July 21, 2003. Excerpt online. http://pulseplanet.com/archive/Jul03/2971.html.

Tonkinson, Carole. *Big Sky Mind: Buddhism and the Beat Generation.* New York: Riverhead Books, 1995.

Toulmin, Stephen. *Cosmopolis: The Hidden Agenda of Modernity.* New York: Free Press, 1990.

Trine, Ralph Waldo. *In Tune with the Infinite: Fullness of Peace, Power, and Plenty.* London: Thorsons, 1995.

Troeltsch, Ernst. *The Social Teaching of the Christian Churches.* Vol. 2. New York: MacMillan, 1931.

Trungpa, Chögyam. *The Myth of Freedom and the Way of Meditation.* Boston: Shambhala, 1976.

————. "Introductory Essay: The Meeting of Buddhist and Western Psychology." In *Buddhism and Western Psychology,* ed. Nathan Katz, 1–10. Boulder, Colo.: Prajña Press, 1983.

————. *The Collected Works of Chögyam Trungpa.* 8 vols. Boston: Shambhala, 2003–4.

Tucci, Giuseppe. *The Theory and Practice of the Mandala: With Special Reference to the Modern Psychology of the Subconscious.* Translated by Alan Houghton Brodick. 1961. Reprint, New York: Samuel Weiser, 1970.

Tuchman, Maurice. *The Spiritual in Art: Abstract Painting 1890–1985.* New York: Abbeville Press, 1986.

Tucker, Evelyn, and Duncan Ryūken Williams. *Buddhism and Ecology: The Interconnection of Dharma and Deeds.* Religions of the World and Ecology Series. Cambridge, Mass.: Harvard Center for World Religions, 1998.

Turner, Frank M. "The Victorian Crisis of Faith and the Faith That Was Lost." In *Victorian Faith in Crisis: Essays on Continuity and Change in Nineteenth-Century Religious Belief,* ed. Richard J. Helmstadter and Bernard Lightman. Stanford: Stanford University Press, 1991.

Tweed, Thomas A. "Night-Stand Buddhists and Other Creatures: Sympathizers, Adherents, and the Study of Religion." In *American Buddhism: Methods and Findings in Recent Scholarship,* ed. Duncan Ryūken Williams and Christopher S. Queen, 71–90. Richmond, Surrey: Curzon Press, 1999.

————. *The American Encounter with Buddhism, 1844–1912: Victorian Culture and the Limits of Dissent.* 1992. Reprint, Chapel Hill: University of North Carolina Press, 2000.

Tworkov, Helen. *Zen in America: Five Teachers and the Search for an American Buddhism.* New York: Kodansha America, 1994.

Vaidya, P. L., ed. *Aṣṭasāhasrikā Prajñāpāramitā.* Buddhist Sanskrit Texts no. 4. Darbhanga, India: Mithila Institute, 1960.

———. *Gaṇḍavyūha Sūtra.* Buddhist Sanskrit Texts, no. 5. Darbhanga, India: Mithila Institute, 1960.

Varela, Francisco J., ed. *Sleeping, Dreaming, and Dying: An Exploration of Consciousness with the Dalai Lama.* Boston: Wisdom, 1997.

Varela, Francisco J., Evan Thompson, and Eleanor Rosch. *The Embodied Mind: Cognitive Science and Human Experience.* Cambridge, Mass.: MIT Press, 1991.

Verheoven, Marin J. "Americanizing the Buddha: Paul Carus and the Transformation of Asian Thought." In *Faces of Buddhism in America,* ed. Charles S. Prebish and Kenneth K. Tanaka, 207–26. Berkeley: University of California Press. 1998.

Victoria, Brian. *Zen at War.* 2nd ed. Lanham, Md.: Rowman and Littlefield, 2006.

von Stuckrad, Kucko. "Re-enchanting Nature: Modern Western Shamanism and Nineteenth-Century Thought." *Journal of the American Academy of Religion* 70, no. 4 (December 2002): 771–99.

Wallace, B. Alan. "Introduction: Buddhism and Science—Breaking Down the Barriers." In *Buddhism and Science: Breaking New Ground,* ed. B. Alan Wallace, 1–29. New York: Columbia University Press, 2003.

———. *Contemplative Science: Where Buddhism and Neuroscience Converge.* New York: Columbia University Press, 2007.

Wallace, B. Alan, and Arnold P. Lutzker, eds. *Buddhism and Science: Breaking New Ground.* New York: Columbia, 2003.

Watts, Alan. "Haiku." In *The World of Zen: An East-West Anthology,* ed. Nancy Wilson Ross, 121–28. New York: Random House, 1960.

———. *This Is It: And Other Essays on Zen and Spiritual Experience.* 1958. Reprint, New York: Vintage Books, 1973.

———. *The Way of Zen.* 1957. Reprint, New York: Vintage Books, 1989.

Weber, Max. *The Protestant Ethic and the Spirit of Capitalism.* Translated by Talcott Parsons. New York: Scribner's, 1958.

Williams, Duncan Ryūken. *The Other Side of Zen: A Social History of Sōtō Zen Buddhism in Tokugawa Japan.* Princeton: Princeton University Press, 2005.

Wilson, A. L. *A Mythical Image: The Ideal of India in German Romanticism.* Durham, N.C.: Duke University Press, 1964.

Woodhead, Linda, and Paul Heelas. *Religion in Modern Times: An Interpretive Anthology.* Oxford: Blackwell, 2000.

Woodward, F. L., trans. *The Book of Gradual Sayings (Aṅguttara Nikāya) or More Numbered Suttas.* 5 vols. London: Oxford University Press, 1932.

Woolf, Virginia. "Jane Austen." In *The Common Reader,* 1st series, 134–45. New York: Harcourt Brace Jovanovich, 1984a.

———. "Modern Fiction." In *The Common Reader,* 1st series, 146–54. New York: Harcourt Brace Jovanovich, 1984b.

———. "A Sketch of the Past." In *Moments of Being*, 2nd ed., ed. Jeanne Schulkind, 61–160. Orlando, Fla.: Harcourt Brace, 1985.

———. *Mrs. Dalloway*. New York: Penguin Books, 2000.

Wordsworth, William. *William Wordsworth—The Major Works: Including the Prelude*. Edited by Stephen Gill. New York: Oxford University Press, 2000.

Wu, Duncan, ed. *Romanticism: An Anthology*. 2nd ed. Malden, Mass.: Blackwell, 1998.

Yokoi, Yūhō. *Zen Master Dōgen: An Introduction with Selected Writings*. New York: Weatherhill, 1976.

Yusa, Michiko. *Zen and Philosophy: An Intellectual Biography of Nishida Kitarō*. Honolulu: University of Hawaii Press, 2002.

Index